Additional Praise for *Be the Solution*

"Michael Strong and his coauthors sketch out a provocative and appealing vision of what you might call 'bleeding heart libertarianism.' Regardless of where you fit on the ideological map, they will challenge the way you think about social progress. So if you're interested in how to make the world around you a better place, take the challenge and read this book."

—Brink Lindsey, VP for Research, Cato Institute;
Author of *The Age of Abundance*

"If you want to contribute to making a better world and you have an indomitable entrepreneurial spirit, this is the book for you. Ours is the age of doing good by doing well. The notion that market competition is all about greed is just a monumental error that you can help a new generation to avoid."

—Herbert Gintis, Santa Fe Institute and
Central European University

"In *Be the Solution* Michael Strong, John Mackey, and other visionary authors organically develop a new framework for capitalism so that the beneficent and transformational potentials of entrepreneurship and free market can be powerfully unleashed for societal good. *Be the Solution* cogently argues that the essential feature and primary virtue of capitalism is not profit-motivated exchange of commodities but voluntary exchange of abilities. *Be the Solution* demonstrates that when capitalism is rightly framed and entrepreneurship is properly nurtured in a culture of freedom, the entrepreneurial spirit of humanity will bring forth new innovative solutions to many of the persistent and pervasive problems of the world. At once informative and inspirational, *Be the Solution* will provoke you not only to think outside the existing paradigms but also to act for the realization of your vision by invoking in you the highest value and the innermost virtue of humanity—freedom and creativity."

—Yasuhiko Genku Kimura, Founder and Chairman,
Vision-In-Action, Author of *Think Kosmically Act Globally*

"Be the Solution is out on a frontier of thought where no one has travelled before. It redefines the word 'prescient.' A breathtaking integration of futuristic thinking about economics, politics, social justice, and human happiness, it is nothing less than a blueprint for a transcendent tomorrow for humanity. Once or twice in a lifetime you come across a vein of thinking like this—one that that makes you feel as if life and the world are suddenly new again. The inspiring future *Be the Solution* paints for us will be the very motivation we have needed to pursue it."

—Dan Palotta, Author of *Uncharitable:*
How Restraints on Nonprofits Undermine Their Potential

"Be the Solution will undoubtedly be added to my 'must read' book list for those who inquire about the causes of world poverty and what can be done to solve these problems."

—Philip Sansone, President and Executive Director,
Whole Planet Foundation

"This is a desperately needed synthesis of the work of the world's most insightful thinkers on how to solve the problems of poverty. It lays bare fallacies in policies that annually misdirect billions of dollars into development of initiatives that don't work. And it offers situation-contingent guidelines for programs that will. A must read."

—Clayton M. Christensen, Professor,
Harvard Business School; Author, *The Innovator's Dilemma*

Be the Solution

*How Entrepreneurs and
Conscious Capitalists
Can Solve All the
World's Problems*

Michael Strong
CEO, FLOW®

Foreword by John Mackey

WILEY
John Wiley & Sons, Inc.

Published by John Wiley & Sons, Inc., Hoboken, New Jersey.

Published simultaneously in Canada.

For general information on our other products and services or for technical support, please contact our Customer Care Department within the United States at (800) 762-2974, outside the United States at (317) 572-3993 or fax (317) 572-4002.

Wiley also publishes its books in a variety of electronic formats. Some content that appears in print may not be available in electronic books. For more information about Wiley products, visit our web site at www.wiley.com.

Library of Congress Cataloging-in-Publication Data:

Strong, Michael, 1960-
    Be the solution : how entrepreneurs and conscious capitalists can solve all the world's problems / Michael Strong ; foreword by John Mackey.
        p. cm.
    Includes index.
        ISBN 978-0-470-45003-1 (cloth)
        1. Entrepreneurship.   2. Problem solving.   3. Capitalists and financiers.   I. Title.
    HB615.S773 2009
    658.4'08—dc22   2008052152

Printed in the United States of America
10 9 8 7 6 5 4 3 2 1

To the Entrepreneurial Spirit in Each of Us

Contents

Contents

Foreword

I grew up in Houston, Texas, during the 1950s and 1960s. My family and friends were fairly typical of the middle class in the southern United States during that era. I spent my late teens and early 20s trying to discover the meaning and purpose of my own life. Before I started my business career, I serially attended two different universities, the University of Texas at Austin and Trinity in San Antonio, where I accumulated about 120 hours of various electives, majoring in philosophy and religion. After dropping out of school for the sixth and final time in 1977, I had earned no degree. During my tour of duty in higher education, I never took a single business class. I am convinced now that this gap in my formal education actually worked to my advantage in the business world. When I started out as an entrepreneur, I had no way of knowing how many accepted business practices I was ignoring and that gap gave me the opportunity to innovate freely without the burden of too many legacies to overcome.

My search for meaning and purpose led me into the counterculture movement of the late 1960s and 1970s. I studied eastern philosophy and religion in college and on my own, and still practice both yoga and meditation. I studied ecology and developed a strong commitment to living lightly on the planet. I was drawn to the concepts of organic farming and natural foods early on. I chose a vegetarian lifestyle (I am currently a near vegan—only deviating by eating eggs from my own chickens), lived in communal housing, and grew my hair and beard long. I was, and still am, one of those crunchy-granola types. Politically, I drifted to the left and embraced the ideology of my peer group that business and corporations were essentially evil because they selfishly sought profits. Along the lines of this reasoning, I viewed government as good because its employees altruistically worked for the public's interests. I worked part-time when I was low on cash, played a lot of pickup basketball with my friends, and continuously read books on dozens of diverse topics.

With that background, I felt well prepared to launch my business in 1978, with a grand total of six months of actual experience working in a small natural food store in Austin. My initial business, a small natural foods market called Safer Way, was located in a charming, rickety Victorian house in central Austin. I started Safer Way with my girlfriend, Renee Lawson, using $45,000 in initial capital that we raised from friends and family for the venture. Renee and I were very idealistic and we started the business because we thought it would be both fun and a way for us both to engage in a right livelihood—supporting ourselves while having fun and helping other people. We were right—we had a blast, and although Renee went on to do other things with her life, I continued to have a great time running Whole Foods Market, the business that Safer Way evolved into, over the last 28 years.

At the time I started my business, the political left had taught me that both business and capitalism were based on exploitation: exploitation of consumers, workers, society, and the environment. I believed that "profit" was a necessary evil at best, and certainly not a desirable goal for society as a whole. However, going into business as an entrepreneur completely changed my life. Everything I believed about business turned out to be wrong! The most important thing I learned about business in my first year was that business was not based on exploitation or coercion at all. Instead I realized that business is based on voluntary exchange. At least in the United States, and certainly in most of the developed world, no one is forced to trade with a business; customers have competitive alternatives in the marketplace for their purchases; employees have competitive alternatives for their labor; investors have thousands of alternatives and places to invest their capital. Investors, labor, management, suppliers—they all need to cooperate to create value for their customers. If they do, then the value created by the business will be divided amongst the creators of the value approximately equal to the contribution each market participant made in creating that value through the competitive dynamics of the market process. In other words, business is not a zero sum game with a winner and loser. It is a win, win, win, win game—and I *really* like that.

However, I discovered that despite my idealism and my newfound certainty of the voluntary nature of marketplace exchanges, our customers thought our prices were too high, our employees thought they were underpaid, the vendors would not give us large discounts, the community was forever clamoring for donations, and the government was slapping us with endless fees, licenses, fines, and taxes.

Were we profitable? Not at first. Safer Way managed to lose half of its capital in the first year—$23,000. Despite the loss, we were still accused of exploiting our customers with high prices and our employees with low wages. The investors weren't making a profit and we had little money to donate. Plus, with our losses, we paid no income taxes. I had somehow joined the "dark side"—I was now one of the bad guys. According to the perspective of the political left, I had become a greedy and selfish businessman.

At that point, I rationally chose to abandon the leftist philosophy of my youth since, in my experience, it failed to explain how the world really worked. With my previous interpretation of the world now shattered, I looked around for alternative economic and political explanations for making sense of the world.

I somehow stumbled into reading Milton Friedman, Friedrich Hayek, Ludwig von Mises, and Ayn Rand—I read them all and said to myself, "Wow, this all makes sense. This is how the world really works. This is incredible." I quickly came to identify myself as a Libertarian. I am one of those people who actually votes Libertarian and have voted almost strictly Libertarian since 1980. What I love most about the freedom movement, another name for the Libertarian platform, are the ideas of voluntary cooperation and spontaneous order that when channeled through free markets lead to the continuous evolution and progress of humanity. I believe that individual freedom in free markets when combined with property rights and the rule of law and ethical democratic government results in societies that maximize prosperity and establish conditions that promote human happiness and well being.

But, unlike many people in the freedom movement who view the responsibility of business solely as returning a profit to investors, I have long been a strong proponent of the social and environmental responsibility of business. Businesses have multiple stakeholders. When all stakeholders are cared for and flourish together, the business has a much higher probability of being profitable over the long term. And with higher profits, giving back to our communities and protecting the environment are simply the right things to do. Indeed, I strongly believe that once more businesses are managed on behalf of all of their stakeholders that many of the challenges we collectively face throughout the world will be effectively and efficiently addressed and reversed.

Along with my youthful explorations in political and economic theory, over the years I maintained my quest for personal growth and expanded consciousness, continuing my study of the great philosophers from all over the world, as well as pursuing a 20-plus-year dedicated study and practice of A Course in Miracles. I also practice a variety of consciousness-altering disciplines such as meditation, yoga, and holotropic breathwork. I introduced my own philosophy of personal empowerment and accountability into Whole Foods Market and structured the business to foster an atmosphere of stakeholder accountability through having a strong business mission, team member empowerment, and continual creative experimentation. Guess what? This philosophy has been incredibly successful and the business has flourished tremendously.

I first met Michael Strong through a mutual friend back in 2002. I liked him immediately. Michael was the first Libertarian I had met who was also idealistic and who shared my commitments to both economic and political freedom as well as personal growth, social responsibility, and environmental stewardship. Like me, Michael wants to use these philosophies and practices to help make the world a better place. Most Libertarians I know are committed to economic and political freedom but not to the other three. Most of my friends who were committed to personal growth and social and environmental responsibility don't believe in economic freedom, and continued to view business and capitalism as inherently exploitative, and the source of the problems instead of the solutions.

Although Michael lived in New Mexico at the time working as the headmaster of a charter school, we began a long dialogue via e-mail in which we shared our ideas about how to make the world a better place and discovered increasingly that we had remarkably similar views on a myriad of issues. In the fall of 2003, Michael invited me to join him at a meeting in Angel Fire, New Mexico, to explore whether we wanted to foster a community of people who shared our vision and ideals. After a great deal of brainstorming and discussion we decided to try to create an organization that would serve as a beacon to liberty, human potential, and making the world a better place. We decided to call it FLOW* in honor of Mihaly Csikszentmihalyi's wonderful book by that title. Since that seminal meeting in the mountains east of Taos, we have been slowly but steadily evolving our ideas about what FLOW is, why it exists, and what we hope to accomplish with this organization. This book is our most complete statement to date about what FLOW offers to the world.

What is FLOW? To sum it up in one simple phrase: FLOW is about liberating the entrepreneurial spirit for good. Our world faces many tremendous challenges, from AIDS to global warming to large population growth to malaria to war and nuclear proliferation to many, many other challenges. FLOW is dedicated to the proposition that creative entrepreneurs can help solve all the challenges in the world. When we talk about entrepreneurs, however, we are not restricting the meaning of the word to business entrepreneurs. Business entrepreneurs will, of course, continue to play a very important role in creating solutions to our challenges, but so will various other types of entrepreneurs including social entrepreneurs, educational entrepreneurs, health entrepreneurs, political entrepreneurs, and spiritual entrepreneurs. At FLOW, we believe that the human capacity for creativity is limitless and that entrepreneurship effectively channels that creativity into real-world solutions for our challenges. Every person alive has the potential to learn and grow and to contribute their unique creativity toward making the world a better place. FLOW is dedicated to liberating each person's entrepreneurial spirit and helping that entrepreneurial spirit creatively flow toward the collective good of all humankind.

—JOHN MACKEY
CEO, Whole Foods Market
Co-Founder, FLOW®

---

*FLOW is a registered trademark of Freedom Lights Our World, Inc.

Preface

Michael Strong

An increasing number of people, of all ages, want to dedicate their lives to making the world a better place. So many people in the developed world now have more than enough stuff, and they now crave meaning and experience more than they crave more goods. At the same time, those who have a comfortable life want to maintain their comfortable lives, and those who do not yet have a comfortable life want to obtain a comfortable life while also working towards making the world a better place. Who doesn't want to "be the solution"?

And, indeed, there are many calamities, present and future, that we should rightly wish to avoid. And both out of a sense of compassion and self-preservation we should work together to create a world that works for all.

In the past those who have felt the most urgency regarding making the world a better place have often expressed themselves through anger and outrage, attempting to motivate others through fear and shame. While there will no doubt be contexts in which such approaches continue to be useful, there is also a tremendous amount of good work to be done by means of creating and supporting new enterprises, for profit, for benefit, non-profit, and everything in between, that transform society for the better in profound ways. This book is for those who believe, with us, that the most important work for the future is to be done by means of creating enterprises or, in the words of Michelangelo, by "Criticizing by Creating."

John and I created FLOW because both of us were frustrated at the fact that the vast majority of those who care about personal growth, compassion, and mindfulness were largely ignorant of economics, and those who were more knowledgeable about economics often ridiculed those writers and practices that were working to reduce our propensities towards egotism and selfishness.

For me, doing good is the most natural thing in the world; I have no appetite for material goods, and am happy living quite simply—at the age of 48, I recently moved across the country and all of my possessions (with the exception of books) fit into my salvaged 1999 Saturn, which I subsequently gave to my daughter and finished my move with only those possessions that I could carry onto an airplane. I simply don't understand why people want things, nor why they enjoy most forms of entertainment. I would rather spend all day, every day, educating young people than "having fun" or being entertained in any other way.

Consistent with my joyful passion to educate the young, I spent 15 years working to create better schools, starting as a public school reformer and then creating several private and charter schools. The last school I created, a charter school in Angel Fire, New Mexico, was located in a region without any serious academic ambitions; the first year the school was operating a representative of the nearby University of New Mexico—Taos stopped by to talk about college options, and the topic of Advanced Placement (AP) courses came up. She said point blank, "Students in northern New Mexico are not capable of passing AP courses."

Despite her informed opinion (she had more than a decade of experience with students in northern New Mexico, and I had none), I nonetheless implemented an AP program at Moreno Valley High School (MVHS). There is a ranking system of U.S. high schools nationally, created by Jay Mathews, an education journalist for Newsweek and the

Washington Post. Mathews' list ranks schools based on the number of AP tests taken at each school divided by the number of graduating seniors. Mathews argues that this is an important ranking system because it turns out that simply taking AP courses, which are more difficult than many freshman college courses, is an excellent predictor of college success—students know what to expect and how to study for a real course.

The second year that MVHS was open, it was ranked in the top 150 schools in the U.S. on Mathews' list. The third year MVHS ranked number 36, with a passing rate for AP exams that was more than double the national average. Most of the schools ranked more highly on Mathews' list than MVHS were either very wealthy suburban schools in places like Palo Alto or Westchester County, or magnet schools that drew the best and the brightest from an entire urban region. Although MVHS was in a higher income region than the surrounding region, the student population was not from high income families, and for the most part the school served as a neighborhood school rather than a magnet (more than 80 percent of the students were local). I had created one of the most rapid turn arounds, in terms of creating a subculture of learning in a region that had previously lacked any such subculture, of any school in the United States. Our students had taken more AP exams and done better on them than possibly any comparable school in the United States, starting from scratch in just three years.

But in the meantime I had been forced out of the school because I did not have an administrator's license. Throughout my 15 years' career in education, I had never become a credentialed teacher nor had I become a licensed administrator. In private schools it had not been necessary and, when I started the school, it had not been required either. I was a victim of a change in New Mexico charter school law, and despite our school's performance, the State Department of Education would not relent on the certification issue.

I describe this anecdote in some detail because there are several ways in which the perspective that John and I have created in FLOW differs from that of more mainstream movements promoting social entrepreneurship and socially responsible business. Most of those who promote social entrepreneurship and socially responsible business identify with the political left, and belong to a social tribe that bonds together by means of hatred and ridicule of the political right. Most of academia shares this social bonding process. The Stanford Social Innovation Review, for instance, a generally excellent publication documenting the contemporary social entrepreneurship movement, rarely publishes anything that would be outside the accepted boundaries of Democratic Party political positions.

As a consequence, there are certain ideas which are simply not stated in polite company because they are identified with the enemy tribe; support for charter schools, or school choice, is one of them. That fact is gradually changing with respect to charter schools—Presidential candidate Barack Obama, to his credit, came out in favor of charter schools in the midst of the heated primary battle with Clinton, who toed an establishment teachers' union party line, but it is still considered poor taste to say anything positive about other forms of school choice in polite (read: liberal) company.

The former 1970's Marxist Herbert Gintis, now turned complexity theorist at the Santa Fe Institute for Complexity, has written that "the left-right dichotomy is a sick joke." Gintis, who was formerly very much a man of the left but who has learned to respect the arguments of classical liberals such as Hayek, realizes that opportunities for doing good are undermined by means of the two-hundred year old attachment to the left-right dichotomy.

I give John great credit for "coming out of the closet" as a libertarian, given his prominence, because the vast majority of Whole Foods Market employees and consumers identify as "left" and bond by means of hating the right and everything with an allegedly conservative hue. John and I are creating a new tribe that might better be described as "upwing" rather than "left" or "right." We are doing so because in order to create a world in which entrepreneurs and Conscious Capitalists can solve all the world's problems, we need to escape the "sick joke" of partisan political categories.

There are three specific ways in which escaping partisan categories can empower us to solve all the world's problems:

1. Entrepreneurs in health, education, and community formation need the same level playing field and freedom that have allowed entrepreneurs in technology to transform the world.
2. In order to escape poverty, the world's poor need access to the same Entrepreneur's Toolkit—secure property rights, rule of law,

and economic freedom—that are enjoyed by virtually all residents of developed nations.

3. Creating property rights solutions to environmental problems, in many cases using the environmental trusts advocated by Peter Barnes in Capitalism 3.0, will allow entrepreneurs to create a more environmentally sustainable world.

All three of these approaches are often ignored by tribalists on the left, including many such tribalists in academia. And yet none of these proposals are new; free market economists have been advocating these structural solutions in some manner for decades and, in some ways, for centuries.

Insofar as those on the right advocate selfishness or religious or ethnic tribalism, we are adamantly opposed to them. Our ideals are very much those of universal compassion, inclusiveness, and peace. From my perspective, the simple awareness of the scale of suffering in the world should incline us all to devote all of our time to helping others. But, as it turns out, in order to help billions of others most effectively, we need to incorporate some knowledge of classical liberalism into our desire to help.

Thus if you are looking for an inspirational book on Conscious Capitalism that repudiates all economics and business as bad, you may be frustrated by those sections of the book that explain basic economic concepts. If you are looking for hard, concrete, detailed economic and regulatory (or anti-regulatory) policy suggestions you may be frustrated by those sections of the book that may seem to be so much inspirational fluff. Political tribalists on the left may be frustrated by our support for markets, and political tribalists on the right may be frustrated by our constant emphasis on doing good. And all of these frustrations are exactly what we believe that the world needs today.

Enjoy what you will and, where you are annoyed, join us in Criticizing by Creating. A world of six, going on seven, billion optimistic, empowered creators will provide billions of new solutions to problems that will allow us to overcome obstacles. We don't claim to have a perfect solution to getting from here to there, but we believe that we are pointing in an important direction that has not yet been adequately recognized.

We can't prove this, of course, because that which has not yet been created can never be shown to exist. Prior to the creation of Whole Foods Market, one could not have proven that a health food store could become a Fortune 500 corporation. Prior to the creation of MVHS, one could not have proven that it was possible for a school in northern New Mexico to become a top-ranked school in the U.S. Indeed in these, and in almost all cases of creation, all of the "evidence," all of the "proof," is that every act of creation is impossible. This is one of the reasons why academic social science will always be blind to the creative possibilities of a free civilization. And yet almost all of us alive in the world today, and almost every moment of health and well-being that we experience, would not exist were it not for two thousand years of "impossible" creation—borne by individuals—that has come before us.

There are many different voices in this book, not all of whom agree with each other. Some of them, such as Candace Smith, Muhammad Yunus, Donna Callejon, Hernando de Soto, Don Beck, and myself might best be described as social entrepreneurs—individuals who have contributed to change primarily through organizations that were not originally organized as profitable corporations. Others, such as John Mackey, Kartar Singh Khalsa, Brian Johnson, and Jeff Klein, have been leaders of for profit corporations—but always with a strong social mission. But in the end, as John likes to say, the difference between for-profit and nonprofit is arbitrary—good for profit corporations and good nonprofit organizations share 98 percent of the same DNA. All of us are united by a desire to do good, and the organizational form through which we do good is less important than is our ability to carry out our mission.

Many of the people who might normally be inclined to read some of the voices, such as those focusing on inspirational personal development, might not usually be inclined to read some of the more economic voices, such as the arguments on economic freedom. But it is our belief that this fragmentation of perspectives is itself one of the obstacles to creating sustainable peace, prosperity, happiness, and well-being for all. We take the view that everything—from personal well-being to physical health to societal strength and peace is all connected. Think of our world, your world, as we are increasingly coming to see personal health: It's not just your diet or just your exercise or just your mental state of being—but all that interconnect and influence each other.

We invite those of you who are weary of partisan hatred, who are poised to release yourself from the desire to force others to conform to your will, and who are willing to live and let live, to work with us in creating a better world.

FLOW offers three public programs, which provide a point of entry and opportunities for action:

1. Peace through Commerce®
2. Accelerating Women Entrepreneurs™
3. Conscious Capitalism®

Though these program you can learn about the movements they represent and meet like-minded individuals who share passion and commitment to making the world a better place through entrepreneurship and markets. More generally, FLOW offers FLOW Activation Circles, where FLOW-oriented individuals can learn, network, and support each other in various cities—write contact@flowidealism.org for information on how to join of start a FLOW Activation Circle in your community.

We also invite you to join our on-line community, at www.flow idealism.org—and receive our newsletters, participate in conversations, meet others, and develop your wiki page to position yourself as a socially minded entrepreneurial individual.

Finally, we invite you to donate to FLOW, which is a 501(c)(3) nonprofit educational organization. You may donate at our web site, www.flowidealism.org, or by contacting us a contact@flowidealism.org.

Peace,
Michael

Acknowledgments

Thanks to the FLOW board, Jim Von Ehr, Vidar Jorgensen, Susan Niederhoffer, and Randy Eisenman, as well as to all who have donated to FLOW, including Dick Cornuelle, Ken and Frayda Levy, Gerry Ohrstrom, Harvey Cody, Kartar Singh Khalsa, Mark Finser, Christiana Wyly, Sam Wyly, and hundreds of others. I would also like to thank Philip Sansone, Jim and Maureen Tusty, Mark Skousen, Tim Fort, and Barbara Barrett. Thanks to Candace Smith, Bert Loan, Marsha Enright, and Malcolm Roberts as early fellow travelers on the path that later became FLOW. Thanks to Gary Becker and the late Paul Heyne for being honorable individuals with deep integrity who also understand entrepreneurs and markets. Thanks to Paul Edwards, Giancarlo Ibárgüen, and Jeff Sandefer as institutional leaders sympathetic to our vision. Thanks to Gary Hoover, the godfather of FLOW, who introduced me to John, and thanks to Milton Friedman, whose early sympathy helped broaden our circle of support in a crucial early stage, and Bob Chitester who introduced John and me to many key contacts. Thanks to Muhammad Yunus and Hernando de Soto for their inspirational, path-breaking work, and support. Thanks to all the FLOW supporters and activists who have taken initiative in various ways. Thanks to my hard-working colleagues who are devoted to this work whether or not they are getting paid, especially Philomena Blees and Jeff Klein. And most of all, thanks to John.

Part One

The Entrepreneurial Spirit and How to Liberate It

The entrepreneur in us sees opportunities everywhere we look, but many people see only problems everywhere they look. The entrepreneur in us is more concerned with discriminating between opportunities than he or she is with failing to see the opportunities.

—MICHAEL GERBER

Chapter 1

Context

Michael Strong
CEO and Chief Visionary Officer, FLOW

A mong the first teachings of the Buddha is the understanding that "mind is the forerunner of all things." If we believe it is impossible to make the world a better place, we will create a self-fulfilling prophecy. If we believe we can make a difference and set about doing so with a clear-eyed vision, passionate focus, persistence, and courage, then we can achieve extraordinary things.

In the language of business, each human being who is dispirited is a loss to the balance sheet of global goodness, whereas each human being who is an inspired, energetic, and thoughtful change agent is an enormous asset to global goodness. Optimistic creators such as Apple's Steve Jobs and Google founders Sergey Brin and Larry Page have produced billions of dollars of wealth and immeasurable happiness and well-being that would not have existed had they not founded the businesses they and their teams created. By championing the practice of microlending, Muhammad Yunus empowered tens of millions of poor women to become entrepreneurs and create value for their families and communities. Maria Montessori created a whole new way of understanding children, and in addition to the tens of thousands of schools that follow her method she influenced child-raising in numerous ways, including the creation of the idea of child-sized furniture. We believe that every human being is capable of creating something of great value, and that at present the vast majority of us only create a tiny fraction of the value that we could create for ourselves and others.

So how do we create a world in which happiness and well-being are ubiquitous and endlessly abundant?

The Importance of Progress

To begin, we highlight the importance of progress, and illuminate the existence of far more progress than is usually acknowledged. People in general like to do things they are good at and in which they are making progress. If we play a sport or a game, we are more likely to keep playing it if we find ourselves getting better and better at it. If we focus on and believe all the doom and gloom we hear from the media and the negative doomsday predictions from both ends of the political spectrum, it is no surprise that many of us are ready to throw in the towel. But if we see the profound progress humanity is making on many levels, we can become ever more engaged in the game of making the world a better place.

What if, instead of (or in addition to) getting excited about playing a game, we got excited about our ever-increasing ability to make the world a better place?

The work of psychologist Martin Seligman clearly demonstrates that we are more effective for a longer period of time when we believe that we are successful and that such a belief will help ensure we will continue to be successful in the future.[*]

Stop and breathe. Have you ever been in a room with too many people yelling, too many televisions and radios blaring, perhaps horns honking outside, and so much stress and anger that you can barely hear yourself think?

While it is wonderful that news is now widely available, being immersed in news and its principally negative orientation, confuses us and prevents us from seeing the world clearly.

---

[*]For a wealth of resources on positive psychology, visit the Positive Psychology Center (www.ppc.sas.upenn.edu/).

The problem is not that what happens on the news is false (though occasionally some is), nor even that the news fails to tell us many important things (which it often does), but more deeply the problem is that the news doesn't encourage us to see the big picture. The news, by its nature, is focused on problems and bad things that happen. And its ubiquitous presence and compelling and penetrating effects distort our perception of reality.

If we want to liberate our potential to do good work in the world and to have a positive effect on the world, we need to believe that what we do matters. And to believe what we do matters, it helps to see that what others are doing and have done for thousands of years makes a difference. The doing of good work may take time, and it may not be obvious how you will achieve your goals. Two hundred years ago almost everyone on earth was poor and famines, in which people literally starved to death, were a regular feature of life around the world. The people who created the steam engine and constitutional government had a general attitude that practical problems could be solved, and they worked hard and long to solve problems, but they did not fully realize that they were creating the beginning of the end of starvation as a routine family experience.

We have good news: What people do matters a tremendous amount.*

Peace Is Breaking Out All Over

Thus, the first fact that we ought to stop and consider is that, despite the steady barrage of news concerning wars that are happening and that might break out in the future, from a deeper perspective the fact is, shockingly enough, that peace is breaking out around the world:

> By 2003, there were 40 percent fewer conflicts than in 1992. The deadliest conflicts—those with 1,000 or more battle deaths—fell by some 80 percent. The number of genocides and other mass

---

*For a data-rich review of the positive context we are all operating in, see Gregg Easterbrook's book *The Progress Paradox* (Random House, 2003), a follow-up to a 1998 article, "America the O.K. Why Life in the U.S. Has Never Been Better" (*The New Republic*, http://phe.rockefeller.edu/g_easterbrook_11jan1998/).

slaughters of civilians also dropped by 80 percent, while core human rights abuses have declined in five out of six regions of the developing world since the mid-1990s. International terrorism is the only type of political violence that has increased. Although the death toll has jumped sharply over the past three years, terrorists kill only a fraction of the number who die in wars.[*]

Prior to 1992, war was far more common around the world than it is today. Wars with more than 1,000 battle deaths are down by 80 percent! The Cold War, in which the planet was divided between Communist countries and capitalist countries, resulted in endless wars throughout the developing world, many of which we barely heard about. While the end of the Cold War has not brought complete peace, it is significant to notice that despite the fact that ongoing televised casualties in Iraq bring the horrors of war into our living rooms, nonetheless from a global perspective we haven't lived in such a peaceful world since the nineteenth century.

Poverty Vanishing More Quickly than Ever Before

Well, so war is on the decline; what about the horrors of poverty? It turns out that poverty is also decreasing on a global scale the likes of which the world has never seen before. Although poverty in Africa remains a very serious problem, the good news is that economic growth in India and China is raising the standard of living of more people more quickly than has ever taken place in history.

The first thing to realize about India and China is that they are each home to more than a billion people. Together they account for about 40 percent of the global population. In the past 20 years, about half a billion people in these two nations have been raised out of poverty. Now, a negative person might point out that three quarters of

---

[*]See "Peace on Earth? Increasingly, Yes" by Andrew Mack in *The Washington Post* (December 28, 2005). The source for this article is a report of a study produced by the Human Security Centre in British Columbia, which Professor Mack heads (www.humansecurityreport.info/index.php?option=content&task=view&id=33& Itemid=68).

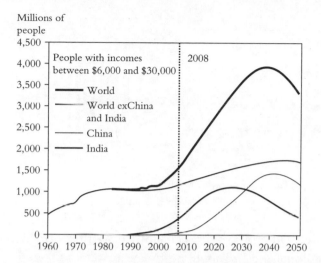

Figure 1.1   The Expanding World Middle Class
SOURCE: Used with permission from Goldman Sachs Global Economics Paper
No. 170, "The Expanding Middle Class: The Exploding Middle Class and Falling
Global Inequality."

them are still poor; but half a billion no longer in poverty is more
than the entire population of the United States. For countries that
have been symbols of mass poverty for hundreds of years to have a
quarter of their populations lifted out of poverty in merely 20 years is
mind boggling. More important, at current rates of economic growth,
China will reach the current U.S. standard of living around 2030,
and India will reach the current U.S. standard of living a few decades
later.* See Figure 1.1.

Defining the middle class worldwide as having an annual per capita
income between $6,000 and $30,000, Goldman Sachs estimates that
before 2040, 4 billion people will qualify. After that the number of people in the middle class by this definition declines primarily because the
Chinese will have become wealthier than that.†

Thus, although there are relatively poor people in the United
States, from the perspective of Chinese or Indian poverty even the U.S.

---

*From The Globalist, April 15, 2005 (www.theglobalist.com).

†Goldman Sachs research cited by Paul Murphy, "The Relentless Rise of the
Bourgeoise," The Financial Times Blog, July 11, 2008 (http://ftalphaville.
ft.com/blog/2008/07/11/14423/the-relentless-rise-of-the-bourgeoisie/).

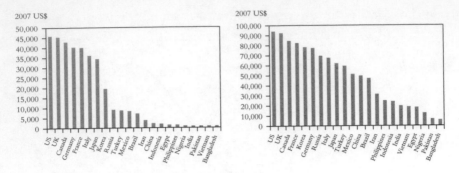

Figure 1.2   Income per Capita in 2007 and 2050
SOURCE: Used with permission from Goldman Sachs Global Economics Paper No. 170,
"The Expanding Middle Class: The Exploding Middle Class and Failing Global Inequality."

poor are well fed and mostly well housed. Within our lifetimes, mass poverty in China and India will no longer exist.

Note the difference in scale between the two graphs in Figure 1.2; by 2050, Goldman Sachs estimates that income per capita in Turkey, Mexico, China, and Brazil will all be higher than it is in the United States today.*

Moreover, it is not only in China and India that economic growth is rapidly eliminating poverty: Ireland, for instance, moved from being one of the poorest nations in Europe 15 years ago to being the wealthiest. Many (but not all) nations from the former Soviet Union are growing well. Chile, Costa Rica, and Mexico are doing well in Latin America. The outlook throughout Asia is generally positive: Forty years ago Japan was a poor nation, thirty years ago Singapore, Hong Kong, Taiwan, and South Korea were all poor, now Thailand and Vietnam have joined India and China in successful economic growth and are on their way to joining the no-longer-poor portion of the world.

Clearly, there is much to do and we should not rest on our laurels. But we also should not despair over global poverty. It is decreasing more rapidly than it has ever decreased in history, with more people attaining higher standards of living than the world has ever known. While very serious problems remain in much of the world, the fact that we are making so much progress so quickly ought to inspire us to more effective action rather than despair.

---

*Murphy, op. cit.

Paradoxically, the alleviation of poverty around the world concerns many people. A headline on economic growth in China expressed environmental concerns with the question, "Too Many Toyotas?" The downside, of course, of nine billion human beings (the expected peak global population later this century), each with a U.S. standard of living, is the demand for natural resources on a colossal scale. Most people assume that such an enormous use of natural resources necessarily implies extraordinary environmental damage. Does it?

The End of Environmental Destruction?

Yes, serious environmental concerns do exist and the possibility of catastrophic climate change is among them. That said, in order to solve the problems facing us it is important to acknowledge the significant progress that has been made in the past and to consider the strategies and techniques that succeeded in driving this progress.

The decline of acid rain is a good place to begin to understand the nature of progress on environmental issues. In the 1970s there were widespread concerns that acid rain would destroy ecosystems throughout the United States. Sulfur dioxide, a pollutant that was emitted largely by power plants, combined with various gases in the atmosphere to create rain that was more acidic than is natural. As a consequence, numerous plants and fish began to die.

Subsequently, a law was passed in the United States that set up a sulfur dioxide trading system: power plants that produced sulfur dioxide had to buy rights to continue to do so. Some companies then began to add antipollution equipment to reduce their sulfur dioxide emissions. As a consequence, they were able to sell their pollution rights to companies that had not yet installed the anti-pollution equipment. Although many environmentalists were originally against this system because they did not like the idea of companies owning a "right to pollute," what happened was that companies suddenly had an incentive to invest in the very best antipollution equipment. The faster they could install better equipment, the sooner they could sell their pollution rights to other companies. Soon it became cheaper, in many cases, to install the innovative antipollution equipment than to buy more pollution rights. As a result, sulfur dioxide emissions in the United States have been cut in half in the last 20 years and most ecosystems that had been damaged by acid rain are now well on the way to recovery.

As important, the cost of adding these scrubbers was less than a tenth of what had been expected. The innovation dynamic catalyzed by the market in pollution rights created a circumstance in which pollution decreased both more quickly and more cheaply than anyone had imagined possible.[*]

The growth of forests in the United States is a good place to begin to understand how our environment may be restored. Deforestation in the United States took place at the highest rate during the nineteenth century as pioneers cleared forests in order to create farms. From 1920 to 1990, the percentage of the country covered in forest was stable. Since 1990, the percentage of the country being re-covered in forest has steadily increased, so that now we are returning about two million acres of land to forest each year.[†] Indeed, the rate of reforestation in the United States is now so high that some scientists believe that the country is absorbing as much in new carbon emissions as it is emitting. U.S. forests now contain 40 percent more wood than they did 50 years ago and, by some measures, despite the fact that the United States is the largest producer of greenhouse gases, due to our heavy levels of reforestation, the U.S. may actually be carbon neutral with respect to net annual emissions.[‡]

Patrick Moore, a founder of Greenpeace, believes that "trees are the answer."[§] He points out that the more wood and paper we use, the more trees are planted, and the more trees that are planted, the more carbon is absorbed into the atmosphere.

Without going into more details here, the primary points are:

---

[*]"Acid Rain Control: Success on the Cheap" by Richard A. Kerr, published in *Science* magazine (Volume 282, November 1998).

[†]Index of Leading Environmental Indicators, 2003, published by the American Enterprise Institute.

[‡]"The International Challenge of Climate Change" by Steve Raynor, November 24, 2004, 12 (www.cspo.org/ourlibrary/documents/EACmemo.pdf).

[§]It is for this reason that Patrick Moore's Greenspirit claims generally "trees are the answer" and backs using more wood to support a larger forestry products industry (www.greenspirit.com/trees_answer.cfm).

1. We have solved environmental problems in the past (decreased sulfur dioxide emissions, increased forest cover).
2. We can continue to solve environmental problems in the future.

Although there are some people who believe that fear of catastrophe is necessary to get people to take action, it is also important to be aware that real progress has been made and continues to be achieved.

As countries develop and poor nations become richer, environmental conditions generally improve. Economists have noticed what they call the "environmental Kuznets curve," whereby economic growth can be detrimental to the environment in countries where average annual per capita incomes range between $2,000 and $8,000, but thereafter, environmental improvements take place. Economist Benjamin Friedman summarizes the evidence:

> In cross-country comparisons, sulfur dioxide, nitrous oxide, carbon monoxide, smoke, and lead from automotive emissions all show increasing atmospheric concentrations up to some income level but a decreasing concentration thereafter. A similar pattern obtains for fecal contamination in rivers, as well as contamination by heavy metals such as lead, arsenic, cadmium, mercury, and nickel, all of which carry well-established health risks. Conversely, the level of dissolved oxygen in rivers (a key sign of biological vitality) appears to decrease at first with economic development and then increase.
>
> Benjamin Friedman, *The Moral Consequences of Economic Growth,* Knopf, 2005, 383

As incomes increase in each country, individuals and governments do what it takes to improve the environment. Although we would like to reduce the extent to which these harms take place, the long-term prognosis for the effects of economic growth on the environment is positive.[*] Although problems do exist and will need to be solved, our track record for solving environmental problems is far more positive than is often acknowledged.

---

[*]See also Jack Hollander, *The Real Environmental Crisis: Why Poverty, Not Affluence, Is the Environment's Number One Enemy* (University of California, 2004).

Health and Well-being in the Developed World

Some of the positive developments in this area are almost unbelievable: The average American lived to 54 only 50 years ago. Now, our average life span is 76 years and climbing. The number of Americans living past 100 is exploding ; currently there are 71,000, three times that many are predicted to reach the milestone in the next 20 years, and who knows how many living up to what age beyond that. Cancer is on the decline, AIDS is on the decline, suicide is on the decline, fatal accidents are on the decline. By almost all measures our health is improving.[*] The major exception is obesity. If we could only exercise more and eat more healthily we would defeat the single greatest obstacle to dramatically improved health.

Meanwhile, we live in larger and better houses than ever before. It takes fewer hours of labor to buy food, clothes, and most consumer goods than it did 50 years ago. In the 1960s long-distance telephone calls were a luxury; now most teenagers have cell phones and Skype Internet long-distance service is free. Almost every poor American has a refrigerator and a color television, items that were considered luxuries only affordable by the rich not long ago. Indeed, almost every item that was once available only to the very wealthy has become common even among the poor in the developed world.

Health care and education are two of the very few items that have become more expensive and, even there, in many ways they have become cheaper. For instance, although university tuitions have increased rapidly, MIT now has a project through which it offers all of its courses online for free. Although it requires considerable discipline to study the material on one's own, the Internet has made access to vast educational resources essentially free to anyone with access to the Internet. The very best encyclopedias on earth even 20 years ago could provide only a tiny, tiny fraction of the information that is instantly available through Google.

Health care is more expensive primarily because there are such sophisticated options available. One hundred years ago, doctors could do very little to improve health; every local pharmacy today provides far higher quality health care, at a lower cost, than was available from

---

[*]Again, see Easterbrook op. cit. for evidence on positive trends.

the best doctors that money could buy in 1910. And, although access to cutting-edge contemporary health care remains a problem, 75 percent of the $1.4 trillion dollars in health care costs spent annually in the United States go to the treatment of chronic diseases, most of which are preventable through lifestyle choices. Eat well and exercise and, in essence, you have solved the single greatest health care problem in the United States in your own small way. Encourage your friends and family to do likewise, and the amount of resources devoted to health care will decrease dramatically.

Goodness and Beauty as the Growth Industries of the Twenty-First Century

Moreover, a significant and growing portion of our population is actively engaged in doing good. Many of the fastest growing companies, and the most desirable corporations to work for, are explicitly committed to doing good: Google, Whole Foods Market, eBay, Southwest Airlines, and Toyota are all socially responsible corporations, and they are just the tip of the iceberg. If corporations want to succeed in the twenty-first century marketplace, they will have to satisfy demanding customers, employees, and investors that they are, in fact, honorable companies. There are numerous indicators that this movement is growing, as documented in Patricia Aburdene's book *Megatrends 2010: The Rise of Conscious Capitalism*.

Meanwhile, from another direction, it is noteworthy that in 2006, for the first time, the Nobel Peace Prize was awarded to Muhammad Yunus and the *for-profit* organization, Grameen Bank, he founded. Grameen Bank has been the leader in the global microfinance movement, through which tens of millions of impoverished women have received micro-loans that allow them to engage in entrepreneurial activity. In 1968, John Kenneth Galbraith expected that the age of the entrepreneur was over. Shortly thereafter, Yunus began giving tiny loans to women to purchase chickens, bicycles, scales, and other capital goods to empower them to launch their own businesses. The age of micro-entrepreneurship was launched even as expert observers had come to believe that the entrepreneurial role was obsolete.

Anyone can be an entrepreneur now. In the 1970s, as Marxist theorists were discussing the final days of "late capitalism," Steve Jobs and Steve Wozniak were creating Apple Computer, Bill Gates and Paul Allen were creating Microsoft, and thousands of other high school and college dropouts were creating thousands of other companies that resulted in the technology revolution of the last 30 years. Because of their efforts, I can now develop entrepreneurial projects with individuals in Sri Lanka, Uganda, Romania, and Nepal in 24 hours. Using the Internet, we can all work together immediately. Andrew Hyde's Startup Weekend gathers small groups of software developers to start a new project or company over the course of an intensive 54-hour weekend.

Sugata Mitra's Hole-in-the-Wall project has shown that illiterate, uneducated ghetto children in Delhi can learn to use the Internet on their own in the course of days, with no outside guidance or instruction whatsoever and immediately engage with the enormous world of the Web. Those of us who want to help others develop their own projects already face an endless sea of opportunity for helping the world's poor improve their lives.

Meanwhile, the astounding success of Wikipedia reveals an unlimited appetite for openly and freely producing and sharing information. The Open Source software movement demonstrates that even very high-quality software can be produced collaboratively, for free. As mentioned earlier, MIT is in the process of putting its entire curriculum online and allowing free access. And with the $100 laptop developed for the One Laptop per Child program and broadband costs collapsing around the world, millions of new people are getting plugged into the global economy and the universe of global knowledge faster than ever before. Ori Brafman and Rod Beckstrom document the "unstoppable power of leaderless organizations" in *The Starfish and the Spider*, as eBay becomes one of the largest economies on earth.

Daniel Pink, in *A Whole New Mind*, makes a compelling case that the growth industries in the twenty-first-century economy in the developed world will be based around the production of goods and services into which meaning, beauty, empathy, and other soft values are integrated. In the developed world, there is a thriving "green" consumer sector. But Pink also points to the ubiquity of design: from the elegant Apple iPod to the fact that Wal-Mart carries "designer" toilet bowl brushes. Much of the value added to products in the future will come from improved aesthetics and richer, more rewarding experiences rather than bigger and more. BMW has engineers who specialize in the acoustic experience of driving a BMW. There are professionals with business cards that read "Cultural Strategist" and "Organizational Storyteller." The world of meaning, design, and aesthetics will generate enormous new industries in the twenty-first century, as all of the old mechanical and commodity-based industries, which operated strictly on price criteria, fall prey to competitors that are ahead of the curve in the meaning dimension of their products and services. Many of the great entrepreneurs of the twenty-first century will be entrepreneurs who create exceptional enterprises that are preeminent producers of beauty and grace, culture and experience, happiness and well-being.

The poet Frederick Turner describes the twenty-first-century growth industries as the "Charm Industries:"

> Once manufactures and information have become vanishingly cheap to produce and therefore are not very profitable or labor intensive, the major form of profitable production in the twenty-first century will be cultural production—the irreducibly labor- and capital-intensive human activities that I call the Charm Industries: tourism, education, entertainment, adventure, religion, sport, fashion, cuisine, personal service, gardening, art, history, movies, ritual, psychotherapy, politics, and the eternal soap opera of relationships. Those industries are subject to diseconomies of scale—that is, they are less effective when pursued by large units of production, such as big nation-states, and more efficient when they take place in small units such as cities, regions, and traditional ethnic areas. Therefore we should remove the political obstacles to the present trend toward greater regional autonomy in culture, while opening all the technological and economic gates of world communication.
>
> Fred Turner, "Make Everybody Rich,"
> *Independent Review,* Summer 2002, 135

Through Pink and Turner we can glimpse a world of never ending economic growth in which the bulk of the growth is in education, culture, and diverse forms of human development and experience. We'll expand on this glimpse when we look at the consequences of liberating entrepreneurs of happiness and well-being to create new and better subcultures and ways of life.

This is the context in which truly extraordinary flows of goods, services, capital, people, and knowledge are taking place. We can no longer afford to be parochial or to support parochialisms anywhere. *The World Is Flat*, in Thomas Friedman's sense. The markets of the future will demand a *Whole New Mind*, in Daniel Pink's sense. And soon we will all be engaged in "Social Business," in Muhammad Yunus' sense of business engaged in a social purpose.

Are Women Entrepreneurs Real Entrepreneurs?

A Whole New Mind, A Whole New Gender, A Whole New World

The world of entrepreneurs is a male-dominated world. The great entrepreneurs of the nineteenth century and the first half of the twentieth century were industrialists, inventors, and salesmen: Andrew Carnegie, Thomas Edison, P.T. Barnum, Henry Ford, Thomas Watson, the railroad builders, the retailers, the newspaper publishers, and so on.

The great entrepreneurs of the second half of the twentieth century were tech entrepreneurs and media moguls: Bill Hewlett and David Packard; Intel's Robert Noyce, Gordon Moore, and Andy Grove; Steve Jobs and Steve Wozniak; Bill Gates; Ted Turner; Richard Branson; and so forth.

First we were a manufacturing economy, then we became an information economy. In both cases, the world we lived in and the wealth that transformed our standard of living was largely created by men. In a recent survey ranking history's great entrepreneurs, the most highly ranked women were Mary Kay Ash and Oprah Winfrey: both highly successful, but makeup and a talk show about relationships?

Daniel Pink's book *A Whole New Mind* makes the case that in the twenty-first century, the most important growth industries will be in the realms of beauty, empathy, harmony, and other aesthetic and quality of life values. He makes the case that Asia, Automation, and Abundance will dictate this transformation. Low-cost manufacturing in Asia has already displaced much of the manufacturing base in the developed world and even some of the manufacturing in Latin America. Meanwhile, automation of manufacturing is continuing at a rapid pace, such that fewer and fewer human beings will be required in manufacturing processes in any case. And, finally, due to abundance, most of us in the developed world are already at the point at which we really don't need any more stuff. We have enough quantity. From here on out, quality will matter far more than it has in the past.

The successful entrepreneurs of the future will be those who can improve the quality of the products and services we consume, especially insofar as those improvements result in improved quality of life. The growth industries of the future will be led by entrepreneurs who specialize in excellence in beauty and design, in style and fashion, in taste and elegance, in better living environments and better social environments, in more harmonious workplaces, more empathetic and patient-respectful health care, in more humane education, and the like.

Pink's notion of "a whole new mind" refers to a future in which both the left brain—analytical—and the right brain—intuitive and holistic—will be more valued than they have been in the past, especially when used together. Although it is not politically correct to make gender generalizations, precisely because in the past women have had to prove their proficiency in a male-dominated world, it seems likely that the future will favor women entrepreneurs to a greater and greater extent. Now that we have enough big cars and powerful computers, maybe we need more wonderful environments in which to live, work, and socialize; better human interactions with our colleagues and from our professional service providers; more design, beauty, style, and taste incorporated into every object we use, every thing we taste, every surface our eyes see.

Most business training is 100 percent oriented toward the analytical side of business. It is mostly by men, for men, to create male businesses, even when occasionally women go through the pipeline. But what if the next generation of business training is far more focused on art, design, style and taste, and on improving the quality of human interactions?

What if women are the real entrepreneurs of the twenty-first century, the ones who create not only the wealth, but more important the well-being, that we all so crave? What if they are the ones who finally shift us from a world based on quantity to a world based on quality? From a world based on ugliness, aggression, and stress to a world based on beauty, empathy, and peace?

Getting a Perspective on Liberating the Entrepreneurial Spirit for Good

Serious problems remain and, as you know if you listen to the news, you will hear about them constantly. But emotional responses, such as anger and depression, do not in and of themselves solve problems. Go ahead and listen to bad news, but remember to discipline yourself to keep a longer term perspective in mind, both with respect to the extraordinary progress that has taken place in the past as well as the extraordinary progress that can take place in the future, if we take initiative and work together.

The Tibetan Buddhists, who have seen as much deliberate destruction of their lives and their culture as almost any people on the planet, are committed to a 500-year plan to create a better world. While most of us believe that it won't take 500 years, sometimes it is worth thinking about what you as an individual can achieve over the course of a lifetime. The Renaissance artist Lorenzo Ghiberti is famous for completing two sets of bronze doors in his lifetime. The first set took him 21 years to complete. The second set took him 27 years to complete. Each door is covered with amazingly beautiful and detailed sculpture, doors that will be famous for as long as they exist. In our world in which life moves so quickly it is worth reflecting on the kind of commitment to excellence that could motivate someone to spend the first half of his life perfecting a set of bronze doors (he started on them when he was 21), and then, when he finished, to spend the second half of his life on a second set.

What if you committed yourself to making a powerful difference in the world over the course of your lifetime? Realize that making a difference is not about a feeling that you have now but a focus on doing good and a commitment to personal excellence that you make for the long haul. You may not know exactly what your contribution is and you may have a number of different ones. As long as you develop your abilities and apply them on behalf of doing serious work for good, you will create your own bronze doors. The historical record shows that the world has become more peaceful, more prosperous, more environmentally healthy, and more comfortable than it was in the past. What can you do to create a better world over the course of your lifetime? What will your bronze doors be?

An Organic Approach to Climate Change?

Jim McNelly became fascinated with composting in the 1970s. He began simply as an enthusiast who practiced composting, studying it, and later writing books and articles about it. He became an expert based on his love of composting.

Gradually he began composting for others, working with larger and larger clients to transform their organic wastes into superb soil supplements. As he worked with larger clients, he needed to solve numerous technical problems that had not been necessary to address on smaller scales. Eventually he created a patented technology for automatic industrial scale composting based on containers modified from the standard container ship unit. His composting containers now produce a super-enriched soil supplement from organic refuse automatically, without releasing significant gases during the process (uncontained composting can release ammonia and methane during the decomposition process).

The resulting soil supplement has a sufficiently high nitrogen content in a "bio-available" form to outperform all commercial fertilizers and yet it almost certainly qualifies as organic. (Not officially as yet because in order to get the nitrogen content up there he has to add a small amount of nonorganic nitrogen and this technique is under review by the U.S. Department of Agriculture.)

Jim's small company, with three full-time employees and various contractors, had its first profitable year last year. This year they expect to see explosive growth, with every year looking brighter beyond. Indeed, based on the prospective size of the global market for his product, Jim is applying for the $25 million Branson/Gore Carbon Sequestration Prize.

What? Composting could become the leading carbon sequestration technology of the twenty-first century? Well, maybe. Jim's calculations are based on the global issue of soil depletion. Commercial farming techniques combined with erosion have depleted the nutrients in tens of millions of acres around the world. The application of commercial chemical fertilizer is running into decreasingly marginal returns in many places. If he can produce high-nitrogen compost that outperforms chemical fertilizer at a lower price, suddenly it becomes profitable for farmers around the world to buy his high-nitrogen compost rather than chemical fertilizer, with the added advantage that applying it each year enriches the soil rather than depletes it. Strictly as a by-product, this massive scale composting would sequester many hundreds of billions of tons of carbon by plowing them back into the earth as a component of this super-soil. And it would eliminate trillions of tons of rotting organic matter from

(continued)

landfills and other stockpiles where large accumulations of plant matter generate fugitive methane (CH_4), another significant carbon-based greenhouse gas (indeed, some scientists consider the methane issue to be more serious than the CO_2 issue). Finally, "nutrient pollution," much of which stems from fertilizer runoff, is the single largest water pollution issue on the planet—and stabilized nitrogen-rich composted soil, tilled into the ground, results in a tiny fraction of the nutrient pollution caused by chemical fertilizers.

Will all of this happen? We don't know. Right now, McNelly's market is relatively small because the up-front cost of his composting containers is high. At present, they are primarily used in places where there are advocates for industrial scale composting, or where sensitive aquifers place strict limitations on the runoff from chemical fertilizers. But as with all product innovation cycles, as his market grows his company will produce a higher quality product for a lower price. How to accelerate this process?

Peter Barnes advocates environmental trusts as a solution to environmental problems. Environmental trusts are private entities with a legal obligation to steward specific environmental assets. They are a property rights solution to the tragedy of the commons problem; thus they represent a new manifestation of The Entrepreneur's Toolkit. With a river trust, for instance, rivershed trustees would be responsible for protecting the integrity of the river's water quality. At present, there are rivers where bass fishermen protect the water by suing upstream polluters—it turns out that bass fishermen are a large, well-organized, aggressive constituency who want the rivers clean and full of bass. A river trust would engage in similar protections of the river regardless of the particular species of fish in the river. If fertilizer runoffs were polluting the river, the trusts would sue either the farmers or the fertilizer companies for letting the runoff contaminate the stream. Merely the threat of such a lawsuit would make less toxic fertilizers a better investment for the farmers or fertilizer companies. Thus, if river trusts were created, they could impose a sufficiently higher cost on farmers and/or fertilizer companies so that Jim's composting containers would obtain a large commercial market.

Other paths to scalability are also possible: As soils become more thoroughly depleted and as Jim's nitrogen-rich compost becomes better known, direct market demand from farmers could stimulate growth. Or if Jim is able to modify the chemical component so that his compost qualifies as organic under U.S. law, demand will increase. Or perhaps Jim's existing product will be considered organic in some country even though it may not yet meet U.S. standards. The rate at which demand for his product will grow depends on numerous variables, including the cost of his inputs,

> the interest rate, the cost specified by landfills for accepting organic refuse, the cost of competitors; products, and so on. If demand drives Jim's company to produce millions of composting containers, it will be a very profitable company and he will become a very rich man. But at no point was money ever the purpose of his work. Jim is just a hippy geek who loves compost.
>
> The primary reason for telling this story is not the ultimate fate of Jim's business. It is, instead, to show one of millions of means by which entrepreneurial creation will ease our growth pains.
>
> Jim's story is interesting because it is unexpected and far-reaching—who would have imagined that composting could do so much? We might well find ourselves in a world some years hence, with eight billion people all enjoying a U.S. standard of living, but with less air pollution, less water pollution, richer soils, and a healthier environment than we have today.

Making the World a Better Place through Entrepreneurship and Markets

The public sector has failed. Or at least it is on the way out despite our best efforts. Bureaucratization cushioned by subsidies, economic and political protection, and lack of transparency is killing it off. It has become a playground of corruption. What started out with good intentions became a road to disaster. . . . Government doesn't have the answers and never will. It is up to social entrepreneurs to solve our problems.

—Muhammad Yunus

While liberating the entrepreneurial spirit is good, while being oneself for a living is good, and while Conscious Capitalism is good, what about the very serious problems facing the world?* What about poverty, war, and environmental degradation? What about crime and homelessness in the developed world? How can entrepreneurial creativity alleviate these problems? Is "being good" good enough? Looked at from another direction, are there limits to what Conscious Capitalists and

---

*Conscious Capitalism is a registered trademark of Freedom Lights Our World (FLOW), Inc.

Conscious Entrepreneurs can achieve or not? If there are such limits, how can we change the policy environment so that more good can be done more quickly and so that seemingly intractable problems may be solved? Can we design and create a world in which all problems may be solved entrepreneurially?

Ideally we want to create a world in which those individuals and organizations that are adding the most authentic value to the world are rewarded with the most revenue, so that they have the power to take advantage of new opportunities to do more good by adding more authentic value. Conversely, we want to create a world in which those individuals and organizations that are harming human beings and the environment are not rewarded for doing so; ideally no one would be rewarded for harming human beings, and all financially sustainable organizations would make life better for people and for the planet.

At present, even though there are clearly niches in which Conscious Individuals and Conscious Capitalists can succeed, aren't there also many niches in which not merely unconscious individuals and capitalists, but actively evil individuals and capitalists are also succeeding? How can we change the rules of the game so that we create an operating system for capitalism in which we ever more closely approximate a world in which only those who make positive contributions succeed in the world?

At the same time, we want to make the world a better place; we want to create sustainable peace, prosperity, happiness, and well-being for all. How do we create an operating system for Conscious Capitalism that will allow the good guys to win more consistently? More significantly, how do we create an operating system for capitalism that will lead to sustainable peace, prosperity, happiness, and well-being for all?

We won't be able to provide definitive answers to these questions here, but we hope to encourage thinking through these issues under a new paradigm. For most of the past hundred years, well-intentioned people have tried to solve these problems directly, by means of proposed government solutions. But even to the extent that those solutions have worked, they have often caused other problems, unintended consequences.

A short history of twentieth-century economic and political thought might be summarized as:

- Market Failure! Markets don't work as well as the classical economists thought and therefore we must control them (1900–1960).

- Government Failure! Governments don't work as well as democratic theorists thought, and therefore we can't depend on them to do the right thing either (1960–2000).

What do we do after we discover the phenomenon of systemic government failure?

The metaphor of a "new operating system" for capitalism is one in which instead of attempting to solve problems directly by means of government managed programs, we artfully design an operating system, a set of legal rules, within which entrepreneurs and Conscious Capitalists are more likely to be able to create positive enterprises and within which positive enterprises are more likely to succeed financially.

But hitherto most advocates of a more Conscious Capitalism have taken for granted that existing levels of government control are largely benign. We believe it is very important to break from this subconscious prejudice on behalf of existing legal structures and create a new, more Conscious Capitalism that is acutely aware of the diverse ways in which governments at present inhibit the solution of many world problems. The reflexive rejection of free market thought has been one of the great tragedies of the twentieth century. Conscious Capitalists need to be aware of the extent to which their ability to create a new and better world depends crucially on The Entrepreneur's Toolkit, secure property rights, rule of law, and freedom of contract.

One of the paradoxes that we must address is that innovation is key to making the world a better place, and yet innovation requires freedom. Just as free speech necessarily allows negative speech as well as positive speech, the freedom to innovate will require freedom to act both negatively and positively. We will suggest ways to think about an operating system for Conscious Capitalism that integrates protection for the environment with the freedom to create new and better ways of living. Our belief in the power of creativity, innovation, and entrepreneurship to transform the world will bring a libertarian, or classical liberal, flavor to many of our solutions.

The extent to which our direction may be described as libertarian is strictly practical; entrepreneurial solutions work faster and better, whenever possible, than government solutions and centralized, bureaucratic control. Moreover, government solutions usually involve creating a frozen, self-interested constituency that prevents urgently needed change later on. The humane protections enacted on behalf of farmers in the 1930s have become obscene agricultural subsidies today. Timber and mining subsidies, likewise, originally justified as humane interventions to help struggling industries many decades ago, have now become multibillion dollar subsidies by the government to damage the environment and inhibit investment in innovation. Green Mountain Energy, the largest clean energy retailer in the United States, finds Texas the most hospitable state in which to do business, because Texas has the least regulated electricity market. In all other states the electricity regulators favor the existing utility companies through a host of pricing and regulatory strategies.

For more than a hundred years, most progressives have reflexively argued against free markets and for government control. In hundreds of ways this is now changing:

- Barack Obama came out in favor of charter schools during the heated presidential primary with Hillary Clinton against the opposition of the teachers' unions. Indeed, he refers to himself as a "University of Chicago Democrat," thus nodding respectfully toward Milton Friedman.
- Jason Furman, Obama's chief economic advisor, is most famous for defending Wal-Mart as a "progressive success story" because it brought low prices to the poor.
- The global antipoverty NGO Oxfam now lobbies to reduce trade barriers in the developed world in order to alleviate global poverty.
- Progressive Peter Barnes' concept of environmental trusts is an innovative private sector solution to secure sustainable environmental stewardship.
- Amory Lovins' Rocky Mountain Institute argues for a real free market in energy that includes the full cost of oil and gas, because he believes that such a free market would make many innovative energy conservation measures profitable. Former Republican Secretary of State George Shultz wrote the foreword to Lovins' most recent book.
- Worldwatch Institute's David Malin Roodman, in his *The Natural Wealth of Nations: Harnessing the Market for the Environment*, documents hundreds of environmentally harmful subsidies and regulations, some of which were mentioned above.

- Progressive educator and twice-named New York State Teacher of the Year John Taylor Gatto is a signatory of the Alliance for the Separation of School and State, an organization that wants to eliminate all government involvement in education.
- Progressive educator Larry Rosenstock, founder of the celebrated High Tech High charter school in San Diego, is now struggling against the public school establishment as he seeks to replicate his charter schools in working-class neighborhoods.
- Lifelong Democratic economist William Easterly wrote a book criticizing foreign aid while at the World Bank and was fired for doing so.
- Fellow Democratic World Bank economists Dennis Whittle and Mari Kuraishi left the World Bank to found Global Giving, a private philanthropy, because they were convinced that private philanthropy could do more good than the foreign aid given by the World Bank.
- Gore speech writer Daniel Pink describes himself as a founding member of Democrats for School Choice because of his analysis of the skills needed to succeed in the twenty-first-century job market, and his apt conclusion that government-managed schools cannot develop the creativity and innovation that our children will need to succeed.
- Organic farmer Joel Salatin has written an article titled "Everything I Want to Do Is Illegal," showing how health and safety regulations prevent him from having an organic teaching farm where he could train the next generation of young people in his natural farming techniques.
- Montessori schools have lobbied against universal preschool because they rightly fear that such a government program would destroy Montessori education as we know it.
- Alternative health care practitioners, including midwives, herbalists, chiropractors, and others are constantly under siege by the mainstream medical establishment.

These are but a small glimpse of the thousands of ways in which traditional free market principles are being adopted, knowingly or unknowingly, by individuals and organizations that have traditionally identified themselves as "progressive" or "leftist." We believe it is time for progressives to look deeply at many long-standing prejudices against free market thinking and be willing to rethink fundamental perspectives— for the sake of creating sustainable peace, prosperity, happiness, and well-being for all.

How Free Markets Brought Peace to Northern Ireland

Twenty years ago, Ireland was one of the poorest countries in the European Union; it is now one of the richest countries, per capita, in the EU and the fourth richest country per capita in the world. This amazing economic growth in Ireland has simultaneously reduced violence in Northern Ireland, the most violent region of Northern Europe for the past 40 years. (See Figure 1.3.) Since the mid-1990s the IRA has observed a ceasefire, and in 2005 it declared an end to its campaign.

Although negotiators and leaders deserve credit for stopping the violence, so does the miraculous rate of economic growth in Ireland and the related high growth

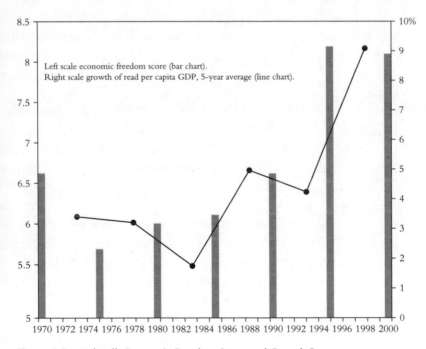

Figure 1.3   Ireland's Economic Freedom Score and Growth Rate
SOURCE: Benjamin Powell, "Economic Freedom and Growth: The Case of the *Celtic Tiger,*" Cato Journal, Vol. 22, No. 3.

in Northern Ireland. A series of trade agreements between Ireland and Northern Ireland led to a 44 percent increase in trade between the two entities, allowing Northern Ireland to benefit to an increasing extent from the economic growth in Ireland.[*] The miraculous rate of economic growth in Ireland was caused by steady increases in economic freedom.[†]

In 1984, unemployment in Northern Ireland was nearly 15 percent, with youth unemployment exceeding 20 percent. (See Figure 1.4.)

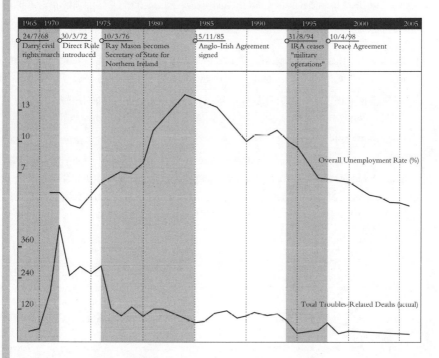

Figure 1.4   Northern Ireland's Unemployment Rate
SOURCE: "Economics in Peacemaking: Lessons from Northern Ireland," *The Portland Trust,* 2003, front material.

---

[*]Economics in Peacemaking: Lessons from Northern Ireland," *The Portland Trust,* 2007, 27.
[†]Although some claim that EU subsidies led to the burst of economic growth in Ireland, clearly economic freedom contributed as well, consistent with the extensive literature on economic freedom and growth. William Easterly, among others, has shown in *The Elusive Quest for Growth* (MIT Press, 2001), that foreign aid alone has not led to growth.

(*continued*)

Today, the unemployment rate in Northern Ireland is 4.5 percent, one of the lowest unemployment rates in all of Europe. Although it is true that poverty does not cause violence and that the vast majority of poor people are nonviolent, chronic unemployment and poverty provide recruiting grounds for those who wish to address other grievances violently. Desperate, angry, marginalized young men with nothing to lose are more likely to try to regain their dignity and seek revenge through battle and bombings. Although the leading figures of terrorist movements are typically more highly educated than average, their popularity as heroes among their peoples stems from the fact that they are perceived as addressing a grievance or an injustice.

Thus, even more important in reducing the level of violence than the change in the overall rates of unemployment was the reduction in the discrepancy between Protestant and Catholic unemployment rates in Northern Ireland. (See Figure 1.5.) In 1985, there was a 14 percent discrepancy between the unemployment rates of Protestants and Catholics; by 2004 this was down to a 3.5 percent discrepancy.[*]

Naturally, when there is a large discrepancy in unemployment rates, the level of resentment is much higher. The combination of overall high unemployment rates, with much higher Catholic unemployment, heightened the religious conflict. Often, the differential rates of unemployment are perceived by the less economically successful group as persecution by the more economically dominant group. As a more dynamic

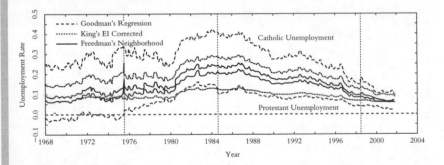

Figure 1.5 The Ratio of Catholic to Protestant Unemployment in Northern Ireland, 1968–2004 (different lines show different approaches to estimating differential rates of unemployment by religion)
SOURCE: Taken from Honaker, J., "Unemployment and Violence in Northern Ireland: A Missing Data Model for Ecological Inference." Paper presented at the annual meeting of the Midwest Political Science Association, Palmer House Hilton, Chicago April, 15, 2004 (www.allacademic.com/meta/p83125_index.html).

[*]"Economics in Peacemaking: Lessons from Northern Ireland," The Portland Trust, 2003, p. 9.

economy reduces unemployment for all, thereby reducing the differential rates of unemployment, the perception of persecution is reduced and the rate of violence declines. While Conscious Capitalists should certainly make a proactive effort to hire so as to minimize such ethnic and religious disparities in employment, there is no substitute for a dynamic, fast-growing economy.

Can the Irish success story be repeated around the world? Gracia Burnham, a U.S. missionary who spent 377 days in captivity with Abu Sayyaf, an Al-Qaeda-related terrorist group in the Philippines, said of the terrorists she knew so intimately:

> So many of the kids weren't bent on jihad . . . [in a world of extreme poverty, Abu Sayyaf was] . . . a career move. . . . Whether they were bent on jihad or not, all those guys wanted was to die in a gun battle so they could bypass the judgment of God and go straight to paradise. If they couldn't die in jihad, their next choice was to go to America and get a good job. (As quoted by Eliza Griswold, "The Believers," *The New Republic,* June 4, 2007)

Hope, and the opportunity to create a better life for oneself and one's family, is a universal aspiration.

Both the terrorists of the Irish Republican Army of the past hundred years, as well as the Islamic terrorists that frighten so many people today, are mostly young people who want opportunity and respect and want their peoples to have opportunity and respect. There will always be ideologues and individuals full of hate, but in a world of opportunity for all, hate-filled individuals will be marginalized as dangerous loners rather than heroic leaders of terrorist movements.

In today's Northern Ireland, few want to see violence destroy the recent prosperity and take away the good jobs they increasingly have. InterTradeIreland, an island-wide economic development agency, aspires for the entire island of Ireland to be one of the five richest economies in the world by 2020. The good news is that in order to achieve that goal, InterTradeIreland projects that the region's economy need only grow at a rate of 4.5 percent annually, more slowly than it has grown in the last 10 years.[*] With Ireland already ranked at number nine, this is primarily about improving the economy in Northern Ireland, which would not yet rank among the top 30 nations in terms of GDP per capita if it were an independent nation.[†]

---

[*] www.intertradeireland.com/module.cfm/opt/25/area/News/page/News/id/195/year/2005/month/10.
[†] Estimated ranking from data obtained here: www.bized.co.uk/current/leisure/2004_5/300505.htm and CIA World Factbook, www.cia.gov/library/publications/the-world-factbook/rankorder/2004rank.html.

The FLOW Ideal: A World of Healthy, Happy People Doing Good through Meaningful Fun

When we are motivated by goals that have deep meaning, by dreams that need completion, by pure love that needs expressing, then we truly live life.

—GREG ANDERSON

I want to do good and have fun doing it. I expect that most people would also like to be doing good and having fun doing it. We can help to create a world in which most of human life, most of the time, consists of doing good and having fun doing it.

In order to do so, we need to dramatically change many of our institutions, not just once, but over and over and over again. We need dramatic, ongoing change in all of the institutions of our society. We need to embrace the process of creative destruction enthusiastically; we need to celebrate the forward motion of an ongoing process of innovation and entrepreneurship that will bring happiness for all into the world.

In Abraham Maslow's hierarchy of needs, once people's more basic needs for food, shelter, and safety have been met, they then crave love, esteem, and self-actualization. In the developed countries, almost everyone's basic needs have been met. Regarding the emerging economies, we know that opening the world will allow the basic needs of almost everyone on the planet to be met. Thus the fundamental problem is how to allow people's needs for love, esteem, and self-actualization to be met more effectively.

We are entering the age of meaning. An increasing percentage of us, an increasing percentage of the time, will have the time, leisure, ability, and interest to choose to engage in meaningful activity that we enjoy rather than meaningless activity that we dislike. Everything about work, leisure, entertainment, education, and family time is in flux. The ongoing inertia of choices made in the past, those patterns of consumption, employment, and investment that determine every aspect of the world we have created, are all undergoing a profound transformation. We are ready to create a new world.

Meaning comes from engagement in positive work that challenges our personal capacity combined with knowledge that our positive work is making a larger contribution to the overall well-being of humanity and life on the planet. There will be an ever-increasing demand for meaningful work. We intend to help show the way to create an ever-increasing supply of such work so as to create a virtuous circle in which all benefit.

Whether people work for themselves or for others, they increasingly want to understand how their actions are contributing to a greater good. They will want to be engaged in work that contributes to society. Many will create new enterprises that are explicitly dedicated to doing good—the current social entrepreneurship movement is the tip of the iceberg in this respect. Many more will want to work for enterprises that provide them with both autonomy and meaning—workplaces such as Google are the tip of the iceberg in this respect. How can we create a society in which everyone has meaningful work? How can you find meaningful work today?

A World of Flow

Many attitudes and institutions today are relics of a time in which conflict was more pervasive, in which many people were more desperate than they are now. In the developed world, in particular, the vast majority of people have more than they need to live comfortably. Indeed, many people are in search of meaning more than money. Many of those who continue to search for money are really searching for meaning through status and consumption. What if those already in search of meaning found it in productive flow play? What if those who thought that they were finding meaning in status and consumption were to discover a more direct and satisfying path to meaning through flow?

Flow is:

> Being completely involved in an activity for its own sake. The ego falls away. Time flies. Every action, movement, and thought follows inevitably from the previous one, like playing jazz. Your whole being is involved, and you're using your skills to the utmost."
>
> Mihaly Csikszentmihalyi, *Flow* (Harper Perennial, 1991)

What if we could create a world in which all seven billion human beings on the planet could be engaged in flow most of the time? What if most people, most of the time, spent time in productive work that was joyously identical to play?

Psychologist Mihaly Csikszentmihalyi developed the flow concept from studying people who loved what they did, who engaged in an activity for its own sake, not for extrinsic rewards. The key element was that people found their capacities challenged by their work/play without being overwhelmed by the challenge. Indeed, individuals engaged in the flow of optimal experience, of full engagement in life, were happier than were those who were spending time with entertainments.

Maslow described a hierarchy of needs. People first need to focus on basic needs such as food and security; starving people are not apt to philosophize. But after their basic needs have been met, they then experience needs to belong and to be esteemed. Only after their needs to belong and be esteemed have been adequately met does their primary purpose become self-actualization. While people may not move directly up the hierarchy, there is a general movement beyond the needy self.

Many of our political conflicts are premised on a world of self-interested individuals. But we live in a world in which an increasing percentage of the population seeks self-actualization, flow, love, and ecstatic mystery more than they seek money, status, or consumption. In the future, an increasing percentage of young people will naturally and unselfconsciously be devoted to creating meaningful careers for themselves. In order to do so, they will need to take responsibility for their own well-being, and they will do so joyfully. And, just as joyfully, they will encourage those around them to be responsible for their own well-being.

The Course in Miracles (Foundation for Inner Peace, The Course in Miracles, www.acim.org) makes the point more simply: Love is the opposite of fear. We no longer need to act out of fear.

Doing Good through Meaningful Fun

To date, Csikszentmihalyi's insights have been used primarily by game designers to develop an endless appetite for game playing. What if the flow experience was characteristic of life experience while doing good rather than play experience in imaginary universes?

We believe that it is possible to create a world in which we are all engaged in meaningful work that makes the world a better place and to engage in that work in a flow-like state that is profoundly satisfying. In order to create this world, we will have to work together both on the systems in which work takes place as well as on the focus, vision, and ethos that each of us brings to the public sphere. As a consequence, we will cover a wide range of issues, ranging from tax policy and economics to personal and spiritual growth. At no point do we claim to have the final word; but we do believe that we have gathered together the foundation for a perspective that can dramatically increase human well-being.

Capitalism is the dominant form of social organization in the world today. And yet many people are concerned that capitalism is harmful to the environment and harmful to human well-being. How can people feel as if their lives are meaningful when they are working within a system through which they harm the world on a daily basis?

It is important to realize that having a meaningful life doesn't imply that everything that we are doing right now is perfect. But it does imply that we are making progress toward a greater good, that our daily efforts contribute to making the world a better place. We offer here a road map to sustainable peace, prosperity, happiness, and well-being for all. By means of this road map, we intend to provide people with an understanding of how each and every one of us can contribute to the greater good of humanity.

Eckhart Tolle, *The Power of Now*

Eckhart Tolle was a research scholar at Cambridge University when, at the age of 29, "a profound spiritual transformation virtually dissolved his old identity and radically changed the course of his life." He subsequently wrote *The Power of Now* (New World Library, 1999), a short, simple book, which became a word-of-mouth best seller with over two million copies sold.

Opinions about the book vary widely; *O: The Oprah Magazine* says, "It can transform your thinking. . . . The result? More joy, right now!" *Time Magazine*, on the other hand, describes it as "mumbo jumbo."

Tolle is an excellent example of a spiritual entrepreneur. He was, and is, not interested in money—he left a traditional path toward what is normally considered

(*continued*)

a "good life" as an academic researcher and spent years with almost no posses-sions at all. But Tolle is also not some bizarre, esoteric spiritual guru. Many of Tolle's insights are extremely simple but not often practiced.

For instance, a primary theme of his book is that most of us spend the bulk of our time either worrying about the past or worrying about the future. He points out that we need not spend our time anxious and worried. We can, instead, choose sim-ply to detach from our ego-mind and experience the present moment, the "Now."

All of us have had spontaneous moments in which we were so struck by the freshness and beauty of a cloud, a mountain, a rainbow, or some other natural phe-nomenon that for a moment we were simply witnessing, without ego-awareness. For many of us, we may have to think back to childhood to recall distantly the experience of such moments because we have become so habituated to the business of life that we no longer are struck so spontaneously by natural beauty that we forget ourselves.

Tolle not only reminds us of these natural, spontaneous states of being, but he also provides us with ways to escape our egos to experience a similarly peaceful state of awareness anytime, anywhere. Although using such language as "escaping egos" may be a case of the "mumbo jumbo" referred to by *Time*, Tolle makes a com-pelling case that many writers in traditional philosophical and religious traditions often pointed to a similar source of inner peace.

For instance, Tolle writes, "Many people are in love with their life drama. Their story is their identity. The ego runs their life. They have their whole sense invested in it." His advice, to escape the anxious ego drama to which many of us are addicted, is similar to that given by the Stoic philosopher and Roman emperor Marcus Aurelius nearly 2,000 years ago, "Accept whatever comes to you woven in the pattern of your destiny, for what could more aptly fit your needs?" Neither Tolle nor Aurelius are claiming that we should not use our minds to solve problems, both to improve our own lives and those of others. Their message is consistently that we should not allow the thought processes needed to solve problems to become addictive emotional states that destroy happiness and well-being.

It turns out that escape from ego and developing the ability to be at peace in the present moment, requires some practice for most people. Tolle's message, along with that of many Greek and Roman philosophers, Christians, Sufis, Buddhists, and others is that we can take responsibility for our personal happiness by means of disciplining our minds and transcending our egos. Buddhist meditation, Christian Centering Prayer, Sufi prayer, Taoist Tai Chi, and Kundalini Yoga are but a few of the many means by which we may train ourselves to escape from ego neediness and pain and from the countless subtle anxieties about the world of which we are often barely aware.

Much human misery, both self-inflicted and harm inflicted on others, is caused by acting from the neediness of the ego. Whatever sources are helpful to you in escaping from the self-imposed pain caused by your ego, we encourage developing some kind of personal practice that empowers you to be free from the emotional pain or neediness whenever you please and to support the cultivation of such practices in others.

Chapter 2

The Entrepreneur as Hero

Candace Allen
Educator and Essayist

I do not consider myself to be a remarkable person. But I am intensely curious about the things that I see around me. And this curiosity, combined with a willingness to assume risks, has been responsible for such success and satisfaction as I have achieved in life.
—CLARENCE BIRDSEYE

What is a hero? For some, a hero represents a person who lives up to age-old values such as honesty, integrity, courage, and bravery. For others, a hero is someone who is steadfast or someone who sets a good example to emulate in the future. To many, being a hero means self-sacrifice, even of life itself, for the sake of others. And many find heroic those who are celebrities, as celebrities receive notoriety and attention that anybody might want.

Originally published in *Economic Insights,* Vol. 2, Number 1, Federal Reserve Bank of Dallas. Used with permission.

Joseph Campbell, who was considered to be the most renowned expert on world mythology and literature, demonstrated the universal path of the hero across time and culture. I venture to speculate that he would probably say that none of the ways I have just mentioned of looking at heroes are wrong; rather, they are incomplete, representing aspects or qualities of the hero.

In his many works, Campbell demonstrated that every society has and needs heroes. Heroes reflect the values we revere, the accomplishments we respect, and the hopes that give our lives meaning. By celebrating our heroes, we honor our past, energize our present, and shape our future. In studying all known cultures, Campbell discovered that though details of heroic action change with time, the typical path of the hero can be traced in all cultures through three stages.

The first stage involves departure from the familiar and comfortable into the unknown, risking failure and loss—a venturing forth for some greater purpose or idea. The second stage is the encountering of hardship and challenge and the mustering of courage and strength to overcome or discover. The third is the return to the community with something new or better than what was there before. Ultimately, the hero is the representative of the new—the founder of a new age, a new religion, a new city, the founder of a new way of life or a new way of protecting the village against harm; the founder of processes or products that make people in their communities and the world better off.

What I will contend here is that in our modern world, the wealth creators—the entrepreneurs—actually travel the heroic path and are every bit as bold and daring as the heroes who fought dragons or overcame evil.

In the first stage of the heroic journey, we find the entrepreneur venturing forth from the world of accepted ways and norms. He asserts, "There is a better way, and I will find it." Unlike many of us who are overwhelmed by the challenges of our immediate world, the entrepreneur is an optimist, able to see more of what might be by taking what is here and seeking to rearrange it. Giving up the conclusions of others about what is or is not possible leads the entrepreneur in his quest to go beyond the satisfaction of the present. In this first stage, those who are spurred to risk leaving the familiar world are motivated by many things.

Some wish to become rich or famous. Some wish to make themselves, their families, or their communities better off. Some seek pure adventure, and some wish to challenge their own limits.

Entrepreneurs are characterized by boundless energy, brimming vision, and bold determination to push into the unknown. They are alert, watching for new opportunities to change the status quo, and often through failure develop a better than average sense of timing, learning to balance patience and immediate action. This brings us to the second stage of the classic heroic journey.

In this stage the entrepreneur finds himself in the uncertainty of uncharted territory. All is at stake. The hero self-sacrifices to an idea or purpose or vision or dream that he sees as greater than himself. His immediate comfort and security become irrelevant. No general agreement exists as to just what that greater, more noble sense of purpose must be. In my own profession, for example, an entrepreneurial teacher who wishes to find a more profitable and beneficial way to provide education to youngsters as an alternative to government schooling may have a profound sense of purpose that drives him onward. And yet, we within the profession might see him as a traitor. Imagine a teacher getting out from under our protected bureaucratic canopy and setting up an English or an economics instruction firm that contracts out to schools or parents. Regardless of that to which he gives himself up, the second stage of the heroic quest involves the surrender to an intense, driving force.

In this stage, the entrepreneur tackles unpromising resource situations and attempts to fashion present resource arrangements into something different and more valuable. Today, the creation of wealth depends much less on discovery of the earth's physical resources and much more on the strength of mind to rearrange and reorganize resources. The entrepreneur's tremendous energy provides him the resiliency to keep coming back after every wrong turn or failure, and his tenacity and enterprising nature are the invisible workings that fuel the efforts that give his ideas tangible form.

This high-risk activity is the electric and dynamic discovery process. It is a test bed of ferreting out profitable opportunities. It is in this stage that he is criticized or opposed by those special interests who control the status quo.

The third stage of the classic heroic journey begins when the entrepreneur returns to the community with the hope of gaining its acceptance of his product, process, or service. By buying new products or services, the customer acknowledges entrepreneurial success. The more profit that is generated, the greater the value of wealth produced. Profits are the reward for increasing benefits to individuals in society, and serving in the capacity as wealth creator, the entrepreneur becomes a social benefactor. The heroic entrepreneur will continue to anticipate what the future will demand of him. He is no ordinary businessperson whose main priorities are simply to turn his profits, avoid losses, or seek to maintain his market share. Nor does he seek government subsidy or monopoly status. For him, the quest is to venture forth again and again into the unknown to create and bring back that which individuals in society value.

Not all people who venture forth on these heroic quests succeed. Approximately 80 percent of new businesses fail within a short period of time. But we must keep in mind that over three-quarters of all new jobs each year come from businesses no more than four years old. Though large, well-established corporations are more visible, small business ventures are where the entrepreneurial action is.

Role models in business best sellers usually come from large, successful corporations, but Hermann Simon, author of *Hidden Champions: Lessons from 500 of the World's Best Unknown Companies*, argues that little known super performer companies made up of 2, 3, or 20 highly entrepreneurial folks have control of worldwide market shares of 50 percent, 70 percent, even 90 percent. For example, St. Jude Medical has 60 percent of the world's market for artificial heart valves. In today's world, it is the individual (or small groups of them) who is embarked on the bold quests that are changing the face of society so rapidly.

The lesson offered to us is that the market is a harsh judge, but even so, some individuals are willing to risk failure, and in doing so time and again, they have become successful, learning that no defeat has to be final. The cumulative effect of this entrepreneurial attitude is that we can all look to the future with optimism, as opportunities abound for entrepreneurial adventure. Many of the heroes today go unnamed, as their contributions are coming so quickly that the time needed to become well known individually isn't available. This is all the more reason to understand the function of the entrepreneur on the heroic path.

If we all focused on just one or two processes that we take for granted, we would see how much our lives have changed due to entrepreneurial activity constrained by the tight discipline imposed on it through market forces.

When I was a little girl, penicillin had just been developed and mothers no longer were losing their babies to minor ear infections. Television wasn't available, but I remember listening to *The Shadow* through the static and crackle of a vacuum tube radio. Telephones were still luxuries in the little farm town of Hugo, Colorado, where I grew up. My Aunt Luella's number was 17 and I could get her by contacting Alma, the local operator. Long-distance calls were a rarity and international calls were simply not made. The first transatlantic cable was not laid until 1956, and it could transmit only 36 calls at any one time. As late as 1966, only 138 simultaneous calls could take place between Europe and all of North America, as compared with the more than 1.5 million simultaneous calls between North America and Europe today. Now telephones are everywhere, and many of our students carry cellular phones with them as casually as I did a bag of jacks or marbles.

And of course, being a baby boomer born in the late 1940s, I had never heard of a computer. It has been estimated that if we had made the same progress in automobiles we have made in computers over the last 30 years, the best Mercedes Benz on the road today would cost about $1.19 and get more than 4 million miles per gallon.

In 1952, economist John Kenneth Galbraith said, "Most of the cheap and simple inventions have been made." This statement seems pretty silly to us today. The changes we have seen since we were children will pale in comparison to the changes we will see in the next decade.

Why, then, are entrepreneurs typically ignored or downplayed at best, or worse, castigated as modern day robber barons who exploit others? Why isn't the entrepreneurial function hailed as heroic?

There are several reasons why entrepreneurs are more likely to be castigated than celebrated. One major reason for the castigation of successful entrepreneurs lies in the political bias against them. As government control over the economy has grown, so has the incentive for politically influential interests to disparage entrepreneurs. Few, if any, economic forces are more disruptive than entrepreneurship. Successful entrepreneurs make bold leaps that break contact with the familiar and leave behind a clutter of obsolete products and processes. In Joseph Schumpeter's words, they effect "creative destruction."

And while most people recognize that creative destruction is essential to general progress, each act of this destruction harms some individuals and groups whose wealth is capitalized into the status quo. Each group wants to benefit from the progress that imposes costs on others while being protected against the progress that imposes costs on themselves. But the more groups that succeed in securing such protection, the less everyone benefits from the economic progress that might have been. And the larger government becomes, the more it becomes a force against progress. While the entrepreneur with a superior idea can draw large numbers of customers from existing corporate giants in market competition, he can't mobilize large numbers of citizens against government obstacles to that competition.

Another reason entrepreneurs are condemned is that the connection between their innovations and economic progress is often indirect and difficult for most to understand. For example, few people understand the depth of the contributions made by Michael Milken and Bill Gates. When this lack of understanding becomes political fodder, those entrepreneurs who do the most to promote economic progress are at risk of being depicted as antisocial scoundrels.

A major reason for the hostility toward successful capitalists and the capitalist system that makes their success possible exists for other than political reasons. Few people understand how capitalism works and most tend to see the concentrated costs inflicted by market competition and take for granted the diffused benefits made possible by that competition. Trying to explain how the invisible hand works to folks already hostile to the ideas of competition and profits is not an easy task. Many who are not entrepreneurial resist the idea that the economic system rewards those who create wealth and that wealth is created on the basis of superior contributions.

Ludwig Von Mises, founder of the neo-Austrian School of economics, recognized that the person who observes others achieving far greater economic success than he, resists the notion that the creators are more deserving of wealth than he.

Furthermore, educated people's perceptions are influenced more than most realize by the opinions of intellectuals at elite colleges and universities—intellectuals who typically despise what they view capitalism to be and the entrepreneurial energy that propels it.

Within our colleges and universities, academics (like every other group anywhere else) like to exert influence and feel important. Few scholars in the social sciences and humanities are content to merely observe, describe, and explain—most want to improve society, and as economist Thomas Sowell repeatedly says, they take on the role of the anointed in assuming that they can and should promote social progress through well intended government action, guided, of course, by their own expertise. Achieving academic distinction by becoming one of the authorities on social change is an opportunity that most can't pass up.

One of the most striking points to make in understanding why entrepreneurs aren't given more recognition is that even the staunchest supporters of the capitalist system often diminish and even dismiss the importance of entrepreneurs. The economists who have developed the subdiscipline referred to as the "new economic history" have been among the most effective at explaining the causal links between the market and economic progress. Yet most of the new economic historians downplay the importance of entrepreneurs and would argue against our placing them in the category of heroes.

Robert Thomas of the University of Washington argues, for example, that individual entrepreneurs just don't matter. According to Thomas, a successful entrepreneur is no more important to the economy than the winning runner in a 100-yard dash is to the race. The winner gets all the glory, but if he had not been in the race, the next runner would have won by crossing the finish line a fraction of a second later, and the spectators would have enjoyed the race just as much. If Henry Ford or Bill Gates or any other successful entrepreneur had not made his pioneering contribution, someone else would have quickly done so. So, as Thomas tells the story, it is hard to justify special celebration of their accomplishments. But this view ought to be challenged.

Go back to Thomas' race analogy. If the runners and their preparation before and during the race are simply taken as givens, it is no doubt true that removing the winner of the race would do little to reduce the benefits of winning. But the identity of the runners and their preparation and effort can't merely be taken as a given. They are influenced by the social acclaim and praise afforded the winner. When champion runners are esteemed in the public's eye, those with the greatest talent are more likely to become runners—to train harder and run faster.

The fact that the entrepreneur receives profits if he is successful is hardly a persuasive argument that entrepreneurial motivation is unaffected by public attitudes.

The point I am making here is that the public attitude is really a sum total of individual attitudes of citizens. If individual citizens do not value the qualities that make entrepreneurs able to go beyond the limits of what is considered to be possible and do not value the environment that allows and rewards those who do, then those citizens empower politicians and their special interest clients who consistently look for justification to tax away the financial gains of successful creators.

It is no coincidence that over the last century, as public respect for entrepreneurs has eroded, so have the constitutional barriers against what is best described as the punitive taxation of economic success.

Just as the society that doesn't venerate winners of races will produce fewer champion runners than the society that does, the society that does not honor entrepreneurial accomplishment will find fewer people of ability engaged in wealth creation than the society that does.

There is one last reason to explain why, though on the heroic path, entrepreneurs are seldom viewed as heroes. When defining the hero and giving credence to what he accomplishes, the focus is often on the giving up—on the self-sacrifice, rather than on the creation and the bringing back to society that which makes individuals a little or a lot better off. As long as the profit, which the hero receives as reward, is viewed negatively as part of a zero-sum game in which the entrepreneur benefits at the expense of others, he will be denigrated and at best treated with disinterest.

And when this attitudinal obstacle plays out politically in the form of restrictive government regulations, trade restrictions, monopolized special interests supported by government, and high tax burdens, we all lose.

Liberating Entrepreneurial Solutions to Housing the U.S. Poor

In an effort to reduce the stigma (class bigotry) associated with manufactured housing, a few years ago The Field Museum of Chicago presented an exhibit designed to transform these attitudes. Titled "Out of the Box: Design Innovations in Affordable Housing," the catalog expresses a fresher design perspective as well.

Contrary to popular belief, manufactured homes have long been an affordable and high-quality housing option. The history of these prefabricated dwellings transcends time and cultural boundaries, reflecting a long and colorful history. Native American teepees, yurts in Central Asia, Sears and Roebuck "kit houses," and the mobile home are but a few examples.

In the last decade, almost 25 percent of new home construction in the United States is prefabricated or uses prefabricated components. The exhibition's designers seek to dispel the stigma associated with the "trailer" home, using cutting-edge technology and innovative design concepts to accommodate consumers' unique lifestyles. Contemporary designs offer consumers endless possibilities—from high-rise apartments designed with stackable modules to single-family one- or two-story homes. A variety of designs accommodate disabilities or feature energy efficiency and include choice amenities such as vaulted ceilings and home gyms.[*]

If low-cost housing is seen as an interesting, beautiful, and original design challenge, then it will draw interesting talent from design, social entrepreneurship, financing, and elsewhere in order to create change.[†]

Indeed, Seattle's Noji Gardens is just such a project. HomeSight, an organization dedicated to creating affordable housing, has created a project in which two-story manufactured homes, designed to look like site-built homes (these days it can be hard to tell the difference) are being sold new for 10 percent less than equivalent used homes.[‡]

As with many of the current generation of social entrepreneurship efforts, the Noji Gardens development is a project that was developed on the scale of a cottage industry: 11 single-family homes and 64 townhomes. This is not to denigrate the efforts of the developers of Noji Gardens, but to point out that effective solutions need to take place on a much larger scale.

There are legal obstacles that prevent such an outcome, however. Roberta Feldman, curator of the "Out of the Box" exhibit, points out:

---

[*] www.uic.edu/aa/cdc/files/OutoftheBox.html.

[†] Indeed, there is an entire movement promoting economical, ecological, and aesthetic design as a solution to global problems. Designer Bruce Mau's Massive Change Project, ground zero of this movement, is an excellent complement to the FLOW project.

[‡] Karen Jenson, "Manufacturing a New Kind of Affordable Housing: Seattle's Noji Gardens," Fannie Mae Foundation, 2001, www.knowledgeplex.org/kp/text_document_summary/article/relfiles/fmf_0510_noji_gardens.pdf.

(*continued*)

It would be very expensive to produce a prototype of many of them [the innovative home designs]. At this point they read like boutique housing, but it doesn't have to be boutique if it were produced in large numbers. The Model T Ford, if they only produced one or a hundred, would have cost a fortune. . . . Maybe we should be questioning why we're not building houses the way we build cars. . . . We're very willing to accept cars off an assembly line. We've come to recognize our manufacturing plants can create a great diversity of consumer products and meet consumer demand, yet in our housing somehow we insist that it has to be site-built to be a good home. [But] we have what's called prescriptive building codes, which tell you, not in every instance, but in most of our code, what materials you have to use. Whereas a performance-based building code, which, for example, most European nations are moving toward, will say what kind of performance they expect: A wall has to have a fire rating of two hours, which means a fire can't go through a wall for two hours. The city tried to encourage the industry to come in, especially to provide units in lower-income communities, and it didn't fly, because by the time they met the building codes, it just wasn't cost effective. It doesn't mean it's lower quality. It's not. Largely that is to support unions, which I believe in. We're in a double bind here. I think labor should get higher wages [but] our housing codes go beyond health, safety, and welfare to include other norms and other special interest groups. (www.lynnbecker.com/repeat/beyondtrailer/designinnovations.htm)

Social entrepreneurs and innovative designers interested in supplying affordable housing, working in conjunction with manufactured home producers, could create much larger scale solutions if a movement existed to reduce housing regulation nationwide. Indeed, in a sufficiently unregulated housing market, housing costs could come down dramatically just as costs for so many other goods have come down.

With respect to many necessities, especially food and clothing, the much-maligned Wal-Mart has been one of the most effective providers for the poor in history (for those who have access to the stores). There are estimates that Wal-Mart has saved U.S. consumers (especially low- and middle-income consumers) approximately $263 billion per year.[*] Relative to the 1970s, household consumables other than housing, transportation, and health care have generally improved in quality while decreasing in price with the poor being the primary beneficiaries. Real wages for the

---

[*]Jason Furman, "Wal-Mart: A Progressive Success Story," http//www.americanprogress.org/atf/cf/{E9245FE4-9A2B-43C7-A521-5D6FF2E06E03}/WALMART_PROGRESSIVE.PDF.

working poor have stagnated if one doesn't include benefits. If one includes benefits, however, wages for the working poor have increased since the 1970s.[*]

But not all of the working poor have received those benefits and, even for those who have, the additional benefits, while valuable, do not help with month to month budgets. With static real wages and declining costs of consumer goods, the working poor would have experienced an increasing standard of living. But there is one major culprit that has undermined any hope that the working poor could make significant economic progress: housing, which takes up 30 to 50 percent or more of household budgets among the poor.

Housing costs have increased by 72 percent since 1970. As a Harvard study on housing in Manhattan points out, "there were 13,000 new units permitted in Manhattan in 1960 alone, only 21,000 new units were permitted throughout the entire decade of the 1990s. In spite of skyrocketing prices, the housing stock has grown by less than 10 percent since 1980."[†]

The nationwide explosion in housing regulation and antigrowth policies have been catastrophic for the poor in the United States. Almost half of all renters spend more than 30 percent of their income on rent (categorized as "unaffordable") and nearly a quarter of all renters spend more than 50 percent of their income on rent (categorized as "severely unaffordable").[‡] The great irony is that while housing costs have nearly doubled, construction costs have decreased.

If construction costs are decreasing, how can housing costs increase? In a rigorous empirical analysis, Harvard economists looking at a variety of evidence concluded that at least 40 percent of the increase in housing costs since 1970 is due to increased regulation. The increase in land values appears to account for only about 10 percent of the increase in cost. The rest may be attributed to increases in housing quality (some of which may have been required by regulation).[§] The authors then go on to explain the numerous causes of increased housing regulation since the 1970s.

---

[*]W. Michael Cox and Richard Alm, *Myths of Rich and Poor: Why We're Better Off Than We Think* (Basic Books, 2000).

[†]Edward L. Glaeser, Joseph Gyourko, and Raven E. Saks, , "Why Is Manhattan so Expensive? Regulation and the Rise of House Prices," Harvard Institute of Economic Research Discussion Paper Number 2020, Nov. 2003,http://post.economics.harvard.edu/faculty/glaeser/papers/Manhattan.pdf.

[‡]See Mark Treskon and Danilo Pelletiere, "Up Against a Wall: Housing Affordability for Renters," National Low Income Housing Coalition, Nov. 2004, http//www2398.ssldomain.com/nlihc/doc/uaaw.pdf.

[§]Edward L. Glaeser, Joseph Gyourko, and Raven E. Saks, "Why Have Housing Prices Gone Up?," Harvard Institute of Economic Research Discussion Paper Number 2061, Feb. 2005, "http//post. economics.harvard.edu/hier/2005papers/HIER2061.pdf.

(*continued*)

Most people are highly aware of the extraordinary power of technological innovation and, correspondingly, of steadily improving quality and decreasing cost in the field of technology. Unfortunately, most people are not aware that this relentless increase in value is the result of free enterprise; it is not the result of technology. The comparison of IT progress in the United States with that in the former Soviet Union was based on this fact. The Soviets put enormous investments into some areas of technological progress, including weapons programs, a space program, and a supercomputer. Again, when they mobilized their resources on behalf of a very small number of very specific goals they were relatively successful. But the texture of day-to-day life for millions of people cannot be improved by government mobilization toward limited goals. It is crucial to allow for widespread free enterprise.

Free enterprise results in relentless improvements in all fields when it is allowed to do so. Every action taken and every interaction is a potential opportunity for creative improvements. We can never say beforehand which person in which interaction will make which improvement anymore than we could determine which mutation in an evolutionary software system will result in which lasting improvement. There is no substitute for massive, parallel, unpredicted experimentation and innovation.

Cotton was once a luxury good only available to the rich. Prior to the Industrial Revolution the poor mostly wore the same woolen clothes year after year. But by 1812, the price of cotton was one-tenth the price of cotton in the 1770s. By 1860, it was less than one-hundredth of its price prior to the Industrial Revolution. Contrary to popular belief, this took place while average working class wages were steadily increasing: All credible economic historians now acknowledge that Karl Marx was simply wrong when he claimed that "the rich get richer and the poor get poorer." In fact, the Industrial Revolution created the first massive middle class in history in the United States and Britain. For the first time ever anywhere on earth, working families could afford luxuries like cotton and tea, cotton clothing, newspapers and magazines, travel, entertainment, etc.[*]

In order to understand how to help the poor, it is very important to know what has worked in the past in helping the poor. And while there continue to be quibbles about the exact characteristics of successful markets, it is not significantly disputed that large-scale free enterprise is an amazing system for generating wealth for all.

As we have seen, however, housing prices have not fallen the way that so many prices have. We do not see a trajectory by means of which housing prices are on their

---

[*]Paul Johnson, *The Birth of the Modern* (New York: Harper Perennial, 1992) pg. 300 and elsewhere.

way to falling to a tenth or a hundredth of their current prices. Although construction prices have fallen slightly, progress does not appear significant.

By contrast, however, manufactured homes have become both cheaper and higher quality than they were in the 1970s. The median family income of owners of manufactured homes decreased in constant 1993 dollars from $24,000 in 1974 to $20,000 in 1993. The median family income of renters of manufactured homes decreased in constant dollars from $19,000 in 1974 to $15,000 in 1993 (again in constant 1993 dollars).[*] Thus, in those regions in which manufactured homes are allowed (mostly rural areas), they provide extremely viable low-cost housing.

The regulatory restrictions that resulted in a 72 percent increase in housing prices since the 1970s have also, invisibly, eliminated opportunities for much larger cost decreases. In the present regulatory environment, construction costs have decreased slightly. In the meantime, manufactured housing has seen a more substantial decrease in costs in those mostly rural areas in which they are allowed. Indeed, on a square foot basis, manufactured homes decreased in cost by 19 percent from 1974 to 1993 whereas single-family traditionally built homes decreased in cost per square foot by only 7.6 percent (without adjustments for increases in quality).[†] While manufactured homes must meet regulatory standards as well, those standards are federally-mandated performance standards that allow for considerable flexibility and creativity in meeting the standards, whereas the motley mix of local building and zoning codes, growth restrictions, and environmental mandates are often highly restrictive.[‡]

Without an increase in wages, if the cost of living across the board decreased by 50 percent, those working poor would experience a 100 percent increase in their standard of living. A 50 percent decrease in the cost of living is not extraordinary

---

[*] Kimberly Vermeer and Josephine Louie, "The Future of Manufactured Housing," Joint Center for Housing Studies, Harvard University, R97-1, January 1997, www.jchs.harvard.edu/publications/markets/R97-1_vermeer_louie_Futmanhousing.pdf.

[†] Vermeer and Louie, op. cit.

[‡] Often codes are extremely prescriptive: Chicago unions insisted on building codes that required the installation of lead pipe in Chicago buildings long after it had been known that lead causes brain damage in children, because the plumbers made more money installing lead pipe than copper or plastic pipe. There are jurisdictions in south Florida in which the landscaping is specified down to the particular species of plants required for specific arrangements. Not surprisingly, it turns out that only one or two landscapers happen to carry that particular species of plant in that particular required size.

(*continued*)

over time when millions of creative entrepreneurs are allowed to discover new and better ways of doing things.

A world in which people make their own decisions, are responsible for their own choices, and thereby able to afford a decent standard of living is a much better world than the one in which we live. The lack of affordable housing is a crisis in the U.S. But creating long-term ever more comfortable and more affordable housing is a better solution than are government housing subsidies. We need to let the millions of creative, innovative, and entrepreneurial individuals get to work making a difference.

If the makers of manufactured housing can create a rural solution that works for those with a median household income of $15,000, why not let them, in conjunction with the designers and social entrepreneurs, create such a solution for urban residents as well?

Chapter 3

The Opportunity

The Creative Powers of a Free Civilization

Michael Strong
CEO and Chief Visionary Officer, FLOW

Man's only limitation, within reason, lies in the development and use of his imagination. He has not yet reached the apex of development in the use of his imaginative faculty. He has merely discovered that he has an imagination, and has commenced to use it in a very elementary way.

—Napoleon Hill

There are estimates that Craig Venter's Celera Genomics was able to sequence the human genome in less than half the time and at one-tenth the cost of the government effort.[*] Burt Rutan's Scaled

---

[*]See Human Genome Project at www.ornl.gov/sci/techresources/Human_Genome/home.shtml.

Composites achievement with SpaceShipOne, was similarly accomplished at about one-tenth the cost and in less than half the time of a comparable NASA project. What if the kind of creativity that makes such astounding rates of progress was applied to the solution of human problems?

Muhammad Yunus launched a structured microfinance movement that now benefits hundreds of millions of women each year. Hernando de Soto has launched a campaign to provide property rights to the urban poor, which is now being implemented in dozens of countries around the world. Both initiatives have outperformed the work of thousands of academic development economists together with thousands of U.N. and NGO development experts. How can we encourage millions more like Yunus and de Soto?

Bill Drayton, founder of Ashoka and the social entrepreneurship movement, is clear about where the real power lies:

> In 1996, when he was elected an Ashoka Fellow, Rodrigo Baggio had a powerful idea and an equally powerful commitment to using it to close the digital divide across Brazil and the world. Rodrigo's movement to democratize the digital era has helped hundreds of local slum communities in a dozen countries across Latin America and Asia successfully build and run computer training schools.
>
> These schools now have over 600,000 graduates—almost all of whom are successfully employed in the new digital economy. How did Rodrigo accomplish all this?
>
> I remember seeing Rodrigo in action in Washington shortly after he was elected. He somehow persuaded the Inter-American Development Bank to give him its used (i.e., extremely valuable) computers. He somehow persuaded the Brazilian Air Force to warehouse and transport these computers. He somehow managed to get them through customs at a time when Brazil was a good deal less relaxed about informatics imports than it is now.
>
> That is how entrepreneurs work. Where others see a barrier, they imagine a logical solution and then turn it into reality.

Getting some of society's biggest institutions to respond to a young, unknown person representing a then unknown organization was simply the right, logical thing to do. That inner confidence, it turns out, is remarkably persuasive.

Bill Drayton, "Where the Real Power Lies,"
Alliance, Vol. 10, No. 1, March 2005

Time and time again entrepreneurs do what other people believe to be impossible, be those others experts, professors, senior officials, or anyone else. Cesar Narys was an art student with no technology background when he talked NASA into letting him use its equipment to set up the first satellite link for live interaction in the 1970s; this "gumption factor" eventually led to a position as VP at AT&T while also consulting around the world helping developing nations set up broadband connections for technology parks.

Fred Smith, founder of Federal Express, submitted a paper outlining the idea for FedEx to a professor at Yale's business school. The professor responded, "The concept is interesting and well-formed, but in order to earn better than a 'C,' the idea must be feasible." The ideas for the Sony Walkman, the CAT scanner, and waffle-sole sneakers were all ridiculed by experts.

Alfred Butts, the creator of the game Scrabble, began working on it, and marketing it, in 1934. It wasn't until 1952, after many permutations and an extraordinary amount of persistence, that Scrabble began to take off, eventually becoming one of the most popular games of all time.

Hundreds of famous writers labored in obscurity for years, receiving rejections slips from hundreds of publishers before becoming successful. J.K. Rowling, who in a few years went from impoverished single mother to the highest earning female in Britain due to the Harry Potter empire, is among the most recent of such success stories.

Individual human beings, believing in individual human visions, despite the evidence, despite expert opinions, despite the odds against them, have been the most powerful creative forces in western civilization. The one thing that Cesar Narys, Fred Smith, Alfred Butts, and J.K. Rowling have in common is the persistence of a vision.

Drayton expands on his account of Rodrigo Baggio and his Committee for Democracy in Information Technology (CDI) and "where the real power lies":

There is another critical element that Rodrigo brought to this process. His work flows from the inner logic of his life—as it does for every great entrepreneur. CDI was not just a clever idea he had two days before. It was rooted both in his personal love for and mastery of the new digital era and, even more important, in deep-seated values. He saw the poverty around him, and focused on the digital divide before there was such a phrase. That combination of love for his field and values then led step by step over many years (starting when he was a teen-ager) to his vision and life commitment.

As a result, when Rodrigo sat across the table from these powerful and much older officials, they were confronting not just confidence in a right idea, but deeply rooted and life-defining values: anon-egoistic faith.

I believe that this values-rooted faith is the ultimate power of a first-class entrepreneur. It is a quality and a force that others can sense and trust. They may or may not understand the idea. They may be afraid to do something out of the ordinary before others have do ne so. But a quiet inner voice tells them they can and should trust Rodrigo.

Drayton here articulates the core FLOW commitment: that values-rooted faith in the rightness of one's vision is the ultimate power of a first-class entrepreneur.

The fact that one is motivated by a commitment to a personal vision often implies that the projects to which an entrepreneur commits his or her life are unproven and unprovable. One of the mistakes that we have made is to limit opportunities for making the world a better place to those projects whose validity can be proven by research. The history of discovery and innovation is filled with monomaniacal individuals pursuing a vision or a dream with no objective evidence that the project will succeed. John D. Rockefeller was very explicit: In a memo to the executive committee of Standard Oil, at a time when low oil prices made oil appear to be a terrible investment, Rockefeller wrote, "Hope if crude oil goes down again . . . our executive committee will not allow any amount of statistics or information . . . to prevent their buying." This commitment to a vision, regardless of the evidence, is what allowed Rockefeller to create the most successful oil company in the world.

We need to bring into being a world in which more people have creative visions, and in which more of them have an opportunity to do their best to bring such visions into being.

A premise of FLOW is that we are dramatically underutilizing the creative powers of the seven billion human beings on the planet. When Yunus proposed helping Bangladeshi peasant women create cell phone businesses, he was told that illiterate peasants couldn't learn how to use cell phones. Six weeks after distributing cell phones (despite the skeptics), Yunus was approached by a proud cell phone lady and asked to give her a phone number, any phone number. He did so and she proudly dialed it rapidly, with her eyes closed. Now cell phone ladies are ubiquitous in rural villages around the world, buying the phones with micro-loans and selling calls by the minute to poor villagers who would otherwise not have access to telecommunications.

Hernando de Soto and his team attempted to open up a sewing business in Peru with two sewing machines—the kind of microbusiness that a microfinance client might launch. They discovered that in order to open up the business legally required nearly 200 discrete bureaucratic steps that took nearly a year of full-time work, going from office to office, waiting, filling out forms, and returning to another office to wait some more. They have since discovered that this absurd level of overregulation is the norm throughout the so-called developing world. Indeed, it is a major reason why the poor in the developing world remain poor. Because of overregulation, they cannot open up businesses legally. As a consequence, they do not have a legal title to their possessions, they cannot use their assets to obtain more credit, they cannot insure their possessions, and they cannot get adequate police protection for their possessions. The most enterprising of the poor are sentenced to ongoing financial insecurity because they are forced to work on the black market. This overregulation does not harm the rich because their businesses are already established and, when needed, they can easily afford the bribes necessary to get things done more rapidly.[*]

---

[*]See Hernando de Soto, *The Mystery of Capital: Why Capitalism Works in the West and Fails Everywhere Else* (New York: Basic Books, 2003).

When I ran an essay contest on "the creative powers of a free civilization," more than 90 percent of the nearly 1,000 essays submitted discussed the theme of creativity as if it were primarily an issue of liberating the imagination by means of new kinds of education or a less oppressive social environment. Although new kinds of education are very important, and social environments that encourage creativity are also important, very few people in our society who think about creativity think about the broader institutional requirements needed to expand the creative powers of a free civilization.

While new ideas, new art, and new literature are important components of social change, without new organizations, new institutions, and new ways of living day-to-day life the ideas, art, and literature remain relatively barren.

As F. A. Hayek says:

> The manner in which we have learnt to order our day, to dress, to eat, and arrange our houses, to speak, write, and use the countless tools and implements of civilization, no less than the "know-how" used in production and trade, all furnish us constantly with the foundations on which our own contributions to the process of civilization must be based. And it is in the new use and improvement of whatever the facilities of civilization offer to us that the new ideas arise, which are ultimately handled in the intellectual sphere.
>
> Thus, the importance of freedom does not depend on the elevated character of the activities that it makes possible. Freedom of action, even action in humble things, is as important as freedom of thought and freedom of belief.
>
> From Friedrich von Hayek, *The Constitution of Liberty* (Chicago, University of Chicago Press, 1960), 34

The sewing machine business in Peru *is* important. The cell phone lady *is* important. Creativity is not merely about cute pictures drawn by kindergartners. It is about the ability to create new enterprises, organizations, and institutions that fundamentally change society.

The developed world has a vast, underutilized asset that is not being leveraged to its best advantage: idealistic people who want to make the world a better place. For most of a century, idealistic people have been encouraged to use anger, protest, lobbying, and legal action in order to make the world a better place. While most certainly some of these behaviors and activities were necessary, we have reached the point at which the social benefit of such behaviors is decreasing. We have reached the point at which creation, rather than attack, ought to be the first obligation of reformers. The social entrepreneurship movement is the first tip of this iceberg.

We want to create a world in which all idealists realize that the creation of new enterprises is the most powerful way to make positive change in the world. If all the energy that is currently invested in zero-sum political conflict was gradually transferred to the committed creation of sustainable enterprises, the cumulative impact on behalf of good would be extraordinary.

Millions of creative, innovative, and entrepreneurial individuals, working in a system of free enterprise, given time, produce staggering improvements in whatever realms of life in which they are allowed to do so.

As John Sparks writes,

Private ownership, private initiative, the hope of reward, and the expectation of achievement have always been primarily responsible for the advancement of mankind. Continued progress—be it spiritual, mental, or material—rests squarely upon a better understanding of the idea of individual freedom of choice and action, with personal responsibility for one's own decisions.

For the purpose of illustrating this idea, let us suppose you had lived in 1900 and somehow were confronted with the problem of seeking a solution to any one of the following problems:

1. To build and maintain roads adequate for use of conveyances, their operators, and passengers.
2. To increase the average span of life by 30 years.
3. To convey instantly the sound of a voice speaking at one place to any other point or any number of points around the world.
4. To convey instantly the visual replica of an action, such as a presidential inauguration, to men and women in their living rooms all over America.

5. To develop a medical preventive against death from pneumonia.
6. To transport physically a person from Los Angeles to New York in less than four hours.
7. To build a horseless carriage of the qualities and capabilities described in the latest advertising folder of any automobile manufacturer.

Without much doubt you would have selected the first problem as the one easiest of solution. In fact, the other problems would have seemed fantastic and quite likely would have been rejected as the figments of someone's wild imagination.

Now, let us see which of these problems has been solved to date. Has the easiest problem been solved? No. Have the seemingly fantastic problems been solved? Yes, and we hardly give them a second thought.

It is not accidental that solutions have been found wherever the atmosphere of freedom and private ownership has prevailed wherein men could try out their ideas and succeed or fail on their own worthiness. Nor is it accidental that the coercive force of government—when hooked up to a creative field such as transportation—has been slow, plodding, and unimaginative in maintaining and replacing its facilities.

John Sparks, "If Men Were Free to Try," *The Freeman*,
February 1977, Vol. 27, No. 2, originally
published in 1954, available online at fee.org

Over time, the creative powers of millions of free, enterprising individuals, allowed to create their own institutions and communities, create miracles. We have allowed enterprising individuals to create miracles in technological realms. There are so many other problems in life; we need to allow for the creation of miracles in spiritual, artistic, social, and other types of entrepreneurship so that, in half the time and at one-tenth the cost, problems can be solved more effectively than we could have imagined.

Creativity requires freedom to act. Every constraint on freedom is a constraint on creative action. While some constraints on creative action are no doubt a good thing (we don't want or need creative activity that involves detonating nuclear weapons or torturing children), it is time to rethink the extent to which creative individuals are allowed to create new products, services, and institutions. There are many thousands of unnecessary laws that limit creativity and constrain human potential.

This was not the case when the Industrial Revolution was created; it was created by ordinary workmen with extraordinary initiative and drive:

> How did the Industrial Revolution occur in Britain in the first place? . . . [Samuel] Smiles noted that . . . "One of the most remarkable things about engineering in England is that its principal achievements have been accomplished not by natural philosophers nor by mathematicians but by men of humble station, for the most part self-educated." . . . Even more than the scientists—Dalton, Davy, and Faraday—the technocrats came from nowhere and had nothing given to them except what they earned with their hands.
>
> George Stephenson ("the greatest engine designer and builder of the age") began as a cowherd; Thomas Telford (canal, road, and bridge builder who almost single-handedly created the infrastructure of England, "the most remarkable man of all, in an age of remarkable men"), a shepherd's son, as a stonemason. Alexander Naysmith (Da Vinci-like artist, designer, and architect of engineering) started as an apprentice coach painter . . . Joseph Bramah, the machine tool inventor, creator of the first patent lock, the hydraulic press, the beer pump, the modern fire engine, the fountain pen, and the first modern water closet, started as a carpenter's apprentice and got his essential learning and experience from the local blacksmith's forge. Henry Maudsley, perhaps the ablest of all the machine-tool inventors . . . began work at 12 as a powder-monkey in a cartridge works and graduated in the smithy.
>
> Paul Johnson, *The Birth of the Modern,* (New York: Harper Perennial, 1992), 571–572

There are literally dozens and dozens of such examples: Almost all of the extraordinary engineering that we all take for granted in the transition from rural to industrial society, was created by uneducated workmen. The idea of a metal bridge or a machine tool simply did not exist in 1750. As Naysmith, one of the creators listed, concluded in *The Birth of the Modern* (p. 573), "I believe that *Free Trade in Ability* has a much closer relation to national prosperity than even Free Trade in Commodities."

There is a myth that advanced formal education is necessary to succeed in today's world because of the complexity of technology. And yet . . . our most recent technological revolution was largely created by high school and college dropouts, much as was the Industrial Revolution. Steve Jobs, Bill Gates, Michael Dell, Linus Torvaalds, and many thousands like them transformed the world. Although their work did build on the work of thousands of academic mathematicians, scientists, and engineers, as well as progress created by both corporate entities (such as IBM) and government (especially the U.S. Department of Defense), without the thousands of uneducated dropouts progress could not possibly have been as deep, diverse, or widespread.

By the mid-1980s, a University of Chicago computer scientist estimated that any decent university in the United States had more computing power than the entire Soviet Union. Moore's law, that computing power doubled every two years, simply did not apply to the Soviet Union. Although they successfully created a few supercomputers, they were completely incapable of creating a vast, idiosyncratic, innovative IT industry. Apple, Atari, Microsoft, Lotus, and others changed the world because anyone could create his own software or device and start up his own company. In economists' jargon, there were no "barriers to entry." And, in fact, many thousands of high school and college dropouts who were engaged in flow experiences, creating gadgets for the fun of it, changed the world.

Silicon Valley, "the largest legal creation of wealth in history," was built largely by unprofessional amateurs using math, sand, and the institutions of freedom. The Soviet Union had the greatest mathematicians on earth, and plenty of sand, but without the institutions of freedom their brilliant mathematicians were not empowered to create those devices that are changing the world.

The "Free Trade in Ability" mentioned by Naysmith was crucial to the achievements of both the Industrial Revolution and the Silicon Valley Revolution. There were neither educational requirements nor licensing laws, no barriers to entry, for engineers in the nineteenth century. That is precisely why working class men entered the field in such droves. There were likewise no barriers to entry for teenage geeks who wanted to mess around with computers; if only licensed electrical engineers had been allowed to do the work, our IT industry would still be focusing on mainframes and expensive minicomputers for large businesses, all more or less controlled by IBM.

The personal computing revolution, the democratization of knowledge and information, would never have taken place. In order to democratize humanism, and make humane institutions available to all, we need to remove barriers to entry and obstacles to creation.

John Stuart Mill, in his famous essay *On Liberty*, made a compelling case that freedom of speech allows for a discovery process to take place in which, over time, humanity benefits through the ongoing discovery of new truths. Mill makes the case that even speech that is often considered to be harmful ought to be allowed, both because it is difficult for authorities to determine what speech really is harmful and because harmful speech often provokes thoughtfulness that results in new and better understandings. Friedrich von Hayek makes a very similar argument for freedom of action:

> Freedom granted only where it can be known beforehand that its effects will be beneficial would not be freedom. If we know how freedom would be used, the case for it would largely disappear. We could then achieve the same result by telling people to do what freedom would enable them to do. But we shall never get the benefits of freedom, never obtain those unforeseeable new developments for which it provides the opportunity, if it is not granted also where the uses made of it by some do not seem desirable. It is therefore no argument against individual freedom that it is frequently abused or used for ends that are recognized as socially undesirable. Our faith in freedom rests not on demonstrable results in particular circumstances but on the belief that it will on balance release more forces for the good than for the bad.
>
> From Friedrich von Hayek, The Constitution of Liberty
> (Chicago: University of Chicago Press, 1960), 31

Alan McConnell makes the point more succinctly: "If it can't be abused, it's not freedom." For those who respect the archetypal wisdom of ancient myths, it is worth pointing out that the Judaic God gave the angels and men freedom together with the power to abuse it. Satan's freedom to fall was a necessary aspect of a perfect Creation; more than one theologian has recognized this as evidence of God's wisdom. It might be considered God's deepest insight.

Some of the most exciting work in software development comes from those who use evolutionary techniques to develop new software. Mutating software programs replicate in a custom-designed environment, which is designed so that, after many generations of replication, the evolved software, which has been selected for over many generations, is extraordinarily effective at fulfilling the function for which it has been selected. Brain researchers have discovered that our infant minds grow based on a process of selection and reinforcement: those neuronal connections which are most useful and effective in accessing the environment in the manner needed by the infant are re-enforced and grow, those neuronal connections that are less useful and effective disappear. As Michael Rothschild points out in *Bionomics*, economies are organic selectionist processes in which millions of individuals pursuing millions of individual goals produce the circumstances in which businesses evolve to fit an ever expanding range of never-before-discovered niches.*

With all selectionist or evolutionary processes, it is important to understand how the environment selects for winners. It is also important to allow for abundant variation. If the environment is selecting for the "wrong" winners, as in evolved software, then the designers will want to change the environment so that better winners evolve. But if one has a positive environment, then one wants abundant variation in order to ensure that ever more wonderful outcomes exist. If one was trying to evolve good software, and if one had a properly structured environment for the evolution to take place, then one would want to have as much freedom and variation as possible in order to optimize outcomes.

In the realm of human action, the legal structures created by governments, together with the cultural characteristics of the participants in those legal structures, create the environment in which humans create

---

*Michael Rothschild, *Bionomics: The Inevitability of Capitalism*, Time Warner Paperbacks, 1992.

new institutions. It is unfortunate that often those who are unhappy with social outcomes attack freedom itself rather than focusing on the changes to the legal structures that would be needed to allow for more positive outcomes to evolve from free institutions.

In order to maximize the creative powers of a free civilization, we will focus instead on creating those changes to the legal structures and cultural characteristics needed to create global peace, prosperity, happiness, and sustainability by means of free institutions. The cultural transformation sketched in the first section, from fear to love, from neediness to self-actualization, is among the many cultural changes that might accelerate these positive outcomes while allowing freedom. There are also changes to the legal structure that we will want to consider.

We do not expect to define a specific set of public policy proposals. We only wish to sketch a way of thinking about the world that will allow all problems to be solved entrepreneurially, which will allow creators, innovators, and entrepreneurs to create global peace, prosperity, happiness, and sustainability in the next 50 years. Done correctly, freely evolving institutions are faster and more effective than are zero-sum conflict institutions. We hope that an increasing percentage of those who are devoted to zero-sum conflicts will direct an increasing percentage of their time, energy, and resources toward win-win free solutions. We want to apply the dynamism of Silicon Valley to the problems of the world; we want to create a "Silicon Valley of well-being" that takes place around the world.

Much of what we propose has been inspired by, or discovered and advocated by, thinkers who have been advocates for free markets. The expression "free market" has many negative associations for many people. In order to avoid this confusion, we will focus on the distinction between coercive action, taken by governments, and voluntary action, taken by mutually consenting adults. It is important before doing so, however, to acknowledge that voluntary action is only beneficial when there are not harmful externalities, when no one else is harmed by the exchange. Because there are often harmful externalities, we must seek to discover creative means of internalizing externalities, such as including the full environmental costs of goods, before fully celebrating free exchange. Our chapter on sustainability will address this issue more closely.

It is also worth noting that the extent to which free exchange takes place is independent of the nature and extent of a social safety net. There is a case to be made that the Scandinavian countries, which are some-times considered socialist, might better be described as "free market welfare states." Their policies are, by and large, capital-friendly; Finland is often among the most highly ranked countries in the world on the Economic Freedom of the World Index (created in part by Milton Friedman). Whether or not to provide particular social services is a com-pletely different issue from regulating interpersonal interactions. The emphasis on voluntary exchange here is thus largely separate from most environmental issues (which we understand are serious), on the one hand, and from social safety net considerations.

Thus assuming internalized externalities and a safety net, there are two primary systems for achieving social goals:

1. Government action
2. Voluntary action

The first is a slow, cumbersome process. Indeed, in the healthiest democracies government was intended to be a slow, cumbersome process in order to minimize abuses of power. Politics is war by other means, and action initiated by government often exacerbates conflict. Implemented decisions are few and relatively rare, and each governmental entity typically carries out one set of policies. Although government may provide useful "rules of the game," the more that we are able to limit government to rule-making rather than hands-on management the better we all will be.

By contrast, voluntary action in a free society does not involve con-flict. In addition, it is radically experimental: Millions, or billions, of human beings have millions, or billions of opportunities to create and to innovate. In whatever realms in which freedom exists, as compared to those realms constrained by law, millions more nodes of experimenta-tion and creativity are possible. Again, although there may occasionally be realms in which the costs of mistakes exceed the benefits of creative improvements, there are reasons to believe that those realms are far more isolated than is currently represented by our legal system.

Milton Friedman, mistakenly considered to be conservative by many—he has long explicitly claimed that he was not a conservative, and in fact has always favored most of all an innovative society—makes these points well:

The preservation of freedom is the protective reason for limiting and decentralizing governmental power. But there is also a constructive reason. The great advances of civilization, whether in architecture or painting, in science or literature, in industry or agriculture, have never come from centralized government. Columbus did not set out to seek a new route to China in response to a majority directive of parliament, though he was partly financed by an absolute monarch. Newton and Leibnitz; Einstein and Bohr; Shakespeare, Milton, and Pasternak; Whitney, McCormick, Edison, and Ford; Jane Addams, Florence Nightengale, and Albert Schweitzer; no one of these opened up new frontiers in human knowledge and understanding, in literature, in technical possibilities, or in the relief of human misery in response to governmental directives. Their achievements were the product of individual genius, of strongly held minority views, of a social climate permitting variety and diversity. Government can never duplicate the variety and diversity of individual action. At any moment in time, by imposing uniform standards in housing, or nutrition, or clothing, government could undoubtedly improve the level of living of many individuals; by imposing uniform standards in schooling, road construction, or sanitation, central government could undoubtedly improve the level of performance in many local areas and perhaps even on the average of all communities. But in the process government would replace progress by stagnation, it would substitute uniform mediocrity for the variety essential for that experimentation which can bring tomorrow's laggards above today's mean.

> Milton Friedman, *Capitalism and Freedom,* 40th Anniversary
> Edition (Chicago: University of Chicago Press, 2002)

It has been a terrible mistake for our society to have politicized this issue. For much of the twentieth century, belief in voluntary action was considered "conservative" and belief in government action was considered "progressive."

While there were most certainly abuses in the realm of voluntary behavior in the nineteenth century, the reaction against voluntarism, throughout most of the twentieth century, was extraordinarily overblown.

Few understood the extent to which innovation relies on the individual initiative of thousands of unknown amateurs, nor the extent to which government would largely clunk along in the service of established elites (including established corporations, established unions, established academic institutions, established medical organizations, and so on.) Laws will always tend to favor the established and visible over the not yet visible, unproven "gleam in the eye" of the unknown amateur.

The nineteenth century saw the first Industrial Revolution created by uneducated amateurs, tinkerers, and engineers. The Silicon Valley Revolution transformed the world with the help of uneducated geeks and rebels (the come-on line for a Silicon Valley billboard advertising the new VW bug calls out "Helllloooooo Rich Hippies!"). The twenty-first century needs a Humanist Revolution based on the unleashed power of those adventurers of the spirit who are exploring the outer boundaries of self-actualization and wellness. The leaders of the two previous revolutions were mostly male. The leaders of this revolution may be mostly female; indeed, if we allowed them to do so, so they might be teenage or 20-something young women, just as the Industrial Revolution and the Silicon Valley Revolution were largely led by teenage or 20-something young men.

For too long, people who have desired to make the world a better place have accepted leadership from those who have directed them toward anger and acts of aggression. This path has resulted in much damage to human life in the past and much impotence and depression today.

FLOW proposes instead that those who desire to make the world a better place engage in lives of constructive action and meaningful work so that we can achieve those goals that have so long eluded us. If everyone who desires to make the world a better place takes positive action, instead of continuing on a path of impotent rage and frustration, we can quickly create sustainable peace, prosperity, and happiness for all.

Why Are Do-Gooders Angry and Punitive So Often?

Does it ever strike you as odd that the people who talk the most about making the world a better place are often bitter and angry? If the motivation is truly altruistic, truly based in compassion for those who need help, truly based in a principled commitment to doing good, then why the anger? Are altruists occupationally prone to anger?

Well, it turns out that they are, in fact, biologically inclined to be angry and punitive toward those who they perceive to be not being helpful.

Evidence from complementary fields suggests that:

- Altruists are perceived as high status in tribal communities.
- An important component of perceived altruism is exhibiting punitive sentiments toward those who contribute less to the good of the tribe.
- Those who contribute most to the community good are most motivated to punish "free riders," those who are not contributing to the good of the tribe.
- A secondary, but important, dynamic is that the perceived altruist should not only punish those who contribute less but also punish those who do not punish those who contribute less.

A recent study of an Ecuadorian tribe by an evolutionary psychologist confirmed that:

> . . . perceived pro-community altruists are indeed high status and suggest that (1) community residents skillfully monitor the altruism of coresidents, (2) residents who engage in opportunities to broadcast desirable qualities are high status only to the extent that they are considered altruistic, and (3) individuals who sanction coresidents based on coresidents' contributions to the community are themselves relatively high status.
>
> Michael E. Price, "Pro-Community Altruism and Status In a Shuar Village," Human Nature, vol. 14, Number 2, June 2003, 191–195

Evolutionary psychologists believe that status is correlated with perceived pro-community altruism because in part it was in our evolutionary interest to prevent free riders, those who failed to participate in the provision of collective goods. Models show that:

> . . . willingness to contribute to a public good can be evolutionarily stable as long as free riders are punished, along with those who refuse to punish free riders. . . . Punishment needs to be visited on free riders on the original public good, and on those who do not punish free riders, and on those who do not punish those who do not punish free riders, and so on.
>
> Michael Price, "Punitive Sentiment as an Anti-Free Rider Psychological Device," Evolution and Human Behavior, vol. 23, issue 3, 203–231

(*continued*)

Thus, from the fact that human groups do demonstrate a willingness to contribute to the public good in a manner that is not consistent with rational choice theory, we might infer that we have evolved an evolutionarily stable set of capacities that enable this, including a propensity to punish those who do not so contribute and to punish those who do not punish.

This model-based hypothesis is further supported by independent evidence from psychological experiments that we are willing to punish those who do not contribute to collective action even at a cost to us, another finding that is inconsistent with rational choice. More specifically, experimental results show that:

> Subjects' punitive sentiments sensitively tracked their risk of suffering a fitness disadvantage relative to free riders in a collective action. . . . In other words, the relationship between willingness to participate in a collective action and desire to punish free riders was specific, selective, and uniform. This evidence of special design suggests the presence of an adaptation that was designed for eliminating the adverse fitness differentials that producers would otherwise incur relative to free riders in collective action contexts.
>
> Michael Price, "Punitive Sentiment as an Anti-Free Rider Psychological Device," Evolution and Human Behavior, vol. 23, issue 3, 203–231

Thus, the more willing we are to contribute to solving the problems of the community, the greater is our desire to punish those who do not. If we had not developed the instinctive correlation between eagerness to contribute to the good of the community on the one hand, and eagerness to punish those who do not contribute to the good of the community on the other, the genes of those of us who are more genetically prone to contributing to the good of the community would have lost out to the genes of those who were more narrowly selfish. It is striking that there exists a "specific, selective, and uniform" relationship between eagerness to contribute to the community good and eagerness to punish.

If we had not evolved a propensity to punish free riders, free riders would have had an evolutionary advantage. But by punishing those who free ride, and punishing those who do not punish those who free ride, and punishing those who do not punish those who do not punish those who free ride, and so forth, in our tribal context we have evolved to ensure that those who free ride do not gain an evolutionary advantage. Thus, the very fact that we have moral impulses to support the public good is necessarily intertwined with the fact that we have moral impulses to punish those who do not (and to punish those who do not punish those who do not, and so on). In the absence of this specific moral machinery, the free riders among us would have dominated our genetic pool, and had we survived as a species would have, in fact, been entirely focused on their "inclusive fitness," that is, the well-being of their immediate families. But we clearly have evolved moral impulses that transcend the motivation to protect the interests of our immediate genetic kin.

With respect to our innate moral propensities, there appears to be a distribution of behaviors, just as there is a genetically grounded distribution of height, intelligence, and other features. Just as both height and intelligence are the result of a deep synergistic combination of environmental and genetic factors, so too, would we expect moral propensities to have a genetically-determined range as well as an environmentally conditioned distribution of expressions of that range.

Thus, do-gooders, those who contribute to the public good, are also more inclined to punish those who do not contribute. Just as the rest of us need to consciously monitor our genetic propensity to eat fat and sugar, so too do the do-gooders need to consciously monitor their genetic propensity toward punitive behavior. As Leda Cosmides and John Tooby, summarize these findings,

> Whether it is sensible now or not, our psychology is designed so that the more we contribute to a collective action, the more punitive we will feel toward those we perceive as free riders.
>
> Leda Cosmides and John Tooby, "Know Thyself:
The Evolutionary Psychology of Moral Reasoning and
Moral Sentiments," in R. E. Freeman and P. Werhane (Eds.),
Business, Science, and Ethics. The Ruffin Series
No. 4. Charlottesville, VA: Society for Business Ethics, 113

In a small tribe of 150, their punitive instincts were likely to be effective. In a complex world of six billion, the same instincts will rarely be effective and may often be destructive.

This instinct is especially harmful when used to punish those who are perceived as not punishing free riders. This is the source of the bigotry against market economics among the do-gooders: It is believed that those who describe the positive outcomes of free enterprise are not doing their job to behave punitively toward free riders, and that therefore they, too, must be punished. In a large, complex market with billions or trillions of transactions, there will be enormous numbers of transactions that are harmful or bad. And the most altruistic among us will be most inclined to engage in public expressions of punitive behavior towards those bad people engaged in harmful activities. Indeed, one can imagine a moral and cultural dynamic arising in which the moral high ground is held by those who want to prohibit all possibility of harmful actions taking place—whether or not they are actually able to prohibit all harmful activity, the most altruistic public posturing will always lead to competing claims to be the most punitive towards those who commit harms. But this instinct, which worked so effectively in motivating others to working together in a small tribe, destroys possibilities for creativity, innovation, and entrepreneurship in a large, pluralistic society.

More darkly, this instinct is also the reason why so many authentically altruistic people became so hate-filled and murderous because of the communist ideal and, more frightening still, the most hate-filled among them often held the moral high ground.[*]

---

[*]For a chilling personal account of the hatred of the most morally-minded communists, read Jung Chang's *Wild Swans: Three Daughters of China*, Anchor, 1992. After reading what the communists did to her parents, one is struck by the extraordinary restraint she shows towards those American intellectuals who enthusiastically supported Mao throughout the Cultural Revolution.

Part Two

Conscious Capitalism

Business social responsibility should not be coerced; it is a voluntary decision that the entrepreneurial leadership of every company must make on its own.

—JOHN MACKEY

Chapter 4

Creating a New Paradigm for Business

John Mackey
CEO, Whole Foods Market and
Co-Founder, FLOW

D o we need a new way to think about business, corporations, and capitalism for the twenty-first century? Do we need to create a new business paradigm? Corporations are probably the most influential institutions in the world today and yet many people do not believe that they can be trusted. Instead, corporations are widely perceived as greedy, selfish, exploitative, uncaring, and interested only in maximizing profits. In the early years of the twenty-first century, major ethical lapses on the part of big business came to light including scandals at Enron, Arthur Anderson, Tyco, the New York Stock Exchange, World-Com, Mutual Funds, and AIG. These scandals have all contributed to a growing distrust of business and further eroded public trust in large corporations in the United States.

Increasingly, many people believe there must be something wrong with both corporations and capitalism. The antiglobalization movement is primarily an anticorporation movement. Many people have come to the conclusion that corporations want to dominate and control the world—for example, David Korten wrote an interesting book called *When Corporations Rule the World*. While many critics, including myself, take issue with Korten's assertions, the book reflects this relatively common belief that corporations are slowly, steadily taking over the world. Along this line of reasoning it follows that this corporate hegemony is not a good thing for the world since corporations are greedy, selfish, and uncaring. In short, corporations and capitalism are not generally in favor, and both have serious branding problems.

Our first theories of economics were developed during the Industrial Revolution. Prior to that, economics did not exist as a discipline. Economics was created as one explanatory response to the Industrial Revolution and initial economic models were based on industrial models of the economy. Although economic theory has evolved since Adam Smith wrote *The Wealth of Nations* in 1776, many economists continue using industrial and machine metaphors to explain how the economy works. Now that we are well into the postindustrial Information Age, these metaphors have become outdated and mislead our thinking about business. For example, recall the trinity of labor, land, and capital as "factors of production," and therefore as merely a means to the end of efficiency and profits. According to this model, business operates like a machine—business owners input various amounts of capital, labor, and land at the start. Profits then spit out on the other side of the metaphorical machine. As most modern economists continue to see it, very much like this model, the purpose of business is to transform factors of production into profit for the benefit of the investors.

The world has become much more complex since those simple machine metaphors were first developed. Unfortunately, current business thinking does not easily grasp systems interdependencies, and therefore often lacks ecological consciousness or a sense of responsibility for other constituencies, or other stakeholders, besides investors. Large corporations are still grounded in a theoretical model that does not acknowledge the complex interdependencies of all of the various constituencies. For business to reach its fullest potential in the twenty-first century, we will need to create a new business paradigm that moves beyond simplistic machine/industrial models to those that embrace the complex interdependencies of multiple constituencies. This is the reality in which corporations exist today, and our economic and business theories need to evolve to reflect this truth.

I intend to raise several questions about current business thinking and practice in this chapter. Because my experience as co-founder and CEO of Whole Foods Market is in the retail grocery business, many of my examples, especially for new business thinking, will feature innovations and standard operating procedures at my own company. I encourage you to take my examples and use your creative imagination to see the possibilities that exist for all current businesses to escape outdated thinking and action. My hope is that you will build upon the Whole Foods Market model for any future businesses or organizations you create as part of a new paradigm.

Voluntary Exchange

In a capitalistic market economy, business is ultimately based on voluntary exchange; all the main constituencies of a business (such as customers, employees, suppliers, and investors) voluntarily exchange with the business to create value for themselves and for others. No constituency is coerced to exchange against its will. This voluntary exchange for mutual benefit is the ethical foundation of business and capitalism. For example, if customers are unhappy with the prices, the services, or the selection at Whole Foods Market, they are free to shop at another competitor. If our team members are unhappy with their wages, benefits, or working conditions, they are free to seek a job with a different firm that provides more of what they seek. If investors in a public corporation such as Whole Foods Market are unhappy with the economic returns being generated, they are free to sell their shares and invest their money in some other alternative. If suppliers want better terms or different product placement than we are willing to give they are free to seek alternative outlets to sell their products. All the constituents therefore exchange voluntarily for mutual benefit, and they are free to exit the relationship whenever they wish.

This voluntary exchange for mutual benefit creates the ethical foundation of business and that is why business is ultimately justified to rightfully exist within a society. This ethical foundation of business doesn't necessarily mean that everything any particular business does is always ethical, but only that voluntary exchange for mutual benefit is itself an ethical process. A business is still expected to behave ethically in its voluntary exchanges and to be responsible for any negative impacts it may create, for example, environmental pollution. So voluntary exchange provides the ethical foundation of business, but what is its purpose?

The Purpose of Business

Have you ever asked yourself what is the purpose of a business? Most business people never ask themselves this interesting question. If you think about it, what is the purpose of a doctor or hospital? Is their purpose to maximize profits? This isn't what they teach in medical schools or what most doctors advocate. A doctor's purpose is to help heal sick people. What about the purpose of a teacher or a school? Do they exist to maximize profits? No, their primary purpose is to educate the young and prepare them to live successful lives in society. What about the purpose of lawyers or courts of law? All lawyer jokes aside, the purpose of a lawyer is to pursue justice on behalf of a client, and our courts exist to settle disputes and bring wrongdoers to justice. All of the other professions put an emphasis on the public good and have purposes beyond self-interest. Why doesn't business?

What then is the purpose of business and who has the right to define it? Economists routinely teach that the purpose of business is to maximize profits for the investors. However, they seldom offer arguments to support this point of view beyond asserting that the business is owned by its investors who have a legal right to hire and fire the management, through the board of directors they elect, and who also have a legal claim on the residual profits of the business. Both of these assertions are true, but these legal rights do not necessarily equate to defining the purpose of a business—why it exists and what its purpose and goals are. In most cases the original purpose of a business is decided prior to any capital being received from investors. While the capital from investors is very important to any business, there is one participant in business who has the right to define what the purpose(s) of the business will be: the entrepreneur who creates the business in the first place. Entrepreneurs create a company, bring all the factors of production together, and coordinate them into a viable business. Entrepreneurs set the company strategy and negotiate the terms of trade with all of the voluntarily cooperating stakeholders—including the investors. When we recruited our original investors at Whole Foods Market they understood that Whole Foods Market had other purposes besides maximizing profits. Entrepreneurs discover and/or create the purpose of a business—not investors, or politicians, or lawyers, or economists.

I've known many entrepreneurs in my life, and with only a few exceptions most did not create their business primarily to maximize profits. Of course they wanted to make money, but profit was just one of the reasons they started their businesses. The following are plausible scenarios for why entrepreneurs create businesses. Perhaps the entrepreneur was unable to work for anybody else, had strong authority issues, and therefore need to be his or her own boss. Or they needed to be in charge of their own enterprise because that is how they derive their sense of self-worth, value, and self esteem. Maybe the entrepreneur has something to prove to his parents, siblings, or friends and creating a successful business will exorcise unconscious childhood demons. It could be that the entrepreneur is a very creative individual who has ideas that he or she wants to see tested in reality to see whether they work. Possibly the entrepreneur is an idealist and wants to make the world a better place, and his primary motivation for creating a new business is to improve the world. Some entrepreneurs likely create new businesses for the sheer fun of it. There are many, many reasons why people create businesses. There are certain entrepreneurs who create a business primarily to maximize profits; however, in my life experience they are definitely a minority.

The founding entrepreneurs determine the initial purpose of their business, but eventually these entrepreneurs will retire or leave the businesses that they created. Does the founding entrepreneur's original purpose remain in perpetuity or can it evolve over time? I believe the purpose of any business can evolve over time. This evolution of purpose is the result of the dynamic interaction of the various interdependent stakeholders with each other and with the business itself. Customers, employees, investors, suppliers, and the community all influence business purpose over time. While the investors will have the ultimate legal claim on the residual profits of the business, the purpose of the business itself evolves over time through the cocreation of the interdependent stakeholders.

This is a fascinating discovery I've made about Whole Foods Market during the previous 28 years. Whole Foods Market's co-founders created the original purpose of the company in 1980, but the interdependent stakeholders have worked together to drive its evolution over the years. We started with a few simple ideals and core values for the company and then created very simple business structures to help fulfill those ideals. However, over time, as the company grew a process of self-organization took place and layers of organizational complexity evolved year after year to fulfill the original core values. As the original core values were expressed over time, deeper meanings of those core values were discovered and/or created by the interdependent stakeholders. Whole Foods Market's purpose has become deeper, richer, and more complex as it has evolved over the years.

The persistent myth claiming that the ultimate purpose of business is always to maximize profits for the investors originated with the Industrial Revolution's earliest economists. How did this myth originate? The classical economists formulated their theories by observing and describing the behavior of various entrepreneurs and their businesses. They observed correctly that successful businesses were always profitable and that, indeed, the entrepreneurs who organized and operated these successful businesses always sought to make profits. Businesses that were not profitable did not survive for very long in a competitive marketplace because profits are essential to the long-term survival and flourishing of all businesses. Without profits entrepreneurs will not be able to invest the necessary capital to replace their depreciating buildings and equipment and won't be able to make the necessary investments to adapt to the always evolving and competitive marketplace. The need for profit is universal for all businesses in a healthy market economy.

Unfortunately, early economists went far beyond merely describing how entrepreneurs always seek profits as an important goal, to concluding that maximizing profits is the only important goal of business. They actually took it one step further; the economists soon concluded that maximizing profits is the only goal they should seek. The classical economists went from describing the behavior in which they observed successful entrepreneurs engage while operating their businesses, to prescribing that behavior as the correct behavior that all entrepreneurs should always engage in all of the time. How did they come to this conclusion?

One possibility is that the classical economists became enchanted with the efficiency and the productivity of the industrial enterprises that they studied. Industrial and machine metaphors became the primary metaphors used to explain how the world really worked since this reflected the Newtonian scientific world-view that came to dominate the consciousness of the age. Every business was seen as a type of machine with various inputs and profits being the output. Profits from business became the primary capital that investors and entrepreneurs used to not only upgrade and improve existing enterprises, but also the capital used to begin new enterprises. The progress of the larger economy was dependent upon this capital accumulation, through the profits of enterprises being saved and reinvested.

In the United States we often take for granted the availability of large pools of capital to invest in new businesses because our economy has been producing them for more than 250 years. However, at the beginning of the Industrial Revolution capital was quite scarce. The ability of successful enterprises to accumulate profits and the redirection of accumulated capital by the entrepreneurs and investors into new and promising opportunities was largely unprecedented in history. Therefore it isn't too surprising that classical economists became enamored with the importance of profits, because profits had historically been very rare and they were essential to the continued improvement and progress of society. Industrial Age entrepreneurs had discovered a form of a "perpetual motion machine"—enterprises organized to maximize profits and through the reinvestment of these profits, the promise of indefinite continued growth.

Great Companies Have Great Purposes

If most entrepreneurs don't create their businesses for the primary purpose of maximizing profits, what are their primary goals? The answer varies tremendously from business to business; there are potentially as many different purposes for businesses as there are businesses. Entrepreneurs create their businesses for a diversity of reasons. However, I believe that most of the greatest companies in the world also have great purposes that were discovered and/or created by their original founders and that still remain at the core of their business models. Having a deeper, more transcendent purpose is highly energizing for all of the various interdependent stakeholders, including the customers, employees, investors, suppliers, and the larger communities in which the business participates. While these deeper, more transcendent purposes have unique expressions at each business they also can be grouped into certain well known and timeless categories. Philosophy credits Plato with expressing the timeless ideals of "The Good," "The True," and "The Beautiful" that humanity has sought to create, discover, and express for thousands of years. If we add the ideal of "The Heroic" to the above three we have the framework of higher ideals that most great businesses seek to express in some form or fashion. The following examples present these four ideals as created and expressed by great, modern businesses.

The first great purpose that great businesses express is The Good. The most common way this ideal manifests in business is through service to others. Authentic service is typically based on genuine empathy for the needs and desires of other people. Genuine empathy leads to the development, growth, and expression of love, care, and compassion. Great businesses dedicated to the great purpose of service to others also develop methods to grow the emotional intelligence of their organizations, an emotional intelligence that nourishes and encourages love, care, and compassion toward customers, employees, and the larger community. While any category of business can be motivated by the deeper purpose of service to others, we find businesses that primarily depend upon the goodwill of their customers to be the most likely to wholeheartedly express this particular deeper purpose. Some of the great businesses that best express the great purpose of service to others include Southwest Airlines, JetBlue Airways, Wegmans, Commerce

Bank, Nordstrom, REI, and The Container Store—all of them retailers and service businesses. Whole Foods Market also aspires to express the great ideal of service to others as its primary purpose. Devotion to service to others is a deeply motivating purpose, one that provides tremendous emotional fulfillment to individuals who truly embrace this ideal.

The second great purpose to animate great businesses is The True, or the excitement of discovery and the pursuit of truth. How very exciting to discover what no one has ever discovered before, to learn what has never before been known, to create a product or service that has never before existed and that advances the well-being of humanity! This great purpose is at the core of some of the most creative and dynamic companies. Google, Intel, Genentech, Amgen, and Medtronic are all examples of great companies motivated by the excitement of discovery and the pursuit of truth. Through their successful fulfillment of this great purpose, all these companies have greatly benefited humanity.

The third great purpose that we find at the core of great businesses is The Beautiful, which can best be expressed in business as the search for excellence and the quest for perfection. A company that expresses beauty enriches our lives in numerous ways. While we more commonly experience The Beautiful through the work of individual creative artists in music, painting, film, and artisanal crafts, we can also see it expressed through certain special companies that have tapped into this powerful purpose as they pursue perfection in their chosen endeavor. Some great companies that express this purpose include Apple, Berkshire Hathaway, and Four Seasons Hotels. True excellence expresses beauty in unique and inspiring ways that make our lives more enjoyable.

The fourth great purpose that inspires many great businesses is The Heroic, or changing and improving the world through heroic efforts. The heroic business is motivated by the desire to change the world, not necessarily through service to others or through discovery and the pursuit of truth, or through the quest for perfection, but through the powerful promethean desire to really change things—to truly make the world better, to solve insoluble problems, to do the really courageous thing even when it is very risky, and to achieve what others say is impossible. When Henry Ford first created the Ford Motor Company it could be viewed as a heroic company. Henry Ford truly changed the world in the early part of the twentieth century. Microsoft changed the world in the later half of the twentieth century. In the twenty-first century The Bill and Melinda Gates Foundation seeks to solve many of the world's major health problems, from AIDS to malaria. One of the best examples of a truly heroic enterprise is Grameen Bank, begun by Muhammed Yunus. His heroic dedication to ending poverty in Bangladesh and throughout the world garnered him the 2006 Nobel Peace Prize. I recommend his book *Banker to the Poor* for an inspiring tale of heroic enterprise. Most heroic enterprises are begun by charismatic, heroic entrepreneurs and the organization's biggest challenge is to successfully institutionalize the heroic purpose after its founding entrepreneur dies or moves on. Very few heroic enterprises have been able to do this over the long term.

Finally, I recommend two books that present the importance of business purpose. The first is *Built to Last* by Jim Collins and Jerry Porras. The other, from which I have drawn heavily for this essay, is *Purpose: The Starting Point of Great Companies* by Nikos Mourkogiannis.

The Paradox of Profits

My thesis about business having important purposes besides maximizing profits should not be mistaken for hostility toward profit, however. I do know something about maximizing profits and creating shareholder value. When I co-founded Whole Foods Market in 1978, we began with $45,000 in capital; we only had $250,000 in sales our first year. In 2006, Whole Foods Market had sales of more than $5.6 billion, with net profits of more than $200 million, and a market capitalization over $8 billion. Profits are one of the most important goals of any successful business, and investors are one of the most important constituencies of public businesses. Although it may seem counterintuitive, the best way to maximize profits over the long term is to not make them the primary goal of the business.

I will use an analogy to explain the best way to create long-term profits. The analogy is happiness because, based on my life experience, happiness is best experienced by not aiming for it directly. A person who focuses his life energies on striving for his own self-interest and personal happiness is often someone who is also a narcissist, or someone who is self-involved and obsessed with his own ego gratification. Ironically, chances are high that such individuals won't actually achieve their goal of happiness by pursuing happiness along this path. In my experience, happiness is a by-product of other things; happiness comes from having a strong sense of purpose, meaningful work, great friends, good health, learning and growing, loving relationships with many people, and helping other people to flourish in their lives. If we have a strong sense of all of the above, it's very likely that we will also experience happiness in our lives on a frequent basis.

Happiness is a by-product of pursuing those other goals and I think that analogy applies to business as well. In my business experience, profits are best achieved by not making them the primary goal of the business. Rather, long-term profits are the result of having a deeper business purpose, great products, customer satisfaction, employee happiness, excellent suppliers, community and environmental responsibility—these are the keys to maximizing long-term profits. The paradox of profits is that, like happiness, they are best achieved by not aiming directly for them.

Long-term profits are maximized by not making them the primary goal. A business is best not thought of as a machine with various factors of production working in tandem to maximize profits. A business model more in touch with our complex, post-modern, information-rich world is that of a complex self-adaptive system of interdependent constituencies. Management's role is to optimize the health and value of the entire complex, evolving, and self-adaptive system. All of the various constituencies connect together and affect one another. If business managers optimize the health and value of the entire interdependent system and the well-being of all the major constituencies, the end result will also be the highest long-term profits for the investors as well.

Conversely, if a business seeks only to maximize profits to ensure shareholder value and does not attend to the health of the entire system, short-term profits may indeed result, perhaps lasting many years, depending upon how well its competitor companies are managed. However, neglecting or abusing the other constituencies in the interdependent system will eventually create negative feedback loops that will end up harming the long-term interests of the investors and shareholders, resulting in suboptimization of the entire system. Without consistent customer satisfaction, employee happiness and commitment, and community support, the short-term profits will probably prove to be unsustainable over the long term.

The most common objection to the above argument is that several thousand businesses are highly profitable and are not actively managed to optimize the value for all of the stakeholders. Instead they put the interests of their investors first and they are also highly profitable. Doesn't this disprove my argument? Not at all. Most businesses are simply competing against other similar businesses that are organized and managed with the same overall values and goals—maximizing profits. The real question is, how does a traditional profit-centered business fare when it competes against a stakeholder-centered business? The only study I know that tries to answer this question is detailed in the book *Firms of Endearment: The Pursuit of Purpose and Profit* by David Wolfe, Rajendra Sisodia, and Jagdish Sheth (2007, Wharton School Publishing). The authors identify 30 companies that are managed to optimize total stakeholder value instead of focusing strictly on profits. They track the long-term stock performance of those that are publicly traded compared to the S&P 500.* Figure 4.1 illustrates this comparison.

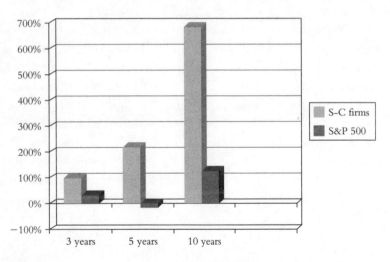

Figure 4.1   Investment Performance of Stakeholder-Centered (S-C) Companies
SOURCE: Adapted from Wolfe and Sisodia, Firms of Endearment.

---

* The publicly-traded companies included in the study include: Amazon, Best Buy, CarMax, Caterpillar, Commerce Bank, Costco, eBay, Google, Harley Davidson, Honda, JetBlue, Johnson & Johnson, Progressive Insurance, Southwest Airlines, Starbucks, Timberland, Toyota, UPS, and Whole Foods Market.

As Figure 4.1 indicates, companies that are managed to create value for all of their stakeholders have had extraordinarily high stock market returns both over the short term and the long term. This is no accident in my opinion. Rather, it is the result of all 30 firms creating a superior business model—the business model that I believe will become dominant in the twenty-first century.

Stockholders Maintain Legal Control

Optimizing value for all the interdependent stakeholders does not mean, however, a loss of legal control of the business for the investors. The owners/investors must legally control the business to prevent their exploitation by management and by the other stakeholders. However, the owners/investors do get paid last. What do I mean by this? The customers get paid first in their relationships with the business in that they come in, find products or services they desire, purchase those products or services, receive those products or services fairly quickly, and often pay after the product or service has been rendered to them. For example, they eat before they have to pay at a café. Next, the employees render their services and get paid on a short-term, periodic basis. Whole Foods Market team members receive their pay every two weeks. The suppliers get paid, according to agreed upon terms and time frames, and government taxes are remitted monthly and quarterly. The owners/investors are paid last, after everyone else has received goods, services, wages, or payment. The investors are entitled to whatever is left over, the residual profits. Because they are paid last, investors must have legal and fiduciary control of the business to prevent management or other stakeholders from shortchanging them. Investors usually demand these conditions as a requirement for investing their capital in a business.

Management does have legal and fiduciary responsibility to maximize long-term shareholder value. However, the best way to maximize long-term shareholder value is to simultaneously optimize value for all the major constituencies, because they are all interdependent upon one another. This is the most important business lesson that I learned while creating and growing Whole Foods Market. Occasionally there

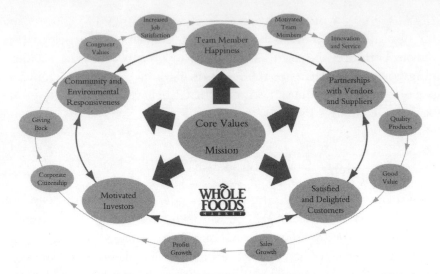

Figure 4.2   An Illustration of "Conscious Capitalism"

are conflicts of interest among constituencies, but in general a "harmony of interests" exists between the different constituencies, since they are so dependent on one another. The best way to maximize long-term shareholder value is to simultaneously optimize the value for all other constituencies. The health of the entire system is what matters the most. Figure 4.2 illustrates one example of what I mean by the phrase "Conscious Capitalism."

Whole Foods Market's Conscious Capitalism

At the center of the Whole Foods Market business model illustrating holistic interdependence, you'll find our core values and business mission. Everything else extends from the business purpose reflected in the core values. Surrounding the central purpose are the various constituencies: customers, team members, suppliers, investors, and the community and environment. All are linked interdependently. Retail business provides a simple model to illustrate that management's role is to hire good people, train them well, and do whatever it takes to have those team members flourish and be happy while they are at work. The team member's job, at least at Whole Foods Market, is to satisfy and delight the customers. If we have happy customers, we will have a successful business and happy investors. Management helps the team members experience happiness, team members help the customers achieve happiness, the customers help the investors achieve happiness, and when some of the profits from the investors are reinvested in the business, you end up with a virtuous circle. I find myself continually astounded about how few business people understand these linkages. But market analysis increasingly illustrates that the businesses with a sole purpose of maximizing profits, in other words, those that do not understand that their profits are produced by an interdependent system of constituencies, are less successful over the long term.[*]

Core Values

When businesses have a purpose beyond maximizing profits, this purpose is often expressed in the business mission. Core values constitute the guiding principles the business uses to realize its purpose. Whole Foods Market's core values very succinctly express the purposes of the business—purposes that include making profits but also creating value for all of the major constituencies. I want to talk briefly about Whole Foods Market's core values. Our business talks and walks our values; we share them with our constituency groups, and invite feedback in the form of dialogs. The core values are: selling the highest quality natural and organic products available; satisfying and delighting our customers; supporting team member happiness and excellence; creating wealth, profits, and growth; and caring about our communities and environment.

Selling the Highest Quality Natural and Organic Products Available

Whole Foods Market is the leading retailer of natural and organic foods in the world. We developed strict and explicit quality standards, which we review regularly. We are very proud to have helped improve

---

[*]Sisodia, Rajendra, Wolfe, David, and Sheth, Jagdish, *Firms of Endearment: The Pursuit of Purpose and Profit,* (Philadelphia: Wharton School Publishing, 2007).

the health, well-being and longevity of millions of people and that we have proven that good health and pleasurable eating are compatible goals. Whole Foods Market resists the continuous trend toward the degradation of the quality of our food through the industrialization of food production. While this industrialization of our food supply has increased production efficiency and lowered the cost of many food staples, both of which are beneficial to society, the process has also resulted in many negative unintended consequences. Several of the practices developed for the industrialized food system have resulted in lower nutritional quality for our food and negative environmental impacts such as pesticide contamination and concentrated animal waste products from CAFOs (Concentrated Animal Feeding Operations). We see this particularly in our animal foods production. Widespread factory farm production of our animal foods results in a tremendous cost to the well-being of the animals, along with severe, negative impacts to food safety and human health that are only recently coming to light in the public arena. To combat this assault on multiple fronts, and to walk our core values, Whole Foods Market is very proud to be developing animal compassionate production standards, working in concert with concerned stakeholder groups in North America.

Satisfying and Delighting our Customers

The customer is our most important constituency, since with no customers, we have no business. We always maintain awareness that our customers shop voluntarily—they are not coerced to shop. If they are unhappy with our business they will go trade someplace else. Because of the voluntary nature of business, we design our business model around the customer, who must be treated as an end and not as a means. What I mean by this statement is that the well-being of the customer must be seen as the most important goal overall and not as a means to profit for the business. In my experience, businesses that think of customers as means to the end of profit do not have the same commitment to service, empathy, and understanding of customers' well-being as the business that treats customers as ends instead of means. Customers are very intelligent! They know when someone is doing a sales job on them, and they know when someone genuinely cares about their well-being.

Supporting Team Member Happiness and Excellence

In order to treat the customers as an end we have empowered our team members to satisfy and delight our customers. New team members are trained to do whatever it takes to satisfy our customers. Happy customers create happy investors. In order to have happy customers we also need to have happy team members because the team members are primarily responsible for creating happy customers. When team members are frustrated, dissatisfied, and unhappy in their work they are unlikely to give the high levels of customer service that the business needs to flourish.

Within a complex interdependent self-evolving system, team members must also be treated as ends and not means. Their well-being and happiness must be an end in itself, not merely a means to the profits of the business. Our internal business model within each store is the self-managing team, which are truly the organizational cells of the business. The teams do their own hiring, work scheduling, and product procurement. They are running their own small business within the store, and they have full responsibility for the business. Each team is empowered on many levels, not only in customer satisfaction.

I also believe that it is absolutely essential to trust team members, and one way to show that trust is through open information. Whole Foods provides open financial information—on all levels since want to be as transparent an organization as possible—without making ourselves overly vulnerable to our competitors. I think it essential that the team members have a sense of shared purpose and power. If team members can align around the values and purpose of the business, they are going to have a greater commitment to the business. They will likely unleash greater energy and creativity through that sense of alignment and shared purpose. At Whole Foods, we consciously reject the command-and-control management style. This top-down, "do it my way" approach is the opposite of team member empowerment. We also teach the importance of "shared fate," and by shared fate I mean that the better the company does, the better the customers do, the better the team members do, and the better the investors do. Once again, I reference the interdependent nature of the relationship of all the constituencies: happy team members create happy customers, happy customers create happy investors.

Another innovative practice at Whole Foods is the sharing of salary information, so that what everyone gets paid is open information. I believe this is the best way to deal with envy, which exists as part of human nature and in any organization. To deal directly with envy, a business must open up and become more transparent. When unjust employment compensation exists, the situation will be noticed and a feedback mechanism will develop to correct it. Conversely, by having such transparency, people can see what skills and qualities are most highly valued and rewarded in the organization so that they can know what to strive for with their own career objectives. We also have a salary cap at Whole Foods, which is currently 19 times the average pay (Figure 4.3); more about that in a moment.

Yet another innovation is our benefits vote, wherein team members vote every three years on what benefits they can enjoy. After fielding repeated and ongoing requests for various benefits as I traveled around to our stores to meet with team members, I realized that I was not smart enough to figure out the right mix of benefits for Whole Foods Market. Our team members were forever asking me if they could have this or that additional benefit. Requests for addition benefits are endless. But this is also true for every stakeholder—the desire for a better deal. Every stakeholder is always looking for more. Customers are always looking for lower prices and higher quality. Investors want higher profits. Team members want higher pay and additional benefits. The government wants higher taxes, and the community wants larger donations. I realized

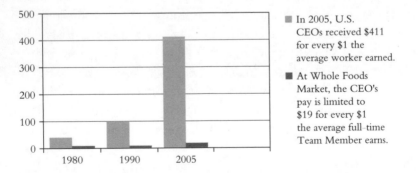

Figure 4.3   U.S CEO Pay as a Multiple of Average Worker's Pay
DATA SOURCE: Business Week (1980–2000) and Institute for Policy Studies—United for a Fair Economy (2006).

that I was not smart enough to figure out the right mix of benefits for Whole Foods Market's team members; instead the executive leadership now decides what percentage of the total revenue will go toward benefits for the company, and then assigns a cost for every potential benefit. Every three years our team members prioritize and vote on the benefits that they most prefer. This process results in benefits that reflect the needs and desires of the majority of the team members in the company.

I also believe in promoting gain-sharing to the largest extent possible. Gain-sharing means creating incentive-based compensation for every team member working at a company. Through this process, team members basically receive their just rewards for efforts expended, and full participation in teamwork is critical to success. Businesses are well-served to clearly define what behavior they want to reward and then set up incentive programs around those criteria.

We have instituted fully paid health insurance for all of our full-time (30 hours per week) team members, or close to 90 percent of all the people that work for Whole Foods. The remaining 10 percent part-time (less than 30 hours per week) team members are encouraged to buy our discounted health insurance if they wish. We also offer personal wellness accounts that allow team members many additional options for their health spending, and health saving accounts. These allow team members to cover the deductible for the health insurance plan or to pay for health services that are out of coverage, such as acupuncture and chiropractic. Money not used rolls over to the next years' wellness account or into a health savings account. We also grant stock options to all team members who have three years of service with the company, with an unprecedented 93 percent of our stock options going to nonexecutives (Figure 4.4).

When team members provide us with feedback, we respond. We are very proud of the fact that Whole Foods Market has been named by Fortune Magazine as one of the 100 best companies to work for during the last nine consecutive years through 2006. Does an emphasis on team member happiness pay off for investors? In a zero sum world it would not. Team member gains would necessarily mean investor losses. Fortunately we don't live in a zero sum world. Rather, we live in an interdependent world where the flourishing of the various stakeholders creates mutual benefits among the different constituencies.

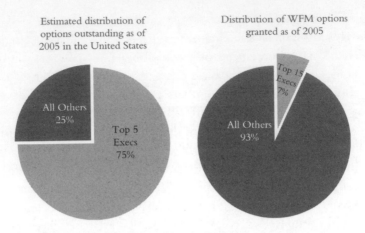

Figure 4.4   Distribution of Stock Options
DATA SOURCE: Institute for Policy Studies—United for a Fair Economy (2006),
Profits with Principles (2004).

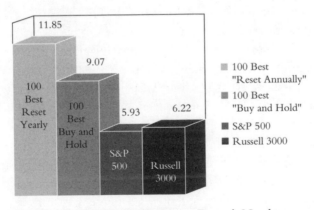

Figure 4.5   Employee Happiness Doesn't Need to
Come at the Expense of Investors
DATA SOURCE: Russell Investment Group.

Figure 4.5 clearly shows that creating a great place to work and
employee happiness do not necessarily come at the expense of the investors in the business. The companies comprising *Fortune* magazine's list of
the 100 Best Companies to Work For have significantly outperformed
both the S&P 500 and the Russell 3000 indices since the list was first

created in 1998. This strong evidence completely supports the ideas articulated in this chapter.

Creating Wealth, Profits, and Growth

While creating value for both customers and team members is very important, so is creating value for the investors. All three stakeholders are interdependent upon one another and all must flourish together. As one of our core values, we feel that Whole Foods Market has a responsibility to create prosperity through profits and growth. We consider ourselves stewards of the investors' money and because of this, frugality is important. We strive never to waste the investors' money. Profits are created through voluntary exchange for mutual benefit, not through exploitation of people. This very important truth reveals as false the many critiques of capitalism, such as Marxism, which argues that all profits should belong to labor because labor creates all of the value of the business. However, this Marxist theory of labor value doesn't bear up under testing in reality.

All value in business is not created through labor, although of course labor does create a significant portion of value (and also receives the appropriate share of the value it generates). Management also creates value with strategic direction, proper resource allocation, and through organizing the business in effective and efficient ways. Investors create value through the capital they have invested. Without sufficient investment capital businesses are unable to buy necessary equipment or invest in necessary leasehold improvements to operate the business or make investments in research and development for the future. Investors deserve competitive returns on their business investments; otherwise they will withdraw their capital from the business and redirect it to alternative investments that give them higher returns.

The different suppliers trading with the business also deserve fair returns in exchange for the goods and services they provide to the business, as do the landlords who provide the real estate to operate the business. Everyone trading with a business is trading voluntarily and their own profits are created through exchange with the business. Any money left over from the myriad of voluntary exchanges is justly owned by the investors in the business. This is their profit and they are paid last—after all the other voluntary traders have completed their exchanges.

Profits create wealth, prosperity, and additional capital. Capital inputs fund most technological innovation and progress. For example, 200 years ago 95 percent of the world's population was considered poor. Today, about 60 percent of the global population is still poor. In the last 200 years we have seen the poverty rate drop from 95 percent to 60 percent. At the current rate of growth, we are going to see world poverty drop considerably in the next 50 years; by the year 2050 only about 25 percent of the world's population will remain below the poverty level. We are seeing this happen right now with the explosion in the economies of two of the most populated countries in the world: China and India. These two economies are growing at extremely rapid rates and hundreds of millions of people are being lifted into the middle class and moving out of poverty. This illustrates what I believe to be one of the most important purposes of business. Business has the fundamental responsibility to create prosperity for our society and for the world.

The Whole Foods Market system of Conscious Capitalism and managing the business for the benefit of all its stakeholders works very well and it creates tremendous long-term shareholder value. Whole Foods is the fastest growing—and the most profitable—public food retailer, percentage-wise, in the United States. Our same-store sales have averaged close to 10 percent for the last 10 years. Comparing this growth rate to conventional supermarket companies such as Kroger's, Safeway, Albertson's, Wild Oats, or Wal-Mart you'll see that our same-store sales are somewhere between 300 and 500 percent greater than same-store sales at conventional markets. Our sales per square foot currently exceed $900, more than twice as high as any of our previously identified competitors. Our store return on after-tax invested capital is 34 percent overall, and higher for stores that have been open for more than one year. Whole Foods' stock price has increased almost 2,500 percent since our IPO in 1992. The sum of $10,000 dollars invested during our IPO would be worth nearly $250,000 today.

Suppliers Are Partners

The fourth stakeholder group consists of thousands of suppliers that provide us with invaluable goods and services. Without our suppliers we wouldn't have anything to sell and the business would quickly cease to exist. I believe the best attitude toward the various suppliers of any business is to view them as essential partners in the enterprise. To keep the system of interrelated stakeholders healthy, most of the suppliers of a business should also flourish through their voluntary trade with the business. While in the competitive marketplace it is impossible for all suppliers of a particular business to simultaneously succeed—inevitably some will fail through a lack of quality or efficiency—it is essential that most suppliers flourish in order to have the capital to improve their quality and the efficiency of their products and services. Honesty, fair trading, and a willingness to help suppliers learn, grow, and continuously improve are valuable attitudes to have in relating to the vendor stakeholder group. As suppliers improve the quality and efficiency of their goods and services, this will also improve what the business can offer to its own customers. I've watched the suppliers in the natural and organic products marketplace continuously improve for almost 30 years. A large part of Whole Foods Market's success has been the result of the continuous improvements and countless innovations of our vendor community.

Caring about Our Communities and Environment

The fifth constituency is our community and the sixth is the environment. I believe that business is best thought of as a citizen existing within the communities where it transacts business. Business even enjoys the same legal status as a person. As citizens, businesses have responsibilities to their communities just like every other citizen. These responsibilities are not infinite, just as we do not have infinite responsibilities as individual citizens to our government or to the local communities in which we live, but we do have some. Most community responsibilities are met through following all the laws that exist in the communities and by paying all the taxes assessed on the business. However, just as individuals may choose to give additional community support beyond simply complying with all laws and paying their taxes, so may business. Vital, dynamic communities need philanthropic support from both individuals and businesses that participate within the community.

I believe philanthropy is consistent with citizenship and should be managed prudently and efficiently just like every other aspect of a business.

Philanthropy, executed properly, can also contribute to shareholder value through increased goodwill with customers, team members, and communities. In my experience, philanthropy is not a win/lose situation, where money is being taken away from investors and shareholders and given to someone undeserving. Instead, with business viewed as an interdependent system of various constituencies, if you manage the business for the health of all the constituencies, optimizing the community constituency provides positive feedback effects on the shareholder constituency. For example, when our stores do the right thing by our communities, we create goodwill with our customers and team members so that they both feel good about the business. We also tend to generate good public relations by doing the right thing in our communities, leading to positive media attention. We are enhancing the long-term brand and viability of our business and all of the above ultimately pays benefits to our investors.

In meeting our responsibilities as citizens, Whole Foods donates five percent of our after-tax profits to nonprofit organizations, with nearly 75 percent given away on a local basis. Whole Foods Market stores support various food banks, local community events, school functions, and Boy Scouts and Girl Scouts—whose families might also patronize our stores. We likewise support health initiatives such as fighting AIDS and breast and childhood cancers. With 198 stores currently, we give to thousands of local organizations. Many of our customers belong to or volunteer with the organizations we support, and as they trade with Whole Foods, we are in turn supporting them in the communities in which we live and do business. Many of our stores also compensate team members for community service work, either on an individual basis or as a group.

Whole Foods Market trades throughout the world and we recognize our responsibilities as global citizens, as well. Poverty remains one of the most serious global challenges, and one of the ways we are trying to be good global citizens is through the creation of Whole Planet Foundation. Our mission with Whole Planet Foundation is to create economic partnerships with the poor and developing world communities that supply our stores with products. Through innovative assistance for entrepreneurship, including direct micro-credit loans, as well as intangible support for other community partnership projects, we seek to support the energy and creativity of every human being we work with in order to help create wealth and prosperity in emerging economies.

Whole Planet Foundation's current efforts center in Costa Rica, Nicaragua, and the Lake Atitlan district of Guatemala, in villages from which Whole Foods purchases pineapples, bananas, and coffee. Additional projects are being set up in India and Honduras, and eventually we will have micro-credit projects throughout the world. Whole Planet Foundation partners with Grameen Bank, which pioneered micro-lending to the poor (both Grameen Bank and its founder, Muhammed Yunus, won the 2006 Nobel Peace Prize). Most loans will go to women, who tend to be the most economically and socially marginalized constituents in many rural communities. Grameen's work in other parts of the world has shown that women have a huge impact on their communities when given access to credit with which to start small businesses. The system Whole Planet Foundation employs is consistent with Whole Foods Market's long-standing internal philosophy of empowerment. For more information on the Whole Planet Foundation go to www.wholeplanetfoundation.org.

The voiceless stakeholder is the environment. All of our other constituencies can speak up when they are unhappy about something. We consider the environment as closely linked to our community constituency. As a business, we exist within both a local and global environment. Whole Foods Market wants to be a responsible citizen in the environment in which we live. We do this by supporting organic and sustainable agriculture and by selling sustainably-harvested seafood.

From its start in 1978 as Safer Way, Whole Foods Market has promoted organic food and the agricultural systems from which it derives. By helping to develop markets, customers, distribution networks, and even the national standards for labeling for organic foods, Whole Foods has also promoted the environmental benefits that accompany the increasing number of organic farms, dairies, ranches and sustainable agricultural practices. For example, organic farms utilize no synthetic fertilizers and pesticides, resulting in reduced usage of fossil fuels, and less chemical contamination entering food chains and water supplies. While some products are transported long distance to meet consumer demand, Whole Foods Markets also stock as many locally-grown and/or manufactured products that meet our quality standards as are available in our market areas.

Organic and sustainable agricultural methods, in addition, build healthy, vital, soil rich with microorganisms and nutrients, featuring superior moisture retention and a resistance to erosion. Other benefits include increased biodiversity when compared to the vast monocultural fields found on industrial farms, and the maintenance of food safety and the integrity of soil and crops by prohibiting the use of genetically modified organisms. Organic agriculture typically acknowledges the role food animals have in our provisioning systems and preserves the integrity of meat and dairy products by prohibiting the use of antibiotics and artificial growth hormones.

Whole Foods Market is working toward animal compassion with livestock animals and eliminating cruel practices in commercial livestock production. Whole Foods refuses to sell commercial veal from tethered calves, *foie gras* from force-fed ducks, or live lobsters, feeling that the methods used to produce and market these animals are too inhumane. Helping create alternatives to the "factory farm" methods of raising livestock is a goal that Whole Foods is strongly committed to, and we have created animal compassionate standards through a multistakeholder process to try to raise the bar. Our standards can be seen in more detail at: www.animalcompassionfoundation.org/standards.html.

Industrial pollution and overfishing cause tremendous damage to our oceans. Coral reefs have declined by 30 percent in the last 30 years. Scientists estimate that the total number of whales in the world has declined 90 percent in the last 100 years. World supplies of cod, swordfish, marlin, halibut, skate, and flounder have been reduced by over 50 percent in the last 50 years. We are fishing out the oceans and it is happening in our lifetimes. Whole Foods Market refuses to sell seafood species such as Chilean sea bass and blue fin tuna that are considered to be endangered species by a consensus of seafood experts. We have long supported The Marine Stewardship Council (www.msc.org) financially and through participation on their board of directors.

Whole Foods addresses its energy usage in several ways. We track our energy use by store and are drilling down to the equipment level so that we can track when outdated appliances need to be replaced. We utilize solar energy and other green building practices in our newer stores and harness the idealistic energy of many of our younger team members in our Green Mission teams. Green Mission team members throughout the company are empowered to work together to systematically lessen our environmental impacts. Our Green Teams have been highly effective in moving the company forward to greater and greater environmental integrity through numerous reusing, recycling, and reeducation initiatives.

Finally, in 2006, Whole Foods took the lead as the largest corporate purchaser of wind energy credits in the nation as we offset 100 percent of our building energy needs with wind energy credits. Each store and office has a comprehensive recycling program, and we open up many of our recycling initiatives to our customers.

In summary, Whole Foods Market meets its responsibilities to both local and global communities, often with innovative programs, and has led by example in many proenvironment initiatives. Whole Foods is also aware that its operations provide many opportunities for improvement in the future. As with our other constituency groups, we have no intention of becoming complacent.

Creating a New Paradigm for Nonprofit Organizations

I want to briefly discuss the limitations of the current nonprofit models that exist in the world today. In my opinion, most modern U.S. nonprofit organizations operate with a mentality that creates inefficiencies, waste, and stagnation; most nonprofits are ineffective in fulfilling their missions. Fully 99 percent of nonprofit organizations are dependent upon donations from the business sector or private citizens in order to exist; in other words, they're not sustainable on their own. Most nonprofits feel pretty good about themselves because they have idealistic, altruistic goals—they have stated purposes beyond maximizing profits. They are do-gooders, trying to do good things in the world. But these good intentions beg the question: Are altruistic goals, by themselves, enough to make nonprofit organizations good and ethical, and do these goals also make them effective? Are the noble purposes by themselves enough? And just because the goals are idealistic does that mean that a nonprofit organization is able to completely transcend self-interest? From my viewpoint, probably not.

It's my position that nonprofit organizations also need to evolve to a more holistic model, just as business needs to. Here we have a great collage of the good, altruistic nonprofits versus the evil, selfish, greedy corporations (Figure 4.6).

A wall exists between the nonprofits and the for-profits consisting partly of the stereotypes that exist in our society today. Nonprofits are viewed as good because they have altruistic, idealistic goals. As you can see on the graphic, nonprofits often believe that money "grows on trees," and because their ideals are altruistic, they are seen as "angels". Nonprofits sponsor idealistic events like AIDS walks and they have an environmental consciousness. On the other side of the wall you see the clear contrast with the for-profit sector of business. You see the stereotype of the greedy businessman with dollar signs in his eyes, grasping after money, and smokestacks popping up all around the world. The angel is transformed into a devil because again, the only goal is to maximize profits and that is seen as simply selfish and greedy.

These stereotypes have outlived their usefulness. As a global society we need both nonprofit and for-profit organizations to become holistic and integral; the wall that separates them needs to be torn down

Good Altruistic	Versus	Evil Selfish and Greedy
(Nonprofit)		*(Corporations)*

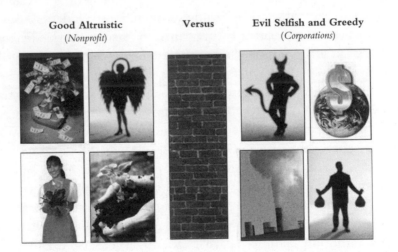

Figure 4.6   Good versus Evil

and the polarities integrated. Corporations need to become more conscious and identify deeper and more comprehensive purposes for why they exist. They must evolve past machine metaphors and learn how to think holistically in terms of creating value for all their interdependent constituencies. Likewise, nonprofits must become economically sustainable and realize that money and profits are good, not evil, and that they are a necessary part of a healthy, holistic organization.

A great example of an economically sustainable nonprofit is Asian-based Grameen Bank, founded by Muhammad Yunus. Grameen has not only helped millions of people lift themselves out of poverty, but it has also become financially sustainable, so much so that it is now technically a for-profit organization—Grameen borrowers are shareholders who receive a dividend when the company does well (though Yunus and the employees are not shareholders and do not earn dividends). Grameen Bank provides a great model to which other nonprofits can aspire. Started in 1983 by Yunus in his native Bangladesh, Grameen Bank offers small, collateral-free loans to (predominantly) poor women who meet certain criteria. Founded on the basis of trust and solidarity, Grameen (Village) Bank works with its customers on their business plans and requires a particular code of conduct that emphasizes community building behaviors and actions. Principal and interest from the loans, typically repaid in small weekly installments, go back into the borrower's local operating funds, to fund new loans. By providing financial opportunity to traditionally underserved clients, Grameen Bank has realized a repayment record of more than 97 percent (one of the best bank repayment records in the world). This contrasts with a repayment rate of less than 60 percent over the same time frame in the traditional Bangladesh banking world that caters to middle and upper class clients. In the more than 20 years Grameen Bank has been in business, the income of more than half of the families of Grameen borrowers has risen above the poverty level.

In Bangladesh today, Grameen operates more than 1,000 branches, serving over 2.1 million borrowers in 37,000 villages. On any working day, Grameen collects an average of $1.5 million in weekly installments. Of the borrowers, 94 percent are women. Although operating in the realm of philanthropic organizations in that it has altruistic goals and ideals, Grameen Bank employs a model that is self-sustaining. And while it welcomes donations, the alternative bank does not rely on the business or private sector for its operating expenses. Grameen methods are now applied in projects in 58 countries, including the United States, Canada, France, the Netherlands, and Norway.

Once the conceptual wall separating nonprofits and for-profits is torn down, it becomes clear that businesses and nonprofits are potentially much more alike than they are different. They both can become holistic, and at a higher integral level, nonprofits and for-profit businesses look remarkably similar. An ideal nonprofit's organizational model looks very similar to the Whole Foods Conscious Capitalism model introduced earlier. The nonprofit expresses core values and it has similar constituencies to a business: employees, customers, suppliers, and investors/donors. The donors want the organization to achieve its societal mission, and if it does the donors will be happy and will send increased financial resources to the nonprofit organization. Just because it has a social mission does not exempt the nonprofit from community and environmental responsibilities. The holistic nonprofit has a very similar model to the holistic business, an important point I want to underscore. Figure 4.7 illustrates the holistic model for nonprofit organizations.

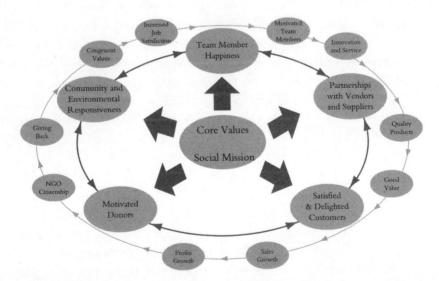

Figure 4.7   The Holistic Model for Nonprofit Organizations

Conclusion

The old paradigm of maximizing profits and shareholder values as the sole purpose of business has created negative unintended consequences. Businesses and corporations are seen as greedy, selfish, and evil. Business is seen as despoiling the environment and causing harm in the world. Business, therefore, has a very bad brand. The good news is that we can remove most of the hostility toward business and capitalism if we change the way we think about it. Business needs to become holistic and integral with deeper, more comprehensive purposes. Corporations must rethink why they exist. If business owners/entrepreneurs begin to view their businesses as complex and evolving interdependent systems and manage their businesses more consciously for the well-being of all their major stakeholders while fulfilling their highest business purpose, then I believe that we will begin to see the hostility toward capitalism and business disappear.

In summation, business is fundamentally a community of people working together to create value for other people: their customers, employees, investors, and the greater society. Business interacts within a harmony of interests. At the same time nonprofits need to become economically sustainable and discover that money and profits are good, not evil, and necessary for them to fulfill their purposes. A holistic perspective is essential for nonprofits. A new Conscious Capitalism paradigm will improve the effectiveness of each type of organization.

But on a basic philosophical level, why try to do good in the world? Why isn't the pursuit of our own self-interest enough? Perhaps we need to look more closely again at what Adam Smith wrote. *The Wealth of Nations* was a tremendous achievement, but economists would also be well served to read Smith's other great book, *The Theory of Moral Sentiments*. There, he explains that human nature is not just about self-interest. It also includes sympathy, empathy, friendship, love, and the desire for social approval. As motives for human behavior, these are at least as important as self-interest; for many people, they are more important.

When we are small children we are egocentric, concerned only about our own needs and desires. As we mature, we grow beyond this egocentrism and begin to care about others—our families, friends, communities, and countries. Our capacity to love can expand even further, to loving people from different races, religions, and countries—potentially to unlimited love for all people and even for other sentient creatures. This is our potential as human beings: to take joy in the flourishing of people and other living beings everywhere. Let us each realize our potential for deeper love and extend it out into the world—let us together create this new business paradigm of Conscious Capitalism.

Let me try to clear up a few misunderstandings about the ideas expressed in this chapter via the answers to questions posed at previous presentations of this material:

Q: Why am I opposed to profit?
A: I am not opposed to profit. As I have pointed out, Whole Foods Market is a highly profitable company. Profits are an important part of what business is about, but they are not the sole purpose of business. Business has purposes other than merely maximizing profits. Entrepreneurs who create businesses rarely create businesses solely for the purpose of maximizing profits and entrepreneurs are the ones who ultimately define the purpose of the businesses they create.

Most businesses have purposes besides maximizing profits, because entrepreneurs create them for other purposes. There may be certain occasions where an entrepreneur creates a business and is only concerned with maximizing profits; he is entitled to do so, it is not unethical. But a strictly profit-based business probably won't be as successful or profitable a business over the long-term as it could be. I doubt it will compete well head-to-head with a more holistic and integral business model, if the business strategy and all other things are equal. I am not arguing that a business cannot operate solely for profits, I'm merely stating that many, if not most, businesses are not that way when entrepreneurs first created them. If business leaders become more conscious of the fact that their business it is not really a machine but part of a complex, interdependent, and evolving system with multiple constituencies, they will see that profit is one of the important purposes of the business, but not the sole purpose. They will also begin to see that the best way to maximize long-term profits is to create value for the entire interdependent business system. Once enough business leaders come to understand and accept this new business paradigm, I believe that Conscious Capitalism will reach a takeoff point and the hostility toward business will largely dissipate over the long term.

Q: Does philanthropy equal social responsibility?

A: No, philanthropy is actually just a small part of the social responsibility of business. The social responsibility of business is about creating value for all of its constituencies. If you are creating value for your customers and employees, acting with integrity toward your suppliers, if you are a good citizen paying taxes, if you take responsibility for your environmental impacts, you'll fulfill most of your social responsibilities. However, if a business is responsible to its investors, employees, customers, suppliers, and the environment but refuses to contribute toward philanthropic organizations, it would be neglecting the important community constituency. This business would be perceived a stingy neighbor, but it could still be creating value in the world through the value it creates for its customers, employees, suppliers, government, and the environment. The contrary is also true: A business could be highly philanthropic to its communities, but if it is creating shoddy or harmful products, exploiting its employees, cheating its suppliers, and doing significant damage to the environment it can hardly be considered an ethical or socially responsible business no matter how great its philanthropic efforts.

Philanthropy is not primarily what social responsibility is about, but it is also not "theft" from the investors if a business chooses to contribute some money to the communities where it has a presence. That would be part of its responsibility as a citizen and such donations will not only help the community but will simultaneously create goodwill with customers, employees, the media, and other citizens in the community. I believe that while philanthropy does not equate to social responsibility by itself, philanthropic donations are certainly consistent with being a responsible citizen in the community in which a business exists.

One common objection to philanthropy is where to draw the line? If donating 5 percent of profits is good (as Whole Foods does), wouldn't 10 percent be even better? Why not donate 100 percent of our profits to the betterment of society? But the fact that a business has responsibilities as a citizen in the various communities it exists in doesn't mean that it doesn't have any responsibilities to investors or other stakeholders. It's a question of finding the appropriate balance and trying to create value for all of the stakeholders simultaneously. Whole Foods donates 5 percent of its profits to the community stakeholder, in addition to the taxes we pay. Is 5 percent the right amount to donate to the community? I don't think there is a right answer to this question, except that I believe zero percent is too little. The co-founders of the company arbitrarily decided that 5 percent was a reasonable amount, and as the owners of the company at the time we approved the decision. Corporate philanthropy is a good thing, but it ultimately requires the legitimacy of investor approval, and the investors as the owners of the business have the right and the authority to withdraw their approval if they wish. In my experience, most investors understand that modest philanthropy can be beneficial to both the corporation and to the larger society. They understand that philanthropy is consistent with creating long-term profits for the investors because of the interdependent nature of the business enterprise.

An argument that I frequently field is that corporations or businesses don't have any special competence in philanthropy; therefore corporations should stick to what they do best, which is maximizing their profits and allowing the individual shareholders to engage in philanthropy. This argument is deceptive for two reasons. First, this line of reasoning overlooks the fact that business is treated as a citizen of the community in which it exists from a legal standpoint. If you want to maximize shareholder value in an integrated holistic system, philanthropy can be part of that strategy, and it is the responsibility a citizen has in his or her community in any case. The same people who argue against corporations engaging in philanthropy frequently argue that government is also incompetent in engaging in civic activities. As their argument develops, now they assert that business is incompetent and government is incompetent, so that puts all civic responsibility onto individual citizens. I ask you, are individual citizens inherently more competent in philanthropic endeavors than businesses? I would argue that because business taps into more complex feedback loops and may enjoy the results of more detailed research on the effectiveness of its investments, business probably has the potential to be more competent in philanthropic practice than most individuals.

From my perspective, we need to acknowledge civic responsibility at the individual, corporate, and governmental levels. Civic responsibilities cannot be completely met by the voluntary individual sector of society. Corporations have great contributions to make in philanthropy. Perhaps some corporate philanthropy is misguided and money is wasted, however, I will point out that corporations make poor investment choices all the time. Corporations make mistakes all the time, and they can make mistakes in philanthropy, just like they can make mistakes in other areas of their business such as the people they hire and promote or their investments in new equipment or facilities or their mergers and acquisitions. Not everything a business attempts will succeed, but that simple truth does not negate the business process. Corporations may not always be successful in the philanthropic arena either; they will occasionally make mistakes. These mistakes do not negate the worthwhile value of most philanthropic efforts. In most cases business philanthropy creates beneficial social value.

Q: Who should control corporations, stockholders or stakeholders?
A: One of the objections I frequently hear is that I advocate for stakeholder control of corporations, as opposed to stockholder control. I am certainly not arguing for that. As I have already pointed out, stockholders own the corporation, they get paid last based on residual profits left over from the business and it remains essential that they have the final say, through the board of directors, on who comprises company management. They need to have the ultimate power to fire management if they are unhappy with the performance of the company. Without that power, inevitably the stockholders will eventually be exploited by the management or some of the other constituencies of the business. I am not arguing, and have never argued, for anything that weakens the property rights of the investors and stockholders. That line of reasoning is a simple misunderstanding.

Q: What about conflicts between various stakeholders? How do you create balance between all the conflicting desires and demands of all the different stakeholders? For example: if more is given to the employees doesn't that necessarily result in less being available to the other stakeholders such as the investors and vice versa? How do you avoid conflict and keep all of the stakeholders happy?
A: Conflict between the various stakeholders in a business is inevitable from time to time simply because each stakeholder wants more. Customers want higher quality and lower prices, employees want higher wages and better benefits, investors want higher profits, governments want higher taxes, and community groups want greater donations. The potential

for conflict is always present. However, the fundamental mistake that most people make when thinking about this issue of conflict between stakeholders is that they create analytical separations between the stakeholders and take it no further. They see the stakeholder groups as separate from each other and the business—each pursuing its own interests.

When this type of analytical separation is employed it also engages in a form of reductionism; it ignores the relationships between the stakeholders and the business and with each other. The business is more than just the sum of the individual stakeholders. It is also the interrelationship, the interconnection, the shared purpose, and the shared values that the various stakeholders of the business cocreate and coevolve together. No complex, evolving, and self-adapting organization can be adequately understood merely through analyzing its parts and ignoring the greater system that also exists. This is a very important idea to understand because while the analytic mind will focus on the conflicting interests of the stakeholders it will tend to ignore or fail to see what the intuitive systems mind understands—that the stakeholders are interconnected together in a "harmony of interests." In a healthy, complex, evolving, and self-adapting system the harmony of interests between stakeholders proves to be far more important and resilient than the various conflicts of interest that the analytic mind focuses upon.

A holistic business creates value for all of its stakeholders. Given the desire of each stakeholder for more, how is the value divided between the stakeholders to keep them happy? There is, of course, ultimately no magical formula to calculate how much value each stakeholder should receive from the company. It is a dynamic process that evolves with the competitive marketplace. No stakeholder remains satisfied for long. It is the function of company leadership to develop solutions that continually work for the common good. The art of excellent leadership seeks the win-win-win-win-win solutions in the context of competitive market processes that optimizes the value of the entire business system for each of the stakeholder participants within that business system.

Q: How do you reconcile the famous quote from Adam Smith with your point of view? *The quote is "By pursuing his own interest he frequently promotes that of the society more effectually than when he really intends to* *promote it. I have never known much good done by those who affected to trade for the public good" (Adam Smith,* The Wealth of Nations*).*

A: To me this quote has two parts to it, the first being a reinforcement of Adam Smith's famous "invisible hand" metaphor, which I think was the most profound insight into social history ever made. The metaphor implies that through a voluntary exchange people acting in their own self interest, pursing their own good, create value for the greater society. I do not argue against that. I believe in the invisible hand. The second part of the statement, however, is what I disagree with: "I have never known much good done by those who have affected to trade for the public good." Much of the good that is done in this world is done by people who intentionally do good. The invisible hand metaphor correctly points out that much good is done for the public accidentally, so to speak, by simple pursuit of self-interest. Through voluntary exchange, acting in self-interest, both parties benefit or the exchange wouldn't happen. That process creates a social good, true, but it is also true that much good is done because people have an intention to do good. All the good is not done accidentally.

I believe that the invisible hand of Adam Smith should be supplemented by the invisible hand of intentional "do-gooding," and that individuals, governments, and businesses have endless opportunities to attempt to do good in the world. Business has the opportunity to do good and create value for all the various constituencies that trade with the business voluntarily. I also believe that supplementing the invisible hand, with a "visible hand," if done consciously, on an ongoing basis by individuals and corporations around the world, would help push humanity into an era of accelerated progress that would be unprecedented in world history. That is what Whole Foods Market is trying to do, and that is what Conscious Capitalism really means.

The Roadmap to Transforming Traditional Company into a Conscious Company

- A company needs to first discover its deeper purpose and organize everything around fulfilling that purpose
- Stakeholder Relationship business model replacing Shareholder Value business model

- Team model and empowerment replacing hierarchical command and control
  - Empowerment and Self Responsibility
  - Accountability and Trust
  - Continual learning
  - The power of appreciation
- Responsibilities to communities and the environment

What Then Is a Conscious Business? What Then Is Conscious Capitalism?

The Conscious Business is based on two primary principles:

1. The business has a deeper purpose beyond maximizing profits and shareholder value.
2. The business is managed to optimize value for all of the interdependent stakeholders.

- Conscious Capitalism is simply the larger ecosystem of Conscious Businesses.
- Conscious Capitalism will become the dominant economic paradigm in the twenty-first century because Conscious Businesses have strong competitive advantages versus traditional businesses.

Magatte Wade: From Senegal to Adina World Beverages and Beyond

Magatte Wade is a Senegalese entrepreneur who founded Adina for Life, a beverage company based in San Francisco. She found that when she had returned to Senegal after living in the United States, people were increasingly drinking Coke rather than the traditional hibiscus beverage of her childhood. She knew that the Senegalese would never return to their traditional beverage unless it became respected in the developed world, so she created Adina (which means "Life" in Wolof, the dominant indigenous language of Senegal) to market the traditional hibiscus drink in the United States. Adina today is a multimillion-dollar company that has received three rounds of financing; its products are carried by Whole Foods Market, Wegmans, and other upscale and natural foods grocery chains.

Wade has now transitioned out of Adina to start a new company, dedicated to re-branding Africa through the creation of a prominent lifestyle brand that combines high-end style and design with African-themed and sourced products. She is frustrated with the fact that Africa is currently branded as pathetic, whereby many people in the developed world regard Africa as primarily an object of pity and compassion rather than as a powerful, positive force in the world. As a cosmopolitan entrepreneur, who was raised in Senegal, educated in Germany and France, and launched a successful career in the United States, she understands global quality standards. At the same time, as a child of Senegal, she knows and loves the many beautiful cultural elements of her country, and realizes that most of the world is unaware of these cultural elements. But in order for the world to come to know and love the best of Senegalese, and African culture, it needs to be combined with other high quality contemporary cultural elements—It is time to transcend the tribal and safari stereotypes of Africa, and integrate the best of contemporary Africa into a cutting-edge, cool cultural mélange of contemporary music, design, fashion, and style. Magatte's personal style is a striking exemplification of this possibility. Can she scale it into a full-blown lifestyle brand with diverse product lines?

Quality is critical to Magatte's vision of Africa. She realizes that it is unlikely that Africa will be able to compete with China and India on low cost manufacturing. But Magatte envisions an Africa that can compete globally by catering to the cultural creative demographic (essentially the Whole Foods Market demographic) by marketing very high quality products that are also made in a socially and environmentally responsible manner. Insofar as China, in particular, has been largely branded as a manufacturing source that does not ensure social and environmental responsibility, she sees an opportunity for Africa to enter the world of manufacturing from the start with a higher-quality brand identity. But this vision will not happen on its own; individual entrepreneurs will have to create supply chains in Africa that produce high quality products that are also produced in a socially and environmentally responsible manner.

As someone who has herself gone through the work of creating a supply chain in Senegal that meets not only U.S. quality health standards but also global organic and Fair Trade certification standards, she knows exactly what it takes to train indigenous Sengalese to meet global standards. Moreover, on the branding and marketing side, she is acutely aware that in order to obtain the high value-added prices that are associated with organic and Fair Trade products, it is critical to develop a compelling and sophisticated brand identity. She cringes when she observes the current lack of brand sophistication prevalent in Senegal.

(continued)

One of the most fascinating abilities of entrepreneurs is the way that they are capable of seeing opportunities that are invisible to most people. Wade is a brilliant visionary entrepreneur in this sense: As she travels through Senegal she sees countless entrepreneurial opportunities waiting to be developed. In each case, she is brutally critical of existing Senegalese standards of customer service, professionalism, cleanliness, consistency, and so on. But she also knows, as an entrepreneur, that it is possible to identify good employees, train them, and reward those who perform well. And thus, she sees each entrepreneurial opportunity as simply a matter of work: On the Senegalese side, create the production system and train the employees to perform at world-class standards while simultaneously developing branding, marketing, and distributional channels in the United States through which the new products may be sold. In addition to Adina, she has already developed a few additional small product lines based on these principles, and as far as I can tell, she is likely to be able to create, and help others to create, any number of successful Senegalese businesses that will be able to sell products in the United States and Europe. Ultimately this will create tens of thousands of good jobs that cumulatively will alleviate the grinding poverty in which so many Senegalese live.

But if it is so easy for Wade to do this, why haven't others done it? First, I should be clear, the fact that she has done it doesn't mean that it is easy. Her criticisms of existing Senegalese standards are apt, and the identification and training of good employees is a nontrivial task. Wade has a great eye for talent, an iron will, is uncompromising in her demand for excellence, and is willing to do whatever it takes to get people to perform at their best. Not everyone has these characteristics; not everyone can succeed at training local people to produce to world-class standards.

In addition, Wade has been blessed with an unusual entrepreneurial education. When I first met her, I thought that thinking like an entrepreneur simply came naturally to her. But upon questioning, she acknowledged that she had not thought like that at the age of 16, nor had she thought like that upon taking her first corporate job at the age of 22. Clearly she has learned something in the world since graduation.

It turns out that her husband had been an entrepreneur whom she watched create his company from scratch. She then worked in Silicon Valley for a headhunter during the late 1990s Silicon Valley boom, putting her in close contact with many dozens of dynamic entrepreneurs in the middle of starting up companies. She then worked as Sponsorship Chair for the MIT/Stanford Venture Lab, where she was in close contact with leading tech corporations, venture capitalists, and high net worth individuals. She learned entrepreneurship by working smack dab in the middle of the world's greatest entrepreneurial region, responsible for looking closely at the guts of entrepreneurial start-ups.

To an entrepreneur, one of the most obvious of truths is that entrepreneurs create value. Entrepreneurs like Wade see flowers growing wild (hibiscus) that Senegalese take for granted and launches a multimillion dollar business (when I told some Senegalese students that Wade had created a successful company that began by selling hibiscus drink, their jaws dropped with wonder—it was simply unimaginable to them). With secure property rights (including secure intellectual property—Wade is acutely aware that brands are valuable if and only if you can defend their IP) and fair contract enforcement, entrepreneurs create value where none existed before.

For Wade, entrepreneurship is a tool for transforming Senegal. While she is absolutely committed to socially and environmentally responsible practices, those are the beginning, not the end, of her approach to using entrepreneurship to do good. At the most basic level, she rightly sees entrepreneurship as an approach to creating urgently needed new private sector jobs in Senegal. More concretely, she sees entrepreneurship as a means of supplying higher quality nutrition, sanitation, financial literacy, education, and other fundamental goods to the people of Senegal. More ambitiously, she sees entrepreneurship as transforming Senegalese culture, style, and identity: As she helps more and more Senegalese products and services succeed in the global marketplace, she intends to fundamentally transform her people's identity from one of helpless dependence (an identity largely exacerbated by the countless NGOs in Senegal) to one of the leaders of global culture.

Chapter 5

Social Business Entrepreneurs Are the Solution

Muhammad Yunus
Managing Director,
Grameen Communications

M any of the problems in the world remain unresolved because we continue to interpret capitalism too narrowly. In this narrow interpretation we create a one-dimensional human being to play the role of entrepreneur. We insulate him from other dimensions of life, such as religious, emotional, and political dimensions. He is dedicated to one mission in his business life—to maximize profit. He is supported by masses of one-dimensional human beings who back him up with their investment money to achieve the same mission. The game of free market works out beautifully with one-dimensional investors and entrepreneurs. We have remained so mesmerized by the success of the free market that we never dared to express any doubt about it. We worked extra hard to transform ourselves, as closely as possible, into the one-dimensional human beings conceptualized in theory to allow smooth functioning of free market mechanisms.

Economic theory postulates that you are contributing to the society and the world in the best possible manner if you just concentrate on squeezing out the maximum for yourself. When you get your maximum, everybody else will get their maximum.

As we devotedly follow this policy, sometimes doubts appear in our minds as to whether we are doing the right thing. Things don't look too good around us. We quickly brush off our doubts by saying all these bad things happen because of "market failures"; well-functioning markets cannot produce unpleasant results.

I think things are going wrong not because of market failure. It is much deeper than that. Let us be brave and admit that it is because of "conceptualization failure." More specifically, it is the failure to capture the essence of a human being in our theory. Everyday human beings are not one-dimensional entities; they are excitingly multidimensional and indeed very colorful. Their emotions, beliefs, priorities, and behavior patterns can be more aptly described by drawing analogy with the basic colors and millions of colors and shades they produce.

Social Business Entrepreneurs Can Play a Big Role in the Market

Suppose we postulate a world with two kinds of people, both one-dimensional but having different objectives. The first is the existing type, that is, the profit maximizing type. The second is a new type, people who are not interested in profit-maximization. They are totally committed to making a difference to the world. They are social-objective driven. They want to give a better chance in life to other people. They want to achieve their objective through creating and supporting sustainable business enterprises. Their businesses may or may not earn profit, but like any other business, they must not incur losses. They create a new class of business that we may describe as "non-loss" business.

Can we find the second type of people in the real world? Yes, we can. Aren't we familiar with do-gooders? Do-gooders are the same people who are referred to as "social entrepreneurs" in formal parlance. Social entrepreneurism is an integral part of human history. Most people take pleasure in helping others. All religions encourage this quality in human beings. Governments reward them by giving them tax breaks. Special legal facilities are created for them so that they can create legal entities to pursue their objectives.

Some social entrepreneurs (SE) use money to achieve their objectives; some just give away their time, labor, talent, skill or such other contributions that are useful to others. Those who use money may or may not try to recover part or all of the money they put into their work by charging fees or setting prices.

We may classify the SEs who use money into four types:

1. No cost recovery.
2. Some cost recovery.
3. Full cost recovery.
4. More than full cost recovery.

Once an SE operates at 100 percent or beyond the full cost recovery point he has entered the business world with limitless possibilities. This is a moment worth celebrating. He has overcome the gravitational force of financial dependence and now is ready for space flight! This is the critical moment of significant institutional transformation. He has moved from the world of philanthropy to the world of business. To distinguish him from the first two types of SEs listed above, we'll call him "social business entrepreneur" (SBE).

With the introduction of SBEs, the marketplace becomes more interesting and competitive. Interesting because two different kinds of objectives are now at play creating two different sets of frameworks for price determination. Competitive because there are more players now than before. These new players can be equally aggressive and enterprising in achieving their goals as the other entrepreneurs.

SBEs can become very powerful players in the national and international economy. Today, if we add up the assets of all the SBEs of the world, it would not add up to even an ultra-thin slice of the global economy. This is not because they lack growth potential, but because conceptually we neither recognized their existence nor made any room for them in the market. They are considered freaks and kept outside the mainstream economy. We do not pay any attention to them, because our eyes are blinded by the theories taught in our schools.

If SBEs exist in the real world, it makes no sense that we should not make room for them in our conceptual framework. Once we recognize them, supportive institutions, policies, regulations, norms, and rules will come into being to help them become mainstream.

The market is always considered to be an institution utterly incapable of addressing social problems. Indeed, the market is recognized as an institution that contributes significantly to creating social problems (environmental hazards, inequality, health issues, unemployment, ghettoes, crime, and so on). Since the market has no capacity to solve social problems, this responsibility was handed over to the state. This arrangement was considered the only solution until command economies were created where the state took over everything, abolishing the market.

But this did not last long. With command economies gone, we are back to the artificial division of work between the market and the state. In this arrangement, the market is turned into an exclusive playground of the personal gain seekers, overwhelmingly ignoring the common interest of communities and the world as a whole.

With the economy expanding at an unforeseen speed, personal wealth reaching unimaginable heights, technological innovations making this speed faster and faster, globalization threatening to wipe out the weak economies and the poor people from the economic map, it is time to consider the case of SBEs more seriously than we have ever before. Not only is it not necessary to leave the market solely to the personal-gain seekers, it is extremely harmful to mankind as a whole to do that. It is time to move away from the narrow interpretation of capitalism and broaden the concept of market by giving full recognition to SBEs. Once this is done, SBEs can flood the market and make the market work for social goals as efficiently as it does for personal goals.

Social Stock Market

How do we encourage creation of SBEs? What are the steps that we need to take to help the SBEs to take up bigger and bigger chunks of market share?

First, we must recognize the SBEs in our theory. Students must learn that businesses are of two kinds: (a) business to make money, and (b) business to do good for others. Young people must learn that they have a choice to make: which kind of entrepreneur would they like to be? If we broaden the interpretation of capitalism even more, they'll have wider choice of mixing these two basic types in proportions just right for their own tastes.

Second, we must make the SBEs and social business investors visible in the marketplace. As long as SBEs operate within the cultural environment of current stock markets they'll remain restricted by the existing norms and lingo of trading. SBEs must develop their own norms, standards, measurements, evaluation criteria, and terminology. This can be achieved only if we create a separate stock market for social business enterprises and investors. We can call it the "social stock market." Investors will come here to invest their money in the causes they believe in and in the companies they think are doing the best in achieving particular missions. There may be some companies listed in this social stock market that are excellent in achieving their mission at the same time they are making very attractive profits on the side. Obviously these companies will attract both kinds of investors, social-goal oriented as well as personal-gain oriented.

Making a profit will not disqualify an enterprise from being a social business enterprise. The basic deciding factor for this designation will be whether the social goal remains the enterprise's overarching goal and is clearly reflected in its decision making. There will be well-defined stringent entry and exit criteria for a company to qualify to be listed in the social stock market and to lose that status. Soon, companies will emerge that will succeed in mixing both social goals and business goals. There will be criteria established to determine up to what point companies qualify to enter the social stock market and at what point they must leave it. Investors must remain convinced that companies listed in the social stock market are truly social business enterprises.

Along with the creation of the social stock market we'll need to create rating agencies, appropriate impact assessment tools, and indices to understand which social business enterprise is doing more and/or better than others so that social investors are correctly guided. This industry will need its own *Social Wall Street Journal* and *Social Financial Times* to publish all the exciting, as well as the terrible, news stories and analyses to keep the social entrepreneurs and investors properly informed and forewarned.

Within business schools we can start producing social MBAs to meet the demand of the SBEs as well as prepare young people to become SBEs themselves. I think young people will respond very enthusiastically to the challenge of making serious contributions to the world by becoming SBEs.

We'll need to arrange financing for SBEs by establishing new bank branches that specialize in financing social business ventures. New "angels" will have to show up on the scene. Social venture capitalists will have to join hands with the SBEs.

How to Make a Start

One good way to get started with creating social business enterprises would be to launch a design competition for social business enterprises. There could be local competitions, regional competitions and global competitions. Prizes for the successful designs will come in the shape of financing for the enterprises or as partnership for implementing the projects.

All submitted social business proposals should be published so that these can become the starting points for the designers in the next cycles or ideas for someone who wants to start a social business enterprise.

The social stock market itself can be started by an SBE as a social business enterprise. One business school or several business schools can join hands to launch this as a project and start serious business transactions.

Let us not expect that a social business enterprise will come up with, from its very birth, all the answers to a social problem. Most likely, it will proceed in steps. Each step may lead to the next level of achievement. Grameen Bank is a good example in this regard. In creating Grameen Bank I never had a blueprint to follow. I moved one step at a time, always thinking this step will be my last step. But it was not. That one step led me to another step, a step that looked so interesting it was difficult to walk away from. I faced this situation at every turn.

I started my work by giving a small amount of money to a few poor people without any collateral. Then I realized how good the people felt about it. I needed more money to expand the program. To access bank money, I offered myself as a guarantor. To get support from another bank, I converted my project to the bank's project. Later, I turned it into a central bank project. Over time, I saw that the best strategy would be to create an independent bank to do the work that we do. So we did. We converted the project into a formal bank, borrowing money from the central bank to lend money to the borrowers. Because donors became interested in our work and wanted to support us, we borrowed and received grants from international donors. At one stage we decided to be self-reliant. This led us to focus on generating money internally by collecting deposits. Now, Grameen Bank has more money in deposits than it lends out to borrowers. It lends out half a billion dollars a year in loans averaging less than $ 200 to 4.5 million borrowers, without collateral, and maintains a 99 percent repayment record.

We introduced many programs through the bank—housing loans, student loans, pension funds, loans to purchase mobile phones to become the village telephone ladies, loans to beggars to become door-to-door salesmen. One came after another. If we create the right environment, SBEs can take up significant market share and make the market an exciting place for fighting social battles in evermore innovative and effective ways.

Let's get serious about social business entrepreneurs. They can brighten up this gloomy world.

Muhammad Yunus and Grameen Bank

Muhammad Yunus, Grameen Bank, and the microfinance movement beautifully exemplify FLOW's commitment to "liberating the entrepreneurial spirit for good."

Yunus was a Bangladeshi economist at Chittagong University in the early 1970s, when Bangladesh was going through some of its most painful years. A devastating cyclone in 1970 was followed by the bloody war of independence from Pakistan. The war was then followed by severe famines, with people dying in the street. Yunus' heart was breaking as he taught academic economics that wasn't alleviating the horrifying poverty he saw around him.

In 1974, he decided to go to a village to learn directly from the people what the obstacles to alleviating their poverty were. He discovered that there were women engaged in handcrafts who were paying interest rates to local moneylenders that were as high as 10 percent per week. If they only had access to a few dollars of

(continued)

capital, they could improve their condition considerably. Yunus began making small loans to these women out of his own pocket, starting with just 27 dollars. In order to provide assistance to more women, Yunus created Grameen Bank, meaning "village bank."

Early on, Yunus discovered that when women borrowed money and generated revenues from their businesses, most of the benefit went toward their children. This was not necessarily the case when men borrowed the money. Therefore, Grameen Bank early on began loaning almost exclusively to women. Gradually Yunus developed a system through which groups of women would receive loans together and, if they all paid back the loans, they would all be eligible for subsequent loans. These groups, typically of five women, would act both as support groups and as a source of peer pressure to ensure that loans would be paid back. As a consequence of this system, in many years Grameen Bank's repayment rate exceeds 98 percent, which is in the repayment range of high-grade corporate bonds, far better than most loan portfolios. Grameen Bank today has 1,084 branches, with 12,500 staff serving 2.1 million borrowers in 37,000 villages. The global microfinance movement, catalyzed by Grameen's high profile success, now reaches more than a hundred million of the world's poor.

Grameen Bank borrowers are required to commit to the "16 Decisions":

1. We respect the four principles of the Grameen Bank—we are disciplined, united, courageous, and hard workers—and we apply them in all areas of our lives.
2. We wish to give our families good living standards.
3. We will not live in dilapidated houses. We repair them and work to build new ones.
4. We cultivate vegetables the whole year round, eat plenty of them, and sell the surplus.
5. During the season for planting, we will plant as many seedlings as possible.
6. We intend to have small families. We shall reduce our expenses to a minimum. We take care of our health.
7. We shall educate our children and see that they can earn enough money to finance their education.
8. We see to it that our children and homes are clean.
9. We build latrines and use them.
10. We only drink water drawn from a well. If it is not, we boil the water or we use alum.

11. We will not accept a marriage dowry for our son and we do not give one to our daughter at her marriage. Our center is against this practice. We shall not practice child marriage.

12. We cause harm to no one and we will not tolerate that anyone should do us harm.

13. To increase our income, we make important investments in common.

14. We are always ready to help each other. When someone is in difficulty, we all give a helping hand.

15. If we learn that discipline is not respected in a center, we go along to help and restore order.

16. We are introducing physical exercise in all centers. We take part in all social events.

While Yunus has sometimes been criticized for the apparent paternalism of the 16 decisions, he regards Grameen as primarily an educational institution. The purpose of Grameen is not simply to provide loans—it is to provide its clients with a path toward a better life. Every individual decides voluntarily whether to become involved with Grameen; thus, each client decides to accept the 16 decisions.

Once when he was visiting a Grameen village, a woman came running up to him, tears streaming down her face, thanking him profusely. When he asked her why she was thanking him, she explained that prior to the 16 decisions, she had spent her entire life waiting for darkness before she could relieve herself. She was grateful because now she was free to take care of her needs any time, night or day. Who could have imagined that an academic economist who decided to visit a local village would end up transforming lives by bundling the requirement that a village build latrines with tiny loans to the poor?

When Iqbal Qadir, a Bangladeshi investment banker, joined with Yunus to create Grameen Phone, through which they proposed to provide cell phones to Grameen borrowers, they were told that these illiterate women were not capable of learning how to use cell phones. But they persisted, and now Grameen Phone has more than 50 percent of the Bangladesh market, with 10 million customers, and it is the most profitable segment of Grameen Bank. A few weeks after distributing the first phones to village "phone ladies," Yunus visited a village where a phone lady ran up to him, closed her eyes, and asked him to give her a number. He did so, and she dialed it rapidly, accurately, and without looking.

(continued)

A recurring theme throughout this book is that entrepreneurs identify possibilities in situations in which no one had believed that possibilities existed. In particular, there will be many thousands of academic experts in diverse areas of academic expertise who believe that FLOW's proposal to solving world problems through entrepreneurship is impossible. It is very important to understand that, at any give point in time, those academics who claim that entrepreneurial solutions are impossible *always have the facts on their side.* There was no evidence whatsoever in 1974 that illiterate peasant women could pay back hundreds of millions of dollars in loans by working in groups of five and making 16 commitments together. As with many entrepreneurial visions, there was no evidence whatsoever that Grameen Bank would work, let alone inspire a model of microfinance that would reach more than 100 million women around the world.

Imagine the reaction among the world's leading academic experts if Yunus had gone to them for support of his project in 1974. At the time, academic beliefs regarding poverty alleviation were divided between Marxists, who believed that communist revolutions were the only credible solution to poverty alleviation, and development experts who believed that a "Big Push" through massive foreign aid was the best strategy. Yunus' beliefs concerning poverty alleviation would have been regarded as reactionary and evil:

> Grameen believes that charity is not an answer to poverty. It only helps poverty to continue. It creates dependency and takes away individuals' initiative to break through the wall of poverty. Unleashing of energy and creativity in each human being is the answer to poverty.
>
> Muhammad Yunus, "What Is Microcredit?," Grameen Bank, October 2008, www.grameen-info.org/index. php?option=com_content&task=view&id=28&Itemid=108

Since that time, communism has been thoroughly discredited and Big Push-style foreign aid has largely been discredited. It has turned out that arguably one of the most successful antipoverty initiatives in the past 30 years started with an academic who walked out of the classroom and into the village to loan $27, and thereby "unleashed the energy and creativity in each human being."

Chapter 6

Business as Service

"Doing Well to Do Good"

Kartar Singh Khalsa
CEO, Golden Temple of Oregon and Makers
of Peace Cereal and Yogi Tea

Our perspective on business is pretty straightforward. It begins with our perspective on life, which is: The purpose of life is to serve. Through service, you can move from individual consciousness, through group consciousness, to universal consciousness. And if your purpose is to serve, to give something to others and to the world, you have to have something to give. Business is a way to produce and present what you have to give and a way to generate more resources to enable you to serve even more.

While some businesses can be seen as self-serving and even damaging to society, in most cases those businesses have a limited life span, even if it is decades. In the long run, the organizations that survive are those that truly deliver service to society, enhancing the quality of our lives, and elevating our sense of what is possible.

Our perspective on business was shaped by our spiritual teacher, Yogi Bhajan. His core teaching was that the purpose of life is to serve. We started our business as a reflection of our commitment to service; so service is a core of what we do day in and day out. It drives how we manage ourselves and our business.

We recognize the opportunity to serve through business on many levels:

- Service to our internal community—providing our owners, managers, and employees with the means to enhance their lives both at work and outside of work.
- Service to our customers and suppliers.
- Service to community and humanity through our product and services, the example we set, and the broader contributions we make.

Business starts in stages. In the beginning stages of a business you have to spend more time on self-interest. First you have got to be profitable; you have got to make money to stay in business. You have to build an organization, you have to build your vendor relationships, and focus on all your networking. But as the business grows and goes through these stages the ultimate stage is service to society, which is where Golden Temple wants to focus: reaching that upper stage so that we can spend more of our time and effort and more of our money serving our local community and humanity in general.

We started about 34 years ago in late 1972. There was a group of us in our early 20s, part of a spiritually based community. We needed jobs to provide for ourselves. If you looked like we did back then not everyone wanted to employ you. That's okay. We wanted to develop something based on our natural lifestyle, to provide products so we could share some of the values and benefits of our lifestyle with other people.

Six of us started the Golden Temple Bakery in the back room of our friend's business, the Springfield Creamery, makers of Nancy's Yogurt. We had 600 dollars and wondered what were we going to do with it. Six hundred went a longer way back then. So we bought some pizza deck ovens and we started making natural bread.

Being young and thinking that bigger is better and not really knowing that much about business we basically learned through the school of hard knocks. We made this bread that was fine in the wintertime; it was all natural, no preservatives in it. Come summertime, the new bread delivered one day was already green with mold the next day. We ended up with a lot of green bread but not much green in our pockets.

We expanded out and expanded our communities. A friend of ours sold us his granola business for about 50 dollars. He had built a natural foods distribution business so we expanded that, too.

I used to be out on the road but was eventually persuaded to come on inside, join the management team, and help figure out what was going on. One day as I was going through the books I figured out why we were the single largest distributor of this Haiku juice product in the world. Somehow we figured out how to sell a case of this for 10 cents less than it cost us. We weren't worried though, we'd make it up on volume!

That kind of business practice dug us a pretty deep hole in the late 1970s. People were telling us it was about time to file for bankruptcy. But we started this business with the value in mind of being able to serve people and serve society and we weren't going to back off. We arranged to pay back all the people we owed money to over three years. Every month, we made these payments. We paid back every penny and got out of the hole we dug. There was a guy who used to head the huge corporation IT&T. He said: "When you are young if you can get paid in money or paid in experience, get paid in experience so you can build on that for the future." We definitely got a lot of experience!

Around 1984 we got out of this debt situation. We were doing about $400,000 in sales and by 1990 we were doing about $10 million in sales and we were actually profitable—so we must have learned something. At that time we took on a couple of other businesses of associated organizations in Los Angeles—the Yogi Tea business and Sunshine, which is a body care business, and brought them all together.

By the year 2000, we were about $25 million in sales. That is the first 25 years. There is a saying: "Trust in God but tie up your camel." The first 25 years were pretty much the trusting God years. The last five years we've focused more on tying up our camel, which to us means practicing business fundamentals. We figured out if you want an opportunity to serve then you have to be financially successful.

We got our management team together and said that we were tired of having one or two good years then two bad years and going up and down on this roller coaster. We committed, got really focused, and set a clear goal: a financial bottom-line goal of $1 million dollars in 2001.

We more than doubled that in the first year, and since then we have strongly increased profits every year as well as the top line. A lot of that is because of the development of the management team—a bunch of great people who really committed to each other, to working and serving each other and the business and really practicing the fundamentals of business. We plan and we set goals. We measure those goals, we report on them, and we hold ourselves responsible to them. This has made a huge difference. In June, at the end of this five-year period, our global sales were close to $100 million. We will have grown three or four times in the last five years.

The management team that has put us where we are today has committed to continue this strong growth. We've committed to grow at least two to three times over the next five years. We expect by some time in 2011 that this company should be doing $200 to $300 million in sales, investing $50 million in improvements and expansion, and creating hundreds of new jobs.

Golden Temple is part of a larger organization that includes other for-profit and nonprofit organizations. My job is to oversee the heads of all these other entities.

In addition to Golden Temple, we have a security business called Akal Security, based out of New Mexico. About 25 years ago, one of our friends wanted to become a state policeman in New Mexico. They said: "No turban and beard, sorry." So our teacher said: "Start your own business." Today, it is the fourth largest security guard company in the United States; it employs about 15,000 people. We handle the majority of the security for the federal courthouses, in conjunction with the U.S. Marshals service. We see security as another important service to the community. If we are safe, secure, and nourished, we can focus on cultivating higher levels of consciousness and serving others.

We have operations in Europe and India, as well. On the nonprofit side, we have a boarding school in India where we focus on developing our children as global citizens and future leaders.

We started ourselves on this path of service with Yoga and meditation, and we continue to teach that whenever and wherever we can. Yogi Bhajan was our teacher. He brought the powerful ancient practice of Kundalini Yoga to the West, which had been a secret practice available only to a select few. Yogi Bhajan said hogwash to that and made it available to all. Kundalini Yoga is now one of the fastest growing forms of Yoga, reaching millions of people around the world. We have a nonprofit called 3HO, the Healthy, Happy, Holy Organization, that promotes the teaching of Kundalini Yoga, and the Kundalini Yoga Research Institute, which studies the powerful effects of Kundalini Yoga on health and well-being through rigorous scientific research.

As part of our service, we are committed to making Golden Temple a truly sustainable business.

The first thing about being sustainable is being around. We've been around for 33 years and we intend to be around for a long time.

Sustainable business these days refers to the triple bottom line. First is the financial bottom line; of course you have to stay financially sound.

Then there is the environmental bottom line, you've got to treat your environment right. I saw this quote from the chairman of Canon. He said: "If there is no future for the earth, we have no future." We have to be concerned about how we treat our planet and, specifically, where we live and work.

The most important to Golden Temple and to me is the third bottom line: the social part of the bottom line, the social equity. How do you deal with the community around you to have a positive impact on that community? We have a line of cereal products that we started about 10 years ago called Peace Cereal. A substantial portion of the Peace Cereal profits are dedicated to supporting organizations that work for peace. We provide grants every year that support those organizations to advance peace in the world—supporting families and children, feeding people, and teaching peace-building skills. This is very important to us.

Sustainable business in general is an adult response to what we face in the world today. It is looking at using our resources efficiently. Making sure we are supporting our communities. Business is responsible for serving communities; it is responsible for more than just itself. When business really acts well it is serving the whole community.

Golden Temple feels that we have a responsibility to enhance the lives of the people we come in contact with, whether they are our employees or our customers or our suppliers. One way or another, how we work together should make our lives better.

On a personal level, as a leader, part of my service is to stretch and push others to be the best they can be, to continue to grow and develop, so they can serve at even higher levels—serving themselves by realizing more of their potential, serving their families and communities, and serving through the work we do together.

And the profits we generate, the green energy, provide more opportunity to serve. As Yogi Bhajan used to say: "Money is what money does." We are committed to doing well, in order to do good.

I slept, and dreamt that life was joy. I awoke and saw that life was service. I acted and beheld that service was joy.

Rabindranath Tagore

Marcella Echeverria and Surevolution

Marcella Echeverria is a Colombian native who was educated in the United States. As a journalist covering travel, style, design, and food she became increasingly interested in handcrafts from cultures from around the world, both the similarities and differences between crafts on the one hand, and the elite worlds of fashion, style, and art on the other. And she decided to create a global brand to bridge the gulf. As she puts it:

> The vision is to create a universal brand that brings the world and work of artisans to the luxury market while also contributing to the preservation of heritage and developing a sustainable business model for the artisanal world. Imagine: you go to the markets in Ecuador and Bolivia and you see these exquisitely made products sold on the ground by very poor people whose choices are limited to either making cheap ceremonial pieces or souvenirs

for tourists. But where is the excellence of the craft? How will it continue? It always struck me as strange that someone would pay $3,000 for a Louis Vuitton bag, which is very nice but produced by a machine, and not $300 for a handmade mochila bag. These are luxury products and deserve to be treated as such.

www.indagare.com/passions/5/departments/173/3336

Surevolution is the brand that she created.

Five years later, she has succeeded fantastically. She has developed a relationship with fashion designer Donna Karan and had her company's products shown in museums and art galleries. She has identified dozens of sources around the world capable of producing art-quality pieces. She is providing consumers in the developed world access to authentic, unique, beautiful items, while simultaneously providing crafts workers from around the world the opportunity to produce and market their highest quality work.

One of her product lines is produced by The Tecnovo Foundation in Colombia, a group that trains ex-guerrillas and ex-paramilitary militia members to produce beautiful crafts. Many of these are teenage boys who have never known a life other than as a child soldier. They welcome the opportunity to have a real job and to learn how to do something they are proud of.

Although she doesn't speak of it much, the endless violence in Colombia, caused by the conflicts between the drug lords and the government, has taken the lives of many people with whom she has been close. Creating jobs in Colombia is a very personal vocation for Marcella.

Chapter 7

Leveraging Entrepreneurship for Social Change

Donna Callejon
COO, GlobalGiving

J ust as entrepreneurs change the face of business, social entrepreneurs act as the change agents for society, seizing opportunities others miss and improving systems, inventing new approaches, and creating sustainable solutions to change society for the better. While business entrepreneurs are primarily motivated by profits, social entrepreneurs are first and foremost motivated to improve society. Despite this difference, social entrepreneurs are just as innovative and change oriented as their business counterparts, searching for new and better ways to solve the problems that plague society. Often the strategies they employ include devising methods of funding that render them largely self-sustaining (for example, revenue-generating strategies). While this approach is not mandatory to be considered a social entrepreneur, it is often the case.

In recent years, social entrepreneurs have emerged as a powerful force for social and economic development around the world as well as in the United States. The hallmark of social entrepreneurs is their systemic approach to change. They shift behavioral patterns and perceptions, building a broad base of support to create positive change throughout society. The most recognized of these individuals is Muhammad Yunus of Bangladesh, who is showing the world that the poor are bankable and that "hand ups" have higher impact than handouts. Yunus' organization, the Grameen Bank, has made loans to 3.12 million borrowers—people previously thought to be unworthy of credit. To date, 46 percent of Grameen borrowers' families have crossed the poverty line.

Today, social entrepreneurs are being heralded as a driving source for international development. Often operating in developing countries, these entrepreneurs frequently lack access to funding. GlobalGiving, itself an innovative organization, is creating a platform that addresses this need.

Following are two inspiring examples of the initiative of social entrepreneurs.

Women Make the Economy Go Round

When Maria Petron Urquia Chavarria asked her female village elders if she could join the Adelante Solidarity Group in her Honduran village to obtain a small loan, she was turned down. Fortunately, a local woman who had experienced the benefit of micro-credit herself decided to loan Maria some of her personal savings. Maria used the loan not to purchase goods for her own family but instead to further fund her budding food stand business.

This "test" was more than enough for the female elders. They decided to allow Maria to join the Adelante microlending program in her village. Maria is currently investing her fourth loan of $497, diversifying her food business to include clothing manufacturing. Adelante encourages its recipients to diversify their business opportunities so they are not at the mercy of the success of just one product. Maria has seen the benefit of this process and is well on her way out of extreme poverty. Her business brings her about $270 a month, which is enough to repair her roof, expand her business further, and send her children to school.

GlobalGiving donors such as Lorig Charkonian of Silver Spring, Maryland, have donated nearly $11,000 to provide Maria and women like her with micro-loans. These loans are allowing women to pull themselves and their communities out of the vicious cycle of poverty. The impact of donations through GlobalGiving is immense; just $50 provides capital for one initial loan while $1,000 can sponsor a loan group serving up to five women for an entire year. These women already possessed the knowledge to fight the cycle of poverty; they just needed the financial capacity to do so. Because of the support of donors through GlobalGiving, they have begun to realize their goal.

This Little Piglet Went to . . . Save a Child from Slavery

Experts estimate that between 25,000 and 40,000 young girls in Nepal have been sold into bonded slavery—by their parents. These parents are so poor that they depend on the income generated by selling their daughters to help feed their families. Most families receive between $40 and $70 a year for their daughters, which is approximately one quarter of an average annual wage. The girls see no benefit themselves, as most do not receive any kind of schooling or training. Some will even be forced into prostitution. When the Nepalese Youth Opportunity Foundation (NYOF) was alerted to this widespread problem, it immediately jumped into action.

Started in 1990 by retired California Supreme Court clerk Olga Murray, NYOF quickly became deeply involved in the Katmandu area. NYOF began its operation as one small children's home in Katmandu, which soon became two. After launching a Nutritional Rehabilitation Home for malnourished children and mothers, NYOF learned of the indentured servitude suffered by many young girls in Nepal. The solution was simple: Offer the family an alternative way to generate the same income they would receive from selling their child. Instead of dispensing loans, NYOF decided to give each family a piglet, an animal that could further their future income when raised and sold. NYOF also offered a regular supply of kerosene to families that agreed to keep their girls at home. The cost to keep a girl out of slavery and with her family is a mere $100.

In addition to keeping the girls out of slavery, NYOF provides them with school uniforms and supplies, and more important, the ability to remain with their families and receive an education. GlobalGiving donors have seen the enormous importance of this project, donating over $20,000 to NYOF. These funds will benefit 200 girls, giving them the opportunity that all children deserve.

GlobalGiving is an online marketplace for international giving. GlobalGiving connects donors directly to social, environmental, and economic development projects around the world. These contributions directly support the entrepreneurial work of project leaders throughout the world, who are bringing innovative, empowering solutions to challenging social problems at the local community level. Since 2003, nearly $3 million has passed through GlobalGiving to over 500 social entrepreneurs worldwide.

GlobalGiving is an innovative collaboration between two entities—the GlobalGiving Foundation and a socially oriented enterprise called ManyFutures, Inc. The foundation handles all due diligence on projects, along with disbursement of funds to projects and tax receipts to donors. The foundation also provides a variety of services to project leaders in the field, including networking and training.

ManyFutures is responsible for the development and operation of the Web site, along with marketing to donors, corporations, and other organizations. ManyFutures and the foundation have partnered with a number of corporations, affinity groups, financial advisors, and other types of donor aggregators to help bring donors to the foundation and the projects in its network. Partners include Hewlett-Packard, The North Face, eBay, Google, and Yahoo!, among others. All donations made to projects go through the GlobalGiving Foundation, a registered 501(c) 3 entity, and are fully tax-deductible.

Sarah Endline and Sweetriot

Sarah Endline is a Harvard MBA who has lived, traveled, and worked in more than 50 countries. She knew early on that she wanted to be an entrepreneur and that she wanted to create an international business. She also had a passion for Conscious Capitalism and was following the progress of all the early Conscious Capitalist companies while she was still in school. But she wasn't sure what business, so while working for others after business school she kept looking for the right product in the right niche.

She knew she loved candy and chocolate, and then she discovered the power of raw cacao nibs. Cacao nibs are small bits of the edible portion of the cacao bean. Raw cacao has more antioxidant flavonoids than any other food tested so far, including blueberries, red wine, and green tea. Raw cacao is also the source of the positive, mildly psychotropic effects of chocolate, raising the levels of serotonin (an antidepressant), endorphins (the source of the exercise high), phenylethylamine (the "in love" chemical), and anandamide (the "bliss" chemical). It is also rich in vitamins and minerals. Cacao nibs are a great health food, sometimes eaten as a sort of nut-like food directly or sprinkled on cereals or used in smoothies.

But they are not especially sweet. One of the reasons why they are healthier than chocolate is that they have all the positive impact of chocolate, in a concentrated form without all the fat and sugar. Sarah decided to create chocolate-covered cacao nibs—thus providing all the positive health impact of the nibs, but as a sweet, candy treat that would bring nibs to a larger, more mainstream market. Her chocolate "peaces" are all natural; and packaged in recyclable, reusable containers, featuring emerging artists. Everything about the company is consciously designed in an effort to leverage her business to do good. As Sarah says, "It's not about writing checks."

Calling her company "sweetriot"

A sweetriot is a joyful celebration of culture, diversity, and understanding—
it is the opposite of a civil riot, which is dangerous, violent, and oppressing.

and calling herself the "Chief Rioter," Sarah deliberately designed a product line that could be produced and packaged in the countries in which she sourced the product.

One of the trends in Conscious Capitalism that Sarah and others are developing is to produce as much value-added in developing nations as possible, in contrast to, for instance, the large chocolate companies that purchase raw cacao beans at global commodity prices, then ship the beans to developed nations for processing. One of the approaches to alleviating poverty more aggressively is a conscious commitment to increasing value-added as much as possible in those nations where the need is greatest.

Part Three

What Do We Need to Do So That Entrepreneurs and Conscious Capitalists Can Solve All the World's Problems?

The entrepreneur is our visionary, the creator in each of us. We're born with that quality and it defines our lives as we respond to what we see, hear, feel, and experience. It is developed, nurtured, and given space to flourish or is squelched, thwarted, without air or stimulation, and dies.

—MICHAEL GERBER

Chapter 8

Solving All Environmental Problems

Michael Strong
CEO and Chief Visionary Officer, FLOW

S ustainability advocates are passionately trying to create a new value system, based on ecological sustainability, and they are passionately trying to evangelize to others that they, too, should accept the growing sustainability value system. A U.N. press release captures the prevailing notion well:

> WORLD'S MIND-SET—SHORT-TERM, WEDDED TO FOSSIL FUELS—MUST CHANGE TO ACHIEVE

> SUSTAINABLE DEVELOPMENT, SAYS SECRETARY-GENERAL, ACCEPTING ENVIRONMENT PRIZE

With the sense that the fate of the planet depends on it, they are urgently trying to convince billions of people in different cultures around the world that their patterns of consumption must change.

There is certainly nothing wrong with trying to do this, and the sustainability movement is slowing the pace of environmental degradation and paving the way for innovative technologies that could have an enormous positive impact. At the same time, it is important to realize that creating a value system, changing the world's mind-set, or raising consciousness is not going to result in an environmentally sustainable world. Indeed, Conscious Capitalist companies will not save the environment in the absence of additional legal protections for the environment.

Instead, as some leading thinkers in the sustainability movement have recognized, a systems approach, based on the creation of new institutions, will be necessary. In the long run, which is what really matters with respect to environmental sustainability, we will need to create property rights solutions of some kind in order to preserve all environmental commons sustainably.

In 1968, economist Garrett Hardin analyzed situations in which a "commons," such as a fishery, or our water supply, or the global atmosphere, was used by many different people. His conclusion was that unless a system was devised to prevent overuse, a "tragedy of the commons" would take place in which the fishery would be depleted, a water supply would be overused or overpolluted, or in which the global atmospheric commons would be overpolluted. Hardin himself realized that reliance on personal conscience (or value system or mind-set) would not be adequate to secure such environmental commons from degradation.

How Property Rights Create Sustainable Fisheries

It is increasingly being recognized that indigenous peoples often relied on property rights to ensure the sustainability of the natural resources on which they relied. This description of how the Alaskan Tlingits managed their salmon fisheries before the arrival of the white man is one such example:

> House or family groups controlled access to locations where the sockeye could be caught, while the clan determined the fishing locations. Each group had exclusive rights to its fishing locations. When an outsider infringed on a location, the trespasser was required to compensate the owners or potentially face violent consequences.

The eldest clan male, the *yitsati*, generally possessed superior knowledge about salmon runs, escapement, and fishing technology and became the custodian or trustee of the hunting and fishing territories. He also assisted in parceling out goods that had been produced collectively to members of the clan. Rights initially could not be transferred to those outside the group. This allowed the exclusion of those who might not abide by customary norms.

Donald Leal, "Community-Run Fisheries,"
www.perc.org/perc.php?id=652&subsection=6

The important fact with respect to sustainability about this anecdote is that the Tlingits did not rely on a value-system or mind-set alone, but rather on specific institutions: a set of property rights and corresponding norms about transfer of those property rights.

In the tribal context in which we evolved, it made sense to influence those around us by means of persuasion and criticism. Just as we have an evolutionarily propensity to eat fats and sugars at every opportunity, so, too, we have an evolutionary propensity to criticize those who are engaging in harms to the community and to the environment. Indeed, in a tribe of 150 who lived their entire lives together, such criticism was an effective force for constraining behavior. But praise and blame, our natural tools for socializing each other, are no longer adequate tools as our communities become larger than the evolutionary tribe.

The Tlingit population of southeastern Alaska was about 15,000 at the time of contact with the white man. The value system or mind-set of their original culture had most likely been an inadequate means of managing the salmon fisheries for many thousands of years. There is a fascinating research study showing that under many circumstances, people spontaneously develop norms for resource allocation; Robert Sugden gave this famous example in his ground-breaking article on norms, "Spontaneous Order":

In a fishing village on the Yorkshire coast there used to be an unwritten rule about the gathering of driftwood after a storm. Whoever was first onto a stretch of the shore after high tide was allowed to take whatever he wished, without interference from later arrivals, and to gather it into piles above the high-tide line.

Provided he placed two stones on the top of each pile, the wood was regarded as his property, for him to carry away when he chose. If, however, a pile had not been removed after two more high tides, this ownership right lapsed.

Robert Sugden, "Spontaneous Order," *Journal of Economic Perspectives,* vol. 3, no. 4, Fall 1989, 85

No doubt, many generations in the past, the Tlingit began to evolve norms for salmon fishing rights much as the Yorkshire villagers had evolved norms for driftwood gathering.

Formal property rights, now enforced by law throughout most of the world, are an essential prerequisite to the large scale, complex societies in which we now live. These property rights originated in tribal customs, but have since been integrated into our current system of legal documents, courts, and policing.

There is a sense in which all of our environmental challenges are the result of the fact that property rights solutions, similar to what the Tlingit independently discovered thousands of years ago, have not been created rapidly enough to keep pace with economic growth and population growth. This does not mean that such solutions are not possible; it simply means that we need to focus our energies on creating such solutions.

In order to get a sense of how such solutions might work in the modern world and what new institutions need to be created, let's look at some recent institutional innovations in contemporary fisheries management. In order to see the power of well-designed institutions, it is worth reviewing the history of Alaskan halibut fisheries, which show the dramatic contrast created by good institutions:

The Alaskan halibut fishing season once lasted for almost 10 months. When regulators decided that overfishing was a problem, they began reducing the length of the season. Before long, however, the season was down to 48 hours, with almost no change in the amount of fish caught. The motivation to catch as many fish as possible, as quickly as possible, remained, and so ingenuity and technology overcame restrictions.

Michael De Alessi, "One Fish, Two Fish, I Fish, You Fish," Fraser Forum, July 2003, www.reason.org/ commentaries/dealessi_20030700.pdf

I happened to live in Homer, Alaska, when the halibut season was 48 hours long. Thousands of fishermen, owning hundreds of millions of dollars worth of big, fast, fishing boats with sophisticated fishing detection equipment would prepare for weeks for the race to the halibut grounds. Although most of them had other jobs or participated in other fisheries at other times of the year, the halibut fishery represented a significant portion of their annual income. Their families depended on them to get out there fast and catch as much as they could.

The result was grim:

> To take advantage of this narrow window, crews went out for 48 consecutive hours, working through the night and—at times—in dangerous weather conditions. Boats and lives were lost. With no time to waste, crews wouldn't bother struggling with tangled long-lines. They would simply cut them loose and cast new ones, even though the old lines continued to lure and kill fish (a destructive process known as "ghost fishing"). There was no time to sort each haul either, so undersized halibut and other species that would normally be released were torn apart and thrown overboard dead or dying. "Bycatch," as these innocent victims are called, is always an environmental cost of fishing, but this cost escalated significantly during the 48-hour season.
>
> www.etei.org/case_study_2.htm

Millions of tons of fish were simply left in the water to rot, the sort of sickeningly wasteful behavior reminiscent of the massive buffalo slaughter of the nineteenth century. In the eagerness to get their share, fishermen would sabotage each other's boats, shoot at each other when another boat came near them, and cut each other's fishing lines, thus wasting more fish in the horrid feeding frenzy.

It is very important to realize that this wasteful and vicious behavior was not caused by western civilization, or capitalism, or value systems, or mind-sets. It was caused by poorly designed institutions—a lack of property rights in the halibut fishery. In 1995, a system of property rights in the halibut fisheries was created based on Individual Transferable Quotas (ITQ) whereby a total limit of 37 million pounds of halibut to be caught each season was allocated among existing fisherman based on a complex (and controversial) system of historical catch.* The ITQ could then be traded, though it remained a provisional privilege granted by the government rather than a real property right.

Immediately after the ITQ system was implemented the insanity of the halibut fisheries came to an end. Again, the fishermen's behavior did not change because they had a new value system or mind-set. It changed because they faced far more sensible incentives. After the ITQ system was passed, the halibut season once again extended to months and fishermen settled into less wasteful practices. The beliefs or person-alities of the fishermen had not changed.

Critics of the halibut fishery in Alaska after ITQ point that the Alaska fishermen are still not proactively investing in the fishery. But once again, the problem is not values, mind-sets, or beliefs: it is flawed incentives. New Zealand hoki (a flaky whitefish that is New Zealand's most important fish) fisheries have combined a more flexible ITQ market (closer to a real property right) along with weaker antitrust laws (fishermen cooperating on ITQ shares would violate U.S. anti-trust law); as a result the hoki fishing community has been more proac-tive.† Because the hoki fishermen have secure property rights, a futures market in ITQs had developed, and because it is in the fishermen's long-term interest to increase the value of the ITQ, they now have an incentive to preserve the fishery.

After the system was established, the hoki fishermen collectively decided to catch 50,000 metric tons less fish than the government proposed—not because they had become environmentally enlightened, but because such a decision increased the long-term value of their fish-ery. Because of these well-designed institutions, there is every reason to believe that the hoki fishery is now sustainable; the fishermen are proactively committed to ensuring that sustainability.

At the most mundane level, people like the Alaskan halibut fisher-men do not regard themselves as bad people—they are just ordinary folk out to earn a living. Again, the problem is not extraordinary greed

---

*Indeed the issue of allocating ITQs fairly was so contentious that other fisheries insisted on passing a federal moratorium on ITQs that only recently expired.

†Michael De Alessi, "One Fish, Two Fish; I Fish, You Fish," *Fraser Forum*, July 2003, 24.

(among the Tlingit or the halibut fishermen) but merely ordinary people engaged in ordinary behavior.

Why Encouraging Changes in Values Won't Be Enough

More deeply, in a pluralistic world, it is unlikely that we will ever be able to obtain anything approaching unanimity with respect to values, beliefs, norms, or behavior. Again, the human psychology that drives sustainability advocates to exhort others to engage in similarly conscientious behavior is a human characteristic that was optimized for tribal groups of 150 or so. Face to face, day after day, in a community in which everyone shared the same culture and cosmic beliefs, it may have been possible to persuade others that they must engage in sustainable practices.

But in a world of more than six billion, in which even within a given nation-state there are diverse beliefs about morality (and reality), it is unrealistic to expect that everyone will be persuaded. People react to incentives and disincentives. Moral suasion is useful in projecting a values system, but if the persuasion lacks a meaningful, tangible incentive structure, the values are likely to be ignored. Carrots and sticks work far better than words and, when manifested in the price system, they allow for nearly instantaneous "sustainability" decisions to be made worldwide.

In addition, the structure of tragedy of the commons problems is often such that a few bad apples can destroy the commons—and in a world of six billion and growing, we are apt to have more than a few bad apples.

In *A Place for Winter*, Paul Tiulana, an elder from King Island, a small island in the Bering Sea, describes what life was like before the white man came. His tribe of Eskimos lived alone on King Island in one small village of about 200 people. Among his many fascinating memories he tells of how from time to time there would be a young man who would do things that people didn't like, who violated the norms of the village. After a number of people asked him not to do these things on a number of occasions, eventually someone would kill him, and the rest of the village would be grateful.

The romance associated with indigenous peoples, especially among advocates of sustainability, should not blind us to the fact that human beings have always included a range of personalities. Even in the pristine original condition of tribes before western civilization encroached, there were some people who were, to be blunt, either jerks or criminals. Even when survival itself is at stake (conditions at King Island are very harsh) and even when all the social pressure of a tribe of people who share a common culture, common myths, common cosmology, and a common belief concerning right and wrong—even then some people, albeit only about 1 percent (apparently there was more than one such case in Paul's lifetime), are just plain jerks.

The selfish human being is not an invention of civilization—though life in large, pluralistic, anonymous societies may increase selfish behavior. But suppose only one out of every 200 people was selfish enough to have warranted killing on King Island (just to be clear, this is not a remedy we endorse in the modern world). In a nation of 300 million, that translates to 1.5 million jerks, and in a world of six billion it means 30 million jerks. Moreover, this assumes that the other 199 out of each 200 are well behaved, perfect citizens with respect to environmental sustainability. Realistically, there is likely to be a continuum of behavior; the point here being that even under very modest assumptions the "change in consciousness" premise of environmental change is completely unrealistic.

Once we have sensible incentive systems in place, such as the Tlingit created or like those that were created for the New Zealand haki fishermen by the New Zealand legislature, then we have created a sustainable world—without changes in value systems or mindsets. We know nothing about the New Zealand fishermen; most likely there were some who were environmentalists and some who were not, some who were selfish and some who were not, some who cared about what other people thought of them and others who did not. But if, through the futures markets for their ITQs, they were able to see immediately that not taking as much fish now increased the value of their ITQ in the future, they immediately did the right thing.

Thus, changes in value systems and mindsets are neither a necessary nor a sufficient condition to ensure environmental sustainability. In a world of democratic governments, creating new property rights institutions is indeed a necessary and sufficient condition to ensure environmental sustainability, but the creation of those institutions is a matter of effective coalition building rather than a matter of changing value systems or mind-sets.

While creating those coalitions may, indeed, involve changing the mindsets of some individuals, it is likely to require changing their mind-sets in a manner diametrically opposed to the manner encouraged by the most passionate environmentalists. Coalitions are built by means of pragmatic compromise rather than impassioned and uncompromising moralism. Mutual understanding is the key mind-set shift, not the ardent embrace of environmental ideals.

How Environmental Righteousness Prevents Progress on Achieving Environmental Solutions

Paradoxically, the ardent embrace of environmental ideals may delay the implementation of effective sustainability solutions. Evolutionary psychologists have shown, both through laboratory studies and anthropological research, that those individuals in a group who are most committed to working to solve a problem together are also the most punitive to those free riders who are not working to solve the problem. Again, in a tribe of 150, this punitive approach worked well. But in modern nation-state democratic politics, a punitive approach toward those with whom one disagrees is not helpful in coalition building. Thus, the required mind-set is contrary to our natural tribal impulses, where those of us who led community initiatives found that our uncompromising moralism was typically rewarded with success.

Reuniting America is a group founded by Joseph McCormick, a Republican activist who ran for Congress as a self-identified "hard-Right Christian" in Jimmy Carter's old district after having spent a decade in Republican activism. His account of his transformation is worth hearing in his own words:

> After losing my race in 1998 my life spun out of control. My wife left, I found myself in a power struggle with my partners for control of my business, and my sister who more or less raised me began a losing battle with cancer. By 2001, I had walked

away from or watched the collapse of everything I had carefully built—my political career, my business, home, marriage. I had lost my identity. I ended up living alone in a mountain cabin in Floyd, Virginia, disillusioned, powerless, rolling the essential questions of life over and over in my mind: Who am I? Why am I here? The answers, even now, are unclear, but during this time I experienced a shift from living my life as if I knew who I was and why I was here, to living my life as more of an inquiry into these questions. This inquiry took on the form of a journey toward personal integrity, that is, reconciliation of the various sides of myself.

Joseph McCormick, "The Story of the Democracy in
America Project and Reuniting America,"
www.reunitingamerica.org/about-us/history/history

While living in Floyd, McCormick became friends with Pat Spino, a midwife from the alternative community there, a "hippy," from McCormick's perspective. Building on this one transpartisan friendship, McCormick and Spino have built a national organization dedicated to encouraging dialogue across partisan divides, dialogue that transcends partisan bickering.

Constructive solutions to environmental problems will require transpartisan cooperation (in all nations). In partisan battles, the environment will usually be the loser, as special interests will exploit partisan differences to continue in their same destructive patterns. Few people realize, of course, that the United States government subsidizes environmentally destructive activities, paying oil and gas, agriculture, mining, and timber interests hundreds of millions of dollars to engage in environmentally damaging activities. Worldwatch estimates that if the U.S. government stopped paying for environmental destruction, every family in the United States would receive a $2,000 tax cut per year.*

There is a Green Scissors Campaign in the United States, an alliance between environmentalists and taxpayer organizations that is attempting

---

*"Worldwatch Institute Proposes $2,000 Tax Cut Per Family to Save the Planet," Common Dreams Newswire, September 12, 1998, www.commondreams.org/pressreleases/Sept98/091298a.htm, based on David Roodman's book, *The Natural Wealth of Nations*.

to pass legislation of this type. Similar cuts in Germany, Japan, and most other industrialized nations are also possible. Governments around the world collect taxes from their citizens in order to subsidize polluting industries. As we shall see, this fact is not a curious coincidence: The structure of large nation-state democratic government is designed to ensure that special interests usually win.

Why We Need to Remove Environmental Assets from Government Control

A savvy child is often able to play off his parents against one another, going first to mommy, then to daddy, to get his way. The only way that parents can maintain discipline and raise a child well is to work together to create an appropriate, healthy framework. Similarly, special interests cleverly exploit partisan differences, playing the two sides off against each other, ensuring that they get their way. Likewise, the only way that legislators can create a constructive environmental framework is to work together to create an appropriate, healthy framework.

Property rights solutions will ultimately lead to a sustainable environment more effectively than will government ownership of environmental assets. Modern large-scale nation-state democracy is not a reliable means of protecting the environment. Because of the structure of government, in most cases special interests will win because they have a far greater incentive to ensure that their interests are protected than the rest of us have to monitor any given issue.

To take one of the most notorious examples: since 1982, U.S. taxpayers have spent about $40 million per year to subsidize logging in the Tongass National Forest, about $1 billion in total payments to increase the rate at which we clear-cut one of our last old-growth forests.* There has been a bi-partisan campaign, consisting of environmentalist Democrats and tax-cutting Republicans, trying to eliminate these subsidies, for about 20 years. Year after year, advocates of saving money by eliminating logging subsidies mobilize their troops, only to have the

---

*Sierra Club, "Waste, Fraud, and Abuse in America's Rainforest," www.sierraclub .org/forests/downloads/200505_tongassfactsheet.pdf.

subsidies slipped in again during the course of the legislative process. Some progress was made in the early 1990s in reducing the subsidies, but the Forest Service continues to spend massive amounts building costly roads the only purpose of which is to facilitate logging. In May of 2006, the House of Representatives passed a resolution to end the subsidies once and for all, but the final appropriations bill as signed once again included the subsidies.

The subsidies benefit a couple of pulp mill companies and provide a few hundred jobs; as special interests go, this is a very tiny, localized special interest. By one estimate, the government is subsidizing each logging job to the tune of $200,000 per job. But the Alaskan senators have enough power in the Senate, and are closely enough allied with these particular special interests, that time and again they keep the subsidies in place.

This can happen because while the rest of us are worrying about the war in Iraq, or global warming, or health care, or the minimum wage, or this or that scandal, or whatever, the Tongass timber interests are focused solely on maintaining their subsidies, day after day, night after night. Mohair subsidies have been ridiculed as a joke for decades longer than Tongass timber subsidies. Why, exactly, do we need to pay farmers to produce mohair? The subsidies were initiated in 1954 on the grounds that a stable supply of mohair was needed for uniforms and more than 50 years later they live on. If the public can't even beat the mohair industry, what hope do we have of managing anything by means of a democratic process? While most of us pay attention occasionally to this or that public policy issue, or engage in partisanship of one kind or another, subsidized interests stay focused on their subsidy every minute of every day. They typically support both Republicans and Democrats, so that they maintain a close connection with whatever party is in power.

Although there are many idealistic organizations that urge the public to pay more attention to political issues, the problem here is one of simple arithmetic: the interests have only one issue to which they devote all of their attention, all the time. The rest of us, no matter how idealistic or altruistic we are, have our attention divided among numerous issues, each of which is hopelessly complex to follow. Even the most devoted policy wonk can only master a modest level of detail among a small number of issues. The fact that special interests will get their way in democratic government is not a problem that can be solved by means of public spiritedness, or campaign finance reform, or scandalous exposes, or by means of electing public officials with more integrity. Basic arithmetic will ensure that special interests win most of the time regardless of which party is in office.[*] I used to play chess and one of the mean things to do to a naïve player is to checkmate them in the first four moves. Most players learn soon enough how to forestall this quick checkmate, but some continue to open themselves up to such a defeat time and time again.

The notion that a public spirited campaign of any kind can defeat special interests in general is contrary to simple arithmetic. The delusion is especially hard to give up because a public spirited campaign can always defeat any particular interest—if the Tongass and mohair subsidies were major issues in a national presidential campaign, and the politicians and media focused on them constantly for 18 months, they could certainly be defeated. And, of course, the interests behind the oil subsidies, cotton subsidies, corn subsidies, and so on, would be delighted to have the spotlight elsewhere—so that they can continue to secure their positions. (Actually, due to public ridicule the mohair subsidies were eliminated in 1996. But then public attention turned to other issues, and in 1999 the mohair subsidies snuck back in again).[†] The notion that any particular victory against any particular special interest is somehow a victory against special interests in general represents a failure to understand the arithmetic of focus. There are hundreds of thousands of public issues, and we can only focus on a handful of them at any one time.

---

[*]Jonathan Rauch's *Demosclerosis* is a sadly entertaining and wonderfully accessible book on how this works and why it is necessarily part of the system. Charlotte Twight's *Dependent on D.C.* adds dozens of anecdotes of the extraordinarily ingenious machinations of politicians and special interests.

[†]Stephen Moore, "Getting Business Off the Dole," Hoover Institution, 1999, No. 3, www.hoover.org/publications/digest/3512731.html.

This "public choice" problem (public choice is a term that describes the theory behind this depressing and disillusioning arithmetic) is one of the most important rationales for limiting government control over society and the economy. The larger government becomes, the more aspects of society over which it exercises control, the higher the probability that the public and the environment, on balance, get screwed.

With respect to environmental sustainability, the only secure solution is to limit the extent to which democratic government exercises control. If the Tongass National Forest were private, then it would charge timber companies to cut trees rather than paying the timber companies to cut trees. And thus there are economists who recommend privatizing environmental assets as a form of property rights solution to tragedy of the commons problems.

But this approach has, in this simple form, never met with enthusiasm among environmentalists for the simple reason that they don't trust private owners to preserve environmental amenities. Most private owners might be inclined to preserve the long-term value of forests, but some might simply clear-cut entire forests because they want the immediate cash, and thus a major environmental asset would be destroyed altogether.

Environmental Trusts: A Property Rights Solution Beloved by Environmentalists

For the past 40 years, we have thus been stuck between a rock and a hard spot: Economists point out that the government is reliably poor at managing environmental assets, and environmentalists point out that corporations are sometimes actively destructive of environmental assets. It appeared to be a choice between a long, slow death of all public assets via government versus random destruction of some percentage of those assets that had been privatized.

Gus Dizerega, Randal O'Toole, Peter Barnes, and others have recently developed a fundamentally new strategy that brilliantly reconciles the best solution in terms of overall long-term sustainability, property rights solutions, without allowing for the occasional total destruction that had prevented environmentalists from previously embracing outright privatization as a solution. In Barnes' version, an environmental trust is created that has a legal obligation to preserve the environmental asset in perpetuity, and if the trustees fail to fulfill the conditions of the trust, it may be sued (if the Forest Service pays to clear-cut all our national forests, it couldn't be sued).[*]

Moreover, any revenue derived from the environmental asset would go directly to the citizens via a Citizen's Dividend, modeled after the Alaska Permanent Fund. For several decades now, oil revenues from Alaskan state lands are put into a trust and each Alaskan citizen receives a check from the fund (it ranges in value each year, but has often been around $1,000 per year). Thus Barnes' vision of environmental trusts has the virtues of simultaneously creating incentives for responsible resource management (the trustees of each environmental asset would be held legally accountable for maintaining the integrity of the trust) as well as sharing any monetary value from the asset directly with the relevant set of citizens.

At present, land trusts are common, and thus with respect to land, Barnes' innovation is modest. There are also a few water and aquifer trusts. But Barnes' idea could be applied to any environmental asset including, in principle, the global atmosphere; his book *Who Owns the Sky?* proposed a global Sky Trust to solve climate change. In principle, there could be specific environmental trusts for national parks, national forests, rivers, lakes, aquifers, the ocean, regional air quality, and the global atmosphere.

There could be habitat trusts that were designed to protect specific habitats that crossed various geographical features; a salmon habitat trust, for instance, could have a functional property right that gave it control over, and responsibility for securing, salmon habitats both at sea and in the spawning rivers. If a farmer wanted to build a bridge across a salmon stream, instead of dealing with government regulators she would negotiate with the salmon habitat trust to determine what features the bridge, and its construction, would need to have so as not

---

[*]See Peter Barnes, *Capitalism 3.0: A Guide to Reclaiming the Commons*, which can be downloaded for free at www.capitalism3.com/.

to interfere with salmon spawning. If pesticide runoff from farms was damaging the salmon ecosystem, the salmon habitat could sue those farmers responsible for the pesticide, or in urgent circumstances get a cease-and-desist order. Although this sounds hypothetical, bass fishermen's organizations have sued polluters in order to preserve water quality in bass fishing streams and rivers. Habitat trusts would ensure that not only those species that were popular to an existing interest group, such as bass fishermen, but any species that we wanted to protect, would have a legal advocate.

The Transition from Environmental Righteousness to Transpartisan Coalition Building

In small groups, such as the tribes of 150 in which we evolved, beliefs and norms concerning right and wrong were usually an adequate means of ensuring that the members of the tribe respected each other and the environment in which the tribe lived (though even in those circumstances, as Paul Tiulana reminds us, some people did not behave respectfully). As indigenous communities became larger, such as the Tlingit, they evolved formal property rights in order to ensure that the environmental commons was sustainable. Modern global society is growing so fast that we urgently need to create formal property rights solutions to ensure the sustainability of all environmental commons. Moral suasion is not enough.

The belief that fundamental environmental changes will take place primarily by means of education or moral suasion is moral illusion, analogous to an optical illusion. In our own lives, those of us who are most likely to read material like this, are also those of us who are most likely to make decisions and change our behaviors by means of the ideas and ideals that drive us. We are also responsive to the concerns of others on these issues. We know, with certainty, that we and many of the people we know have, in fact, changed our behavior as a consequence of education and moral suasion. And based on this experiential certainty, we redouble our efforts to educate and persuade others to likewise change their behavior.

Moreover, there have been idealistic public campaigns that have transformed society. Although the idealistic campaign to bring equality to African-Americans, women, and others has by no means completely succeeded, standards of public behavior are dramatically different today as compared to 50 years ago. Today a football coach or college professor can be fired for making statements that were universally made with impunity 50 years ago.

But consumption of wood products, or salmon, or oil is not like public expressions of racism. Public expressions of racism are easily monitored, and thus sanctioned, by others. They are also costless to quit doing. And there was widespread elite agreement that racist attitudes were negative, some considering such attitudes merely inappropriate and others considering them evil.

By contrast, our consumption of different resources involves many billions of decisions by many billions of individuals. Most of those decisions are made invisibly—we have no idea how much wood, salmon, or oil are used by all the people with whom we interact. In addition, it is in some cases very costly for some people to quit using wood or oil. And even if there is some (though by no means complete) agreement that we should use less carbon-emitting fossil fuel, there is no agreement on how much less. The primary focus of the sustainability movement should be the transpartisan creation of new institutions to secure the environment, not the imposition of value systems or mind-sets.

At present, the entire global sustainability movement is focused on creating norms around what they believe to be environmentally sustainable business practices, environmentally sustainable lifestyles, environmentally sustainable belief systems, and so forth. Again, there is nothing wrong with this and their efforts are no doubt launching valuable innovations that have played, and will continue to play, a positive role in creating long-term environmental sustainability.

But there is at present a smaller cadre of institutionally wiser environmentalists who are already working on lasting property rights solutions. These leading thinkers need considerably more support for their initiatives. Moreover, it is important that they receive transpartisan support.

There are several shortcomings with the sustainability movement's relatively exclusive focus on creating new practices, lifestyles, and beliefs:

1. There are some problems for which their efforts are likely to be completely ineffective. Insofar as, for instance, they use less of a commodity for which widespread demand continues to exist, they merely decrease the price of that commodity (however slightly) in a way that may then lead to a corresponding increase in demand from others.

2. The belief that their lifestyle is morally superior to the lifestyles of others, which may or may not be a valid belief depending on thousands of judgment calls in most cases, may exacerbate partisan and cultural polarization. While there is nothing wrong with humble approaches to a sustainable lifestyle, demonizing the "other" is rarely helpful in a democracy, especially when the other is numerically large and powerful.

3. In some cases, advocates of environmental sustainability are also hostile to capitalism and economic growth, attitudes that often result in policies that harm the poor, especially the developing world poor.[*]

And yet, with just a slight shift in emphasis toward the creation of institutions that would internalize environmental externalities, many of the same ideals and energies of the sustainability movement will unambiguously position them as leading innovators and entrepreneurs creating a bright green future for all.

There will be some commons for which direct privatization may be appropriate. There may be others for which privatization into environmental trusts is more appropriate. Here we won't address the innumerable complex issues involved in these decisions. But on balance both private owners and trusts will defend the integrity and sustainability of their property. Because it is in their interest to do so, most of them, most of the time, will charge an appropriate amount for resource extraction (such as Tongass timber sales) or pollution (such as carbon emissions into the global atmosphere) so that the full cost of environmental destruction is included in the price of the goods and services we purchase.

---

[*]See the film, *Mine Your Own Business* for an entertaining and vivid illustration of some specific examples, www.mineyourownbusiness.org/.

Excerpted from "A Personally Transformational Encounter of Left and Right" by Tom Atlee

On June 11, 2004, I was privileged to join in a fascinating meeting of Left and Right organized by Let's Talk America and the Democracy in America Project. This unusual gathering was funded by the visionary Fetzer Institute and generously hosted at its wooded Seasons Retreat Center in Kalamazoo, MI. When we said our good-byes three days later, I knew my worldview had been changed forever.

People from MoveOn.org, ACLU, the AFL-CIO, Sierra Club, and Rolling Thunder (Jim Hightower's group) couldn't make it from the Left. But a couple of former Clinton administration officials came—Shirley Wilcher of Wilcher Global LLC and the National Congress of Black Women, and Carl Fillichio of the Council for Excellence in Government—and a number of other folks who have roots in progressive politics, like myself, Mark Satin of *THE RADICAL MIDDLE* newsletter, and Michael Toms of New Dimensions Radio.

Among the pillars of the conservative movement who attended were David Keene, chair of the American Conservative Union (the largest grassroots conservative organization in the United States); Bill Thomson, national field director and a leading spokesperson for the Christian Coalition; FBI veteran Gary Aldrich, founder of The Patrick Henry Center for Individual Liberty (and author *of Unlimited Access*); and columnist and radio talk show host Bob Barr, former U.S. congressman from Georgia and a board member for the National Rifle Association.

I came to this weekend largely because of Joseph McCormick, the strong conservative who had come to believe that dialogue and deliberation—and, through them, the emergence of an inclusive, dynamic We the People—offer better answers to our predicament than win/lose battles over positions and candidates. His journey had brought him to the same place mine had, but through the opposite door. I had tremendous respect for him, but I couldn't relate to his right-wing past at all. Even as I joined him in our common dedication to dialogue, I couldn't quite figure him out through the lens of my progressive analysis.

What I experienced before and during the weekend gave me a gut-level understanding of how my own ideological righteousness could close my mind and heart. Using Google, I researched the people who were coming to the conversation. I read articles by the conservatives and listened to their radio talk shows—and I got riled up by what they said. I reacted with anger, frustration, and rejection of who they

(*continued*)

were. I thought silent counterarguments and felt the rise of adrenaline. Friends warned me to be careful—some couldn't even imagine going to talk with such people. The dialogic side of me was despairing. I doubted I was up to the challenge. I knew I should set aside my reactions and try to see these conservatives as people, but the task seemed daunting. I was anxious, determined to work hard to be open, and half expected the whole effort to be a disaster.

So what happened? I had a remarkable time. Right at the start, in small mixed breakout groups, we explored what the United States meant to us when we were 12 years old—and now. We told each other what we cherished about the United States. I told my story of growing up in a progressive, activist family that sided with socialist revolutions and learned all the bad things the United States did in the world—and yet how I still held on to the dream that our country had a major, positive role to play in the world, a powerfully positive myth to live out for the benefit of all humanity.

We explored our experiences of political difference. I heard a conservative's story of speaking out in a public forum as a college student. A radical progressive student had responded, "When the revolution succeeds, your kind will be the first to be shot!" The audience had cheered the radical, and this man had never forgotten that. I could understand why. We went on to explore the psychological and tribal dynamics of polarization, and what was lost and gained by seeing others as the enemy and by feeling certain we were right (subjects about which I will write more soon). We came to a place where we didn't want to use those labels at all. We were searching for some other ways to relate that had more positive possibility in them.

Lessons

Perhaps my biggest insight was that if we stepped out of the liberal/conservative, Left/Right dichotomies, we would find ourselves individually very different and usefully unique in our perspectives, with vast areas of workable common ground. The great political dichotomies present us with artificially polarized—and polarizing—differences and little common ground. They lead us to gather together in our tribes, preparing for war and totally losing sight of our actual differences (as unique individuals), our many similarities (offering many diverse possibilities for alliances) and our real common ground (as human beings with universal needs, living in communities, nations, and a struggling world that require our shared attention).

I see my challenge now as nurturing an open curiosity, with less fear, judgment and preconceptions when engaging with those I see as conservative, as well as with everyone else. If they are spokespeople for the Right—as several of the attendees at this meeting were—I now know that their public statements are called forth by the system we live in, as are the provocative statements of the progressive Left or Democratic partisans. I now expect that, on meeting them, I will probably find them different from whatever I may have concluded from their media persona and their Google results. Similarly, if they are ordinary people who happen to be conservative, then I'll likely find, if I really listen to them, that I agree with them more often than not—and even where I don't agree with them, I'll be able to understand where they're coming from, and be able to see their very real humanity under all their opinions. I may even come away wiser, with a more nuanced sense of the issues we discussed and what they really mean in the big picture. As Let's Talk America says, "What if what unites us is more than we realize, and what divides us is less than we fear?"

All that said, I'm not at the point of loving everyone. I realize there are extremists out there who would not tolerate real dialogue or consider recognizing the humanity and legitimacy of the other. But I also realize that such people exist on both sides and are often leaders in creating polarization for their own ends. In fact, extremists exist wherever differences have coalesced into sides and solidified into polarized stereotypes. They are a natural part of polarized systems. But the ideologues are seldom the majority—or even a sizable minority—of either side. Most people are not that unapproachably righteous and dehumanizing. However, the many people on all sides who could potentially hear each other can only show up as the complex, unique, diverse human beings they are, when they are provided with forums that support them in relating to each other across political divides in respectful, nonthreatening ways. Such forums are hard to come by in today's political culture. It is up to us to make them.

The Shift

In the end I experienced a deep, gut-level transformation. I had a profound personal shift away from Left/Right framings that was comparable to my earlier shifts away from sexism and homophobia. As with those other shifts, I still have impulses from my earlier state, but I don't believe in them anymore. I am quite convinced that the whole Left/Right frame is a trap, and that we are deeply embedded in it in ways that are crippling us. It is also clear to me that we have a long, hard slog ahead of us as we try to free ourselves from this worldview, because the deep psychological and tribal impulses driving it are extremely powerful.

(continued)

What personally struck me most, and with tremendous irony, was that I had bought into a frame of reference that prevents us from achieving true collective wisdom. I was indoctrinated into this framework by my culture, my family, and most groups I have been part of. I accepted Left and Right as real without realizing that, through my acceptance, I was collaborating with those who have conquered whole societies by dividing them using these simple, compelling ideological boxes. I enjoyed the benefits of righteous certainty and was able—even eager—to project blame onto others. I dehumanized the other (in my case, those called "conservatives") in ways that prevented me from engaging with them to discover their fuller humanity and their reasoned viewpoints and, perhaps worst of all, from seeing the systemic dynamics that were driving us apart so we couldn't even imagine working together.

Taking lessons from my brothers and sisters across the political spectrum, I can now say that my addiction to the Left/Right worldview is partly my own responsibility (the conservative view) and partly the responsibility of the social systems into which I was born and socialized (the liberal view).

Just as I have earlier had to face the fact that cigarettes were poisonous before I could stop smoking, I now believe that the Left/Right model is most significantly a source of poison, rather than a source of wisdom, pleasure, or power. I believe it is poisoning my own thinking and poisoning us all. Standing in the remnants of my Left perspective, I now suspect that the Left/Right paradigm is killing us far more effectively than the Right ever could. I would hope that some of my colleagues on the Right feel similarly that the Left/Right paradigm is more destructive than the Left. In any case, I personally want to free myself from that poisonous frame of reference so I can better do my work for the world.

So I am done with that. I will dedicate my life to changing the social structures that uphold that polarized way of seeing the world. I will promote and support well-facilitated opportunities to encounter others in creative, loving, intelligent ways that empower us all to take back our future and make it our own, together. I'm not sure anything short of that will save us from the shadows we fear and free us into more inclusive ways of thinking and living that are filled to overflowing with possibilities.

Green Tax Shifts as a More Immediate Solution

Because the full-blown creation of trusts to solve all of our environmental issues will take several decades, especially ambitious international trusts such as the Sky Trust, it will be appropriate to simultaneously work on parallel policy tracks that may have a more immediate impact. Tax policy is the most important such track: in addition to the Green Scissors campaign, mentioned above, a Green tax shift would help jump-start a bright green future for all now.

It is important to understand that the concept of a tax shift is revenue neutral or could even be combined with an effective tax cut (think transpartisan effectiveness); there would have to be guarantees that the result of the shift was not higher net tax revenues. The general strategy of such taxes is to reduce or eliminate taxes on income and wealth creation on the one hand, while simultaneously increasing or imposing taxes on the use of natural resources.

If we had a Sky Trust, it would charge an appropriate fee for carbon emissions such that each time we filled up our gas tank, ate food shipped from overseas, or flew on a vacation, the environmental costs of our activity would be included in the normal prices that we paid for goods. Since we don't, and aren't likely to for several decades, an immediate solution within particular nations is to shift the tax burden from existing tax sources to a carbon tax.

For instance, Al Gore has proposed eliminating all payroll taxes and instituting a tax on carbon that would bring in the same amount of revenue. The fact that he proposed a trade, rather than simply proposing an additional tax, is crucial. Better yet, he wisely identified a tax that is known as "the worst tax" because it hits the poor the hardest.[*] If such a tax shift were gradually implemented, gradually millions of businesses and hundreds of millions of people would face a very different set of daily decisions. On the one hand, business and the economy would benefit: Payroll taxes make it costly for businesses to hire workers, typically adding 30 to 40 percent onto the cost of every worker hired. With their existing budgets, they could add significantly more people to their workforces. The nationwide demand for labor would increase average salaries across the board and decrease unemployment. As employees became more valuable, more companies would invest

---

[*]Payroll taxes have been described as "the worst tax" because they especially hurt the poor directly while indirectly hurting the poor by means of slowing economic growth. See "The Worst Tax: How Payroll Taxes Have Hurt America's Working Class," *Washington Monthly*, July–August 1997, http://findarticles .com/p/articles/mi_m1316/is_n7_v29/ai_19596307.

more in training and in workplace amenities. Most Americans would benefit profoundly in their day-to-day life.

At the same time, millions of businesses and hundreds of millions of people would have to make very different decisions about heating and cooling their homes, about travel plans, about which vehicles they purchased, and ultimately where they chose to live relative to their jobs. The vast majority of ordinary people and ordinary businesses make the vast majority of their decisions based on their personal financial planning: Can I afford to buy a new car? Can I afford that new house? And so on. With higher energy costs, an entire range of energy saving procedures and devices that, at present, are only purchased by zealous green consumers would suddenly be purchased by millions of ordinary Americans.

Those green entrepreneurs who are currently barely succeeding due to the fact that their market consists only of a tiny market of green consumers would suddenly find the demand for their product exploding. Demand for wind energy would increase dramatically. GE, the largest producer of wind turbines, may find its stock price increasing, demand for electric and hybrid cars would increase, a market for low-carbon ethanol and other biofuels would become big business, and so on.

Initially, many people might resist such a green tax shift, because of fear and because there are always losers in every change. It would have to be phased in gradually so that people could adapt. At first glance, there might be some economic analysts who would be critical of such a tax shift on the grounds that the increased energy costs might damage the economy more than the elimination of employment taxes would help the economy. But if the shift was phased in slowly, innovation would ensure that the shift was a net gain. Better yet, if the shift was accompanied by a transpartisan effort to eliminate harmful and unnecessary regulation and reduce the extent of government control over the economy, both the environment and the people could be better off in the end.

In addition to Gore's proposed green tax shift, exchanging payroll taxes for carbon taxes, there is a significant body of literature on increasing the tax on land, but not construction, in order to encourage more efficient land use. Sprawl is essentially a government-sponsored program via the mortgage interest deduction, which subsidizes large houses, and government highway construction, which subsidizes driving. With increased land taxes, the elimination of the mortgage interest deduction, and increased reliance on toll roads, we would begin to see a dramatically different pattern of urban and suburban development.*

The magnitude of these distortions is enormous: Mortgage interest absorbs about 7 percent of national income, represents a third of our annual debt, and is larger than the total value of private housing. Meanwhile, the assessed value of corporate real estate, due to depreciation schedules on buildings, is even more preposterous: In 1993 the Federal Reserve Bank discovered that all corporate land in the United States had a reported net value of negative $4 billion.† Just as timber companies and mohair producers conspire to keep their subsidies in the federal budget, so, too, do banks, real estate interests, and landowners conspire to ensure that their interests are favorably represented in the tax policy. Flat tax advocates believe that a flat tax would be more fair than our present system is because a complex tax structure, like a complex federal budget, multiplies the opportunities for special interests to get their way.

These massive, largely invisible subsidies lend credence to Mencken's cynical truism, "The whole aim of practical politics is to keep the populace alarmed—and thus clamorous to be led to safety—by menacing it with an endless series of hobgoblins, all of them imaginary." Just as magicians perform their tricks by misdirecting our eyes away from what is really happening, so, too, do politicians perform their tricks by misdirecting our attention to the current urgent issue of the day. A new generation of environmentalists is learning to keep its eyes focused where it matters and not where politicians want them to stay focused.

Discoveries such as the legalized distortions in real estate values mentioned previously have shifted the attention of many thoughtful environmentalists away from traditional activism and toward tax policy reform. For instance Jeffrey Smith, a Green Party founder, has since become a

---

*Jason Furman, President Barack Obama's economic advisor, to his credit endorsed George W. Bush's attempt to end the mortgage interest deduction. See Jason Furman, "End the Mortgage-Interest Deduction! Why the Left Should Embrace the Bush Tax Commission's Most Radical Proposal," *Slate*, Nov. 10, 2005., www.slate.com/id/2130017/.

†Fred Harrison, *The Losses of Nations: Deadweight Politics versus Public Rent Dividends*, 72–73.

Georgist libertarian (Henry George was a nineteenth century economist famous for advocating a land tax), focusing largely on land tax policy as the single most important means of reducing environmental damage.* Alan Durning, a former Worldwatch senior researcher and founder of Northwest Environment Watch, has produced excellent material on green tax shifts.† A complete green tax shift could completely eliminate all individual taxes and all corporate taxes, both of which undermine human effort and slow economic growth, while simultaneously guiding us toward an improved environmental stewardship.

Green Taxes—Highlights (From the Sightline Institute)

Taxes are the DNA of the economy: invisible, cryptic, and awesomely powerful. And unfortunately, the tax system penalizes many of the activities Northwesterners want more of—such as work, entrepreneurship, and investment, while encouraging activities that Northwesterners want less of—such as sprawl and the waste of resources.

Tax shifting—an innovation implemented in a dozen European countries—means reducing taxes on paychecks and profits and replacing the revenue, dollar for dollar, with taxes on pollution, resource consumption, sprawl, and traffic. Phased in over years, tax shifts actually boost prosperity and enhance environmental and human health at once.

Sightline Institute's 1998 book *Tax Shift*—available in a full-text download—is a comprehensive guide to the possibilities of tax shifting in the Northwest. Here are a few examples:

- Tax pollution, untax enterprise and work. Each year, Northwesterners send billions of pounds of harmful substances into the region's air, water, and land—many of these end up in living things. Pollution taxes could raise enough money to eliminate most business taxes. And the infrastructure for pollution taxes is already sturdy enough to begin a decades-long transition.

---

*There are many excellent sources for proposed green tax shifts. See www .progress.org/banneker/shift.html and www.progress.org/geonomy/ for some places to start.

†Alan Thein Durning and Yoram Bauman, *Tax Shift: How to Help the Economy, Improve the Environment, and Get the Tax Man Off Our Backs*, www.sightline .org/publications/books/tax-shift/tax/?searchterm=%22tax%20shift%22.

- Tax resource depletion, untax income. Governments could trim income and sales taxes and make up the difference in revenue from levies on water, hydropower, timber, and minerals—activities that cause a disproportionate share of ecological degradation. Washington, for example, whose reliance on sales tax makes its system highly regressive, could cut its state and local sales taxes by one-third if it taxed natural resource-depleting activities.
- Tax sprawl, untax buildings. In every northwest city, vacant lots and rundown, low-rise buildings promote urban decay and push people out to the suburbs. Shifting the property tax partially or entirely off buildings and onto land would create a powerful incentive for investment in city and town centers and adjacent neighborhoods—revitalizing downtowns and reducing sprawl.
- Tax congestion, untax commerce. Governments build roads, but then don't charge drivers for their use. Lacking any price mechanism, urban drivers pay for road use with their time, by waiting in traffic. The solution? Transportation experts widely agree that "congestion pricing"—tolls that rise during rush hour—is the best answer.
- Spread clean technologies with "feebates." Feebates are point-of-purchase incentives that charge a fee for less efficient products and give a rebate for more efficient ones. Best of all, they create a snowball effect, systematically nudging the market toward cleaner designs.*

*Taken from Sightline Institute, Green Taxes, www.sightline.org/research/taxes.

The Unlimited Resource

The only unlimited resource is human initiative and imagination.* Therefore the most important thing not to tax, and not to limit without good cause, is our ability to create and innovate. No human being has any idea what transformations would take place in the economy if, say, gasoline were $10 per gallon due to a gradually increasing carbon tax. It could be that a low-carbon biofuel would be developed that

---

*See Julian Simon, *The Ultimate Resource*, Princeton University Press, 1983, for the original statement of human ingenuity as the ultimate resource.

completely eliminated our dependence on oil while having very little impact on our way of life. Or it could be that we would develop
entirely new building techniques, entirely new recreations, or entirely
new lifestyles. It could be that some aspects of our way of life might
change very little, whereas other aspects, that right now seem trivial,
might change dramatically.

Everything we buy is produced through a long chain of decisions
involving the cost of energy, but even this information does not allow
us to predict how life would be different if energy costs changed. At
any point in that long chain there could be innovations in production,
design, relative cost of inputs, or other areas that could lead to either
an increase or a decrease in the final cost of a product. Current guesses
regarding what products and services are likely to be sustainable are
really just guesses. While in the short term, with modest changes in
energy costs such guesses may have some validity, in the longer term
with larger changes in energy costs, no one knows.

For this reason as well, it is important that proposed changes be
based on "taxing harms" rather than "subsidizing goods." As we saw in
the previous discussion, a subsidy for an alternative fuel today is likely
to survive for many decades, regardless of whether that particular alternative fuel is actually an improvement on our present fuel system. This
is why the existing ethanol subsidies, really farmer and agribusiness
subsidies, rightly make many people very uncomfortable. There is every
reason to believe that corn growers and agribusinesses will promote the
idea of ever increasing subsidies in perpetuity despite the inefficiencies
of corn ethanol.

In the meantime, it is important for the sustainability movement to
support the movement toward green innovation. Worldchanging.com,
leading innovators of the concept of a bright green future through
innovation, recently published a book, also titled *Worldchanging*, that
includes 600 pages of "bright green" innovations. Its web site offers
extraordinary access to many thousands more examples. In the language of Alex Nicolai Steffen, Worldchanging's founder:

> With climate change hard upon us, a new green movement
> is taking shape, one that embraces environmentalism's con-
> cerns but rejects its worn-out answers. Technology can be a

font of endlessly creative solutions. Business can be a vehicle for change. Prosperity can help us build the kind of world we want. Scientific exploration, innovative design, and cultural evolution are the most powerful tools we have. Entrepreneurial zeal and market forces, guided by sustainable policies, can propel the world into a bright green future.

"The Next Green Revolution," *Wired Magazine,* May 2006, www.wired.com/wired/archive/14.05/green.html

Steffen is correct. Entrepreneurial zeal and market forces, guided by sustainable policies, can propel the world into a bright green future. Al Gore gets this:

Free market capitalist economics is arguably the most powerful tool ever used by civilization. As the world's leading exemplar of free market economics, the U.S. has a special obligation to discover effective ways of using the power of market forces to help save the environment.

Al Gore, *Earth in the Balance,* Houghton Mifflin, 2000, 182

In the short run, we need a transpartisan consensus to create a successful Green Scissors campaign, so we quit using taxpayers' money to destroy the environment. This will shift prices slightly toward a more sustainable future.

In the medium run, we need a green tax shift that will more completely align day-to-day decision making for all with environmental sustainability while simultaneously liberating the economy from harmful taxes. This, too, can be based on a transpartisan consensus by means of a forthright appeal to reduce or eliminate taxes on work, effort, and investment.

And as we are working on these provisional approaches, we also need to begin working on a long, steady movement toward lasting property rights solutions to environmental problems, including either privatization or environmental trusts for all land, water, air, and habitats that we want, or need, to preserve. Once these private solutions have been established and government is no longer involved in managing environmental assets, we will then have created a permanent foundation for a bright green sustainable future for all.

The Role of Trusts

When we think of capitalist institutions, the one that immediately comes to mind is the corporation. But there is another institution that is as old and as firmly established as the corporation, and that is the trust.

The essence of a trust is a fiduciary relationship, that is, one that is based on the beneficiary's confidence in the trustee. A trustee holds and manages property for another person or for many other people. A simple example is a trust established by a grandmother so that her grandchildren will have money to go to college. She then appoints a trustee, a bank for example, which by law has a fiduciary responsibility to manage the assets on behalf of the beneficiaries and to assure that the trust's purpose is achieved. Other trusts include pension funds, charitable foundations, and university endowments.

The rules of trust management, which are defined by state statutes and by centuries of case law, include the following:

- Managers must act with undivided loyalty to beneficiaries. If a manager fails this obligation, he can be removed and penalized.
- In most cases, managers must preserve the principal. It is acceptable to spend income, but it is not acceptable to invade the corpus.
- If the beneficiaries of a trust span many generations, the trustee may not favor one generation over another.
- Managers must assure transparency. Information about money flows must be readily available to beneficiaries.

These rules are enforceable by the courts. The basic mechanism is that an aggrieved beneficiary can bring suit against a trustee, and the trustee must then prove that he acted prudently to carry out the mandate of the trust. This is in contrast to the state: The government can give away whatever it wants with impunity. There is no legal recourse, except on rare occasions; the politicians have a free hand.

If we were to design an institution to protect pieces of the commons, we couldn't do much better than a trust. The goal of commons management, after all, is to preserve assets and deliver benefits to broad classes of beneficiaries. That is what trusts accomplish.

What, then, can we say about the state's capacity to serve as a commons trustee? In theory, the state represents all citizens equally and should be able to protect our common assets. But in reality, the track record of the state as trustee of the commons has been far from exemplary. There are at least five reasons for this:

1. The elected officials who run the state do not have a long-term perspective. Just as corporate leaders are focused on the next quarterly statement, political leaders are focused on the next election. They like to please constituents here and now, not worry about future generations.

2. Elected officials, alas, need money to get reelected. It is tempting to trade common assets for private campaign contributions.

3. Elected officials are not accountable to beneficiaries in the same way private trustees are. They can give assets away with virtual impunity whereas private trustees, because of their fiduciary responsibility, cannot.

4. The state and its leaders have many other things to do besides manage common assets. It's easy for this task to get neglected.

5. The state's finances are huge and complex. All sorts of funds are commingled. It's extremely difficult for the public to track money from common assets or to ascertain whether these assets are being well managed.

From Peter Barnes, "Capitalism, the Commons, and Divine Right" (The E. F. Schumacher Society, Great Barrington, MA, 2003), an essay originally presented as the "Twenty-Third Annual E. F. Schumacher Lecture," as edited by Hildegarde Hannum, full essay available at www.schumachersociety.org/publications/barnes_03.html.

Chapter 9

Eliminate Global Poverty

Michael Strong
CEO And Chief Visionary Officer, FLOW

The entrepreneur is essentially a visualizer and an actualizer. . . . He can visualize something, and when he visualizes it he sees exactly how to make it happen.

—ROBERT L. SCHWARTZ

Whenever entrepreneurs have had access to The Entrepreneur's Toolkit:

- Secure and well-defined property rights
- Freedom of contract
- Timely, fair, and reliable enforcement of contracts

they have created wealth by means of transforming undervalued assets into valuable goods and services, and thereby moved societies from poverty to wealth. The Toolkit allows entrepreneurs to transform personal vision into real societal value.*

In order to make plans for the future—and entrepreneurship is all about making plans for the future—it is necessary to know what one can control, thus the need for property rights; it is necessary to be free to create, thus freedom of contract; and it is necessary to know that business relationships will be adjudicated fairly and promptly, thus the importance of contract enforcement. The Entrepreneur's Toolkit is as necessary to the entrepreneurial creativity of entrepreneurs as are canvas, paint, and palette to a painter, or pen and paper are to a writer. Without the Toolkit, entrepreneurs only have their own labor. With the Toolkit, they can design and create a better world through enterprise creation.

The importance of the Entrepreneur's Toolkit was well known to classical liberal thinkers. For instance, consider William Graham Sumner in the nineteenth century:

> Some men have been found to denounce and deride the modern system—what they call the capitalist system. The modern system is based on liberty, on contract, and on private property.
> Sumner, William Graham. *What Social Classes Owe to Each Other* (New York: Harper & Brothers, 1883), 64

This perspective was rejected or ignored throughout most of the twentieth century, not only by Marxists, who explicitly wanted to abolish private property, but also by neoclassical economists, whose models pretended that entrepreneurs and legal institutions were irrelevant or didn't exist. The Solow growth model, the dominant approach to analyzing economic growth for the second half of the twentieth century, assumed that the savings rate, population, and technological change were the only relevant variables that determined growth. As a consequence, as former colonies became independent nations in the 1950s and 1960s, almost all of them either became Marxist and remained poor, or they attempted to implement some type of policy based on a neoclassical growth model, without considering legal institutions and the importance of economic freedom, and remained poor. Sumner

---

*See Richard Epstein, *Simple Rules for a Complex World*, for a more comprehensive statement of the set of legal rules needed for a contemporary commercial society.

understood The Entrepreneur's Toolkit. For most of the twentieth century Solow, Samuelson, and other leading mainstream economists did not (Mises and Hayek did throughout).

Only now are economists beginning to rediscover the importance of free institutions. Compare, for example, Sumner's description of key institutional elements with that from Elhanan Helpman's recent survey *The Mystery of Economic Growth*, which reaches a similar conclusion to that of Sumner, after he has spent 141 pages summarizing the current state of academic debate on economic development:

> Although it has been established that property rights institutions, the rule of law, and constraints on the executive are important for growth, the exact ways in which they affect income per capita are not well understood.

Cautiously, hesitantly, after 120 years during which academic opinion had almost unanimously rejected, in Sumner's words, "the modern system . . . based on liberty, on contract, and on private property," we have come full circle.

If Sumner's clear statement of the Entrepreneur's Toolkit had consistently been considered expert opinion from 1883 onward, and successfully implemented in nations around the world, poverty could have been eliminated long ago. By 1883, Britain and the United States had become the first nations on earth with a steadily increasing standard of living for the working class, thanks to their recognition of the insights of Adam Smith in 1776. At no point had Adam Smith ever been proven wrong; nonetheless the world's intellectual leaders took us all on a hundred year detour through communism, Fabian socialism, and other deviations from sound classical liberal principles.

Israel Kirzner, one of the greatest twentieth century theorists of entrepreneurship, and Frederic Sautet note:

> In order to foster socially-beneficial entrepreneurial activity, policy makers must pay attention to the quality of institutions—especially as they impact profits. Institutions that enable individuals to exercise their creativity to the fullest extent possible, by allowing them to discover opportunities and to reap the gains they have discovered, will foster an entrepreneurial society. It is only in the context of well-defined and enforced property rights

that society can benefit from the fullness of entrepreneurial activity. Institutions should also include the freedom to contract over property rights and a limited interference from government with markets—especially regarding regulation and taxation.[*]

They then go on to endorse measures of economic freedom to judge the quality of the economic environment. Economic freedom is a measure of institutional quality that largely coincides with the extent to which a given society provides an adequate Entrepreneur's Toolkit.

In the 1980s, Michael Walker of the Fraser Institute gathered Nobel Laureates Milton Friedman, Gary Becker, and other prominent economists together to create a formal measure of economic freedom. The result was the Fraser Index of the Economic Freedom of the World, which today uses 38 distinct third-party, objective data sources to measure the economic freedom of most of the nations on earth (a few are not included due to lack of adequate data).[†] Fraser measures economic freedom using publicly available data in five categories:[‡]

1. Size of Government: Expenditures, Taxes, and Enterprises
2. Legal Structure and Security of Property Rights
3. Access to Sound Money
4. Freedom to Trade Internationally
5. Regulation of Credit, Labor, and Business

Such a formal measure of economic freedom is useful precisely because of the endless debates regarding free market economics. Instead of quibbling about whether this or that particular policy improved an

---

[*] See Israel M. Kirzner and Frederic Sautet, "The Nature and Role of Entrepreneurship in Markets: Implications for Policy" Mercatus Center Policy Primer No. 4, June 2006, for a clear analytical statement of this perspective, though it is implicit in Adam Smith.

[†] See Gwartney and Lawson, The Fraser Institute Economic Freedom of the World: 2006 Annual Report, available online at www.freetheworld.com

[‡] Because this index includes data going back to 1970 for some countries, and because it is based on publicly available data sources, the Fraser Index is more frequently used for scholarly research than is the better known Wall Street Journal/ Heritage Economic Freedom Index (though the two are highly correlated). As a consequence, there is a large and growing set of empirical evidence of the consequences of economic freedom on economic growth.

economy, the architects of the Fraser Economic Freedom Index strove to create an objective set of measurable criteria against which the overall levels of economic freedom within nations could be compared over time. While not a perfect measure by any means, it is useful to have such an objective set of criteria that roughly correspond to the extent to which nations make the Entrepreneur's Toolkit available to their people.

Are the Scandinavian Countries More Free Market than the United States?

Well, they weren't quite there in 2006, the latest year for which data are available, but they are far closer than is generally realized.

Of course, of the five categories in the Fraser Economic Freedom Index there is one in which, with the exception of Iceland, they score far below the United States: Size of Government:

Nation	Size of Government Score	Size of Government Rank
Denmark	4.39	123rd
Finland	5.03	110th
Iceland	6.94	51st
Norway	5.80	91st
Sweden	3.73	134th
United States	7.13	43rd

The issue of Size of Government is by far the greatest difference between Scandinavia and the United States. If one looks at the other four categories, however, it turns out that the Scandinavian average, 8.26, is almost exactly identical to the U.S. average, 8.27:

Nation	Legal System and Property Rights	Sound Money	Freedom to Trade Internationally	Regulation	Average
Denmark	8.96	9.36	7.77	8.44	8.63
Finland	9.01	9.52	7.43	7.77	8.43
Iceland	8.80	8.62	5.90	8.76	8.02
Norway	8.91	8.90	6.62	7.48	7.98
Sweden	8.41	9.61	7.72	7.26	8.25
Scandinavian Average	8.82	9.2	7.09	7.94	**8.26**
United States	7.58	9.66	7.53	8.31	**8.27**

(continued)

Indeed, all five score more highly than the United States on Legal System and Property Rights, Denmark and Sweden score more highly on Freedom to Trade Internationally, and Denmark and Iceland have less regulation than does the United States. Both Denmark and Finland's four subcategory average is higher than that of the United States and Sweden's, at 8.25, is almost identical to that of the United States at 8.27. Thus, while it may seem provocative to ask whether Scandinavia is more free market than the United States, it turns out to be not such a stretch.

How has this happened? Since 1980, all the Scandinavian nations have increased their levels of economic freedom whereas economic freedom increased in the United States until the year 2000, peaking after eight years of President Bill Clinton, and since then, after eight years of President George W. Bush, economic freedom has steadily decreased. Indeed, by 2006, the United States was less economically free than it was in 1980 when Ronald Reagan replaced Jimmy Carter:

Nation	1980 Economic Freedom Rating (Chain-Linked)	2006 Economic Freedom Rating (Chain-Linked)	Change
Denmark	6.52	7.85	1.33
Finland	6.90	7.71	.81
Iceland	5.36	7.76	2.40
Norway	6.13	7.45	1.32
Sweden	6.05	7.28	1.23
Scandinavian Average	6.19	7.61	**1.42**
United States	7.99	7.86	**−.13**

Based on this chain-linked version of the index (in which countries are compared in consistent categories from year to year), Denmark's economic freedom score (including Size of Government), 7.85, is now almost identical to that of the United States, 7.86. The overall Scandinavian average, even including Size of Government, is not far from that of the United States. If these trends continue, very shortly Scandinavia will, in fact, be more free market than the United States by this formal measure of economic freedom created by some of the world's most renowned "free market" economists.

Mass Wealth Creation, Leading to Mass Poverty Alleviation, by Means of Providing Broader Access to the Entrepreneur's Toolkit

Given economic freedom and The Entrepreneur's Toolkit, entrepreneurs will create wealth and eliminate mass poverty. This is a simple, reliable claim that should have been universally recognized from the time of Adam Smith.*

Gurcharan Das, the poverty guru from India has estimated that at rates of economic growth in India under socialism, it would have taken until 2300 for India to reach a U.S. standard of living. In the capitalist growth rates experienced by India after the economic liberalizations of the early 1990s, India is now expected to reach a U.S. standard of living around 2050. Only economic freedom, by accelerating economic growth, has the power to bring more than a billion people out of poverty 250 years faster than would otherwise have occurred.

In the past 40 years, Hong Kong and Singapore have gone from poor to rich by means of economic freedom. It is worth recalling that in 1960 they were both poorer than most African nations, and now Hong Kong has one of the highest GDPs per capita in the world, exceeding that of both Switzerland and the United Kingdom. Singapore's is now higher than that of Germany and Japan. In the last 20 years, Ireland and Estonia have gone from poor to rich by means of economic freedom; in 1990, Ireland was the second poorest country in the EU, and now it is the wealthiest.† In 1992, after the collapse of the Soviet Union, Estonia's GDP per capita was 30 percent of the EU average; it is now 65 percent of the EU average and converging

---

*Elements of this chapter were taken from an earlier unpublished paper cowritten by myself and Theodore Malloch.

†For the case of Ireland, see Benjamin Powell, "Economic Freedom and Growth: The Case of the Celtic Tiger," *The Cato Journal*, Winter 2003. For the case of Estonia, see Mart Laar, "The Estonian Economic Miracle," Heritage Foundation Backgrounder #2060, August 7, 2007, www.heritage.org/Research/WorldwideFreedom/bg2060.cfm.

fast. Any nation on earth could become wealthy by means of increasing economic freedom to Hong Kong levels.

Jeffrey Sachs, in *The End of Poverty*, ridicules the notion that economic freedom alleviates poverty by pointing out that there is no correlation between *levels* of economic freedom, on the one hand, and economic growth, on the other.[*] It is unfortunate that this is the extent to which he takes note of the literature on economic freedom, because there are two powerful correlations that he ignores altogether.

There are two key findings from decades of formal study of economic freedom using the Fraser Index, both of which were ignored by Sachs:

1. Per capita GDP is highly correlated with economic freedom: Rich countries are free, poor ones are not.
2. An increase in economic freedom correlates with increased rates of economic growth.[†]

The result: Any nation that continues to increase its Fraser ranking over a 20-year period will almost certainly experience increased economic growth. The surest way to achieve The End of Poverty is by means of increasing economic freedom around the world.

Figure 9.1 shows the correlation between per capita income and economic freedom. Few correlations in the social sciences are as clear-cut as is the correlation between economic freedom and prosperity.[‡]

The other correlation that Sachs ignores is that increases in economic freedom are correlated with economic growth. According

---

[*]Jeffrey Sachs, *The End of Poverty*, (New York: The Penguin Group, 2005), 318–320.

[†]For a review of the literature on economic freedom from a skeptical European perspective that nonetheless concedes the evidence that economic freedom increases rates of economic growth, see Jakob de Haan, Susanna Lundstrom, and Jan-Egbert Sturm, "Market oriented institutions and policies and economic growth: A critical survey," Thurgauer Wirtshaftsinstitut Research Paper Series No. 5, March 2005. See also Gwartney, Holcombe, and Lawson, "Institutions and the Impact of Investment on Growth," *Kyklos* May 2006, vol. 59 Issue 2: 255–273.

[‡]See James Gwartney and Robert Lawson, with William Easterly, *Economic Freedom of the World: 2006 Annual Report*, 33.

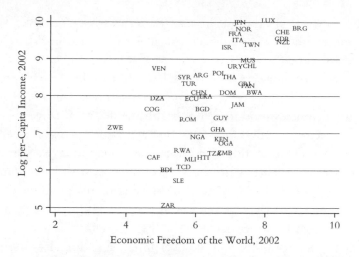

Figure 9.1 Economic Freedom of the World (2002) and Log per Capita Income
SOURCE: From William Easterly, "Freedom vs. Collectivism in Foreign Aid," taken from James
Gwartney and Robert Lawson, with William Easterly, *Economic Freedom of the World: 2006 Annual
Report*, reprinted with permission of The Fraser Institute.

to several estimates, a one point increase in economic freedom on the
Fraser Institute rankings, results in 1 percent or greater increase in rates
of economic growth.[*]

While economic freedom rankings are often perceived as political, due to more than a century of anticapitalist attacks on market-ori-
ented economists, if we look closely at empirical data, the controversy
dissolves. The Fraser Institute Economic Freedom of the World Index
reveals that the so-called socialist economies of Scandinavia actually have
more economic freedom than do any developing world nation. In short,
if every poor country were as free market as Scandinavia, there would
be no more poverty on earth. On this index, with Hong Kong in 1st
place, Iceland is 12th, Finland is 14th, and Denmark is 13th (the United
States ties for 8th with Australia). Bangladesh is 108th.[†] To simplify

---

[*] de Haan, Lundstrom, and Sturm, op. cit.

[†] This and all rankings are taken from James Gwartney and Robert Lawson, with
Seth Norton, *Economic Freedom of the World: 2008 Annual Report*.

exposition, we will continue to use Bangladesh for comparisons, but other poor nations, including almost all African nations, share similar characteristics.

Sweden and Norway have somewhat lower rankings, 23rd and 33rd, respectively, in large part due to their large governments. Relatively free market policies produced the wealth needed to finance these welfare states; between 1870 and 1950 Sweden had the highest per capita GNP growth in the world, with government spending relative to GDP per capita lower than that in the U.S. Only after Sweden became one of the wealthiest nations on earth did government spending increase.[*] Moreover, even in Scandinavia, growth in government peaked in the 1970s, and it has become increasingly free market ever since.[†]

Quite aside from the level of government spending, it is more helpful to regard Scandinavia as "free market welfare states" than socialist. Sweden regulates business less than almost all other nations on earth; it is ranked 10th in level of business regulation whereas the United States is ranked 25th. Bangladesh is 112th. (Iceland is first in the world; Finland is second, each with less business regulation than Hong Kong). With respect to credit market regulation, the United States is ranked 23rd and Finland 10th. Bangladesh is 107th.

These abstract economic freedom ratings have very concrete real world consequences. The Peruvian economist Hernando de Soto and his team have worked in dozens of poor countries estimating how long it takes to open up a legal business.[‡] They have discovered that in poor nations it takes between one and two years, working full-time going from government office to government office, in order to open up a legal business.

Only elites can afford to go through these costly and labyrinthine procedures—or, more likely, to bribe officials so that they don't

---

[*] See Stefan Karlsson, "The Sweden Myth," posted at The Mises Institute, Aug. 7, 2006, and Johan Norberg, "Swede and Sour," Tech Central Station, June 10, 2002.

[†] See historical rankings from James Gwartney and Robert Lawson, with Seth Norton, *Economic Freedom of the World: 2008 Annual Report*.

[‡] Hernando De Soto, *The Mystery of Capital: Why Capitalism Triumphs in the West and Fails Everywhere Else* (New York: Basic Books, 2000).

have to submit to such nonsense. Indeed, overregulation is a primary cause of developing world corruption. The consequence of such overregulation is that when the poor do become entrepreneurs, they have no property rights, no secure contracts, and no insurance, none of the standard protections that every businessperson in the developed world takes for granted. Their opportunities as businesspeople are severely constrained by the absence of an accessible legal system.[*] One recent study estimates that moving from the lowest quartile of business regulations to the highest quartile implies a 2.3 percentage point increase in annual economic growth—depending on the size of the nation; this translates into millions, tens of millions, or hundreds of millions of additional people being brought out of poverty each year.[†]

Secure property rights have long been recognized as a cornerstone of free enterprise. De Soto has also documented how the poor throughout the world also do not have access to governmental protection of their property rights. Again, this is in sharp contrast to Scandinavia, where Finland provides the most secure property rights in the world, Denmark ranks 2nd, and Norway 3rd. On this measure, Bangladesh ranks 131st. The wealthy nations all share secure property rights, rule of law, sound money, relatively unregulated economies and free trade. The poor nations, for the most part, do not have these economic freedoms.

The Fraser Institute 2006 Economic Freedom of the World Report presents numerous positive correlations between economic freedom and other desirable outcomes such as those shown in Figure 9.2.

---

[*] The World Bank Private Sector Development web site has an entire section devoted to papers researching various dimensions of this issue, http://rru.world-bank.org/PapersLinks/Reducing-Administrative-Regulatory-Barriers/. See also the World Bank "Doing Business" rankings and web site, www.doingbusiness.org/.

[†] Simeon Djankov, Caralee McLiesha, and Rita Maria, "Regulation and Growth," World Bank, available online 24 July 2006, http://papers.ssrn.com/sol3/papers.cfm?abstract_id=893321.

Economic Freedom and Access to Improved Water Sources

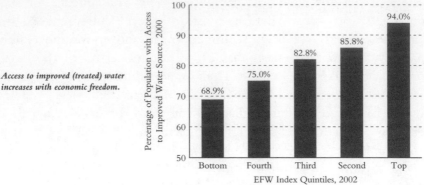

Access to improved (treated) water increases with economic freedom.

Economic Freedom and Human Development

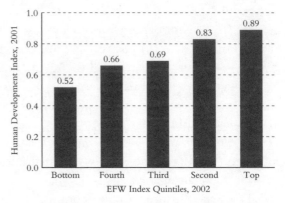

More economic freedom is related to greater "human development" as measured by the United Nations.

Note: The United Nations' Human Development Index is measured on a scale from zero to one: zero = least developed; one = most developed.

Economic Freedom and Corruption

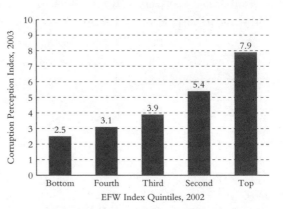

With fewer regulations, taxes, and tariffs, economic freedom reduces the opportunities for corruption on the part of public officials.

Note: Corruption is measured on a scale from zero to 10: 10 = little or no corruption; zero = highly corrupt.

Figure 9.2   The Positive Impact of Economic Freedom
SOURCE: James Gwartney and Robert Lawson, with Erik Gartzke, Economic Freedom of the World Report, 2005, The Fraser Institute, compiled from the sources listed, available on-line at www.freetheworld.com/2005/Chapter_1.pdf. Reprinted with permission from the Fraser Institute.

Preserving Democracy and Preventing Civil War through Economic Freedom

Political scientist Adam Przeworski has studied the relationship of per capita income and the stability of democracies:

> There is no doubt that the probability that a democracy survives increases with per capita income. You can control it for everything from the kitchen sink to the grandmother's attic. That relationship will survive anything. It's monotonic, and it's strong, unbelievably strong.
>
> Adam Przeworski, "Capitalism, Democracy, and Science,"
> Interview with Adam Przeworski by Gerardo L. Munck,
> February 24, 2003 (www.nyu.edu/gsas/dept/politics/faculty/
> przeworski/przeworski_munck.pdf), 17

And as we've shown, the evidence is likewise strong that increasing economic freedom is the most effective means of increasing GDP per capita.

In much of the developing world, civil wars remain an all-too-common reality. Approximately as many people have died in African wars in the past 50 years as in all other wars around the world, and most of those have been civil wars or cross-border conflicts that were stimulated or exacerbated by civil wars. Most fatalities from armed conflicts are now civilians in civil wars:

> In the modern civil war the composition of victims differs radically from the wars of the early 20th century, in that the impact has shifted from military personnel to civilians. At the beginning of the 20th century about 90 percent of the victims were soldiers, but by the 1990s nearly 90 percent of the casualties resulting from armed conflict were civilian (Cairns, Edmund, A Safer Future: Reducing the Human Cost of War, Oxford, U.K., Oxfarm Publication, 1997).
>
> Cited in Paul Collier, Lani Elliott, Havard Hegre, Anke Hoeffler,
> Marta Reynal-Querol, and Nicholas Sambanis, Breaking the
> Conflict Trap: Civil War and Development, A World Bank Policy
> Research Report, 2003 (http://indh.pnud.org
> .co/files/rec/Conflictrap.pdf), 17

Independent research by Marta Reynal-Querol and Simeon Djankov shows that secure property rights and rule of law, measures of which are included in the Fraser

(continued)

Economic Freedom Index, are more important determinants of whether or not a country will collapse into civil war than is GDP per capita itself.[*] In their words,

> Our results indicate that institutions, proxied by the protection of property rights, rule of law and the efficiency of the legal system, are a fundamental cause of civil war. In particular, an improvement in institutions from the median value in the sample to the 75th percentile is associated with a 38 percentage points' reduction in the incidence of civil wars. Moreover, once institutions are included as explaining civil wars, income does not have any effect on civil war, either directly or indirectly.
>
> Simeon Djankov and Marta Reynal-Querol,
> "The Causes of Civil War," World Bank Policy
> Research Working Paper No. 4254

These dry statistics, of course, reflect a life-or-death difference for millions of human beings. The Entrepreneur's Toolkit is not only about alleviating poverty, it is about creating peace. Finally, the political scientist, Erik Gartzke has found that economic freedom, as measured by the Fraser Economic Freedom Index, is 50 times more effective than is democracy at reducing violent conflict.[†] A world in which all countries on earth had as much economic freedom as Scandinavia might well be a completely peaceful world, or very nearly so.

---

[*] Simeon Djankov and Marta Reynal-Querol, "The Causes of Civil War," World Bank Policy Research Working Paper No. 4254.

[†] See "Executive Summary," Economic Freedom of the World: 2005 Annual Report, Fraser Institute, www.freetheworld.com/2005/Executive_Summary.pdf, and also Erik Gartzke, "Economic Freedom and Peace," Economic Freedom of the World: 2005 Annual Report, Fraser Institute, www.freetheworld.com/2005/Chapter_2.pdf.

Economic Freedom as the Means of Economic Development

The economist Miles Cahill, in an article titled "Is the Human Development Index Redundant?," has shown that GDP per capita is statistically indistinguishable from the U.N.'s Human Development Index (HDI) due to the fact that the other metrics included in the HDI, life expectancy at birth and education, are so highly correlated with GDP per capita.[*]

Increased GDP per capita results in improved human development. The only way to increase GDP per capita is through economic growth. As Michael Spence, chair of the U.N. Commission on Growth and Development puts it,

> We chose to focus on growth because we think that it is a necessary condition for the achievement of a wide range of objectives that people and societies care about. One of them is obviously poverty reduction, but there are even deeper ones. Health, productive employment, the opportunity to be creative, all kinds of things that really matter to people seem to depend heavily on the availability of resources and income, so that they don't spend most of their time desperately trying to keep their families alive.
> www.growthcommission.org/index.php?option=com_
> content&task=view&id=96&Itemid=169

There is no charity or NGO on earth that can raise a billion people out of poverty. This is why Nobel Laureate Robert Lucas said, "Once you start thinking about economic growth, it becomes hard to think about anything else." From this perspective, increasing economic growth becomes the ultimate form of charity.

Economists talk about the "demographic transition," the move from large families to small ones. Around the world, every single nation that has experienced sustained economic growth has seen a dramatic collapse in family size. As economist Brad DeLong points out,

> In a poorer country the average level of education is low, and children can be put to work at a relatively early age, thus augmenting the production resources of the household. In a richer

---

[*] Miles Cahill, "Is the Human Development Index Redundant?," *Eastern Economic Journal*, vol. 31, No. 1, Winter 2005.

country the average level of education is high, and children are
a major drain on household cash flow for nearly two decades.

Bradford DeLong, "Cross-Country Variations in National
Economic Growth Rates: The Role of 'Technology.'"
Prepared for the Federal Reserve Bank of Boston
conference on Technology and Economic Growth,
June 5–7, 1996 (www.j-bradford-delong.net/econ_articles/
growth_and_technology/Role_of_Technology.html)

In developed nations, women now average two or fewer children. The transition from many children, used as resources to bring
income into the household, to few children, each of whom is a significant investment, takes place as women become more valuable as
income earners than as producers of children. This transition is also
associated with the move from rural life, where children are used as
labor, to urban life, where women work in factories. It must be said,
as even some Marxist feminists have admitted in Irene Tinker's *Persistent
Inequalities*, that multinational factory work often empowers women
relative to existing alternatives.

But the concentrated power of multinational corporate decision
making all too easily favors crony capitalism. We should promote
a Conscious Capitalism as much as possible that aspires to avoid
crony capitalism. But in addition, we want to promote an open society in which achievement is open to all. The best way that we can
do this is to remove the obstacles to entrepreneurial capitalism and
let millions of microentrepreneurs in the informal sector become
macroentrepreneurs in the formal sector (while also acknowledging
that perhaps only one out of a hundred, or one out of a thousand,
will succeed).

There is a robust case that increasing economic freedom is the *single* greatest means of increasing rates of economic growth, and thereby
increasing GDP per capita, improving human well-being by diverse
measures, improving gender equality, reducing corruption, decreasing violent conflict, and stabilizing democracies. Given a level playing
field, with few legal barriers to entry and appropriate protections for

the environmental commons, entrepreneurial capitalism rewards innovation, genuine service, and value creation.

In the absence of economic freedom, capitalism often degenerates into crony capitalism: a playing field in which the operations of capitalism are systematically biased in favor of the "good ol' boys," where organizations are rewarded in which highly connected individuals (closest to the power structure) reward their loyal friends, family, and fellow partisans with contracts. This is a system that rewards insularity, elitism, and exclusion.*

A pure version of either form has never existed; all existing forms of capitalism are some combination of the entrepreneurial ideal and the crony reality. But because the entrepreneurial ideal is humanity's best hope for widespread, sustained peace and prosperity, it is in the interest of all well-intentioned and socially conscious people to support and promote the entrepreneurial ideal. The promotion of economic freedom should therefore be a primary development goal, and the implementation of economic freedoms should be regarded as one of the highest acts of charity.

A Friendly Wager to Alleviate Global Poverty

In honor of Jeffrey Sachs' proposal that increased foreign aid is likely to eliminate poverty, as well as a claim he made in *Scientific American* that high taxes and large social welfare systems do not inhibit growth, I propose the following reputational bet.†

---

*See also Carl Schramm, Robert Litan, and William J. Baumol, *Good Capitalism, Bad Capitalism, and the Economics of Growth and Prosperity*, for a four-way analysis of types of capitalism; here I am emphasizing the virtues of entrepreneurial capitalism rather than oligarchic capitalism.

†For his claim that foreign aid will end poverty, see Jeffrey Sachs, *The End of Poverty*. For his claim that high taxes and large social welfare systems do not inhibit growth see, Jeffrey Sachs, "The Social Welfare State: Beyond Ideology," *Scientific American*, October 2006, www.sciam.com/article.cfm?id=the-social-welfare-state.

Wager: Let's compare three sets of 20 nations, 20 years from now:

Sachs 1: The 20 nations that have received the most government-to-government foreign aid as a percentage of per capita GDP.

Sachs 2: The 20 nations that have experienced the greatest percentage growth in government (as measured by the Fraser Index).

Easterly: The 20 nations that have experienced the greatest increases in economic freedom as measured by the Fraser Economic Freedom Index.*

I believe that the average GDP per capita increase will be greater among the countries in the Easterly proposal than among either Sachs 1 or Sachs 2. To avoid the ambiguity of outcome associated with a battle of regressions, I will exclude nations that qualify for one of the Sachs' alternatives as well as Easterly: Let's examine a mutually exclusive set of nations, one that exemplifies the characteristics required for economic growth as celebrated by Sachs, the other that exemplifies the characteristics required for economic growth as celebrated by Bill Easterly and others. To give Sachs unreasonably generous odds, I'll call it a win for him if either Sachs 1 or Sachs 2 beats Easterly.

Knowledge is power. The world needs to know the positive impact of economic freedom so that we may liberate the entrepreneurial energies of the world's five billion poorest so that they may make themselves wealthy.

---

*There are reasons to believe that specific subcategories of the EFW index are particularly important to development, especially "legal structure and security of property rights." I thus include as a requirement that the nations experience monotonically increasing scores on "legal structure and security of property rights" and that they each have achieved a minimum score of 5.0 10 years from now. Finally, we should exclude those nations in which more than 25 percent of GDP is due to the export of oil or another natural resource, because oil (or resource) price increases are likely to be the primary driver of growth rather than policy. If Sachs claims that he also accepts some modified version of EFW himself, then I will have achieved the goal of getting him to acknowledge the real state of knowledge concerning economic development. Until he does so, he should be regarded as the leading cause of poverty in 2025 for his failure to provide good advice, given his prominence.

Fair Trade Certified Women's Empowerment Free Zones?

Because of the importance of economic freedom, including secure property rights and rule of law to economic activity means that land that is located within legal systems that provide a world-class business environment is far more valuable than is land that is not. Normally the process of improving the business environment is a slow, irregular process. But by means of free zone designations that include a new legal system, land values can increase rapidly.

There is a growing body of significant, rarely acknowledged evidence that free zones—or special economic zones or free cities—are a proven means of economic liberalization and the creation of sound economic institutions.[*] Such zones have played a key role in the economic liberalization of Taiwan, South Korea, Mexico, Ireland, Mauritius, United Arab Emirates, and China. Hong Kong and Singapore, of course, are free cities that are essentially regime-wide free zones. Given this extraordinary track record in promoting economic growth, free zones should be receiving considerably more attention. They have recently been introduced as a means of increasing the liberalization of India, and diverse experiments with zones are taking place around the world. Although some zones are merely tax concessions, we are most interested in those zones whose design explicitly includes the creation of a world-class legal environment within zone boundaries, including a fast-track regulatory regime, secure property rights, and credible and transparent contract enforcement mechanisms.

There is reason to believe that free zones provide a unique means of untying the Gordian knot of developing states, as discussed in Douglas North's recent work.[†] North states that the stability of most developing countries is dependent on elite groups having a vested interest in limiting the access of most citizens to the formal

---

[*] Most of the information and the ideas contained herein have been taken from conversations with Robert Haywood, executive director of the World Economic Processing Zones Association (WEPZA), and Mark Frazier, CEO of OpenWorld, both of whom have been in the free zone industry for more than 30 years. The fundamental strategy here is Frazier's. See Michael Strong and Mark Frazier, "Creating an Effective Alliance Around Women's Empowerment Free Zones" for more detail (www.flowidealism.org/Downloads/WEFZ%20Coalition.pdf). Key development scholars, including William Easterly, have acknowledged that development economists have simply ignored the role of free zones in economic development.

[†] Douglass C. North, John Joseph Wallis, Steven B. Webb, and Barry R. Weingast, "Limited Access Orders in the Developing World: A New Approach to the Problems of Development" (September 1, 2007). Policy Research Working Paper No. 4359. Available at SSRN: http://ssrn.com/abstract=1015978.

(*continued*)

economy and the government having an interest in maintaining the support of the powerful elite and instituting obscure and exclusionary rules and regulations to protect the elite interests. General economic liberalization is seen as destabilizing by the government and the elite. Because a zone might be supported by a segment of the elite as a private business opportunity and may not be seen by the rest of the elite as threatening their privileges, zones allow for small scale, incremental increases in economic freedom. If designed correctly, they can not only encourage greater economic freedom in the zone but also throughout the hosting nation-state. Eventually they can lead to an increase in political and personal freedoms such as we have seen in Taiwan, South Korea, and Mexico where authoritarian governments were forced to yield control to political opposition through a relatively democratic and peaceful process.

Throughout the developing world, after a piece of land has been designated as a free zone with Singapore- or Hong Kong-class business climate improvements, the value of the land climbs between 500 percent and 3,000 percent or more. A plot of land that was worth $1 million at the outset can rise to between $5 million and $30 million in value following introduction of credible, world-class incentives and institutional practices. From $4 million to $29 million may be created in a short interval due to the increased confidence in a secure legal environment for business.

The amounts vary based on particulars of the situation, and it takes time for the higher values to be achieved; businesses must come to trust that a world-class business environment has been securely established before they begin competing to get into the free zone, the factor that drives up land prices. In the San Isidro free zone in the Dominican Republic, land values rose 2,000 percent after the land was freed of taxes, customs duties, and telecommunications monopolies. In Dubai and Freeport, Bahamas, property value increases have been on the order of 8,000 percent over the initial 12-year period following introduction of free zone incentives. In Shenzhen, China, the World Bank has noted that the country's pioneering Special Economic Zone has attracted four million immigrants and led to annual economic growth rates averaging 34 percent throughout its first 15 years of operation. This compounds to a parallel rise in property values of at least 12,000 percent.

Consider the implications of this process of near-instantaneous wealth creation: Advocates of foreign aid claim that for $160 billion per year we could eliminate poverty. Developed world governments then engage in extended arguments over who will pay how much. Moreover, as mentioned earlier, $160 billion per year in foreign aid would only eliminate poverty if policies in poor nations also changed. Indeed, there is evidence that unless foreign aid is very carefully invested, it can actually harm nations by supporting corrupt governments. Those of us who want to solve problems are frustrated by the endless political battles.

What if instead of lobbying governments to spend $160 billion per year in foreign aid, which may or may not do any good, we simply created $160 billion per year that went directly to local and regional women's and children's causes instead of into the hands of corrupt or ineffective governments by means of Women's Empowerment Free Zones?

Women's Empowerment Free Zones could be designed such that a portion of the land value gains from free zone designation would be channeled into community trusts chartered to benefit women and children. The best way to ensure lasting revenue streams for women's community trusts in a free zone project is to use a Build-Operate-Transfer (BOT) approach. BOT approaches have been successfully implemented in dozens of privately-financed, multibillion dollar infrastructure projects (including power plants, airports, toll roads) in emerging economies.

Under such BOT approaches, a free zone developer, who takes on most of the risk and initiative for making a business park or tech park a reality, starts with a 75 percent stake in the free zone in order to ensure adequate incentive to complete the legal process and build the infrastructure needed to attract business. The developer may be an experienced local organization, a multinational development firm, or an experienced free zone developer such as Dubai or Singapore. In addition, the governments that commit lands for the concession are also given a share in the free zone, say 15 percent, in order to provide an incentive for them to streamline and support the legal concession. This percentage may be complemented by a Singapore-inspired compensation strategy in which government employees are given bonuses in proportion to free zone economic growth to ensure they have an incentive to maintain a transparent business climate for firms of all sizes.

Phase I partners include the local business along with local and global educational institutions that organize a small "quick start" demonstration area. They can be vested in the overall venture (including expansion areas) and its success by means of a 5 percent stake. It is important that the initial free zone partners include high quality innovative educational partners that support entrepreneurial culture and rapid development of core skill sets rather than traditional educational partners alone.

The remaining 5 percent in this model is given immediately to women's community trusts designed to provide funding for women's credit organizations, domestic violence support, and vouchers for children's education and health care. A key

(*continued*)

element in the BOT design is for the percentage stake of the developer to stead-ily decrease over a 30-year period, and the percentage stake of the commu-nity trust to steadily increase. To preserve the quality of the zone, it is important to keep the developer, governments, and Phase I partners vested at some level, say 35 percent of the equity. But after 30 years, the community trust could be receiving income streams that represent 65 percent of the equity of the free zone.

Free zones also have a negative reputation as a haven for money laundering and sweatshop manufacturing. Some of this reputation is justified and some is not. But regardless of past history, in principle, one could design a free zone to be as socially responsible as one pleases (I've even suggested to TransFair, the leading U.S. Fair Trade certifier, that it certify Fair Trade free zones). The benefits of a legal regime that offers a robust Entrepreneur's Toolkit in no way implies that people are not treated well there. Even the most socially-minded entrepreneurs, even the pur-est Yunus social businesses, require the Entrepreneur's Toolkit in order to function efficiently, and most of the world is poor because such a business environment is not available at present.

Elements of this vision have become a reality; now it is time to integrate the pieces to create powerful changes that benefit all. ZonAmerica has proven that IT-based free zones can be as successful as manufacturing free zones have been, and the explosion of growth in tech and outsourcing will ensure that demand for world-class tech park free zones will continue to increase. Dubai and Singapore have proven that their free zone expertise can be transferred to other regions of the world.

One of the greatest challenges, of course, is to create confidence in the new legal environment. Dubai has used one of the most innovative approaches of all by hiring a British judge to apply British Common Law in one of their zones. Insofar as the quality of the legal system is one of the most important determinants of land values, by credibly implementing British Common Law within the boundaries of a zone, Dubai has created a new model for rapid wealth creation. In the past, many free zone developers have provided physical infrastructure, such as roads and ports. In the future, free zone developers will provide both physical and legal infrastruc-ture, identifying the legal systems that are most conducive to rapid wealth creation. In essence, they will become entrepreneurial creators who will discover new legal arrangements that will be even more effective than British Common Law.

In short, it is possible to envision a competitive global free zone industry with numerous suppliers of both physical and legal infrastructure bidding to improve both the physical and legal infrastructure of various nation-states. Because of the dramatic wealth creation possibilities inherent in such a vision, it is also possible to imagine that wealth creation being used to provide an ever-increasing safety net for the women and children of the world in perpetuity. Entrepreneurs creating Fair Trade Certified Women's Empowerment Free Zones could eliminate poverty and improve the lives of billions of women and children very rapidly by means of such an approach if they were allowed to do so.

Once one realizes that poor legal systems are the primary cause of poverty, and that a precedent exists for a nation to allow other legal systems to function within geographically limited areas of its borders, the next question becomes, "Why not let entrepreneurs eliminate global poverty quickly and in perpetuity for all?"

Chapter 10

Is Economic Freedom for Everyone?

Hernando de Soto
President, Instituto Libertad Y Democracia

You Americans began your revolution somewhere about 1811, creating the wider possibility of having business organizations— the first one was in New York—formed without authorization of government or Congress if it had to do with wool or with cotton or with other materials. Pennsylvania followed in 1836 and then Connecticut in 1837. In 1860, about 14 states had general incorporation acts, but it was only at the end of the nineteenth century that in the United States anybody could form a company and get people together in a productive enterprise.

We think that was absolutely crucial to the great U.S. economic success story: If you do not have companies—that is to say, the possibility

From a speech originally given by Hernando de Soto "Is Economic Freedom for Everyone?" delivered at The Heritage Foundation on September 29, 2006.

of associating people with different specialties that may not be part of your family—you're not going to be able to produce those 48,000 pins of Adam Smith. You're going to be forced to work within your family. So if you open up the market and there are enormous possibilities, but you're not given the legal tools to organize and cope with the information that comes from the market, the market's going to overwhelm you. This is what's happening today in developing countries and many former Soviet Union countries, where most people are not organized to create a complex organization that allows them to analyze this enormous amount of information the market produces and detect just what they need to build a product and then get it all together in one place—a legal company that now has the legal tools to grow productively and expand into wider markets beyond family and acquaintances.

We've also been looking at, for example, the history of the early French Libertarians since 1850, led by Charles Coquelin, who started saying, "Look at what the Americans have been doing. We've got to follow up." The main characteristic of the advent of the market is the downfall of the traditional patrimonial and feudal institutions, which were like a rope pulling us in one direction, the state and the people. We're now realizing that to be able to honor the division of labor, we don't need a rope but fine threads that unite us not to government, but to the rest of society. Those fine threads are legal instruments—such as contracts, property rights, and especially the means to create more productive business organizations.

By looking at the *Journal des Economistes*, the bastion of French liberal reform, the different acts and proposals that they brought out to make their case for reform, you see how much resistance they met in France where the argument against those who wanted free enterprise and everybody having the right to get into enterprise was: What you are in effect proposing is the creation of states in miniature. Government, these critics of legal reform argued, has got to be reserved for the public sector for which we can all vote. If you start giving the right to form little governments to little people, one day those governments will take over—probably not such a bad thing, but it seemed a terrible idea at that time.

This fight against little states is actually very much what we're facing in developing countries. The whole idea—careful of those multinationals, which my friend Jagdish Bhagwati calls the B-52s of globalization—is the fear of what people you didn't vote for are going to do to your life.

What was very important is that Coquelin managed, around 1863, to start creating the first laws to allow the French government to grant people the right to have a company simply by complying with formal requirements, bankruptcy laws, and so on. In Britain, where there was similar resistance to these small governments, it began with the Joint Stock Company Act in 1840, which was then perfected again with a Limited Liability Act in 1855 and then again the Joint Stock Company Act in 1856.

These liberal reformers started a major revolution that has not really reached developing countries. The proof of it for us is that the tendency of most people who are interested in helping developing countries like mine or those in Africa or Asia is to say, "But they're from different cultures. These guys aren't built for joint stock companies. They like being in tribes. That makes them feel warm and fuzzy." On the other hand, here's a market. It's like telling everybody you go out into outer space, but you don't have an encapsulated area where you can organize the information of outer space and convert energy into something that can actually be metabolized and allow you to grow.

So markets, yes. We Third Worlders decided that we believed in markets with the fall of the Berlin Wall. There are only about three countries in the world that would say "markets, no," and those would be North Korea, Zimbabwe, and Cuba. The Venezuelans are beginning to say something like that, but they're not quite there yet, and the Bolivians are beginning to say something like that, but they're not quite there yet, either.

The rest of us have got market economies, but we don't have the enterprises that allow people to organize different specialties to be able to deal with that swirling mass of information in the market. Most of the market produces information that is not reliable. The two sides of mankind are, on the one hand, we have enormous imagination, but the Janus-like side of that is that we also lie a lot.

If you think of all your laws in the United States, what are they mainly for? They're out there to find out whom you can trust. The moment I land in a U.S. airport, the first thing they try to find out is if I'm really de Soto. This guy goes out, checks all the things to find out if I'm really who I say I am. He wants to see the facts, and if the immigration people are not quite sure, I'll be put into a back room and checked again. Then, when I cease being confused with a bearded terrorist, I'm finally let out. I go and try to get a little cart to carry my luggage through customs, but I need a credit card, more documentary proof about de Soto—that he's really got the credit to get the cart. All the time, I'm being checked. Why? Because we human beings lie about ourselves, and if the authorities don't have a way of distinguishing the lies from the facts, all the information that's useless from what's essential, the system is not going to work.

And that happens not in the market; it happens in the enterprise.

What is crucial about that? In Latin America, we have enterprises. At the Institute for Liberty and Democracy (ILD), we started doing a very interesting study that began about nine months ago with the Inter-American Development Bank under its new president, Louis Alberto Marino, who said, "I believe in all these things that you people from the Institute for Liberty and Democracy are doing. Let's ask various Latin American countries whether they have what is crucial for the success of their enterprises; let's take 12 countries, going from Mexico down to Argentina, basically the west coast of Latin America, and let's find out how many people are actually working within companies, within business organizations, and let's find out if they've got all the legal tools that are required to move ahead."

What we learned in this recent study confirmed what we had been finding out in the Institute for Liberty and Democracy for more than 20 years: namely, that people all throughout our world are organized in business organizations. Most of these enterprises, however, are what we call the "extra-legal sector" or the "informal sector." (Some of those businesses are actually formal, which is why we prefer the term "extra-legal.")

The question then to be asked is: If Latin American democracies have been starting to give everybody the capsules or cells or warm little ponds within which to organize themselves, have we really given them all the qualities, all the instruments, all the legal devices that you in the rich nations have been fine-tuning over the last 120 years? Or are we giving them something different? So we made a list of questions.

The first question that we asked was: Why is it important to create companies? Coquelin used to call it a readaptation of social intelligence. Before, we got all our information from government and from feudal organizations. Now, by allowing society to disperse itself vis-à-vis this enormous market into different little entities that have to deal with that enormous amount of information outside, we are reorganizing social intelligence so that we're now going to learn from a variety of independent fields and will find ways of putting all that information together, which is what you do at Heritage. It's what you do in your U.S. think tanks. It's what intellectuals do.

And so the next question was: What are, therefore, those things that companies should have to become information-sensitive agents that allow entrepreneurs to filter information so that they can get what you need? The first thing that you need is an organization that is separate from your family. It doesn't mean that you can't own enterprises. Most enterprises in your country are probably family-owned. It just means that when you do business, you do it according to rules that are different from how you operate in your family.

In our countries, the Third World countries, the tendency of government has been to protect the family and say, "Just stay there. We're going to let your family buy and sell. We're going to call that a micro enterprise, or we're going to call it a social interest enterprise or an Aztec enterprise, an Inca enterprise, a Zulu enterprise. It's going to be there." But by doing so, by not creating the separate space, we have not encouraged the collection of correct information. We have created what Maturan and Valdez, two brilliant Chilean philosophers who worked at the Santa Fe Institute, would have called an "autopoietic institution." An autopoietic institution is an organization that is created to deal with the outside, that has a different hierarchical structure. What we have managed is simply to consolidate autopoietic institutions, which are essentially families taking care of their own survival needs, with hierarchies that have nothing to do with what you need to succeed in the market.

You go to a small little micro enterprise in Peru and say, "Who runs this place?" And a good-looking Peruvian with a big black mustache comes out and says, "I do." You know he's the head of the family. But you look over his shoulder and see his wife, who's a pretty imposing lady, and you realize that really she may be the one that runs the place. And if your eye roves to the other corner, you may find the mother-in-law who actually runs the whole thing. You don't really know. When you deal with a company in the United States, it's all determined by law: This is the CEO; this is the CFO. These are their responsibilities, and you know who's liable and who's accountable by law.

When you do not give these other organizations a separate rule, you have not created the first indispensable structure to be able to have something that is accountable to business, whose purpose is to make money and be profitable. You have also not created the vehicle that will allow your society to pass from uniquity to individuality, because the characteristic of all premarket societies is uniqueness. In other words, I may not be an individual, but in society, I know what I am. I'm a soldier, or I am a merchant. Or I am in the business of making shoes, and I belong to this guild. And I feel good because I know what my place in society is. I know who my king is, and I know who my leader is.

When markets came to the West, you had to destroy that order to create one based on meritocracy and individuals. You lost a lot of the comfort of belonging to a specific organization. You could now belong anywhere. You could be in The Heritage Foundation one day; and you could be tomorrow at Lazard Frères. You could be working at McDonald's. You're an individual. You can move around. And the thing that allows you to convert yourself from a unique person within a strict society where people feel good, where people don't need psychiatrists as much as individuals do, but where you can't move around as you can in the market—is an institution that is separate from the church, that is separate from the family, that is separate from the tribe, that is dedicated to business. If you don't have that, the transition from uniquity to individuality will be a very tough one, or so we at the ILD think.

The second thing you need is an identity that is not just your personal identity. When I go home to Arequipa, the Peruvian city where my family is from, most people recognize me because they say, "He's got the de Soto eyes but his mother's eyebrows." Identity is all about redundancy, cross-checking information. But when you get into the commercial world, you need another type of identity, and for that you need a separate structure.

You need to be able to describe your wealth in documents. You need to be able to divide stock into parts. You may be my brother, but I'm not going to give you more than 20 percent of the company because I thought 80 percent of it up, or I am using my collateral to fund it. You've got to be able to capture value in property documents that relate to stock. At the same time, if you're going to look for investment, you've got to be able to issue stock or shares. How else are you going to get investment? You've also got to be able to have property because we know that in the majority of cases, you're going to need property or the information about property to build a track record or use the property itself to collateralize the loan. Otherwise, how are you going to achieve the credibility that is necessary to get credit?

You need asset shielding. Why? Because if everybody supports you with capital, you've got to make sure that when you're dealing with an actual company, that nobody in the company has just decided to leave, taking with them all their assets. You've got to have those assets shielded and put into one place. You need to have capital locked in for that same reason. You need to have going concern value reflected. If I asked, "What's Heritage worth?" and somebody came around and said, "Well, let's see what the price of the American flag is, how much textile there is in that, how much there is in the seats, how many computers do they have,"—that isn't the value of Heritage. The value of Heritage is that plus all its knowledge, its capital, its goodwill, its capacity to influence the course of events in the United States and, therefore, history.

It's the same with a business corporation, but where are all these intangibles reflected? They're reflected in company documents. There's no other place. They're not in the air. They're in company documents, and that's where they get captured.

So, our question at the Inter-American Development Bank and as we went down the west coast of Latin America from Mexico to Argentina was how many Latin American companies have any of these qualities: the property rights, the asset shielding, the capacity to issue shares, and so on? And the reply is 8 percent. In other words, when we sign a free trade agreement with you or you sign it with anybody in the world, you are signing with 8 percent of the businesses in those countries. The other 92 percent are the people who don't understand how you get at that large swirling mass of the universe that people call the market, because they don't have the legal tools to get into the market or the identities or the contracts with which you can actually globalize.

The first thing you have to do if you are going to get into international trade is to fill in a bill of lading on an airway bill. You're going to have to fill in the first thing, which is your name. I'm going to say de Soto. What's your address? Well, what happens if most of us Latin Americans don't have official addresses? We can't even fill in the second line. It's a totally alien world. You can't do without the companies. And that means that in the field of research, which is where we're really at, we have forgotten how important it is to have instruments, legal instruments, to allow us to put things together. We've lost respect for those things.

There used to be a time when we knew that things which in and of themselves didn't look like they had much value but that held things together were extremely important. For example, as I was reading the other day, Thomas Jefferson wrote a letter to a friend who had asked what he was doing. He said, first of all, I've got various family responsibilities. In my family, to begin with, I am the nail maker. In those days, making nails was very important because that's what held the houses together. That's what held carriages together. We hadn't yet learned how to make nails by cutting wire, so nails had to be forged and they had to have a certain type of sharpness to put things together. They were so valuable, as a matter of fact, that the whole history of your conquest of the West is about people making log cabins, advancing a few miles or a couple hundred miles and then deciding to move further west—and then they would burn down the log cabin just to retrieve the nails.

Things that fasten and bind other things together are always very important things. And all those legal instruments I'm talking about are nails. Per se, they're not particularly dramatic, but they actually help you put things together. They may not give you the shape of things, but without them, you cannot put things together. And if you look around this room, there is not one thing here that has been built by one person. Everything has required thousands of persons.

There is this wonderful Leonard Read example of how many companies it actually takes to put together a simple pencil, which contains wood from Oregon, graphite from Sri Lanka that's wedded down with candellia wax from Mexico and sulphuric acid from France. All of that takes about 1,600 companies. Before you were able to put the wood together with the graphite, you had to get the owners or the people who are going to deliver these goods—their hopes, their beliefs, their promises, their statements—onto enforceable statements or that wasn't going to work. The law had to work, and that is essentially business law.

The question, then, would remain: Is the world ready for that? Maybe we have to have massive education programs for which, of course, there's no money, and everybody will tell you that is not what is happening. So we took with glee the opportunity given to us by former President Benjamin Mkapa of Tanzania, who approached us and said, "I believe in the things you're saying. I can see that what you're saying is true, but in my country all the books say we're run by tribes." So we organized in Tanzania a group of 975 Tanzanians to go out in the field and find out what was cooking, what was going on, and these are the things we found.

The first thing we found is that in every village we went into, when we tried to find out whom the land belonged to, we found that only 10 percent of the land is owned by tribes. Ninety percent is privately owned. What happened to the tribes? Somebody is going to have to study that. Was it when the Tanzanians created the republics in the 1960s, the politicians decided to do away with the tribes because they were a parallel structure and they didn't want any competition? I don't know. All I'm telling you is that I found that the tribes, which were mainly the shepherds, only owned about 10 percent of the land. Everything else was privately held.

What did they have? They had titles, very simple ones. And who created those titles? Adjudication committees. That's the way the Roman Empire started. Nobody began with property rights. What happened is that people wanted to avoid conflicts between themselves, and so there was an adjudication committee of elders that said, "all right, the Smiths own this, the Sullivans own that, the Daleys own this, the Valdezes own that." It was essentially a practical move to have peace so that everybody could collaborate. The rights come later when you legislate over adjudications that have already taken place.

In this country of $270 gross national product per capita, which is a very low gross national product per capita, as well as in Ethiopia where we're also beginning to work, which has $70 gross national product per capita, people are adjudicating all over the place, and that isn't the result of any assistance program or any aid program. When we've gone to Tanzania, what we've seen is that they're adjudicating, and they're documenting their adjudications, so property is being created there without anybody's particular support. For us, that makes property an archetype in Tanzania: a pattern of social practices created by the people themselves for themselves.

Every area that we've gone to is documented. Property rights are established by mutual agreement and documented. In each case, maps are coming more into place, and when people can sign, they sign, and where they can't sign, they put their fingerprints. So identity is also being established. Every village has got at least one small room where people are doing record keeping. Sometimes the record keeping is really poor. It may not be color-coded or it may not be in alphabetical order. But the idea of creating records so that you can then identify yourself and build credibility is there. This is what they're doing, but nobody's writing about it, because to write about it, you have to field 975 people. Otherwise, you get one person's experience of what he observed when he visited a third world country.

We started seeing documents that effectively indicate that land and assets are fungible. They can be traded for money—of course, within very restricted and small groups because there's not one standard document. There are many kinds of documents, but at least they have local value the way they did in the United States in the eighteenth and nineteenth centuries. They are being used as collateral.

We're seeing testaments. Those are most of the documents that we find in the record keeping. How can there be a testament if there isn't private property? It's obvious that somebody has decided this land is his land. So you can go someplace, and they tell you, "These are the Bantus, or these are the Shepebos, and they own all of this land, and that's what the records of Spain or France or England say." But inside that so-called sovereign area, people are saying, "This belongs to de Soto, and I want it to belong to my sons, or I don't want it to belong to my sons. I want it to belong to my third wife." So obviously, private property's on the move.

We haven't found one group of people that are associated that don't have some kind of a document—whether they can read or write doesn't matter; there's always a scribe to do it—that puts the constitution of the company onto paper. Basically, these documents say: We've seen division of labor. We've seen that there's a distinction of documents between management and labor. We've seen that in different companies, there are people who are the record keepers. They're keeping the information in place that can then be used to start creating a market economy. We haven't found one bull or one cow in all of Tanzania that doesn't have a private brand on it.

So are we all ready for freedom? The reply is, yes, we are. We just haven't all picked up on it.

That is the basic problem, because it's not as if we're not concerned in the world with institutions. We spend billions of dollars helping developing countries have institutions, but those institutions haven't connected with the social order. Basically, what we've done are legal transplants. This is where we're very good in Peru. If our lawyers have been trained in Spain, they will photocopy Spanish laws and bring them in. Or if they've been trained in the United States, they'll photocopy your laws. The real problem is how do you actually mesh that with people's beliefs? What adjustment do you have to make so that a good rule becomes applicable and culturally recognizable in your own country?

One of the persons who taught me the most about this is my friend John Sullivan, who is here from the Center for International Private Enterprise. He said to have a look at the *acquis communautaire*, which is the process that the Europeans have for integrating their larger European economic unity. For example, in 1978, Spain acceded to the *acquis communautaire*, to the European Economic Community. They didn't go in and say, "Okay, these are the laws of Frankfurt; we're going to apply them." They said, "These are the principles of where we want to head. This is how we understand markets and how we understand law in the European Economic Community, so let's take the Spanish laws as they are and combine them in the direction of unity." These are exercises that can take 10 or 15 years, but essentially, the process of the European Economic Community is a process whereby what you do is bring in the rule of law to these countries, and you try and set standards while respecting local culture.

When you deal with developing countries like mine, then it's PL-480, microenterprise—give them a tractor that will rust in the middle of the field. But it's all about rules. When Europeans deal among themselves, it's rules. When Americans deal among themselves, it's rules. It's about nails. When we deal among ourselves, it's all about logs and things that are important, to be sure, but what's really important in a market economy is how you actually bring things together, and the tools to bring things together are essentially the laws.

I think, to a great extent, that the disorder that we find in the world is actually the opposite of information. Having the right kind of information is what produces order. By definition, disorder is the opposite of information. And to be able to catch the kind of information you need on an everyday basis, you need companies, associations of people that will get that information which is indispensable, and if they don't get it, they will fail.

In effect, when the United States and other Western European countries began creating companies, they were creating the devices that allow you to process the information and that allow you to make sense out of huge, unruly markets. What brings the rules into place is essentially what companies have got: business law and property law. That's what allows you to pass from a society based on uniqueness to a society based on individuals.

Interestingly enough, we have looked at this with a very recent friend of ours, Ashraf Ghani, who is the chancellor of Kabul University and before that the minister of economy and finance for Afghanistan. We are trying to form a coalition of Third World universities so that we can figure out how we create a career path for people who are concerned with this eclectic science of connecting law to local customs, which we think is the missing link to make markets work and to make a Western-type order available to all countries. At that time, when we're able to deal with those things, we will then be able to establish a regime of freedom for the world.

So my reply to the question that Heritage asked me—are we all ready for economic freedom?—is that I'm convinced we are. It turns out that it's more difficult than we thought. It's a very sophisticated process. It has to be documented. It has to be taught. And once we do learn that it's not only about macroeconomic rules but how people can get organized and are getting organized even in the most backward parts of the world, we will be closer to success.

Elena Panaritis and The Panel Group

Elena Panaritis was a World Bank economist for over a decade starting in the 1990s. As she worked on privatizations in Latin America she came to realize that the core element for sustainable economic growth is the establishment of a properly functioning property rights system. She then started and lead the design and implementation of the first full-fledged holistic reform on property rights in Peru, an initiative that was highly unconventional for the World Bank at the time. During her work she collaborated with a variety of academics and visionaries who thought outside the box, including Hernando de Soto and his team. The World Bank awarded her prizes for innovation and recognized her for the development of international best practices. She became the leading expert in the area, consulting around the world on similar work as a World Bank economist, reforms advisor for the past 18 years. She has now set up an entrepreneurial for-profit firm, The Panel Group, designed to promote property rights reform.

How Can One Improve Property Rights On a For-Profit Basis?

As with free zones, property rights reforms increase land values. Panaritis calculates that the property rights reforms in Peru increased land values by $1.7 billion in three years. With wealth creation opportunities like that, the only challenge is aligning the incentives of the various decision makers such that they make, and keep, the agreements needed to implement the reforms. There is certainly some uncertainty ex ante in such a situation, and a great deal of expertise is required to create serious property rights reforms that do, in fact, increase land values. But as Panaritis and The Panel Group create a track record as a profitable investment vehicle, one can imagine extraordinary wealth increases taking place around the world at a rapid pace.

In much of Eastern Europe, for instance, real estate transaction costs run approximately 25 percent of the purchase price. Imagine, as a U.S. homeowner, the loss of equity in your home if, say, you had no title insurance and it had just been discovered that there was a title conflict that would result in transaction costs equivalent to 25 percent of the value of your home. That one discovery could easily reduce the value of your home by half.

Panaritis is, in effect, reversing this story: She is doubling, or more, real estate values wherever she works by reducing or eliminating the countless irrationalities and irregularities in property registries and processing around the world.

Chapter 11

Can Entrepreneurs Help Us Improve Our Understanding of the World?

Michael Strong
CEO and Chief Visionary Officer, FLOW

T he credibility of academia is based on the notion that professors are experts in their field who have achieved their positions by means of track records of exemplary scholarship. In the hard sciences, where exemplary scholarship is based on scientific work that is consistent with empirical research, ultimately grounded in increasingly accurate experimental predictions, this credibility is based on a solid foundation. Outside the hard sciences, the foundation for academic expertise and credibility is more tenuous.

Social scientists superficially appear to be engaged in a process similar to that of hard scientists. In the hard sciences, however, it is much easier to judge whether a theory has been refuted by the evidence: A specific prediction is made and either the evidence confirms the theory or it does not. In the social sciences no specific predictions are made and the evidence often supports a proliferation of possibilities. There are, of course, particular topics in the social sciences that can be supported by empirical research; these aspects of social science may approach the rigor of the natural sciences. But in many areas, academic reputations are built primarily upon the opinions of other academics, and there appear to be long-term speculative bubbles in academic ideas that are sustained for decades merely because other academics like to read and discuss the same ideas.

For instance, an external observer might have expected that *Social Text*, "a journal at the forefront of cultural theory," might have experienced an Enron-like implosion after physicist Alan Sokal submitted a parody that was accepted as authentic. On the contrary, although *Social Text* is a laughingstock among scientists, it retains its legitimacy within the world of cultural theory. It is as if Enron was revealed as a house of cards but continued as if nothing had happened.

The issue would be harmless enough if nothing were at stake, but in fact, lives are at stake.[*] To take a very simple, dramatic example, there were numerous individuals who could have predicted negative consequences from the experiments in forced collectivized agriculture that took place in the Soviet Union in the 1930s and in Maoist China in the late 1950s and early 1960s. Yet even while tens of millions of individuals were dying, many in academia claimed that these regimes were superior to that of the United States. The sociologist Paul Hollander has written several books documenting the extraordinary claims made by academics and intellectuals on behalf of communism,

> The Soviet system, according to Malcolm Cowley, the American writer, "was capable of supplying the moral qualities that writers missed in bourgeoisie society: comradeship in struggle, the

---

[*] See Michael Strong, "The Opportunity Cost of Obsolete Beliefs in Academia," The Free Liberal, Feb. 16, 2006 (www.freeliberal.com/archives/001872.html).

self-imposed discipline, the ultimate purpose . . . the opportunity for heroism and human dignity." Leon Feuchtwanger, the German writer, rejoiced in the "invigorating atmosphere" of the Soviet Union where he found "clarity and resolution." John Dewey compared the ethos prevailing in the Soviet Union to "the moving spirit and force of primitive Christianity," and Edmund Wilson confessed that "you feel in the Soviet Union that you are on the moral top of the world where the light never really goes out." J.D. Bernal, the British scientist, found "sense of purpose and achievement" and was persuaded that "the cornerstone of the [Soviet] Marxist state was the utilization of human knowledge, science and technique, directly for human welfare.

Paul Hollander, "Judgments and Misjudgments,"
in Lee Edwards, editor, *The Collapse of Communism,*
Hoover Institution Press, 1999, 179

These were not minor figures. Dewey was arguably the most prominent public intellectual in the first half of the twentieth century. Edmund Wilson was arguably the most prominent literary critic of the twentieth century. Bernal was a founder of X-ray crystallography whose work led directly to the discovery of DNA. These comments were being made while Stalin was in the midst of murdering tens of millions. Hollander points out the painful irony that often the academics and intellectuals were most vigorously celebrating each new manifestation of communism during their most murderous phases: the Soviet Union in the 1930s, Mao's China in the 1960s, third-world revolutions in the 1970s (just as Pol Pot's Cambodia was revving up its murder machine).

In the hard sciences nonobvious facts, such as the existence of unimagined planets and chemical elements, were predicted in advance of discovery. It is striking that one of the few nonobvious predictions in the social sciences, the prediction by Mises and Hayek that communism would fail due to the lack of price information, was ridiculed or neglected in the social science literature from the 1930s until the 1990s, when it suddenly became accepted wisdom. Paul Samuelson's *Principles of Economics* 13th edition, published in 1989, claimed "the Soviet economy is proof that, contrary to what many skeptics had earlier believed, a socialist command economy can function and even thrive."* The skeptics being sneered at here are Mises and Hayek. Samuelson's economics textbooks, selling more than 4 million copies, represented the apex of expert judgment in economics throughout the 1950s, 1960s, 1970s, and 1980s.

In 1989, when some academic economists were still praising the Soviet economy, I had dinner with an Egyptian reporter who noted that the Soviet Union had to change because a generation of Soviet military advisors, sent to advise "third world" nations such as Egypt, had discovered, to their humiliation, that ordinary Egyptians had cars, refrigerators, and a host of modern conveniences that were only available to the *nomenklatura* of the Soviet Union. Throughout the world more than four million leaders and professionals, the decision makers for much of the western world for two generations, were taught to believe that Samuelson's work was authoritative. His profoundly flawed judgment was a major force for defining economic reality for the entire world throughout the second half of the twentieth century.

Samuelson's expertise consisted of writing papers that interpreted aspects of the economic world in mathematical terms. Samuelson is still considered brilliant by those professors who value the mathematical formalisms of neoclassical economic theory. He made a successful career by publishing papers that his academic peers respected because of his ability to solve certain kinds of complicated mathematical puzzles. The same criticism may be made of Robert Solow's blindness to the role of entrepreneurs and The Entrepreneur's Toolkit in his mid-twentieth century theories of economic growth. *Social Text* continues to believe that it is "at the forefront of cultural theory" because academics in cultural studies respect the complicated verbal games that are played there. But without a responsibility to compare their conclusions with empirical realities, academic disciplines float off into the ozone. Unlike science and engineering, there are no anchors to an external reality beyond the pages of the peer- (and friend-) reviewed journals. Enron eventually had to show a profit; when analysts realized there was no chance of the company

---

*See Mark Skousen's excellent analysis of the history of Samuelson's textbooks, "The Perseverance of Paul Samuelson's Economics" (www.mskousen.com/Books/Articles/perserverance.html).

coming out ahead because of its shenanigans, its stock collapsed. But academic speculative bubbles keep going for decade after decade. We have been mistakenly led to trust academics outside the natural sciences because of the extraordinary achievements of the natural sciences. For the past hundred years we have assumed that university "brand names" that gave us reliable knowledge with respect to science and technology could also supply high quality thought, decisions, and judgment regarding politics and society. We were wrong. What to do now?

In 1990, the polymath Robin Hanson wrote a paper titled, "Could Gambling Save Science?: Encouraging an Honest Consensus," in which he proposed the creation of futures markets in ideas to solve the problems with academic knowledge creation. He was explicitly motivated by the well-documented, systematic flaws with the academic knowledge creation process:

> Academia is still largely a medieval guild, with a few powerful elites, many slave-like apprentices, and members who hold a monopoly on the research patronage of princes and the teaching of their sons. Outsiders still complain about bias, saying their evidence is ignored, and many observers [Gh, Re, Syk, Tu] have noted some long-standing problems with the research component of academia. . . . Peer review is just another popularity contest, inducing familiar political games; savvy players criticize outsiders, praise insiders, follow the fashions insiders indicate, and avoid subjects between or outside the familiar subjects. It can take surprisingly long for outright lying by insiders to be exposed [Re]. There are too few incentives to correct for cognitive [Kah] and social [My] biases, such as wishful thinking, overconfidence, anchoring [He], and preferring people with a background similar to your own. . . . On the whole, current academic institutions seem less than ideal [Ki], with incentives that reward being popular, fashionable, and eloquent, instead of being right.
>
> Robin Hanson,
> "Could Gambling Save Science?
> Encouraging an Honest Consensus,"
> http://hanson.gmu.edu/gamble.html.
> (See original for full set of references cited by
> Hanson to support these claims.)

Although Hanson's paper referred to "idea futures," that is, futures markets in ideas, the term "prediction markets" has become more common.

Since Hanson's 1990 paper, a growing prediction markets industry has sprung up, with dozens of online sites allowing individuals to bet on the outcomes of diverse events. In the United States all such sites use play money, because U.S. securities law has not yet allowed for the creation of real money prediction markets. But there are real money prediction markets overseas.

Could Prediction Markets Have Prevented the 2008 Financial Meltdown?

Nicholas Taleb, who has become famous by showing that there are "Black Swan" events that cannot be predicted, claims that the 2008 mortgage meltdown was just such an event. And in some sense, no doubt he is correct. But he also acknowledges that some Black Swan problems can be shifted into more manageable territory by means of improved information.

Although Taleb ridicules prediction markets as subject to the same Black Swan blind spots as mainstream markets, he is evaluating them based on their existing, relatively simple, manifestations. He doesn't seem to realize that, as a tool, prediction markets are in an early stage of innovation in which we may need dozens, or hundreds, more prediction markets (especially real money markets) to be implemented in various realms to reduce uncertainty by means of discovering, and disseminating, knowledge that had previously been unavailable.

To take one example, anonymous corporate prediction markets have increased the accuracy of sales predictions and product release dates. Michael Abramowicz and Todd Henderson have a paper on using prediction markets to improve corporate governance by overcoming the challenges of obtaining alignment between the leaders of an organization and the desired outcomes of the organization.[*]

Freddie Mac's chief risk officer expressed concerns in mid-2004 leading to his being fired in 2005:

---

[*] Abramowicz, Michael B. and Henderson, M. Todd ,Prediction Markets for Corporate Governance. Notre Dame Law Review, Vol. 82, No. 4, 2007; U Chicago Law & Economics, Olin Working Paper No. 307; GWU Law School Public Law Research Paper No. 221; GWU Legal Studies Research Paper No. 221. Available at SSRN: http://ssrn.com/abstract=928896

> In an interview, Freddie Mac's former chief risk officer, David A. Andrukonis, recalled telling Mr. Syron in mid-2004 that the company was buying bad loans that "would likely pose an enormous financial and reputational risk to the company and the country."
>
> http://econlog.econlib.org/archives/2008/08/freddie_macs_wh_1.html

Suppose Andrukonis and others within Freddie Mac and Fannie Mae had had the opportunity to use internal prediction markets through which their concerns about various aspects of their portfolios could have been expressed? Employees could have bet on the default rate of various elements of their portfolio, at specified dates in the future, with payoffs going to those who most accurately predicted specific portfolio default rates. This approach, when employees are shielded appropriately, is a means of avoiding the "kill the messenger" strategy that forced Mr. Andrukonis out and no doubt kept many others silent as they knowingly watched the tragedy unfold.

Again, Taleb acknowledges that moral hazard increases the probability of Black Swans. For very large quasi-governmental organizations as large as Freddie Mac and Fannie Mae to be firing whistle-blowers, especially chief risk officer whistle-blowers, is a nontrivial event when they are not subject to normal market pressures and incentives. If government-backed financial institutions such as Freddie Mac and Fannie Mae had been required to have anonymous internal prediction markets whose ongoing results estimating their portfolio risk had been transparent to the public, opinions such as that of Andrukonis would most likely have been far more evident to more people at a much earlier date.

To take a second example, a more developed futures market in Housing Price Indices might also have changed outcomes. In retrospect we now know that in November 2005 the Housing Price Index (HPI) peaked and began a long decline. It was only six months later, on May 16, 2006, that the Chicago Mercantile first introduced a futures market based on the Housing Price Indices. It grew in volume slowly, as new futures products often do; by mid-July of 2006 there were only a few dozen open contracts, worth a few million dollars, in the major metro areas for which the market existed. One blog commenter complained as of Nov. 21, 2007, with respect to using the CME futures to evaluate the San Diego (SD) housing market,

> There two problems with using CME Housing futures data to analyze the housing market: (1) lack of free historical data (if anyone can resolve this, let me know) and (2) the relative illiquidity of the marketplace due to its
>
> (*continued*)

size. The Fed Board of Gov's published a nice report on using housing data see: www.federalreserve.gov/pubs/feds/. . . .

It's a bit technical (and now a little dated) but they make good points about using CME data. Note that the open interest in SD housing futures was only 58 contracts or $3.6 million, which obviously wanes in comparison to the total SD real estate market or any other large price setting market mechanism (e.g., stock markets or currency/commodity futures). Note that open interest today (11/21) is only 72 contracts.

http://piggington.com/august_case_shiller_hpi

The fact that historical data was not freely available and that the market was relatively illiquid as recently as November 2007 does not imply that the futures in HPI does not provide valuable information, it only implies that it was a relatively new market which is still in a growth phase. At the time, by the way, the HPI futures at CME were predicting a decline on into 2011.

To take yet another new information source, Realius (www.realius.com) is a real estate prediction market launched in 2007 in San Francisco and available in 2008 for five regional markets. Unlike the HPI, which estimates housing price data through a formula based on historical data, which may introduce various inaccuracies vis-a-vis actual prices, Realius is based on the predictions of on-the-ground local real estate experts estimating the sales price of individual homes, a far richer source of local knowledge than is available through the HPI. The founder of Realius suggested that had his prediction market been working five years ago we might have avoided this mess.

I am not claiming that any of these three specific markets:

1. A hypothetical internal prediction market within Freddie Mac and Fannie Mae, whose real-time results were transparent to the public
2. The CME HPI futures
3. Realius

necessarily would have, on its own, prevented the meltdown. Nor am I claiming that other factors were not involved; they most certainly were.

Instead, I'm proposing that in the coming decades, as hundreds and hundreds of new prediction markets are developed for very diverse niches, our ecosystem of knowledge will change. There will still be Black Swans, for certain. But it is premature to claim that prediction market technologies have failed in this particular instance. We don't know how much information could have been made available had all three of the proposed prediction markets mentioned above, and dozens more not imagined here, all been functioning for 20 years in advance.

It is important to see prediction markets as a versatile new technology about where the desktop computer was in 1980. "Gee, look at the cool stuff it does."And yet, compared to today, a 1980 Apple III looks pretty primitive.

Perhaps there are elements to this particular meltdown that were for some reason completely impervious to the endless possibilities of ever more granular knowledge discovery than I'm imagining. On the other hand, if real money prediction markets were legal in the United States, endless numbers of entrepreneurs would set up diverse for-profit discovery mechanisms, and I would never want to bet against the ingenuity of millions of such human beings.

Prediction Markets as Reputation System and Research Tool

Prediction markets may provide a powerful antidote to academic abuses of power. Just as critical experiments have enforced a reality-based ethos of scientific integrity in the hard sciences, so, too, prediction markets may be used to enforce a reality-based ethos of scientific integrity among those who make claims about society, politics, and economics. When theoretical speculations in the hard sciences repeatedly produce false predictions they are marginalized. We need to create just such a system for the social sciences.

The idea behind prediction markets is simple: People who claim to have any foresight or expertise into a social or political issue bet on specific empirical predictions concerning what will happen in the future. James Surowiecki's *The Wisdom of Crowds* has popularized research showing that under certain conditions crowds outperform experts. Well-designed prediction markets fulfill those conditions: The Iowa prediction markets outperform exit polls in predicting elections; and Florida orange futures markets *outperform weather forecasters* in predicting Florida weather. When we give large numbers of people an opportunity to discover the truth about the world, in a situation in which there are financial payoffs for accuracy, on balance they outperform experts.

More recently, Philip Tetlock conducted a large-scale analysis of expert political judgment and discovered that the better known an expert, the worse his judgment as measured against predictive accuracy.[*]

In the 1980s, the economist Julian Simon famously bet the ecologist Paul Ehrlich that natural resources were not becoming more scarce. Ehrlich agreed to the bet, they settled on the scarcity of five metals based on their inflation-adjusted prices, and the price of all five metals was lower in 1990 than in 1980. Thus, Ehrlich lost the bet and paid Simon. This is the first high profile "reputational bet." The science fiction writer David Brin has proposed that we keep "Prediction Registries" in which prominent individuals who make future prognostications in public should have their predictions tracked to see how accurate they tend to be (and by this standard Ehrlich has a long run of failed predictions).

Paul Ehrlich's bet with Julian Simon concerning his belief that natural resources were becoming scarce—which he famously lost—has not completely undermined Ehrlich's reputation. But what if, instead of one controversial academic betting against another, there were thousands of ordinary people working to make a buck off of the foolishness of academics? Insofar as ordinary people often have much greater insight into social and economic systems than do many academics, the most egregious foolishnesses of academia would rapidly be exposed.

If, in 1989, Paul Samuelson believed, for instance, that the workers' standard of living in 1995 would be higher in the Soviet Union than in the United States, then he could have placed a public bet on a prediction market (which would include a specified means of measuring the empirical outcome and a dispute resolution process). If, say, a plumber in Queens, a bureaucrat in Stalingrad, and a cab driver in Egypt had all bet differently, they would have made money and Samuelson would have lost money. Instead of the limited recognition that Simon's bet with Ehrlich received, people in bars in Queens, Stalingrad, and Egypt would all be focused on the failure of publicly-identified experts.

---

[*] Nick Schulz interview with Philip Tetlock, "What Makes You an Expert?," TCS, Feb. 3, 2006. See also Philip Tetlock, *Expert Political Judgment: How Good is it? How Can We Know?* (Princeton, N.J.: Princeton University Press, 2005).

Moreover, prediction markets are nonideological: the future happens the way it happens. Thus, although Julian Simon beat Ehrlich, there are now scientists concerned about global warming who want global warming skeptics to put their money where their mouths are.

Will teen pregnancy be higher in 2010? Collectively, in the wisdom of crowds sense, teens participating in a cash prediction market may provide better information about this, at least in local contexts, than sociologists can obtain by means of surveys. When storms across the Midwest damage wheat crops, wheat futures reflect this change in condition almost instantaneously. Just as futures markets in wheat are sensitive to storms in the Midwest, so, too, a futures market in teen pregnancy would be sensitive to sexual practices and birth control usage among teens. If a new 10 million dollar abstinence program was introduced, and it had almost no impact on the futures market, we would know more quickly that such a program was likely to be worthless.

At present, monetized prediction markets are not legal. But if they were, we could learn about the efficacy of government programs, the prerequisites for economic growth, the effectiveness of educational policies, and the validity of social theories.

Academic reputations in many fields, based as they are merely on academic publication histories, bear no necessary relationship to real-world understanding in disciplines that lack experimental verification. Yet academic opinions regarding politics, economics, and society nonetheless have both legal force and social prestige that are often completely unwarranted. Insofar as there are areas in which academic experts have superior insight into the workings of society, the validity of their expertise will be valued by prediction markets; such academics will find that their public recognition and respect increase. On the other hand, prediction markets will cause unwarranted respect for academic expertise to decline.

For those of us who believe that excessive respect for academic opinion has led to avoidable poverty, waste, and human misery due to adherence to the misguided policies proposed by academics in the past century, then the need to create a more reliable system for discovering the empirical truth about the political and social realm is urgent. Moreover, prediction markets have the added benefit of allowing ordinary people to make money, possibly fortunes, by exposing those unfounded academic beliefs that are most widely accepted at present. Society wins, ordinary people win, and we create an incentive for people to focus their energy and attention on discovering important facts about the future.

Although there is a common perception that futures markets in commodities are dominated by speculators, the individuals who tend to win in such markets are not speculating, they are gathering knowledge. One wheat trader I knew had a network of wheat farmers across the Midwest with whom he was in regular contact throughout the growing season, systematically assessing an estimate of the year's crop based on the knowledge gathered. A futures trader in cocoa had developed a sophisticated mathematical model that predicted the cocoa crop based on early growth trends taken from carefully identified sample sites. He gathered information regarding the cocoa buds early in the season, which was then used as input into his proprietary models, which allowed him to outperform others in the cocoa markets. These and other individuals are properly seen as "knowledge entrepreneurs" or "discovery entrepreneurs," individuals who have found ways to acquire knowledge that will allow them to outperform the market (until other individuals create even better means of discovering the same knowledge, thereby forcing ongoing competitive progress in real-world knowledge discovery).

This model of real-world knowledge creation and discovery is apt to be far more effective and valuable than is academic expertise alone. The use of real money prediction markets as an entrepreneurial knowledge discovery mechanism does not imply the end of academia. In many cases, those academics who are currently creating useful knowledge will find their work to be more valued by such knowledge entrepreneurs. Just as professors of electrical engineering are often provided endowed chairs by IT companies who value their contributions, social scientists who provide knowledge with real-world value will find that their work will receive increasingly significant financial support from entrepreneurs who need their research.

But using prediction markets to adjudicate many disputes will gradually discriminate between those academics and intellectuals whose claims are unfounded, despite their success within academia, and those academics and intellectuals who have sound track records. As a result we will have a far more reliable system for generating information on how to make the world a better place than we do at present. And knowledge entrepreneurs, making bets in legalized real money prediction markets, investing deeply in knowledge discovery, will lead the way.*

How Anti-Capitalist Bigotry in Academia Prevents Knowledge of Practical Solutions From Being Disseminated

In considering the effectiveness of academia in disseminating valuable ideas, it is instructive to consider the history of property rights solutions to tragedy of the commons problems. The most serious threats to the environmental sustainability of the planet are all due to tragedy of the commons problems, the fact that no individual entity owns the relevant resources.

Over-fishing is among the most serious environmental problems; the U.N.'s 2005 Millenium Ecosystem Assessment lists "overexploitation, especially overfishing" as one of the five most critical environmental issues on the planet. Happily the American Association for the Advancement of Science (AAAS) recently published a study showing the benefits of "catch shares," through which individual fishermen (or corporations) are given rights to a specified portion of a fishery. "Catch shares" save fisheries by giving fishermen a property right in a fishery. But what is most striking about the AAAS press release, is their claim that privatizing the fisheries is a new idea:

> A study published in the September 19 (2008) issue of *Science* shows that an innovative yet contentious fisheries management strategy called "catch shares" can reverse fisheries collapse. Where traditional "open access" fisheries have converted to catch shares, both fishermen and the oceans have benefited.[†]

The notion that "catch shares" is "innovative" in 2008 is dumbfounding. In 1999, the National Academy of Sciences released a comprehensive report endorsing "catch

---

[†] www.eurekalert.org/pub_releases/2008-09/s-nso091208.php

(continued)

---

*Hanson himself has envisioned an entire form of government based on decision markets, prediction markets that allow betting on alternative future possibilities. See his work on decision markets "Decision Markets," IEEE Intelligent Systems, http://hanson.gmu.edu/decisionmarkets.pdf, and "Futarchy, Vote Values, but Bet Belief," http://hanson.gmu.edu/futarchy.html, for more detail.

shares."* But "catch shares," usually in the form of Individual Fishing Quotas, have been implemented in diverse fisheries, including the U.S. around the world since the late 1970s. How is it that a solution that has been in place for thirty years is considered "innovative"?

In fact, economists have understood the logic of property rights solutions to tragedy of the commons problems since at least 1870. Here is Carl Menger, the founder of the Austrian school of economics, analyzing the situation in 1870:

> ". . . when all members of society compete for a given quantity of goods that is insufficient . . . a practical solution to this conflict of interest is . . . only conceivable if the various portions of the whole amount at the disposal of society pass into the possession of some of the economizing individuals, and if these individuals are protected by society in their possession to the exclusion of all other individuals."†

In essence, he is articulating the tragedy of the commons, "when all members of society compete for a given quantity of goods that is insufficient," and proposing a property rights solution, "a practical solution . . . is . . . only conceivable if the various portions of the whole amount at the disposal of society pass into the possession of some of the economizing individuals."

Ludwig von Mises, the great 20th century Austrian economist and free market advocate, articulated both the problem and the solution clearly in 1940:

> If land is not owned by anybody, although legal formalism may call it public property, it is utilized without any regard to the disadvantages resulting. Those who are in a position to appropriate to themselves the returns-lumber and game of the forests, fish of the water areas, and mineral deposits of the subsoil-do not bother about the later effects of their mode of exploitation. For them the erosion of the soil, the depletion of the exhaustible resources and other impairments of the future utilization are external costs not entering into their calculation of input and output. They cut down the trees without any regard for fresh shoots or reforestation. In hunting and

---

*Sharing the Fish: Toward a National Policy on Individual Fishing Quotas, NAS, 1999, www.nap.edu/openbook.php?record_id=6335&page=2

† Quoted in Roy Cordato, "An Austrian Theory of Environmental Economics,", Mises Institute, http://mises.org/story/1760.

fishing they do not shrink from methods preventing the repopulation of the hunting and fishing grounds. In the early days of human civilization, when soil of a quality not inferior to that of the utilized pieces was still abundant, people did not find any fault with such predatory methods. When their effects appeared in a decrease in the net returns, the plough-man abandoned his farm and moved to another place. It was only when a country was more densely settled and unoccupied first class land was no longer available for appropriation, that people began to consider such predatory methods wasteful. At that time they consolidated the institution of private property in land. They started with arable land and then, step by step, included pastures, forests, and fisheries.*

As we saw earlier, the Tlingit Indians developed private property in fisher-ies many hundreds of years ago, as did numerous tribes around the earth. By 1870, Menger had outlined the basic logic behind the need for property rights solutions, and by 1940 Mises clearly stated the problem of the tragedy of the commons as well as the solution. In 1954 H. Scott Gordon published "The Economic Theory of a Common-Property Resource: The Fishery," a high profile, widely cited article that really spawned the subsequent literature on property rights solutions to fisheries. Garrett Hardin's 1968 Science article, "Tragedy of the Commons" mentions privatiza-tion as a possible solution, and by the mid-1970s legislation in several nations actu-ally creates Individual Fishing Quotas (IFQs) in several fisheries. By the 1980s there is an active "Free Market Environmentalism" movement that promotes property rights solutions to tragedy of the commons problems, including IFQs. By 1999, the National Academy of Sciences is on board with their formal study and endorsement.

And yet Jared Diamond's 2005 book *Collapse*, which is essentially about trag-edy of the commons problems, shows that Diamond fails to understand how prop-erty rights solutions can be deployed to prevent tragedy of the commons problems. He dismisses fisheries privatizations as a solution despite the aforementioned evi-dence of their success.† Indeed, he believes that political leaders and free market

---

* Ludwig von Mises, pg. 652, 1940, www.mises.org/Books/HumanActionScholars.pdf

† For excellent analyses of Diamond's failure to recognize property rights solutions, see John Braitland, "On Societal Ascendence and Collapse: An Austrian Challenge to Jared Diamond's Explictations," Working Paper, http://mises.org/journals/scholar/bratland5.pdf. See Rognvaldur Hannesson, "The Privatization of the Oceans," The MIT Press, 2006, for a survey of the issues associated with creating property rights solutions to deep sea fisheries.

(*continued*)

advocates are to blame for failing to address these crucial environmental issues. But the primary opponents of IFQs are environmental organizations such as Greenpeace as well as local interests who are concerned that they will lose out in the transition.[*] Diamond is often listed as one of the world's leading public intellectuals. Surely his book manuscript was reviewed by dozens of the world's leading academics. Environmental issues are the highest profile issue of all for many of the world's well-intentioned people today. How is it that with such intense focus on such a key issue by such illustrious and knowledgeable individuals, there was a total and complete failure to understand a simple economic principle that has been well-known more or less since 1870?

Of course, one could list any number of other high profile environmentalist documents and organizations that also fail to demonstrate such awareness. It is in this context of truly astounding ignorance of obvious principles that in September 19, 2008, AAAS could describe "as an innovative yet contentious fisheries management strategy." Contentious, perhaps. Innovative, not at all. Would anyone describe a computer operating system from the 1970s, the theory of which had been developed a century before that, and an early version of which has been used by indigenous peoples, as "innovative?"

The only plausible rationale for such widespread ignorance of basic economic principles is anticapitalist bigotry. It is true that IFQs often result in a more concentrated fishing industry, as the big corporate fishing organizations tend to buy out the smaller fishermen. This is precisely the reason that Greenpeace is opposed to IFQs—Greenpeace has not contradicted the findings of the NAS, AAAS, and others that IFQs create sustainable fisheries. They just don't like corporate fishing. But if what we really want is environmental sustainability, we should be pursuing solutions that work, not indulging our anti-capitalist bigotries.

---

[*] See Rob King, edited for online by Jay Townsend for Greenpeace USA, "Sinking Fast: How Factory Trawlers are Destroying U.S. Fisheries," http://archive.greenpeace.org/oceans/globaloverfishing/sinking fast.html, which criticizes IFQs, which can be designed and implemented poorly, without acknowledging their real strength as a solution.

Chapter 12

Improving Health, Happiness, and Well-Being

Michael Strong
CEO and Chief Visionary Officer, FLOW

The one essential thing is that we strive to have light in ourselves. Our strivings will be recognized by others, and when people have light in themselves, it will shine out from them. Then we get to know each other as we walk together in the darkness, without needing to pass our hands over each other's faces, or to intrude into each other's hearts.

ALBERT SCHWEITZER,
FROM RABBI GREENBERG'S
THE ART OF LIVING

There are a number of serious human concerns that are not being adequately addressed by capitalism as we know it. Some of the most serious and thoughtful critics of capitalism include:

- Those who care about how the appetites, attitudes, and souls of young people are currently being formed.
- Those who are concerned about the increasing propensity of our society to be dominated by commercialism, sensationalism, materialism, and conspicuous consumption.
- Those who care about the invisible virtues, including justice, honor, love, awareness, kindness, empathy, curiosity, wonder, and wisdom.
- Those who seek a world in which all young people can develop the skills they need to have satisfying, successful, professional lives in the highly competitive twenty-first-century global economy.
- Those who care about creativity, innovation, and entrepreneurship as a means of creating ever greater levels of human happiness and well-being.

Even those who claim that capitalism can be tamed so that it is not harmful to the environment, as well as those who insist that it can eliminate poverty, are not inspired by the kind of life it seems to promote. We in the developed world are certainly wealthier than any class of human being in all of human history. And yet few believe that we are significantly happier or healthier as a consequence of our amazing standard of living.

Here I will propose that the reason that capitalism has resulted in such crass consumerism and materialism is, paradoxically, because we do not have enough of it yet. In particular, by managing health, education, and community formation by means of government, we have prevented the most powerful force for innovation the world has ever known from releasing its innovative powers to improve our health, to improve our education, and to improve our communities.

Martin Seligman is the leading figure in the new field of positive psychology, the study of human happiness. In order to deepen one's happiness, Seligman proposes:

- Cultivating positive emotions about the past by increasing gratitude, forgiveness, and letting go of the notion that the past determines your future.
- Cultivating positive emotions about the future by learning to recognize and dispute pessimistic thoughts.
- Cultivating positive emotions about the present by savoring the moment and practicing mindfulness.

- Cultivating a state of flow.
- Developing virtues that lead toward a sense of gratification.
- Developing your signature strengths in work, love, and parenting.
- Using your signature strengths in service of something larger than yourself.*

Without going into Seligman's detailed description of each of these elements of happiness, it is worth noting that while one could conceivably develop each of these characteristics by means of reading a book, in essence each of them must be internalized as a habit in order to be effective.

It is not enough to read about cultivating positive emotions. The verb "to cultivate" means to nurture and grow. Cultivating positive emotions means developing new intellectual and emotional habits by practicing them on an ongoing basis. As Aristotle, the original philosopher of happiness, knew well, virtues are acquired by means of the habit of acting virtuously. Likewise, while one can run down a checklist of strengths in a book to identify what your unique, signature strengths are (for example, curiosity, integrity, humility), in order to develop them beyond their present state, it is useful to focus on them and practice them regularly in order to improve them and thereby achieve a state of excellence. And, finally, while some individuals may naturally be focused on applying their signature strengths to something larger than themselves, in today's busy, distracting society, an individual who is not focused on something larger than himself may need to develop the habit of transcending his usual solipsism.

Can entrepreneurs help individuals to develop habits? Is there a market in habituation services? What would it take to create a deep, innovative market that could support the development of serious, sophisticated, ever-improving forms of habituation, constantly being updated for a constantly changing world?

Experts in habit formation suggest that it takes at least three weeks, and possibly three months, of consistent new patterning to change a habit. Because it is so difficult, people trying to change habits are

---

*Adapted from Martin Seligman, *Authentic Happiness* (New York: The Free Press, 2002), 248–249.

encouraged to work on changing just one habit at a time. Clearly this approach may work with learning to remember to floss or even exercise daily. It sounds a bit more challenging if the habit to be developed is moment-by-moment mindfulness, or acting virtuously, or acquiring an entire set of new mental and emotional habits, an entire new way of being in the world.

One could make the case that various entrepreneurs support the development of new habits, including therapists, personal coaches, personal growth trainers, radio show hosts, podcasters, authors, religious teachers, and more. Typically they specialize in either habit-encouragement-by-exhortation or, in the case of personal trainers, yoga instructors, and so forth, the acquisition of new physical habits by means of regular instruction.

While all of these service providers no doubt benefit their customers, and while they may indeed help to improve the happiness and well-being of their customers, they certainly don't provide full-blown support for the development of the diverse habits needed to achieve happiness according to Seligman. Seligman himself sells books and tapes on positive psychology—is that the extent to which entrepreneurs of happiness can serve the public?

The Dalai Lama points out that achieving happiness is not a simple process:

> Achieving genuine happiness may require bringing about a transformation in your outlook, your way of thinking, and this is not a simple matter. It requires the application of so many different factors from different directions. . . . Change takes time. . . . But I think that as time goes on, you can make positive changes. Every day as soon as you get up, you can develop a sincere positive motivation, thinking, "I will utilize this day in a more positive way. I should not waste this very day." And then, at night before bed, check what you've done, asking yourself, "Did I utilize this day as I planned?" If it went accordingly, then you should rejoice. If it went wrong, then regret what you did and critique the day. So, through methods such as this, you can gradually strengthen the positive aspects of the mind.
>
>   Dalai Lama and Howard Cutler, *The Art of Happiness*

In traditional Tibetan culture, of course, monks spend many years in rigorous training on a daily basis, for many hours per day, from a young age. The Dalai Lama's own renowned sense of personal serenity is the result of such comprehensive and rigorous long-term training of mental and emotional habits. He did not develop his own deep sense of equanimity and compassion from reading a book and thinking a positive thought every day.

There are a few longer-term experiential options for adults. S.N. Goenka's network of Vipassana centers, for instance, offer 10-day meditation retreats where one meditates daily from 4:30 A.M. until 9:30 P.M., with only short breaks in between. In order to ensure that the mind stays focused, during breaks there is no talking or eye contact allowed, no reading, no writing, no music, essentially no interaction with the world outside one's mind except for the minimum needed to eat, groom, and receive instruction in Vipassana technique. All meals are vegetarian, with only fruit in the evening. No payment is required; one pays as one thinks appropriate at the end of the experience.

Even so, 10 days is less than the three-week minimum recommended to change a habit, and realistically relatively few adults are apt to take 10 days off from their routines and responsibilities in order to meditate. Even the Vipassana experience, one of the deeper experiences available to adults interested in an environment in which they can immerse themselves in a situation that is supports rigorous training in new mental and emotional habits, is limited compared to the years of training the Dalai Lama and other Buddhist monks undergo.

There are also residential treatment centers for the addicted. Precisely because addiction is so difficult to overcome, they typically provide a regimen that not only prevents an opportunity to relapse into addiction but that also strives to cultivate new habits and attitudes in the hopes that such new mental, physical, and emotional habits will reduce the probability of a relapse into the addiction. Youth residential treatment centers are a booming industry, with costs exceeding $500 per day, typical stays on the order of four months or more, behavioral modification programs, and inconsistent outcomes. Moreover, neither addiction treatment nor behavioral treatment for troubled adolescents quite inspires images of entrepreneurs of happiness and well-being, even when such centers do improve well-being.

Brain research is increasingly revealing the physiological challenges to changing habits. It is now clear that habits, in the behavioral sense, are the result of actual neuronal connections that are not only difficult to change, but which revert back to their previous functioning quickly:

> Important neural activity patterns in a specific region of the brain change when habits are formed, change again when habits are broken, but quickly reemerge when something rekindles an extinguished habit—routines that originally took great effort to learn.
>
> "Brain Researchers Explain Why Old Habits Die Hard,"
> Cathryn M. Delude, October 19, 2005
> (http://web.mit.edu/newsoffice/2005/habit.html)

Once we have certain neuronal firing networks established in our brains, there is always the possibility, even after we have learned a new habit, that our brains could revert back to the old firing pathways, which are still sitting there. The old circuits don't go away, they just lie there unused (but ready to be revived) whenever we go to the effort of creating new circuits by means of our three weeks of consistent daily effort.

There is, of course, one portion of our life in which we have the opportunity to develop habits that, if properly designed, could last a lifetime—the first 18 years. What we now know as K–12 education consists of approximately 14,000 hours of education, on which we currently spend approximately $100,000 per child. Malcolm Gladwell's recent book *Outliers* cites evidence that world–class excellence in skill development requires at least 10,000 hours of practice.[*] During the 14,000 hours of K–12 education, if students spent time actually practicing specific cognitive skills, instead of simply sitting and listening or sitting and doing trivial exercises, they could develop extraordinary skills. Thus, the issue is not merely one of creating positive habits; the possibility exists of developing extraordinary abilities among far more young people simply through years of rigorous practice.

With most products in the $100,000 price range, we find an extraordinary drive toward innovation. Other than housing, there

---

[*] Malcolm Gladwell, *Outliers*, Little, Brown, & Company, 2008.

are no other products or services in the $100,000 price range that are purchased by almost all Americans. And even though housing is a highly regulated industry, with building regulations and federal loan agencies dictating many specific design features, it is still a highly innovative industry with many dramatic changes in materials and design in the past decades. But, of course, in the case of education we do not make the $100,000 purchase—the government does.

Public Housing and the Tuition Tax Deduction instead of Public Schools and the Mortgage Interest Deduction

One of my favorite thought experiments is to consider what our world would look like today if, say, starting in the 1840s and expanding to cover a majority of Americans by the 1930s, the U.S. government had chosen to provide free public housing to all citizens and tax deductions for education, rather than public schools for all U.S. children and the mortgage interest deduction for homeowners. For the purposes of the thought experiment, let's add that instead of an 1860s legal decision declaring, "A man's home is his castle," (following a British tradition that dates to feudal times) our legal system had long ago established that "A parent's right to educate his children as he sees fit is sacred." Furthermore, the courts would have made clear that the government has a right to intervene in housing decisions and arrangements as it sees fit, even intervening in private housing arrangements when it was declared to be "in the public interest" to do so.

With a public-spirited commitment to provide free public housing for all, perhaps single adults would get a single room unit with 300 square feet and families would get a standard apartment of 800 square feet with three tiny bedrooms using cutting-edge 1930s building technology. Over time, as it was discovered that some contractors were not building homes that met appropriate standards, a government certified builder's education program would be required for contractors and construction workers to ensure that they consistently produced high quality homes according to the government interpretation of 1930s "best quality" building standards. Our homes would receive periodic inspections from government-certified home inspectors who would repair and replace those defective parts and materials that were listed in the official home repair manual. There would be almost no homelessness, because those who escaped government homes would be caught by the police and forced back into their homes as truants.

There would be a small, marginalized private apartment building industry, but because free public housing dominated the market, the materials used in the private market would be largely the same as those used in the public market. In most states, there would be regulations that forced private builders to build private apartments in accordance with the standards set by public housing using only government certified builders. Because the private apartment industry would be so marginal, units therein would be more expensive and lower quality than in our world. It would be considered normal to live in public housing, and many would consider it elitist and extravagant to pay for an apartment when the government supplied a perfectly good one for free. There would be a national debate about the deteriorating state of public housing, but most would regard their own neighborhoods as adequate even while being concerned about the squalor elsewhere. With everyone living in public towers, those hippies and fundamentalists who went out into the country and built their own units in isolation would be regarded with suspicion and considered undemocratic.

At the same time, with all payments on education tax deductible, we would now have three, going on four generations of U.S. citizens who had had a greater incentive to spend more on education, of all sorts, because those expenses were tax free. A more diverse market in education would exist, with hundreds of thousands of educational entrepreneurs creating surprising innovations. Children would learn more, enjoy the process, have less homework, spend more time with their families, and learn lifelong habits to promote well-being. There would be wealthy educational entrepreneurs who specialize in creating highly customized educational programs for students with special needs, families with special interests, or students with unusual aptitudes. There would also be wealthy educational entrepreneurs who had specialized in mass-producing consistent, high quality, plain vanilla education programs that incorporate the innovations of those programs in the vanguard a decade later.

Highly capitalized education corporations would hire the best expertise in human development, and those individuals who had an unusual ability to design and replicate systems to support human development would be highly sought after professionals with salaries to match. The entire world of education would be highly differentiated with many different kinds of specialized positions we can't imagine, some offering in-home educational opportunities, some offering diverse wilderness and deep cultural experiences, some cultivating the ability to think creatively, others the ability to intuit the feelings of others, some developing entrepreneurial visioning to an extraordinary degree, others developing the capacity for understanding the human body from the inside out. A small attempt at "public schooling" would be rejected after a short period as an embarrassment to those who had originally endorsed it.

In short, instead of a shallow, hedonistic culture with rebellious teenagers living in enormous houses (the average U.S. citizen existing under the poverty line lives in more square footage than the average European), we would today be known as a culture that prized learning, well-being, and human development, while living in small, dull, crowded apartments. Teenagers would be committed to learning and well-being, with their social hierarchies based on who was doing the coolest learning stuff; though perhaps they'd have sullen, angry attitudes about their dull, tiny homes.

Sound implausible? Perhaps. But consider the cultural effects of Soviet communism: vibrant intellectuality in math, physics, and chess, where creative freedom was allowed and a leaden conformity in the social sciences and broadcast media. Talented people want the freedom to create always and everywhere.

A New Vision of Education as Habituation and Cultural Creation

Once one realizes the importance of developing a dynamic, innovative market in habituation and cultural creation services, one realizes that:

1. With the right institutional framework, thousands of us can create new, more positive cultures for our young people.

2. The same institutional framework that will allow for greater happiness and well-being will also allow for the emergence of dramatically better academic performance and workplace skills.

3. It is crucial to change the institutional framework toward greater educational freedom in order to allow this to happen.

4. In the absence of such changes, our world will inevitably become increasingly driven by shallow impulsiveness, a world in which "Children will learn . . . that the accumulation of things and the expression of one's own feelings are the meaning of life."*

Given the right institutional framework, many thousands of people could be creating better schools (and thereby better subcultures) than now exist. I can't predict exactly what kind of schools that they would create. But if they focused specifically on deliberately creating better, more positive school cultures—by focusing on the development of habits and norms; by allowing visionary leaders to staff the school with individuals who exemplified core virtues; and by consistently providing young people with compelling heroes, ideals, and aspirations that were achievable through specific communal practices—then possibilities exist that are quite beyond our current experience.†

This could be the start of a dynamic, experimental, innovative transformation of U.S. education in which thousands of new practices are developed, thousands of new ways of structuring schools are created, thousands of new kinds of human relationships blossom, and thousands of new microcultures are founded, classroom by classroom, school by school. A flourishing society seeded with new, vibrant, school-based microcultures could then transform our macroculture in new, surprising, and beneficial ways.

Right now most wonderful practices are virtually illegal in public schools. But we can change that. It doesn't need to be against the law to improve kids' lives.

---

*Robert Bellah, from his 1989 introduction to *Tokugawa Religion* (New York: The Free Press, 1985).

†St. John's College, Plato and Aristotle, Werner Jaeger's *Paideia*, and Alasdair MacIntyre's *After Virtue,* have all influenced my views offered here. See also Michael Strong, *The Habit of Thought: From Socratic Seminars to Socratic Practice* (Chapel Hill, N.C.: New View Publications, 1997), and David V. Hicks, *Norms and Nobility*.

A Practical Approach to an Idealistic New Social Vision

Aspirations and ideals are crucial to the psyche of Western civilization. Marxism exercised such an extraordinary influence over millions of minds because it promised a better world. Indeed, it boggles the mind that the need for aspirations and ideals was apparently so great that a movement that was more murderous than Nazism, whose murders were repeatedly documented over a 70-year period, nevertheless continued to serve as an ongoing focus for idealism throughout 70 years of mass murder. It seems that we crave a vision for a brighter future.

Since the collapse of communism there have been no widely recognized aspirations for society. The nightmare of communism should not prevent us from having humane aspirations.

Environmentalism, multiculturalism, and antiglobalization—those movements in which the spirit of the Left lives on—are wholly inadequate as visions for the fulfillment of human potential. Conservatives mostly fight against the social changes of the last 40 years, without offering much of a positive vision of their own.

There is a large market for books and workshops on how to live a better life. The *Chicken Soup for the Soul* series and Stephen Covey's *Seven Habits of Highly Effective People* series are but two well-known examples. They have each become small industries in their own right; during a period in the late 1990s a list of the top-selling 100 books of the year contained several volumes from each series and more than half the books overall were either inspirational or self-help. M. Scott Peck's *The Road Less Traveled* has been on the *New York Times* bestseller list for longer than any other paperback. Apparently people crave guidance.

Many people, perhaps most people, would like to become more successful at the art of living. Although individuals may receive inspiration from quotations, inspirational speeches, religious sermons, works of art, or nature, very few individuals are able to learn the art of living from any of them. They must be provided with experiences in which the inspiring approach to life is constantly supported and reinforced. This is why many churches place an emphasis on fellowship. It is very difficult for us to create better lives for ourselves in isolation. We usually need peer communities to support our practice of the good, of wellness, of excellence, however we perceive such goals.

Beyond the genetic component, human beings become who they become based on the daily, moment-to-moment manner in which they live. They learn, or fail to learn, the art of living from those around them. We have no institutions in which young people may learn better ways of living. Schools at present are mostly institutions in which young people learn worse ways of living.

There is a lacunae in our existing set of institutions. Although there are universities that encourage the study of education and human development, schools that follow government rules, and churches and secular organizations that promote spiritual ideals, there are no institutions that allow for the ongoing practical development and implementation of better ways of living. We need to allow for the growth of a new species of institution in which better ways of living may be developed and transmitted to our young.

Reformers have long recognized that education is the solution to our problems.* What has not been generally recognized is the equivocal nature of the term "education." Exhortational billboards or worksheets on self-esteem do not change habits and appetites, norms, and attitudes. Inspiring, healthy adults, who build real mentoring relationships with the young people whom they supervise and who work together as a team to impart the practices of a coherent culture to the young can make a significant difference. We need to create institutions in which the power of such adults is constantly concentrated, enhanced, and developed as they learn those practices needed to transmit a coherent culture. We do not have such institutions at present.

In the absence of government schools and government teacher training (that is, training through state-accredited schools of education mandated by state licensure laws), at this point our society would have nurtured institutions devoted to the practical development, implementation, and continual improvement of better ways of living. Teacher training would have developed along a path that would have been quite different

---

*Kant, "On Education," is an excellent early source on this perspective; Rousseau's *Emile* a very different one. Ultimately, of course, these themes may be traced, in a different form, back to Plato.

from what it is today, much more closely aligned with the optimization of human potential. Schools would be unimaginably different from what they are today, much more closely aligned with the fulfillment of those human needs that would allow for the optimization of human potential.

I have many thousands of hours of experience in creating new classroom cultures along with capable colleagues, in training others to create such cultures, and in creating schools in which new student cultures thrive. I have wanted to create new and better teacher training centers so that I could staff new and better schools reliably. This goal is not possible at present.

My proximate goal as an educator was primarily to increase intellectual performance; I had cohorts of students who gained twice and three times the national average annual gains on the SAT verbal. In northern New Mexico, I created a charter school in a region where no students had ever taken an Advanced Placement (AP) test; a faculty member from the University of New Mexico-Taos told me point-blank that "Northern New Mexico students are not capable of passing AP tests." New Mexico as a whole typically ranks near the bottom of all states nationally, 47th or lower, by various educational measures.

In the school's second year, so many of our students were taking AP tests that we ranked in the top 150 schools in the United States on Jay Mathews' Challenge Index, which is calculated by dividing the number of AP tests taken by the number of graduating seniors. In the school's third year, it was ranked the 36th best public high school in the nation based on the Challenge Index, with students passing AP tests at more than double the national rate. It has remained a top-ranked school, despite the fact that I was forced to leave my position as school principal because I did not have a public school administrator's license. I know how to create new school cultures that are intensely intellectual, even in the most unintellectual environments, that result in extraordinary, measurable intellectual gains.

To create superb intellectual gains, I realized that the ultimate answer lay in changing peer culture to be supportive of learning rather than hostile to learning. This is especially critical if one wants to improve intellectual performance among cultural groups that are not already performing well academically. In order for a school to make a consistent, comprehensive push toward changing a peer culture, the school director needs the freedom to focus directly on those variables that determine patterns of peer interactions.

When I directed a charter school, I worked for the government. My employer, the government, judged my work strictly by whether I hired credentialed teachers; whether my students scored well on certain standardized exams (exams that were not aligned with authentic learning); whether I followed the state procurement code (they actually specified the number of purchase orders allowed in each file folder); and other such trivia. The lawmakers who established these laws were not bad people. The state employees who enforce these laws are not bad people. The thousands of school administrators for whom compliance with the law is the primary focus are not bad people.

And yet, the strictures with which the law forces us to comply are at best very partial and misguided. A busy administrator soon finds most, if not all, of his or her energy consumed by compliance with dictates that utterly fail to reflect human needs and reality. It is not possible to raise young people well by means of general rules passed in the form of laws or bureaucratic decisions by distant legislatures and state boards of education. It is not possible to make the many thousands of adjustments, for particular individuals, particular circumstances, and in a world of pervasive change, while adhering to many strata of inconsistent laws and regulations.*

By means of such well-intentioned compliance with well-intentioned enforcement of well-intentioned laws, over many decades of public education, we have reached a horribly inhuman situation in which young human life is systematically distorted and starved for meaning and inspiration. These distortions and starvations in K–12 education, contribute to much of the dysfunction of our society. In the last 100 years or so, compulsory mass public education has replaced individual human discernment of what the young human spirit needs

---

*Brain researchers estimate that the number of potential synaptical connections in the human brain exceeds the number of molecules in the universe. The human brain is the most complex known entity in the universe. We have thousands of different kinds of shoes; we should have thousands of different kinds of schools. It is simply not possible for legislation and regulation to create educational institutions that adequately reflect the extraordinary diversity of the human mind.

with a bureaucratic system that has been utterly blind to the needs of the human spirit. We have preempted and then betrayed our deepest instincts, and we gradually need to rediscover how to raise our young so that they may be happy and well in the chaotic world of never-ending change in which we find ourselves.

Creativity and the freedom to use it have given more people better, healthier, and more fulfilled lives than any of us fully realizes. The great tragedy of modern times is that the most powerful system for developing and disseminating ever more sophisticated products and services, the free market, has not yet been applied to educating our young. The great tragedy of modern times is that those who believe that only a fraction of human potential, well-being, and happiness has yet been achieved mostly don't believe in the power of free markets, and most of those who do don't envision an unlimited expansion of human potential, well-being, and happiness.

I want to convince those who believe that human potential is as yet largely untapped that educational freedom is the *sine qua non* for the realization of their dreams and to specify how to create those institutions that will allow for the realization of their dreams.

Many of those who believe in human potential believe that free markets are hostile to human potential and fundamentally undermine its development. What they don't realize is that their assessment is, at present, correct precisely because we have not allowed a market in education to form. Current connotations of the term "free market" imply commercialism and consumerism because our current schools are utterly incapable of training appetites. Young people are completely vulnerable to marketing; a course in media awareness does not change the fact that young people today crave the kinds of stimulation that existing markets provide for them. The only way to change the vulnerability of young people to marketing is to cultivate their preferences, to instill in them individually a more valuable set of preferences, and to surround them with a peer culture that supports such alternative sets of preferences.

Initially perhaps, few parents or students will choose schools that develop the human spirit. But if you believe, as do I, that there are marvelous aspects of life that are being lost to contemporary young people because of the avalanche of destruction of creativity that has been let loose upon our culture, then perhaps I can persuade you that educators such as myself, and better, will be able to market the foundations for deep wellness to both parents and young people. I'm inclined to believe that the latent demand for education that satisfies the human spirit is enormous. In such a world, "sales" and "marketing" will have profoundly different connotations than they do at present. Instead of being inundated solely with marketing that appeals to our most shallow impulses, we will increasingly find ourselves in a world in which competing visions of well-being are put forward in tantalizing fashion.

The stage at which we now find ourselves is one in which the most important lesson that the young need to learn is how to live. We need experts on life, integrity, wellness, humor, kindness, love, accepting grace, finding courage, and on being human. We need model human beings who can create new, better ways of living together. We need artists of life who can blend together the astonishingly different cultural patterns, old and new, to create teen cultures devoted to new forms of human adventure that move beyond violence, manipulative and casual sex, bigotry, social cruelty, drugs, whining, self-righteousness, laziness, vanity, and self-indulgence.

We are now at a stage in which the work that is needed is not merely a matter of teaching algebra or grammar or historical facts. It is increasingly the case that the duller parts of all academic disciplines may largely be taught by means of computers. Increasingly, human educators will need to specialize in uniquely human abilities, those skills, habits, attitudes, and norms that technology will never be able to transmit.

If people knew that they could do what they love and share what they love with others, while being assured of a modest salary, they would be crawling out of the woodwork to practice their artistry. We have entered the age of meaning. Now that most of us have had our basic needs for food, lodging, and security met, we long more than anything else to make a meaningful contribution to society.

Exercising our creative powers by means of sharing our individual uniqueness and brilliance with the young is far, far, more satisfying than is shopping or parties or gambling or doing most of the other wasteful things that so many people spend so much time doing. If we were allowed to create better learning communities, most recreation would come to seem boring.

More than anything, we need schools based on love. We need schools in which people passionately love what they are doing, love what they are teaching, love what they are learning, where teachers love their colleagues, students love their teachers, teachers love their students, parents love the school, where everyone is joined by a passionate vision of excellence and human flourishing. Such schools cannot be mandated or created by force. They must be freely chosen by all parties involved.

In a world of educational freedom, parents, students, and educators will choose those educational communities that they love, communities that are based on love. For more than 100 years we have cauterized the love that mothers and fathers feel for their children by coercive educational models.* We must now begin to heal from this violation of the human spirit. As a consequence of allowing love into the world of K–12 education, on a grand scale, we will begin to introduce love into the adult world, very gradually, on an even grander scale.

The Challenges We Face

For much of the twentieth century, social scientists tended to believe that human beings were creatures of culture. The Marxists believed that human selfishness could be eradicated in a post-communist utopia. Anthropologists studying exotic cultures discovered an astounding array of behaviors and concluded that human nature was almost entirely plastic. Feminists, in the battle for equality, argued that traditional male/female stereotypes were culturally-determined rather than based in nature.

---

*From a petition to the King of the Netherlands begging for freedom from forced schooling when it was first begun in the early nineteenth century: "Sire, do not deny us any longer the tender interests of our children. We would rather see our goods consumed than our flesh and blood corrupted." Cited in Charles Leslie Glenn, Jr.'s, *The Myth of the Common School*, 53.

More recently the field of sociobiology has renewed interest in the genetic aspects of human nature, that which is inherited rather than culturally determined. Human beings have certain genetic predispositions, including appetites for sex and for status, that seem to be hard-wired into our DNA. One of our genetic predispositions, however, is to be influenced by our peers. The desire for acceptance, recognition, and respect from our peers and from our society is very powerful.

It is largely futile to try as individuals, or even as families, to form isolated bulwarks against the overwhelming force of pop culture. The fundamentalist Christians realize this, which is why they are so insistent on mobilizing en masse on political issues and why they are eager to home school or send their children to Christian schools. (It is also the reason why they have created Christian rock, Christian radio, Christian bookstores, Christian television stations, and so on. They realize the importance of mounting a coherent, coordinated cultural campaign against pop culture.) Advocates of new culture; advocates of a more just, kind, and humane world, those who believe in human potential—all need to realize that their goals are also best realized by means of freeing education from government control.

Although a certain percentage of the high school population is working hard in order to get into competitive colleges (perhaps 20 to 30 percent), the vast majority of high school students are devoting only a small fraction of their intellectual and moral energies toward learning. For most middle and high school students, school is a social activity, a kind of game in which the goal is to obtain adequate grades while doing as little real learning as possible. The number of hours wasted, the number of dollars wasted, and the sum of human energy wasted, is colossal. No other sector of the economy has as great a potential for improvements in efficiency.

As someone who has brought numerous adult professionals into the classroom, I can say that most professional adults, who themselves worked reasonably hard in school and were reasonably polite (they were almost invariably among the 30 percent who actually worked in school), are shocked when they first teach contemporary students. The level of apathy and indifference to learning—the disrespect for authority—is astounding. *Beavis and Butt-Head* is a joke very much based in reality. Anyone who doubts this should substitute teach in a local government high school for a week. Be sure to get a course schedule that includes a few nonhonors courses; the view from the high end may be misleading.[*]

Adolescence in America is largely a disaster. Bill McKibben, the environmentalist writer and advocate of natural living, is as harsh as any fundamentalist parent: "If one had set out to create a culture purposefully damaging to children, you couldn't do much better than America at the end of the twentieth century." Patricia Hersch, in a book titled *A Tribe Apart: A Journey into the Heart of American Adolescence*, states: "All parents feel an ominous sense—like distant rumbles of thunder moving closer and closer—that even their child could be caught in the deluge of adolescent dysfunction sweeping the nation." According to a *USA Today* poll, although 75 percent of U.S. parents say they have taken steps to shield their children from outside influences deemed undesirable, 73 percent concede that limiting children's exposure to popular culture is "nearly impossible."[†]

---

[*] In 1999, Phi Delta Kappa, one of the most respected educational organizations in the United States, published an article "Give Us This Day Our Daily Dread: Manufacturing Crises in Education." The article makes the case that enemies of public education deliberately manufacture crises in order to undermine support for public education. The author recommends that, in response to many of the alleged failings of public education, we should apply the "So what?" test. One of his examples of a manufactured alarmist finding is the statistic that fewer than 10 percent of students are attentive in their high school science classes. He claims that this is a "So what?" finding that should be ignored. His rationale:

"No 'index of attentiveness' is provided, tempting readers who have not been in recent close contact with large groups of adolescents to infer that 10 percent is a low value."

Thus in an article in defense of public education published by a leading organization of professional educators we are told to respond "So what?" to the fact that only 10 percent of students are attentive in their high school science classes. The author does not dispute this fact, but instead implies that such a statistic is to be expected among those who have been "in recent close contact with large groups of adolescents."

The Indiana University High School Survey of Student Engagement reports that 55 percent of students spend less than three hours per week preparing for all of their classes combined; when one considers that many students who are working hard to get into competitive colleges spend three hours per night, the implication is that vast numbers of students do no homework at all: (www.indiana.edu/~nsse/hssse/pdf/hssse_2004_overview.pdf).

[†] The material in the foregoing paragraph is all taken from a *USA Today* article titled "A Culture Purposefully Damaging," Oct. 1, 1998.

Professional wrestling is the most popular television show among adolescent males. Mary Pipher's well-known book *Reviving Ophelia* makes the case that contemporary teen culture amounts to an assault on teen girls: "America today is a girl-destroying place," she states. Students across the United States acknowledge that the viciousness of high school cliques and hierarchies could lead to another Columbine-style massacre anywhere.

The obvious power of teen culture to shape human lives has only recently been re-recognized. We were much wiser in the nineteenth century. Ralph Waldo Emerson summed up the perspective well: "I pay the schoolmaster, but it is the schoolboys that educate my son." More recently, Judith Rich Harris, in *The Nurture Assumption*, has shown that the majority of evidence of psychological research suggests that peers have a greater influence over young people than do parents: "In the long run it isn't the home environment that makes the difference. It is the environment shared by children. It is the culture created by these children."

The pervasive power of peer influence is most problematic with respect to negative behaviors:

> Research has shown that the best predictor of whether a teen-ager will smoke is whether her friends smoke. This is a better predictor than whether her parents smoke. Teenagers who smoke are also more likely to engage in other kinds of "problem behavior": to drink, to use illegal drugs, to become sexually active at an early age, to cut classes or drop out of school, to break laws. They belong to peer groups in which such behaviors are considered normal.
>
> Judith Rich Harris, *The Nurture Assumption: Why Children Turn Out the Way They Do*, Simon and Schuster, 1998, 281

As a consequence, "Telling teenagers about the health risks of smoking . . . is useless." The only way to affect teen behavior is to change the nature of peer culture. The massive public health and education dollars being spent didactically are almost entirely wasted. An educational approach that intervened in peer culture, instead of futilely talking *at* kids, is the only approach that is worth being described as "an investment."

John Taylor Gatto, twice named New York State Teacher of the Year, describes conventional K–12 education as 13 years' training in passivity and dependence, meaninglessness and incoherence.* The method is the only real lesson learned by the students. Existing K–12 education largely consists of experiential indoctrination in the lesson that learning is boring, humiliating, and meaningless and that therefore the only rewards in life come from intense stimulations. Appetites for community, spirituality, art, and nature are systematically stunted in our young people in the first 18 years of their lives. As adult consumers, they then go on to create the society in which we live.

As traditional cultures erode in the face of the media mass cultures, and as addictive behaviors and substances degrade the lives of increasing millions, those of us who care about human well-being have an opportunity to create new cultures that are more humane while also being suitably adapted to twenty-first-century global society. Innovative, enculturating K–12 education is the only means of raising new generations with the coherence and structure of a culture in the face of the avalanche of commercial stimulation that has become inescapable and will become as addictive as any drug. As the United States debates, and gradually implements, school choice, we face a unique opportunity to transform our world for the better.

The influence of traditional cultures around the world is decreasing. Tribal cultures in Africa, Indonesia, and South America are vanishing. Ethnic sub-cultures in urban areas of the United States are gradually disappearing. A few mass media-supported monocultures are taking over the world: a Muslim mass culture, a Hispanic mass culture, a Chinese mass culture, and an Anglo mass culture. The traditional idiosyncrasies, practices, prejudices, and virtues of those cultures in which mankind evolved are rapidly vanishing. Insofar as traditional cultures are being replaced by new idiosyncratic cultures, for the most part the new cultures are being formed by electronic media rather than by human beings.

Around the world, life with human beings in a common culture is being replaced by daily experiences of flashy, stimulating, electronic

---

*John Taylor Gatto, *Dumbing Us Down: The Hidden Curriculum of Compulsory Schooling*, New Society Publishers, 2002. See especially Chapter 1, "The Seven-Lesson School Teacher."

sounds and images. Electronic stimulation is becoming increasingly potent and seductive. Technology will continue to develop ever more compelling television and video, computer and video games, musical stimulation, and virtual reality. As a teen I read a science fiction novel in which most people no longer wanted to live life; they preferred to experience their virtual realities, complete with electrodes to stimulate the brain so as to simulate physical experiences and mental states. Life consisted of the virtual experience of having sex with the most attractive partners, reliving the most transcendent religious experiences of saints and martyrs, or triumphantly fighting as a gladiator engaged in orgies of violence, all achieved while lying down in a lounger and not moving a muscle.

Each year advances in entertainment technology bring us closer to this world. Readers who are not immersed in this world have no comprehension of the amount of time and money young men spend on electronic games. The gaming world is now a bigger industry, by revenue, than the motion picture industry, and this enormous industry caters to a narrower demographic than does the motion picture industry—mostly young males. These massive revenue streams will result in ever-larger investments in evermore sophisticated virtual experiences that will soon approximate the science fiction vision described in the previous paragraph. Role playing games and virtual reality technologies are rapidly becoming more intensely stimulating and more intensely real. One of the best-selling computer games in recent years, *Grand Theft Auto*, includes an option whereby teenage boys can hire a prostitute, avail themselves of her services, and then murder her.[*] Blowing up heads and splattering human beings, are common gaming

---

[*] Of course, players also have the option to date rather than merely to hire a prostitute: "The main reason to date a girl in this game is to get stuff from her. . . . The easiest way to make your relationship with a girl go down is to abuse her during a date. This means hitting her or shooting her with any weapons. If you hit her just once, the date might not immediately end. However, shooting the girl or beating her repeatedly will instantly end the date. All of the girls can take quite a few hits, including multiple head shots from various weapons. But they can die, and if you kill a girl, she will no longer be your girlfriend." From "a guide to dating female characters in the video game *Grand Theft Auto: San Andreas*" published as "The Gamer's Guide to Girls" in *Harper's Magazine,* October 2005, 22.

options. We should be concerned about the ever-increasing realism of such gaming experiences and the hours of saturation and the consequent tastes and appetites formed among numerous boys.

But it is possible to create new forms of K–12 education based on ever-deepening human bonds and experiences so that real, lived life will be a more compelling direct experience for young people than it is at present. As Mihaly Cziksentmihalyi points out in *Flow*, engaging in creative, challenging activity is an optimal experience. But in order to prepare them so that they can take advantage of life's peak experiences we need to develop young people from a young age so that they have the capacity to engage in such activity. Then we must provide them with constant opportunities to practice such activities— only then will they find real life more engaging than the evermore intensely-stimulating virtual realities coming soon to a neighborhood near you.

Transformative Cultures as a Solution to Public Health and Environmental Problems

The costs of a world in which short-term stimulations are more satisfying than long-term virtues is already immense, arguably on the order of $1 trillion per year in the United States alone. The leading causes of death in the United States are heart disease, cancer, stroke, respiratory disease, and accidents. The rate of incidence of each of these is heavily influenced by lifestyle factors:

> Currently, modern chronic diseases, including cardiovascular diseases, Type 2 diabetes, metabolic syndrome, and cancer, are the leading killers in Westernized society and are increasing rampantly in developing nations. In fact, obesity, diabetes, and hypertension are now even commonplace in children. Clearly, however, there is a solution to this epidemic of metabolic disease that is inundating today's societies worldwide: exercise and diet. Overwhelming evidence from a variety of sources, including epidemiological, prospective cohort, and intervention

studies, links most chronic diseases seen in the world today to physical inactivity and inappropriate diet consumption.

Christian K. Roberts and R. James Barnard,
"Effects of Exercise and Diet on Chronic Disease,"
Journal of Applied Physiology, March, 30, 2005, 98

If we could develop and transmit an improved cultural technology it would reduce death, disease, and the associated costs, at a much greater rate than is possible by means of improved medical technology. A culturally-reinforced habituation education will be more powerful than a public health campaign to eat less fat and sugar. The National Center for Chronic Disease Prevention claims that 75 percent of our $1.4 trillion in health care cost goes toward the treatment of chronic diseases, the incidence of which are largely preventable by means of lifestyle factors.[*] This figure does not include costs associated with accidents, which are also influenced by lifestyle factors. One estimate of the medical costs associated with automobile accidents alone for 1990 was $362 billion.

In addition to chronic diseases and accidents, addictive behaviors are among our most prevalent and intractable social problems. The American Council on Science and Health puts the costs of social addictions to alcohol, tobacco, and illicit drugs at $241 billion. People with healthy relationships and healthy habits, people who are surrounded by others who live healthier lives, people who are engaged in meaningful work in a meaningful community, are less likely to succumb to addictions. A public health campaign on billboards is a weak substitute for a culture that supports well-being. Expensive addiction treatment centers after the addiction has taken hold are a terrible substitute for a culture that promotes healthy behavior. People who

---

[*] And as global wealth increases, these issues are rapidly becoming global issues. A recent article in *Scientific American* (September 2005, *Special Issue: Crossroads for Planet Earth*) by Barry Bloom, dean of Harvard's School of Public Health, summarizing the state of global public health claims: "Globally, infectious disease is waning, but chronic disorders are taking an increasing toll. Many chronic ills are related to lifestyle and are unlikely to abate without action by regulatory and health agencies." Of course, they are also unlikely to abate with action by regulatory and health agencies. I suspect it has never occurred to Dean Bloom to consider minimally regulated school choice as a long-term solution to these problems.

learn the art of living while young will harm society, and themselves, significantly less over their lifetimes.

Our existing medical system is not effective at transmitting techniques for reducing stress, changing diet, and improving physical fitness. Indeed, there are financial and institutional incentives that will continue to result in an emphasis on a "drugs and surgery" approach for many decades rather than a transition to a more holistic wellness approach. Schools, where children's habits and attitudes may be developed for 13 years in a row, is the ideal environment in which to cultivate wellness. Yet existing schools are, for the most part, even worse than our existing medical system when it comes to cultivating wellness. Often, well-raised young people learn bad habits through our existing schools.

Currently there are differential insurance rates for smokers and non-smokers. I envision a world of competing brands of educational programs with competing approaches to learning and wellness (like the tiny, amateurish Montessori and Waldorf movements but with billions of investment capital and diverse types of extraordinary human talent committed to their development and implementation). If certain brands of schooling reliably graduated individuals with healthier habits, graduates of such programs might be eligible for lower insurance rates. With financial incentives combining with parental interest in their children's well-being, all guided by cutting-edge zealots for healthier ways of living, gradually one can imagine a society with significantly fewer health problems and much lower health costs. Preventative medicine could become a reality.

Latter-day Saints (Mormons) provide a dramatic case study of the public health benefits resulting from involvement in a particular culture. The Mormons have created a distinctive culture with remarkable health and welfare benefits. Utah, where 70 percent of the population is Mormon, has the lowest, or near the lowest, rates of smoking, lung cancer, heart disease, alcohol consumption, abortions, out-of-wedlock births, workdays missed due to illness, and the lowest child poverty rate in the country. Utah ranks highest in the nation in number of AP tests taken, number of AP tests passed, scientists produced per capita, percentage of households with personal computers, and proportion of income given to charity.* An epidemiological study of the impact

---

* See www.adherents.com/largecom/lds_dem.html.

of LDS membership on smoking estimated that if non–LDS rates had matched LDS rates among Utah residents between 1994 and 1998, there would have been 24,000 fewer years of life lost.[*]

Utah is often ranked among the best places to live and the best places to raise children. Provo, more than 90 percent Mormon, was ranked by *Self* magazine as the healthiest city for women in the country, because it had the lowest incidence of cancer, violence, depression, and so on.

Within Utah, it is clear that Mormons are disproportionately represented within these positive statistics, and Mormon populations outside Utah share similar phenomenally positive statistics. Indeed, although no academic researcher would dare to propose such a thing, one could conclude that a mass conversion to Mormonism would reduce social problems more effectively than all welfare spending, academic research, and public health initiatives in the last 50 years.

I don't believe that we have to convert to Mormonism in order to obtain these benefits. I think that, given a large, diverse, educational marketplace, secular humanists, new age spiritual educators, and traditional religious educators will all develop better ways of promulgating habits of wellness due to innovations in enculturation technology.

Currently, we spend approximately $430 billion annually on a K–12 educational system that is not only ineffective with respect to academic content, it is also ineffective with respect to inculcating good habits. What if, deployed by means of educational vouchers, that $430 billion saved our society between $500 billion and $1 trillion in health care, lost productivity, and accidental damage costs? These figures don't include the human costs associated with rape, child and spousal abuse, unwanted pregnancies, and other features of contemporary human life that might be reduced by healthy enculturating educations.

Many environmentalists are against economic growth because they perceive economic growth to be necessarily a matter of increased use of natural resources. But under the right circumstances human beings have a greater appetite for achieving their human potential than they

---

[*] R. Merrill, "Impact of LDS church's health doctrine on deaths from diseases and conditions associated with cigarette smoking," *Annals of Epidemiology*, Vol. 13, Issue 10, 704–711.

do for endless material aggrandizement. Economic growth could just as well mean additional demand for art, music, spirituality, and community rather than for gambling, pornography, intoxicants, and status goods. We can create schools that dramatically shift preferences toward those things that we perceive as good, but we will need a lot more freedom in order to do so.

As someone who has been exposed to many different means of expanding human potential, I perceive an unlimited realm of human development with respect to body, mind, and spirit. I could spend many lifetimes exploring various practices and disciplines without ever having any time to watch television or go to the mall. If schools provided meaningful, enculturating educations that provided young people with a profound sense of well-being, many of the concerns of environmentalists would be ameliorated. This approach is certainly more effective than is preachy environmental education. As long as young people have the appetites that they do, enforced by the status hierarchies of existing peer culture, then all the environmentalist preaching in the world will remain impotent.

None of the current outcomes are necessary outcomes. Teens from all social classes can be polite, motivated, and well-educated. Teenage males can treat teenage females respectfully. Teens do not have to be racist. Teens do not have to be cruel. Teens do not have to addle their minds with drugs and alcohol for recreation. Teens do not have to graduate from high school illiterate and lacking basic workplace skills. All teen pathologies are entirely preventable and unnecessary. A steadily increasing percentage of teens, and subsequently adults, could have the opportunity to be healthy, well, whole human beings.

The Power of Culture

Anthropologists have long been aware of the power of cultural differences: African tribesmen who could follow nearly invisible traces in the dust to track animals; Native Americans who could withstand great pain and suffering during rites of passage; Polynesian fishermen who could determine their location while at sea, far from land, by feeling ocean currents with their hands; Japanese samurai who voluntarily committed seppuku to avoid the shame of not fulfilling their duty; Buddhist monks who burned themselves to death in Vietnam in the 1960s to protest the war. These are but a sampling of the extraordinary range of human capacities that are possible due to culture. During the first generations of anthropological discovery, people from one culture were often incredulous when they first encountered the practices of human beings from another culture. Surely human beings are not capable of such things!

Thomas Sowell has documented systematic differences worldwide in the types of work and achievement characteristic of individuals from different cultural backgrounds. For instance, Chinese and Lebanese peoples often own disproportionately large percentages of retail business establishments in diverse nations, despite differences in legal requirements, local cultures, local business practices, and so forth. Germans built pianos; Jews were prominent in the garment industry; Italians have been prominent as architects and as fishermen. These tendencies held true regardless of the various nations to which they had emigrated. Sowell shows conclusively that these cultural disparities are the norm rather than the exception.*

Fareed Zakaria quotes Joel Kotkin's conclusion after studying cultural patterns in his book *Tribes*:

> If you want to succeed economically in the modern world, the key is simple—be Jewish, be Indian, but above all, be Chinese.
> Fareed Zakaria, *The Future of Freedom: Illiberal Democracy at Home and Abroad*, W.W. Norton & Co., 2003, 53

Although it is not politically correct to acknowledge facts so directly, cultural background obviously plays a crucial role with respect to the success of different populations in our current educational system. Asian and Jewish students are admitted disproportionately to elite colleges and score more highly on a range of tests than do students from other ethnic groups. African-American and Native American students score lower on such tests. This is not evidence of genetic inferiority, but rather of a cultural background that does not happen to provide students with the cultural prerequisites to succeed in our

---

*Thomas Sowell, *Race and Culture: A Worldview*, New York: Basic Books, 1995.

existing school system. Why not create schools that provide all students with the cultural prerequisites for success?

There are precedents for deliberately changing the culture of student populations. Medieval students were a raucous bunch, even when they were 10 or 12; violence, drinking, begging, and whoring were common among students from all social classes. It took centuries of civilizing effort on behalf of the church authorities who ran the schools to change these behaviors. A sample of earlier student life from Philippe Aries' *Centuries of Childhood*:

> At Aix the rector . . . after summoning there a great many boys of the fourth and fifth (classes) [whose tender years afforded them no protection against this contagion of violence], and there he pointed out to them the evil in dueling and forbade them to indulge in dueling under pain of severe penalties. . . . This spirit of violence went with considerable license with regard to wine and women. . . . Montaigne tells us, "A hundred scholars have caught the pox before getting to their Aristotle lesson." And the boys read Aristotle young!
>
> Philip Aries, *Centuries of Childhood: A Social History of Family Life*, translated by Robert Baldick, Vintage Books, New York, 1962, "The Roughness of Schoolchildren," 315–336, available at www.webster.edu/~corbetre/philosophy/education/aries/rough.html

Aries concludes:

> It needed the pressure of the pedagogues to separate the schoolboy from the bohemian adult, both of whom were heirs of a time when elegance of speech and dress was limited not even to the cleric, but to the courtly adult. A new moral concept was to distinguish the child, or at least the schoolboy, and set him apart: the concept of the well-bred child. It scarcely existed in the sixteenth century; it was formed in the seventeenth century. We know that it was the product of the reforming opinions of an elite of thinkers and moralists who occupied high positions in Church or State. The well-bred child would be preserved from the roughness and immorality which would become the

special characteristics of the lower classes. . . . The old medieval unruliness was abandoned first of all by children, last of all by the lower classes: today it remains the mark of the hooligan, of the last heir of the old vagabonds, beggars, and outlaws.

Aries traces a long history of thoughtful commentary by this elite of thinkers and moralists (mostly Jesuit educators and priests) that led to specific changes in school policies and practices. Century by century, student behaviors which were once the norm among schoolboys (teen and younger), such as fighting, drinking, and whoring, became increasingly less common.

Of course such behaviors still occur, but not at the scale or with the level of acceptance that was once the case. Medieval books on manners explicitly instruct people not to urinate in the corners of the castle or to blow their noses on the tablecloths.* Such instructions are generally unnecessary today. Culture has changed significantly in the intervening years.

Just as the Jesuits deliberately marginalized hooliganism, and just as the Mormons have deliberately created a more successful and healthy religious subculture, so, too, could other groups create more successful subcultures. Over time, they would learn much from each other, and a multitude of hybrids would be developed. The human race would learn a terrific amount about how to create well-being deliberately.

Skeptics may find the analogy between traditional or religious cultures, such as Jewish or Mormon cultures, and classroom cultures implausible. Given the current state of affairs, the analogy is implausible. My point, however, is that habits, attitudes, appetites, and norms are important to education; that because of this a free market that allowed for the deliberate development of habits, attitudes, appetites, and norms would flourish due to parents' ongoing interest in improving their children's well-being; and that in a free market, an innovation dynamic would develop that would eventually have highly beneficial results—ultimately the results would be far more positive than what we can currently imagine just as the results of today's technology would astound our ancestors.

---

*For a summary of some of these issues, see John Gillingham, "From Civitas to Civility: Codes of Manners in Medieval and Early Modern England," *Transactions of the Royal Historical Society* (2002: Cambridge University Press), 267–289.

In 1930, almost all of the technology we use today would have seemed implausible. Since then, many billions of dollars and many thousands of bright, creative, focused, practical individuals have created technological wonders—and this result is strictly due to the fact that most of the activity took place in a free market. We can't know what might have been the case if similar billions of dollars and thousands of free individuals had been allowed to create new ways of life in a similarly free market. Silicon Valley was created from math, sand, and freedom. The Soviet Union had the best mathematicians, plenty of sand, but no freedom. And by the mid-1980s a decent U.S. university had more computing power than did the entire Soviet Union.

This may be regarded as a parable with profound implications for our educational system.

Human beings in modern society are not what we could be. None of us has lived up to our potential. Our current set of research institutions for improving human well-being, including those institutions staffed by academic psychologists, sociologists, and education professors, has overlooked a critical strategy for improving well-being. In addition, those public health officials who are trying to reduce obesity, heart disease, cancers, suicides, child and spousal abuse, family dysfunction, addiction, and so on, have overlooked a critical strategy for improving well-being. And finally, those activists and idealists who seek to reduce racism, poverty, materialism, greed, and environmental insensitivity have overlooked a critical strategy for improving well-being. The entrepreneurial creation of coherent modern tribal structures (or virtue cultures), initially in the context of what is now known as K–12 education, provides a better means of solving all of the foregoing problems than has been or will be provided by the exertions of academic researchers and public policy experts.

A Market in Cultural Innovation in order to Help the Poor

The poor are particularly harmed by the lack of a market in education in a world characterized by cultural erosion. The upper classes can afford to either protect their children from cultural erosion by means of their choice of private school or public school in upscale neighborhoods, or they can more readily remedy the problems after the fact by means of therapies, detox centers, vacations, lessons, plastic surgery, retreats, spas, and a thousand other options available to those who can pay. The poor, however, are often simply the victims of cultural erosion, and a poor parent has little recourse when her child's well-being has been undermined.

Our existing educational system is designed to support education as training and/or curriculum coverage. It is not designed to support education as enculturation. Insofar as professional success in the twenty-first century depends on the development of critical thinking skills and intellectuality, the traits of innovation and entrepreneurial initiative, and mastery of upper-middle-class social norms, enculturation is the crucial species of education for social mobility. Young people from households or cultures in which these cultural traits are not already developed will be systematically excluded from the professional classes as long as we continue our existing public school system. As an institution public school has evolved to serve most effectively the most "normal" children of upper-middle-class families; it is most damaging in its effects to any student who is outside the norm or any student who lacks the cultural prerequisites implicitly presupposed by the system.

The greatest benefits of educational innovation, as I see it, will be a system for distributing cultural wealth and well-being as effectively as the market has distributed technological wealth so far. Televisions and radios, refrigerators and washing machines, cell phones and pagers, have all become cheap and ubiquitous even among the poor. Why haven't we created a society in which thrift, industriousness, intellectual curiosity, academic focus, self-discipline, respect, and courtesy are equally cheap and ubiquitous? K–12 education ought to be the leading vector for transmitting good habits from one generation to the next and for adapting new norms and habits to the times. Instead of creating amazing institutions for the transmission of the best cultural habits, our schools have suffered from cultural wars that have deracinated any set of common norms from public schools, resulting in K–12 education that teaches young people not to abide by any set of norms whatsoever— except those spontaneously developed by pop culture and peers.

Insofar as the goal of education is the transmission of culture, direct contact with humans who know how to live is crucial. Although innovations in educational technology may help teach the academic component of education, innovations in the human element of education are the only means by which we will be able to make a fundamental difference in the lives of the poor. I say this as someone with solid roots in the working class, someone who has seen some members of my family flourish due to positive habits and attitudes and other members of my family experience misery due to negative habits and attitudes. Based on the dozens of members of my own extended family whose lives I've observed, as well as the hundreds of children of various social classes whom I've educated, it is clear that day-to-day intellectual and emotional habits are the real key to social mobility. And, as an educator who specializes in the development of new intellectual and emotional habits by means of the creation of new classroom cultures, I know that all young people can have access to the habits needed for success.

The poor are among those who would benefit most from such a process of mutation, selection, and subsequent transmission of new classroom and peer cultures. The system of K–12 education that has been established in this country was a reasonably effective system for educating upper-middle-class students 100 years ago. If a student had been raised with the cultural norms of the upper-middle class, then training in biology, chemistry, grammar, history, and so forth might have been an efficient use of time in order to prepare him for entrance into college at the time. Since then, generations of students have wasted time that might have more productively been spent on other activities. Instead of learning biology or grammar in a context in which initiative and intellectual independence was destroyed, they could have been learning initiative and intellectual independence first and foremost, or frugality and industriousness, or emotional awareness and teamwork, or some other combination of more valuable personal traits.

Anyone who saves and invests $2 per day in an index fund from the age of 15 to the age of 70 will, at long-term average rates of equity return (9 percent), become a multimillionaire. Is it utopian to imagine that, if there were schools that provided deep habituation in frugality and industriousness, in our economy today every impoverished student could create a multimillion dollar fortune? Unlike welfare or other stop-gap measures, such a transference of the technology of success to the poor could eliminate poverty permanently. Moreover, only a generation ago such norms of frugality and industriousness were common. They still are among many people from the developing world.

Because human beings are so varied, with different cultural backgrounds and different personal characteristics, in order to optimize future success for the underprivileged we need vastly more variety in education. Given enough freedom we will eventually develop forms of education that are remarkably different from what we see at present. Some need training in manners, some in "how to win friends and influence people," some in frugality and investment, some need education as emotional therapy, and some need to find themselves. In a market, these and other forms of education will be integrated seamlessly into formidably effective, holistic human development programs that will allow for far more social mobility than exists at present. The more K–12 education is forcibly restricted to the existing curriculum administered by the existing government institutions and certified personnel, the more the poor, in particular, will continue to suffer.

Success in our society is not simply a matter of academic achievement. It is well-known that the income distribution fits a log-normal distribution (highly-skewed, with few rich and many poor). This income distribution is almost certainly due largely to the fact that numerous independent variables—such as academic skills, presentation (speaking) skills, strategic intelligence, appropriate class manners, emotional intelligence, and so on—are necessary to succeed in the workplace.

A complex constellation of characteristics are required for success, most of which are not cultivated by existing schools. Although there are some students who fail because they do not learn academics, there are other students who do learn academics and yet who still do not succeed in life. Our present approach does not begin to provide every child with what he or she really needs to succeed in life. Insofar as it claims to do so, the system is telling a lie.

The Idea of Cultural Innovation

Cultural innovation is constantly taking place. Every new song, book, video, movie, game, communication device, software package, home design, bathtub, spatula, toothbrush, tattoo, zoo, museum, sex toy, car, vacation, map, corporation, spiritual practice, parenting practice, marital therapy, food, diet, exercise, piece of sporting equipment, and so forth has some impact on culture. The notion that we should not seek to innovate culturally is absurd. It is happening all around us at an ever-increasing pace (remember Alvin Toffler's *Future Shock?*).

The only relevant question is, "Do we allow cultural innovation to take place in every realm of life except education, or do we also allow a world in which educators may consciously, deliberately learn how to provide better ways of life?"

The most potent cultural innovators are probably in the field of entertainment, broadly construed. There is nothing wrong with enter-tainment per se. But entertainment necessarily is geared toward satis-fying short-term needs, values, and desires. Why should we accept a society in which cultural innovation is almost exclusively determined by means of short-term impulses?

Suppose, hypothetically, that there are human capacities or appe-tites that take 10 or more years to develop; that those aspects of human nature are best developed during the formative years of childhood and adolescence; and that it is necessary to have communities of tal-ented, committed people working in concert over many years in order to best develop those aspects of human nature. If, hypothetically, any such aspects of human capacity existed, we would be largely ignorant of them because the institutions just described do not exist.

With respect to some desirable traditional cultural traits, those who have tried to preserve them find that it has become very difficult to pass them on to their children in contemporary circumstances. In the West, there are plausible claims that attributes such as character and integ-rity, courage and honor are not what they used to be.* In Japan, which experienced a very rapid transition to modernity in the late nineteenth century, older Japanese observed the rapid decline in the Samurai Bushido ethos in a matter of decades. Alaska natives saw an even more rapid introduction to modernity in the mid-twentieth century,

---

* A tough, grizzled old Colorado rancher, a seeming model of probity and integ-rity, humbly acknowledges that his generation doesn't even know what integrity is by comparison with that of his father and grandfather. No comment needed regarding the subsequent deterioration in more recent generations.

in which thousand-year-old survival skills ranging from hunting knowledge to extraordinary physical toughness and prowess, vanished almost overnight. Cultural traits that may have evolved over many centuries disappear in a generation or even within a few years.

A skeptic may suggest: Fine and good, but we don't really need seal-hunting skills, arctic survival skills, samurai self-discipline and shame, or perhaps even old-style honor and integrity. Regardless of what one thinks of the particular examples of skills, my point is that if there were any human characteristics whatsoever that required long tutelage by trained masters in a supportive culture they would be invisible to us at present. There may be amazing capabilities that might allow human beings to adapt to the twenty-first century but which do not exist, which cannot exist, because our society has prevented the development of those institutions that would bring forth such human capabilities.

Traditional cultures, having evolved through centuries of interaction with a relatively stable environment, are models of such integrated, coherent cultures. Education in such cultures was a natural, unconscious experience in which young people gradually learned the practices of their culture. With the exception of the rapidly disappearing vestigial remains of such cultures, human beings today are raised in a more or less incoherent cultural universe. In the absence of a coherent culture, humans are more likely to find themselves prey to impulsive and compulsive behaviors, variously directed toward material goods, status, sex, food, vanity, emotional attachments, gambling, electronic stimulation (television, video games, and so on), or drugs. We are very complex organisms; in order to live as healthy adults, we need to be raised well.

A century and more ago people talked about "formative education" or "the education of character" which was understood to be the deliberate effort to provide young people with the internal stability required to live well. The model that I have described is as true of traditional formative education as it is of transformative education. Indeed, formative education is the model for all my educational interests. I am very impressed by the formative education characteristic of military schools and traditional Catholic schools. Although my goals as an educator are very different from the goals of these schools, the cultural traditions of which these schools are an integrated component are rightly attentive to such currently neglected aspects of education such as heroes, ideals, music, manners, and attitudes.

Most of contemporary academic education is remarkably neglectful of the importance of such details. The extraordinary human phenomena resulting from the development of Spartan discipline or Buddhist awareness would never have occurred as a consequence of a contemporary American education. I have gradually come to realize that although traditional education and traditional culture were deeply flawed, the holistic cultural approaches used in traditional cultures should not have been left behind by modernity. The same kinds of approaches that have been used in traditional cultures for centuries can be adapted and innovated for greater human well-being going forward into the future.

Gradually, the distinctive new cultures will develop reputations as a market develops in which parents need more information to understand which school model is best for each of their children. Just as *Car and Driver* and *PC User* magazines provide detailed, opinionated analysis of their respective products, so too, will education magazines arise that will provide detailed analysis of distinctive educational cultures. New standards of quality will arise. Instead of test score performance (in the case of public schools) or elitist reputation (in the case of private schools) sufficing for measures of quality, gradually there will develop cadres of perceptive education critics, similar to critics found in the worlds of automobiles, computers, food, art, travel, and so on: These critics will discern those schools that develop an especially wonderful sort of emotional intelligence, those schools that develop a distinctive mental originality, those schools in which lifelong healthy habits are reliably developed, those schools in which males characteristically treat females with remarkable grace and consideration, and a thousand other distinctive virtues.

Alasdair MacIntyre, in *After Virtue*, describes the prerequisites for what he calls a "virtue culture."* He intends for these prerequisites to be abstract and general, to apply to any culture that wishes to develop any

---

* Alasdair MacIntyre, *After Virtue: A Study in Moral Theory* (University of Notre Dame Press, 1984).

particular set of human virtues, be they integrity, politeness, courage, compassion, environmental concern, gender equality, or what have you. His prerequisites are:

1. A communal understanding of each individual's life as a meaningful whole, a life in its entirety as a contribution to the community: people must see the value and meaning of their life as a lifelong contribution (or lack thereof) to society. If people interpret life simply as one impulsive entertainment after another, or one political commitment after another, or any set of disconnected events, it is impossible to develop a serious virtue culture.

2. A moral tradition. People, especially young people, must be raised in a morally coherent social universe. Who are the great heroes of the past? What are the great events that led to our present time? What ideals do we aspire to in the future? What actions (or even thoughts) are considered unforgivable transgressions? What leads to exclusion from the community?

3. A set of practices that allow the people to develop, practice, and perfect their virtues. If manners are important, then there will be social settings in which the best manners are modeled. If honor is important, then there will be social settings in which honor is recognized, acknowledged, exhibited. Whatever the virtue, young people will be immersed in a culture in which the human actions that allow them to achieve excellence in that culture will be constantly exhibited. For manners, young people would be provided training in the small points of etiquette as well as the larger social principles behind the etiquette. Schools that developed frugality would provide constant opportunities for students to discover amazing values for very little money. If political participation is the required virtue, young people would be trained in political oratory, analysis, and dialogue. In each case, the training may be implicit rather than explicit; but it must be pervasive in the cultural immersion that constitutes their education.

These conditions are almost impossible to provide today. They certainly don't exist at most public schools.

MacIntyre is of the belief that all cultures prior to modern European culture were based on such a schema. Humans were raised understanding that they had a role and standing in society and that their entire life was a reflection of how well they fulfilled that role. Indeed, in many cultures, this reputational effect was multigenerational: if one violated a cultural norm, it damaged one's children, and one's children's children, and so forth.

Each culture had a vision of excellence in that society. This vision of excellence was transmitted by means of myth and heroic tales, it was transmitted by a multitude of comments, jokes, attitudes, manners, behavioral corrections, and so forth. The very texture of day-to-day life provided a consistent, coherent template that taught young people how they were to behave. From time to time, a member of the society was sanctioned or expelled in a manner that made it perfectly clear what types of behavior were not condoned by the community. And young people were brought up in a set of cultural practices that allowed them to practice the requisite virtues of that society so that they would naturally become respectable adult participants in such a society.

Of course, western civilization has been seeking liberation from these sorts of intolerant virtue cultures for some 500 years. The social rebellions known as the Renaissance, the Reformation, and the Enlightenment in their resistances to traditional authorities unwittingly provided the foundation for the more radical liberations of the twentieth century. In the 1920s and the 1960s it appeared as if radical individual freedom was the final goal.

What none of the liberators seems to have realized is the truth of Goethe's insight that "Whatever liberates our spirit without a corresponding increase in self-control is pernicious." I continue to be committed to the liberation of the spirit; and I have gradually come to realize that as I liberate spirits, I have an absolute obligation to simultaneously provide training in self-control. Else I am responsible for disasters.

Traditional cultures did not seek to liberate the spirit: by and large, they sought to constrain the spirit within very well-defined cultural boundaries. As a consequence, they were often highly bigoted, shaming, and sometimes cruel: *Zorba the Greek* contrasts Zorba's own liberated spirit with the cruel stoning of a young widow. Films continue to celebrate the liberation of the young from the constraints of traditional narrow-mindedness: See *My Big Fat Greek Wedding* and *Bend It Like*

Beckham for recent sweet comedies based on the same theme. Few people who are truly knowledgeable about traditional cultures would want to return to their brutal stasis, conformity, constraints, and judgmental attitudes.*

And yet many people long for community, tradition, ritual, structure, and meaning in their lives. We (including most emphatically Socratic intellectuals such as myself) have ripped traditional societies and norms to shreds. We had to do it. There were gross injustices and bigotries. We must now rebuild more humane, tolerant, decent replacements for those earlier systems.

Again, I don't claim to have a particular solution. While I can offer profoundly better approaches to training intellectuality and independent thought, I have not solved the problems of sexuality and the meaning of life. I know other educators who are better than I am at creating respect and reverence, who are better at creating awareness and self-discipline, who are better at creating physical vitality and rugged toughness, and who are better at creating aesthetic delight and musical joy. We need to be able to blend these and other approaches to discover what works. Each of us needs to be able to choose our own combinations and educational partners.

The more deeply I've thought about how to create a comprehensive educational solution to this problem the more I've been daunted by the scale of the problem. But no one individual should or could solve it. If thousands of individual educators were allowed to work with others to create institutions that exemplified their own solutions, our society would gradually begin to figure out these problems on a large scale. Many thousands of wonderful human beings would, bit-by-bit, here and there, begin to discover, create, evolve, and then disseminate and improve better ways of life.

---

*Indeed this is the ultimate theme of Dinesh D'Souza's book *What's So Great About America?* (Regnery, 2002). A cultural conservative himself, D'Souza ultimately acknowledges that for all of the cultural depravity, American freedom makes it all worthwhile in the end; the value of escaping traditional cultural constraints is that great (D'Souza is an émigré from India).

A transformative education that cultivates the attitudes and appetites, the habits and customs, the fashions and fantasies, the virtues and ideals of future generations offers a virtually untapped resource for increasing human well-being. In addition, many of the chronic problems facing modernity, including such diverse phenomena as environmental degradation, cancer, immune system disorders, poverty, racism, addictive behaviors, crime, and spousal and child abuse may ultimately require for their solution deep cultural changes that can only be achieved by means of transformative educational techniques not yet imagined.

A Vision for the Future

We need to allow entrepreneurs the freedom to create a radical reconstruction of our educational system and, consequently, of our society. Most readers will find it implausible; prior to my career as an educational entrepreneur I would not have believed my own conclusions.

The good news is that it is possible to create fundamentally new peer cultures in our schools, cultures that are more supportive of learning, achievement, politeness, respect, and wellness. The challenge is that it will not be possible to create and disseminate high quality versions of these new peer cultures on a large scale until we have dramatically more educational freedom than we do at present.

For me, the most urgent political issue in the United States today is to gradually transform our existing K–12 educational institutions by means of universal school choice, through vouchers or tax credits, with minimal constraints concerning curriculum, staffing, or structure of schooling. There are three reasons why I regard this issue as the most urgent of all:

1. Because of the relentless pressures of global competition, those in our society who are not currently receiving a great education will find life in the twenty-first-century job market harsh and unforgiving.
2. Because of the collapse of common norms of culture, including those norms that prevent addiction, constrain sexuality, support

industriousness and thrift, and provide a foundation for long-term meaning and purpose, many in our population already find life harsh and unforgiving.

3. Because people at all levels of our society crave greater meaning, purpose, and community in their lives. They find themselves immersed in a society that lacks structures for providing new models of meaning, purpose, and community and in which gambling, pornography, addictive substances, sensational entertainments, consumer culture, and other types of short-term satisfactions are cheap and ubiquitous.

By administering K–12 education through government, a clunky, lumbering, impersonal agent, we have created a society in which it is easier for entrepreneurs to innovate and market short-term stimulations such as gambling and pornography than it is for entrepreneurs to innovate and market sources of long-term well-being such as wisdom and compassion. We need to legalize markets in happiness and well-being by means of legislation authorizing K–12 educational freedom.

Government control of education—through public schools or through excessive regulation of charter or private schools—amounts to granting control over the young human soul to all those who produce short-term stimulations. Either real human beings, with distinctive intentions and ways of life, are allowed to create cultures with integrity—by means of minimally regulated school choice—or bureaucratic rules prevent the formation of appetites in the young, and marketers of all sorts thereby prey on the unformed souls of the young. This is the situation that we find ourselves in today. Educational freedom, rather than government control, is the sine qua non for the creation of happiness and well-being for all.

This argument may be summarized by means of 20 propositions on education and wellness:

1. Culture, habits, and attitudes are the most important prerequisites to education.
2. Historically, traditional cultures have varied widely; human variability due to culture is extraordinary. That variability is currently being lost through the force of those technology-based monocultures that are sweeping the world.

3. Over the course of 13 years of formal education, the average high school graduate is exposed to 14,000 hours of K–12 schooling. It is possible to have a considerable impact on the habits, attitudes, ideals, aesthetics, aspirations, and culture of the students over that time if that were to become the primary focus of educational institutions.

4. Habituation in new cultural norms may be successfully cultivated in the young only when they are educated by adults who consistently, moment-by-moment, support and enforce the new forms of habituation and personally exemplify the new virtues. In order to do this, the adults themselves must exhibit a consistent form of habituation. New cultures cannot be created by innovations in textbooks or software.

5. Except for those few educational approaches that have distinctive teacher training programs (Montessori, Waldorf, and some religious school systems) combined with schools that actively support those pedagogies, existing teacher training does not even begin to ensure consistent habituation. The most consistent habituation faced by K–12 students in government schools today is habituation in passivity and dependence.

6. Cumulatively, deliberately inculcated habits and attitudes may provide a foundation for new cultures. The Jesuits deliberately created a more disciplined and intellectual European culture out of the chaos of medieval education. Montessori and Waldorf education are nascent examples of new cultures being formed today.

7. The existing government-controlled education system acts as a monopolistic standard with a marketshare far greater than that held by Microsoft's Windows standard. Unlike the Microsoft dominant standard, the government schooling standard is enforced legislatively and financed coercively.

8. Only when this dominant standard collapses will great educational innovations begin to be launched.

9. Freedom has been necessary for innovation in the world of ideas, the world of technology, and the world of entrepreneurship. If Galileo had been more effectively censored, Newton and modern physics might not exist. If government had regulated the invention

of electrical devices in the nineteenth century, Thomas Edison's "invention of invention" would never have come into being. If tech entrepreneurs had needed government licenses to do their work, Silicon Valley, the microcomputer, and the Internet would be a pale ghost of their current selves, if they existed at all. Likewise, educational freedom will be necessary for educational innovation.

10. Only visionary organizations, designed and built with a commitment to a distinctive vision, can consistently create distinctive cultures that are powerful enough to compete with the teen culture defined by the media. A distinctive, long-term vision can only be implemented voluntarily. Visionary leaders must be able to hire, fire, and promote faculty based strictly on their own perception of quality.*

11. Markets will supply those goods desired by consumers.

12. Parents want their children to be healthy, well, productive, and happy.

13. In a free educational market there will be a demand for schools that can supply a healthier culture.

14. Innovative educators employed by private, visionary organizations will gradually develop increasingly healthier and more positive versions of teen culture.

15. Peer culture is a more powerful influence on teens than are parents. Currently teen culture is the biggest obstacle to parental ability to raise their children well. Conversely, a positive teen culture could compensate for many of the weaknesses of poor parenting.†

16. Culture by its very nature produces "neighborhood effects," or externalities; once we have created more sources of positive teen culture it will spread to those who don't originally pay for it or even choose it.

17. Many of us develop critical habits as teens; a healthier teen culture will result in a healthier adult culture.

---

* cf. Collins' and Porras' book, *Built to Last: Successful Habits of Visionary Companies,* (Harper Collins 2002).

†Again, Judith Rich Harris' *The Nurture Assumption,* op. cit., abundantly documents this thesis.

18. "Healthier" may be construed widely; the foregoing analysis applies to any positive cultural characteristic.
19. Cumulatively, the long-term effects of an innovative, competitive market for adolescent well-being may produce cultural consequences as profound as, or more profound than, the long-term effects of technological innovation.
20. Cumulatively then, just as technological innovation has had a dramatic impact on the economic standard of well-being, so too, cultural innovation will have a dramatic positive impact on our social, emotional, and moral standard of well-being.

It has been said that the greatest invention of the nineteenth century was the invention of the invention. While there had certainly been inventions prior to the nineteenth century, only gradually did tinkerers and experimentalists begin to become conscious and deliberate about the act of invention. A magnificent turning point was Thomas Edison's creation of a laboratory specifically for the sake of creating inventions.

The worlds of martial arts and eastern spiritual practices contain innumerable lineages, each with a revered founder. The founders of new branches of lineages are rarely described using the rhetoric of innovation, yet that is precisely what they are. They are individuals who have achieved a new advance on a particular discipline or practice, resulting in new techniques that are then passed on to subsequent practitioners of the lineage. Similarly, the founders of monastic orders, such as St. Francis or St. Benedict, are not usually perceived as cultural innovators, despite the fact that they launched new cultural institutions that have survived for centuries.

In western education, individual educators are recognized as leaving a legacy from time to time. Thomas Arnold is renowned for creating a distinctive culture at Rugby School in England in the nineteenth century. Maria Montessori is well known for founding Montessori education, as is Rudolf Steiner for founding Waldorf education. Older alumni to this day feel a powerful attachment to the Hutchins' College, the program at the University of Chicago during the tenure of Robert M. Hutchins as college president, 1930–1950. As with the saints, gurus, and martial artists, with the exceptions of Montessori and Steiner these educators are not usually conceptualized as innovators.

The haphazard cultural inventions that have taken place hitherto, in eastern and western cultures, are analogous to the occasional inventions that characterized western society prior to the nineteenth century. By means of radical school choice combined with a conscious recognition of the power and importance of creating new school cultures, the greatest invention of the twenty-first century may be the invention of new cultural models that continually allow human beings to adapt ever more effectively to a world of ongoing creative destruction while allowing for ever deeper levels of happiness and well-being for people of all races, cultures, classes, and abilities.

In Conclusion

In the Preface, we pointed out that in order for entrepreneurs to solve problems, they need access to "The Entrepreneur's Toolkit,"

- Secure and well-defined property rights.
- Freedom of contract.
- Timely, fair, and reliable enforcement of contracts.

Entrepreneurs create value by manifesting visions of a new world in new enterprises, transforming undervalued inputs into products and services that are valued by others. By means of entrepreneurial vision, they literally create value from nothing but their imagination. We need to provide access to The Entrepreneur's Toolkit so that diverse unknown visionaries from around the world have the tools needed to transform entrepreneurial vision into valued reality.

In each of our three areas of interest, there is a somewhat different primary obstacle to the entrepreneurial solutions of problems.

With respect to environmental problems, there is an absence of secure and well-defined property rights needed to prevent the destruction of environmental assets. Thus, creating property rights solutions to tragedy of the commons problems will be primary here.

With respect to the end of global poverty, nations are poor to the extent to which they are missing all three key elements in the Entrepreneur's Toolkit. Although there are a few qualifications, to a considerable extent nations are wealthy to the extent that their governments provide The Entrepreneur's Toolkit.

With respect to increasing health, happiness, and well-being, legal obstacles to freedom of contract, including laws restricting innovation in education, health care, and community formation, are the primary limitation on accelerating our pace of health, happiness, and well-being.

Because there are ongoing disputes regarding the validity of these notions, despite the evidence in their favor, we will also propose the use of prediction markets, with reputational tracking, as an entrepreneurial approach to knowledge discovery and to the resolution of policy disputes.

Part Four

Living a Life of FLOW

Hell, there are no rules here. We're trying to accomplish something.
                                                    —THOMAS EDISON

Chapter 13

The Upward Flow of Human Development— Maps of the Terrain

From Success to Significance—The Five Bottom Lines of Conscious Capitalism

John Mackey
CEO, Whole Foods Market and Co-Founder, FLOW
Dr. Don Beck
CEO, The Spiral Dynamics Group

O ne of the core philosophical underpinnings of FLOW is our belief in the human species' limitless potential for self-development. We are capable of learning and growing our entire lives. Our ability to learn and grow is not restricted to external knowledge and skills such as those we need for our jobs, or various intellectual disciplines such as history, science, or mathematics. We are also capable of tremendous growth in our consciousness and all the various components that compose that consciousness including our cognitive abilities, motivations, ethics, emotional intelligence, capacity for love, meaning, compassion, and wisdom. We believe that consciousness development engenders a decrease in narcissism and an increase in caring and consciousness; that humans move from egocentric to ethnocentric to world-centric—and beyond—as they develop in consciousness. The upward Spiral of development is at the same time a Spiral of compassion—from *me* to *us* to *all of us*. By cultivating our potential and functioning at higher levels of consciousness, as individuals and groups, we access personal flow states and advance the FLOW vision of creating sustainable, resilient, and emerging societies.

In this chapter we will share a few models of human development that we have found very valuable to our own understanding of how higher consciousness expands. These models are merely guides for you to use if you find them to be valuable—or not to use if you decide otherwise. Being only models they are not "true" in any final absolute sense, because ultimately the truth of reality cannot be captured by any model, which is necessarily an abstract oversimplification of what we believe reality to be. It is our hope, however, that the two models we briefly describe may inspire you to look at your own life in a wider and deeper context and help you to realize that you have far greater potential to learn and grow than you previously thought possible.

No doubt the financial upheavals of the first decade of the twenty-first century, coupled with growing globalization and the environmental threats to our survival, have awakened in most sensitive business leaders the critical importance of leading and managing in a different way. A great deal is at stake for all of us.

Abraham Maslow's Hierarchy of Needs

Abraham Maslow, a U.S. psychologist who lived from 1908–1970, is usually credited with being one of the founders of both Humanistic Psychology and Transpersonal Psychology. His most enduring contribution to the expanding field of psychology was his famous model

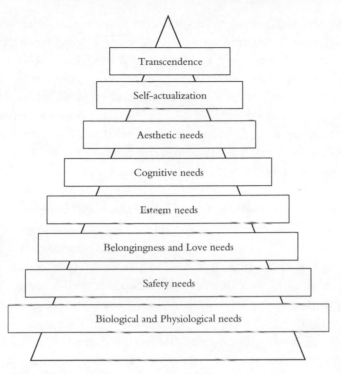

Figure 13.1   Maslow's Hierarchy of Needs Diagram,
Adapted to Eight Levels
SOURCE: Diagram by Anna Madrona, adapted from Abraham Maslow,
Motivation and Personality, New York, Harper and Row, 1954.

and explanation of the human "Hierarchy of Needs." Maslow believed that human motivations could be organized into a hierarchy of various requirements and desires, with the requirements lower in the hierarchy needing to be satisfied before the desires higher in the hierarchy could be met. He used a pyramid model to represent the hierarchy, which can be seen in Figure 13.1.

Deficiency Needs

In Maslow's model, the first four levels of needs are considered to be "deficiency needs" or "D-needs." When a D-need is not met, we feel dissatisfaction and have a strong desire to get the need met. When the need is adequately satisfied, however, we will likely no longer notice it, and will simply "move up" to the next need level. Each need level takes priority over the need level above, until the requirement is satisfied. For example, once our need for security and safety is adequately met, we will find that the need for love and belonging becomes the predominant motivation for us. This process of working to satisfy a basic need and then moving up the hierarchy continues on each level. Further explanation of each D-need is provided below.

Physiological Needs. Our bodies need adequate air, food, and water. Maslow also considered sexuality a physiological need, as well as exercise and bodily comfort. Until these foundational needs are adequately met, they become our highest priority. According to Maslow, these physiological needs can control thoughts and behavior, and can contribute to physical and psychological sensations of sickness, pain, and discomfort.

Safety Needs. Once our physiological needs are met, safety, economic security, comfort, and peace become the most important motivations. For some individuals, security concerns will outweigh requirements to completely satisfy physiological needs. Most Americans, unless living in impoverished, crime-ridden inner-city neighborhoods, take for granted that their safety needs will be met, therefore this requirement may not enter their consciousness frequently. After the terrorist attack on Sept. 11, 2001, and then in the 2008 economic downturn, however, the safety/security need became far more important to many Americans, because they felt that they could no longer take it for granted. Many American citizens have been willing to trade off some of their other important values such as freedom and peace to try to ensure greater safety and security.

Love/Belonging Needs. After our physiological and safety needs are fulfilled at the second level, at the third level our requirements are social. Included in the needs are intimate relationships of all types including friends, family, and a sexual partner/significant other. Human beings form various kinds of affiliations and most belong to a variety of groups having different purposes—our families, work teams, religious congregations, clubs, and, increasingly, online communities. Each of us wants to be accepted and cherished by people within our groups. When this need is not met we usually feel alienated, lonely, and depressed.

Esteem Needs. At this level, a person's requirement is for esteem, defined by Maslow as "a stable, firmly based, usually high evaluation of ourselves." Esteem includes both inner (self-respect or self-esteem) and outward (esteem from others) validation. Self-esteem would include "a desire for strength, achievement, adequacy, mastery and competence, confidence in the face of the world, and independence and freedom." Included in the yearning for esteem of others would be "the desire for reputation or prestige, status, fame and glory, dominance, recognition, attention, importance, dignity, or appreciation."*

Being Needs

Once the deficiency needs have been satisfied, people are free to expand their worldview beyond their immediate world. Maslow called the two levels beyond the D-needs, "Being Needs" or "B-needs." Unlike the pattern of our D-needs which, once filled, disappear from our consciousness while we pursue fulfillment at subsequent levels, our B-needs have staying power. They continue to motivate us further and are intrinsically satisfying to us. The more we pursue meeting these needs, the more we enjoy them.

Aesthetic and Cognitive Needs. Although not fully acknowledged in all explanations of Maslow's Hierarchy, the fulfillment of these needs marks an entry into the Being Needs level. Some of the B-needs at this level include goodness, truth, beauty, purpose, wholeness, and justice. These two need levels roughly correspond to the ideals of "the good, the true, and the beautiful" that the philosopher Plato wrote about 2,500 years ago. Maslow believed that as we move up the Hierarchy of Needs our desires and needs for beauty, goodness, justice, and truth become more important.

Self-Actualization Needs. Self-Actualization is most simply defined as meeting the need to fully realize one's potential. Although

---

*Maslow, Abraham, *Motivation and Personality* (New York: Harper and Row, 1954), 21.

Kurt Goldstein initiated the use of the term self-actualization, Maslow is primarily responsible for it coming into fairly common usage. Maslow provided this explanation:

> Musicians must make music, artists must paint, poets must write, if they are to be ultimately at peace with themselves. What humans can be, they must be. They must be true to their own nature. This need we may call self-actualization.
>
> Abraham Maslow, *Motivation and Personality*
> (New York: Harper and Row, 1954), 22

Maslow considered people who were self-actualizing to be psychologically healthy. Some of the characterizations he gave of self-actualizing people, as compared to those not yet seeking a greater purpose, include:

- They articulate a clearer and more accurate perception of reality.
- They demonstrate greater self-acceptance and acceptance of other people; they pass fewer judgments, engage in less defensiveness.
- They are more spontaneous, natural, unpretentious, and bring greater simplicity to their interactions.
- They are interested in solving problems; this often includes the problems of others; solving these problems is often a key focus in their lives.
- They tend to be centered on solving problems outside of themselves, rather than remaining ego-centered.
- They are generally highly creative and resist total conformity to culture.
- They demonstrate greater autonomy and independence, and have a strong desire for privacy.
- They convey strong feelings of respect, empathy, care, love, and compassion for other people but have meaningful relationships with only a few.
- They possess a strong sense of values and personal ethics.
- They express appreciation continuously.

All of the above qualities or behaviors seem pretty positive, don't they? However, self-actualizing people display characteristics that may not be conventional or grounded in societal norms, and they may mildly threaten people engaged in lower need levels. Among these qualities are:

- They may show many of the "lesser human failings" in that they are saddled with character flaws and bad habits like other people; they can be boring, stubborn, irritating, angry, depressed, petulant, prone to temper outbursts, pride, superficial vanity, and partiality to their own creations.
- They are strong individuals and are occasionally capable of an extraordinary and unexpected ruthlessness; they can display a surgical coldness when it is called for.
- They may recover so quickly from the death of people close to them as to seem heartless.
- They are not free of guilt, anxiety, sadness, self-castigation, internal strife, and conflict.
- They display an acceptance of the nature of self, of human nature, of much of social life, and of nature and physical reality, and are therefore disinclined to commiserate or tolerate less expansive opinions.
- They are more apt to enjoy, even seek out, differences in opinion and behavior than to fear them.
- They may speak realistically and harshly of those who deserve it, and especially of the hypocritical, the pretentious, the pompous, or self-inflated, generally when deserved and for the good of the transgressor.
- They are autonomous, therefore find enculturation difficult; people sense they are different.

In summation, the self-actualized individual is far from saintly, but is most decidedly authentic. As you may infer from the incomplete list above, self-actualization involves a suite of qualities, behaviors, and thought processes that develop over time and at different paces for everyone reaching this level.

How Does One Go about Self-Actualizing?

The process is rarely direct, and indeed, to set a goal to self-actualize may be the most direct way to self-sabotage this Being Need. One of

Maslow's contemporaries explains this seeming paradox in the following manner:

> The true meaning of life is to be found in the world, rather than within man or his own psyche, as though it were a closed system. . . Human experience is essentially self-transcendence rather than self-actualization. Self-actualization is not a possible aim at all, for the simple reason that the more a man would strive for it, the more he would miss it. . . . In other words, self-actualization cannot be attained if it is made an end in itself, but only as a side effect of self-transcendence.
>
> Viktor Frankl, 1946, *Man's Search for Meaning,* 175

Self-Transcendence Needs. At the top of the hierarchy, self-transcendence is also occasionally referred to as spiritual needs. Maslow felt that the cultivation of peak experiences, along with the study of those that others experienced provided a route to personal growth and fulfillment. By peak experiences, he meant unifying, ego-transcending experiences that provided a deep sense of purpose to the individual, along with a sense of the integration of the parts of the whole, or a sense of alignment. While these peak experiences can occur at any level, they will be experienced and described within the framework of that level. Individuals engaged in meeting the Being Needs might have these experiences with greater frequency and to greater end results. He further described this transcendence and its characteristics in an essay in the posthumously published *The Farther Reaches of Human Nature* wherein he makes a point that these individuals experience not only ecstatic joy, but also profound, "cosmic sadness," at the ability of humans to foil chances of transcendence in their own lives and in the world at large.

As a great teacher, mentor, and theorist, Maslow inspired students, colleagues, and admirers who continued to evolve his theories in Transpersonal Psychology and human development, including human moral development. Most notable among them were Lawrence Kohlberg, Carol Gilligan, Clare Graves, and his colleague, Don Beck, who each contributed models they felt better clarified or further refined the original work of Maslow.

Emergent Deep Value Systems and Spiral Dynamics

Clare Graves, who was a peer and friend of Maslow's and who influenced and was influenced by him, developed another system to explain human consciousness development and "the way the world works."

While Maslow's Hierarchy of Needs operates within a *horizontal* development manner within world views, Graves developed models in "emergent deep value systems" that describe the *vertical* levels of development within the human experience.

Graves' work has been extended and applied in what is called "Spiral Dynamics." The official title is "the emergent, cyclical, double-helix model of biopsychosocial development of the adult human being."

Graves discusses his initial model in this manner:

> I am not saying in this conception of adult behavior that one style of being, one form of human existence is inevitably and in all circumstances superior to or better than another form of human existence, another style of being. What I am saying is that when one form of being is more congruent with the realities of existence, then it is the better form of living for those realities. And what I am saying is that when one form of existence ceases to be functional for the realities of existence then some other form, either higher or lower in the hierarchy, is the better form of living. I do suggest, however, and this I deeply believe is so, that for the overall welfare of total man's existence in this world, over the long run of time, higher levels are better than lower levels and that the prime good of any society's governing figures should be to promote human movement up the levels of human existence.
>
> Dr. Clare W. Graves

Graves' work was built upon by one of his chief popularizers, Don Beck, and one of Beck's students, Christopher Cowan. They wrote the book called *Spiral Dynamics: Mastering Values, Leadership, and Change*.

First, you might enjoy taking a little test. Which of these statements below best describe your own viewpoint?

The World Is . . . [*]

  a. A natural milieu where humans rely on instincts to stay alive.

  b. A magical place alive with spirit beings and mystical signs.

  c. A jungle where the strongest and most cunning survive.

  d. An ordered existence under the control of the ultimate truth.

  e. A marketplace full of possibilities and opportunities.

  f. A human habitat in which we share life's experiences.

  g. A chaotic organism forged by differences and change.

  h. An elegantly balanced system of interlocking forces.

Spiral Dynamics Overview

Spiral Dynamics argues that human nature is not fixed; humans are able, when forced by circumstances, to adapt to their environment by constructing new, more complex, conceptual models of the world that allow them to handle the new problems. Each new model includes and extends all previous models. According to Beck and Cowan, these conceptual models are organized around so-called ᵛMeme systems of core values or collective intelligences, applicable to both individuals and entire cultures.

Spiral Dynamics is a biopsychosocial-spiritual framework for understanding core human thought processes. Spiral Dynamics helps identify how people change, organize, develop consciousness, make choices, create strategies, and communicate. This system helps to reveal the hidden codes that shape human nature, liberate global diversity, and drive or hinder social and organizational transformation.

According to the Spiral Dynamics model, human consciousness evolves over time, both in individuals and for the larger society. This evolution of consciousness can be viewed as a hierarchical Spiral that evolves to greater levels of complexity. (See Figure 13.2. This diagram should properly be seen in color. To See a color version of the Spiral, visit Don Beck's web site at www.spiraldynamics.net.) Neither the Spiral nor the hierarchical levels are rigid, but can be rather likened to flowing waves, with much overlap and interweaving. Individuals are not impervious as they move through these levels.

Within this system's model, different colors represent different levels or waves of development, each offering a viewing point for the real

---

[*]Question from The Values Test, © National Values Center.

world according to unique perceptual filters. The colors, which have no significance in and of themselves, are simply a useful abbreviation tool, developed to help us quickly grasp the level of consciousness we are discussing.

In Spiral Dynamics, the term "ᵛMeme" refers to a core value system, acting as an organizing principle, which expresses itself through memes (self-propagating ideas, habits, or cultural practices).

Spiral Dynamics uses the word meme with each color. The word meme was introduced by Richard Dawkins when he wrote *The Selfish Gene*. The small 'v' means "value meme" to indicate that we are referencing value systems. The Spiral Dynamics model currently has defined eight distinct levels of consciousness, but allows for the potential of new, more complex levels emerging.

The first use of the term "memetics" in this context was by Mihaly Csikszentmihalyi in his 1994 book titled *The Evolving Self*. You will recognize him to be the author also of *Flow: The Psychology of Optimal Experience* (1990).

A graphic depicting the levels of the Spiral is shown in Figure 13.2.

The ᵛMemes are like invisible core intelligences. They are both structures of thought processes and broad orienting paradigms that we

Figure 13.2   The Levels of the Spiral

use to interpret the world. Life conditions awaken ᵛMemes, which may emerge, surge, regress, or fade in response to those events that trigger change. No one ᵛMeme is better or worse than another, they are simply less complex and more complex. Note that, as the Spiral turns into greater complexity, it brings with it all of the memetic codes and their successes and failures that have come before.

All ᵛMemes are beneficial and necessary and evolving to more complex ᵛMemes, which require experiencing and living the less complex ᵛMemes first. The ᵛMemes, however, interact with much overlap and interweaving, resulting in a dynamic Spiral of consciousness unfolding. The ᵛMemes can express both healthy (for better) and unhealthy (for worse) qualities; sometimes it is more beneficial to the individual to be healthy at a lower ᵛMeme than to be unhealthy at a higher ᵛMeme. An individual's particular ᵛMeme level can brighten and dim as life conditions change. Each one of us experiences different things that set us off to the next evolution or keep us locked permanently in a lower level.

In general, ᵛMemes follow several trajectories as they evolve. They go from less complex, natural, technological, and human environments to more complex. They likewise go from surviving (for example, in the bush) through the awakening of new consciousness levels to even higher levels of complexity (understanding the entire global ecosphere). Finally, they go from a small piece of land (via migrations across land and information terrains) to the global village and cyberspace (where complex development through shared information becomes possible).

Each memetic code has its own unique way to organize itself, or be motivated, or respond to a host of issues in management. Each will select expressions or representative content, but it is the underlying deep motive that is more important.

The First Tier ᵛMemes

Beck and Cowan recognized and elaborated upon eight core ᵛMemes. The first six are called First Tier ᵛMemes, with the remainder classified as Second Tier ᵛMemes, which we will explain later. We want to provide basic characteristics of the ᵛMemes in the following pages. The following sketch of the eight memes has been adapted from Beck and Cowan's book, *Spiral Dynamics: Mastering Values, Leadership, and Change* (Blackwell Business, 1996).

Beige "Instinctive/Survivalistic" ᵛMeme   The first is the Beige "Instinctive/Survivalistic" ᵛMeme. This first arrived on the scene, or "awakened," more than 100,000 years ago. Its basic premise is: *Do what you must to stay alive.*

The characteristic beliefs and actions of the Beige ᵛMeme are:

- Individuals rely on instincts and habits to survive.
- The distinct self is barely awakened or sustained.
- Food, water, warmth, sex, and safety have priority over anything else.
- Individuals form into family survival bands to perpetuate life.

Where do you find the Beige ᵛMeme expressed? A representative list includes: the earliest human beings on the evolutionary scale, newborn infants, senile elderly, late-stage Alzheimer's victims, mentally ill street people, starving masses, people on bad drug trips, and shell-shocked survivors from wars.

Purple "Magical/Animistic" ᵛMeme   As human consciousness evolves, it next goes into the Purple "Magical/Animistic" ᵛMeme. This second awakening occurred approximately 50,000 years ago. The basic theme for the Purple ᵛMeme is: *Keep the spirits happy and the tribe's nest warm and safe.*

The characteristic beliefs and actions of the Purple ᵛMeme are:

- Animistic thinking; magical spirits—both good and bad.
- Obeying the desires of spirit beings; mystical signs.
- Showing allegiance to chief, elders, ancestors, and the clan.
- Preserving sacred objects, places, events, and memories.
- Observing rites of passage, seasonal cycles, and tribal customs.

Although much of this seems benign, this is the time frame and human development level where slavery and human sacrifice came into the picture. Native American Indians were living primarily in the purple ᵛMeme when the Western peoples arrived on both of the American continents. Do not think of this worldview as primitive and simplistic. It contains nuances that most people in first world societies can neither see nor understand.

Where do we find the Purple ᵛMeme expressed? The following provides a sample: belief in guardian angels and Voodoo-like curses, animism, blood oaths, chanting and trance dancing, good luck charms, mystical ethnic beliefs and superstitions, New Age practices—crystals, tarot, astrology, and Harry Potter's magical world.

The following provides more detail about the typical qualities seen in the Purple Magical/Animistic ᵛMeme:

- Characteristics
  - Mystical spirits, signs
  - Safe clans and nests
  - Powerful elders
  - Our people versus "them" or "the other"
- Decision making
  - Custom and tradition
  - Elders' counsel
  - Signs or the shaman
  - Clan gets the spoils
- Education
  - Paternalistic teachers
  - Rituals and routines
  - Passive learners
  - Family-based learning; oral history to pass down the stories
- Family
  - Extended kinships
  - Rites of passage
  - Strict role relations
  - Protects bloodline
- Community
  - Respects folk ways
  - Honors ethnicity
  - Lets group be itself
  - Guards magic places
- Life space
  - Old country ways
  - Focus on subsistence
  - Fearful, mystical, superstitious
  - Full of spirit beings

A note on the rhythm of the various levels: ^{V}Memes tend to alternate between individualistic and collectively focused. The Purple ^{V}Meme is collectively focused. The next level, Red, is characterized by an individualistic focus.

Red "Egocentric/Narcissistic" ^{V}Meme   The Red "Egocentric/Narcissistic" ^{V}Meme, the third awakening, occurred about 10,000 years ago. Its basic theme is: *Be what you are and do what you want, regardless. "Nobody tells me what to do."*

Many American teenagers are at the Red ^{V}Meme level. Many of us probably remember going through this stage during our adolescence.

The characteristic beliefs and actions of this ^{V}Meme are:

- The individual sees the world as a jungle full of threats and predators.
- The individual breaks free from any constraints to please self as self desires.
- The individual stands tall, expects attention, demands respect, calls the shots.
- The individual enjoys himself to the fullest, right now without guilt or remorse.
- The individual conquers, outfoxes, and dominates other aggressive characters.
- The collective, highly-developed ethnic identity can lead to genocidal wars, slavery, and racism.
- The individual believes that: "*I am special, I will live forever, I am immortal, not like the others.*"

Where is the Red ^{V}Meme expressed? A representative sample includes: the "terrible twos," rebellious youth, frontier mentalities, feudal kingdoms, street gangs, James Bond villains, epic heroes, soldiers of fortune, wild rock stars, William Golding's *Lord of the Flies*, Sauron in *Lord of the Rings*, Voldemort in *Harry Potter*. One can even detect this theme in gangster capitalism or big-boss leadership behaviors.

When adults are centered in the Red ^{V}Meme, we often think of them as immature and self-centered. But in a positive spin, Red energy is often critical for overcoming restrictions and boundaries put on you by other systems.

The following provides more detail about the typical qualities seen in the Red Impulsive/Egocentric ᵛMeme:

- Characteristics
  - Raw power displays
  - Immediate pleasure
  - Unrestrained by guilt
  - Colorful and creative
- Decision making
  - Tough-one dictates
  - What gets respect
  - What feels good now
  - Powerful grab spoils
- Education
  - Rewards for learning
  - Tough-love tactics
  - Work on respect
  - Controlled freedom
  Family
  - Gang-like battles
  - Builds us versus them walls
  - Tests of worthiness
  - Struggles with the system
- Community
  - Predators in control
  - Danger to the outsiders
  - Forms fiefdoms
  - Turf wars and vendettas
  Life space
  - Unconstrained
  - Might makes right
  - Winners and dead losers
  - Attention-seeking

Blue "Purposeful/Authoritarian" ᵛMeme   After the very individualistic Red ᵛMeme, the next level swings to the more communal-focused

orientation. The Blue Purposeful/Authoritarian ᵛMeme, as the fourth awakening, began approximately 5,000 years ago. The basic rules for the Blue ᵛMeme are: *Life has meaning, direction and purpose with outcomes determined by an all-powerful Other or Order.* This ᵛMeme brings discipline to the Spiral because while you are in Blue, you are now following a higher order.

The characteristic beliefs and actions of the Blue ᵛMeme include:

- Sacrificing of the self to the transcendent Cause, Truth, or righteous Pathway.
- Allowing the Order to enforce a code of conduct based on eternal, absolute unvarying principles of right and wrong—there is one right way to live and deviations from the path are punished.
- Following the right path produces security now and guarantees future reward; if you don't follow the path, you have made your choices and must suffer the consequences.
- Displaying missionary zealotry (which can be short on evidence and long on belief and faith), as well as closed minds.
- Engaging in pleasurable acts is seen as frivolous and humor is rare; although there is a lot of talk about compassion, actions tend to be based on judgment, not compassion.
- Operating from a fundamentalist, conventional, traditional, and conformist worldview.

Where do you find the Blue ᵛMeme expressed? A sample includes: Christian and Islamic fundamentalism, Puritan America, Dickensian England, Singapore's strict discipline, witch hunts, codes of chivalry and honor, the Spanish Inquisition, Shia versus Sunni holy wars, the caste system in India, Frank Capra's *It's a Wonderful Life*, Boy and Girl Scouts, and patriotism.

The following provides more detail about the typical qualities seen in the Blue Purposeful/Authoritarian ᵛMeme:

- Characteristics
  - Only one right way
  - Purpose in causes
  - Guilt in consequences
  - Sacrifice for honor
- Decision making
  - Orders from authority

- Do right, obey rules
- Adhere to tradition
- Righteous earn spoils
- Education
  - Truth from authority
  - Traditional stair steps
  - Moralistic lessons
  - Punishment for errors
- Family
  - Seat of truths and values
  - Proper places for all, respect for parents
  - Codes of conduct
  - Teaches moral ways
- Community
  - Peace and quiet
  - Cautious and careful
  - Tidy, green, and neat
  - Born into society
- Life space
  - Law-abiding citizen
  - Places for everybody
  - Seeks peace of mind
  - Rewards to come

The Blue ^{v}Meme is one the core constituencies of the more right-wing and left-wing ideologies, which in fact, share the same value code, but with diverse and even mutually exclusive content.

Orange "Scientific Modernism" ^{v}Meme
The Orange Scientific Modernism ^{v}Meme, the fifth awakening, began only 300 years ago. Its tagline is: *Act in your own self-interest by playing the game to win.*

Some of the characteristic beliefs and actions of this ^{v}Meme include:

- Strongly expressed individualism; Orange breaks away from the conformity of the Blue ^{v}Meme.
- Developed human rights, legal freedoms, free markets, capitalistic democracies.

- Strong faith in science and rationality, which eclipse superstition.
- Seeking to live the "good life" with material abundance.
- Believe that optimistic, risk-taking, and self-reliant people deserve their success.
- Play to win and enjoy competition; very success driven.
- Base principles on ethics, not religion.
- Ignore inner spirituality to a high degree; the subsequent loss of the sacred.

The Orange ᵛMeme is expressed in the following: The Enlightenment, "success" ministries (such as Napoleon Hill and Tony Robbins), America's "Founding Fathers," Ayn Rand's *Atlas Shrugged*, Wall Street, Rodeo Drive, The Riviera, the cosmetics and fashion industries, cosmetic enhancements to the body, emerging middle classes around the world (for example in India and certain parts of China), Chambers of Commerce, corporate America, *Forbes* magazine, materialism, and the stereotypical yuppies. Many of us may relate strongly to this ᵛMeme. Orange is the dominant ᵛMeme in the United States today.

Here is traditional capitalism, reflecting the belief that capitalism based in narrow self-interest always results in a greater good.

The following provides more detail on the typical qualities seen in the Orange Achievist/Strategic ᵛMeme:

- Characteristics
  - Competes for success
  - Goal-oriented drive
  - Change to progress
  - Material gain/perks
- Decision making
  - Bottom-line results
  - Test options for best outcome
  - Consult experts
  - Successful win spoils
- Education
  - Experiments to win
  - High-tech, high status
  - How-to-win niches
  - Mentors and guides

- Family
  - Upwardly mobile
  - Demands attention
  - High expectations
  - Image conscious
- Community
  - Caters to prosperous
  - Displays affluence
  - Buys into society
  - Security for the elite
- Life space
  - Wants to prosper now
  - Competition always
  - Leverages influence
  - Seeks material things

Green "Communitarian/Egalitarian" ᵛMeme The response to the somewhat singularly driven Orange vMeme is found in the Green Communitarian/Egalitarian ᵛMeme, the sixth awakening, which first appeared nearly 150 years ago. The basic theme for the Green ᵛMeme is: *Seek peace within the inner self and explore, with others, the caring dimensions of community.* Another way to think of this ᵛMeme is as "the sensitive self."

Some of the characteristic beliefs and actions of the Green ᵛMeme include:

- Becoming more aware of the suffering of the world, of other sentient beings.
- Freeing the human spirit from greed, dogma, and divisiveness.
- Feelings, sensitivity, and caring supersede cold rationality.
- Sharing the Earth's resources and opportunities equally among all.
- Reaching decisions through consensus processes.
- Antiauthoritarian and against hierarchy; establishes lateral bonding and linking.
- All values are pluralistic and relativistic; no one should be marginalized.
- Environmentalism becomes a socio-political movement.
- Highly idealistic; believes "All people are good; it's society that makes them bad."

- Can create cults of victimhood and censorship through politically correct thinking; can also be politically, if not spiritually, dogmatic.

The Green ^vMeme is seen in the following: John Lennon's music, deep ecology, Greenpeace, animal rights, Woodstock, single-payer health care proposals, ACLU, humanistic psychology, diversity training, multiculturalism, Boulder, Colorado, The Body Shop, politically correct thinking, deconstructionism, postmodernism, *Utne Reader,* Paul Ray's Cultural Creatives, the natural/organic foods movement, and Barack Obama's politics.

Green begins to connect on a global basis to other organizations and individuals with whom it harmonizes to multiply the good all can do working together. With our partnerships, FLOW is recognizing that if we really want to help the world to evolve, we have to link up with other organizations and people with whom we harmonize to extend our influence.

The Green ^vMeme now has about the same amount of power in the United States as the Blue ^vMeme, which is a key factor in the culture wars that now rage in our country. Blue, Orange, and Green ^vMemes all struggle to assert the dominance of their own beliefs and values in the cultural, economic, political, and legal structures of the United States.

The following provides more information on the qualities inherent in the Green Communitarian/Egalitarian ^vMeme:

- Characteristics
  - Seeks inner peace
  - Everybody is equal
  - Everything is relative
  - Harmony within the group
- Decision making
  - Reach consensus
  - All must collaborate
  - Accept any input
  - Communal spoils
- Education
  - To explore feelings
  - Shared experiences
  - Social development
  - Learn cooperation

- Family
  - Grouping of equals
  - Participative activities
  - Highly accepting
  - All feelings processed
- Community
  - Social safety nets
  - Politically correct
  - Open for insiders
  - Invests in self
- Life space
  - Thrives on belonging
  - Needs acceptance
  - Sacrifice feels good
  - Renews spirituality

The Second Tier ᵛMemes

Consciousness continues its upward flow. There is a huge gap between what we have been talking about so far, and the next wave of consciousness. None of the First Tier ᵛMemes can fully appreciate the value of the other ᵛMemes. Each believes that its worldview is the only true perspective and that everyone who disagrees is either wrong, deluded, ignorant, or in some cases evil.

Since there are billions of people on the planet moving through the First Tier memetic codes, each at his or her respective center of gravity, the initial task at Second Tier is to facilitate people's relatively peaceful and productive passage through their various systems. This is where traditional capitalism evolves into Conscious Capitalism, since it now plays a role in the continual movement of human minds and communities through these developmental passages.

Individuals who operate from the Second Tier are capable of fully appreciating the value and necessity of all the ᵛMemes. They comprehend that the health of the entire Spiral, and all the ᵛMemes, is essential. At the Integral (Yellow) level, fear and anxiety largely disappear from consciousness.

People centered in Second Tier are not better people—they are simply different. They are not necessarily happier, nor do they see themselves as elites in any form. They tend to be open systems, without heavy judgment (but displaying strong discernment), yet able to work within each of the other meme codes. They can surf the spine of the Spiral, with a repair kit to unblock the emergence of others through the inevitable zone of emergence.

Yellow "Autonomous/Integrative" ^vMeme   The first level within the Second Tier is the Yellow Autonomous/Integral ^vMeme, which is the seventh "awakening," and it occurred approximately 50 years ago. The Yellow ^vMeme's basic tenet is: *Live fully and responsibly with authenticity.* The thinking mode is systemic, with Natural Design tools.

Some of the characteristic beliefs and actions of the Yellow ^vMeme are:

- Pursuit of learning for its own sake.
- Systems thinking.
- Viewing life as a kaleidoscope of natural hierarchies, systems, and forms.
- Valuing the magnificence of existence over material possessions.
- Prioritizing flexibility, spontaneity, and functionality.
- Valuing knowledge and competency over rank, power, and status.
- Integrating complex systems with ease.

The Yellow ^vMeme is expressed in the following: Carl Sagan's astronomy and Conscious Capitalism. Whole Foods Market, Google, The Container Store, and Southwest Airlines are a few examples of corporations that sometimes operate at the Yellow ^vMeme level.

The following qualities typify the Yellow Integral ^vMeme:

- Characteristics
  - Big picture views
  - Integral structures
  - Naturalness of chaos
  - Inevitability of change
- Decision making
  - Highly principled
  - Knowledge centered
  - Resolved paradoxes
  - Competent get spoils

- Education
  - Becomes self-directed
  - Whole-day package
  - Tuned to interests
  - Nonrigid structure
- Family
  - Shifting roles
  - Expects competence
  - Takes each as is
  - Information base
- Community
  - Does more with less
  - Appropriate technologies
  - Power is dispersed
  - Integral systems
- Life space
  - Life is learning
  - Intrigued by process
  - Freedom to just be
  - Rarely fearful

Turquoise "Holonic" ^vMeme   Beyond the largely individualistic Yellow ^vMeme, the Turquoise Holonic ^vMeme, as the eighth awakening, began expressing about 30 years ago. The basic premise of the Turquoise ^vMeme is: *Everything flows with everything else in universal living systems.*

Some of the characteristic beliefs and actions of the Turquoise ^vMeme include:

- Experiencing the world as a single, dynamic organism with its own collective mind.
- Acknowledging the self as both distinct and a blended part of a larger, compassionate whole.
- Viewing everything connected to everything else as incredibly beautiful ecological alignments.
- Experiencing energy and information as permeating the Earth's total environment.

- Thinking that is holistic and intuitive, with an expectation of cooperative actions.
- Synthesizing science and religion into a universal spirituality.

The Turquoise ᵛMeme is seen, for example, in Pierre Teilhard de Chardin's "noosphere," and envisioned as Gandalf the White from *Lord of the Rings*.

Some of the differences to note are that the Yellow ᵛMeme creates solutions to problems and paradoxes on an individual basis. The Turquoise ᵛMeme has a communal orientation.

The following qualities define the Turquoise Holonic ᵛMeme:

- Characteristics
  - Scans the macro
  - Synergy of all life
  - Safe, orderly world
  - Restore harmony
- Decision making
  - Blend natural flows
  - Look up/downstream
  - Plan for long range
  - Life gets spoils
- Education
  - Access to world
  - Blends feelings and technology
  - Bring past to life
  - Maximize the brain
- Family
  - Global awareness
  - Grows consciousness
  - Broad interest ranges
  - Seeks outreach
- Community
  - Interconnected
  - Highly diversified
  - Not isolationist
  - Information rich

- Life space
  - Belong to universe
  - Fit into chain of being
  - Do something here
  - As one with life force

Until the life conditions of the Yellow system that will awaken the eighth code become apparent and spread widely, one will not be able to detect a full version of Turquoise.

Are there any ᵛMemes beyond Turquoise? New ᵛMemes will continue to be created as the evolution of human consciousness so requires. Beck and Cowan claim that a new ᵛMeme, Coral, is emerging but that it still lacks a sufficient number of people to be statistically meaningful.

Supporting the Entrepreneurial Shift

Now, how is Spiral Dynamics relevant to FLOW? Spiral Dynamics is a useful model for understanding one's personal values and current level or wave of consciousness. Spiral Dynamics is also a useful model to better understand what is happening in the world today.

In addition, Spiral Dynamics is a useful model for understanding organizations and businesses. Most corporations in the United States are rooted firmly in the Orange ᵛMeme; a few are in the Green ᵛMeme, as are many nonprofits. There are very few Second Tier corporations, businesses and nonprofits, and this is the very gap that FLOW wants to help fill by supporting enlightened entrepreneurs to make the shift from Orange into Green and beyond. The good news is that information is increasingly available regarding the organizations that might be considered to show Second Tier traits or have internal programs that reflect Second Tier values.

The Five Bottom Lines

Here is a practical framework for integrating the concepts of Spiral Dynamics into the design and operation of business organizations. Can you identify the memetic codes in each of these five bottom lines?

1. Noble **PURPOSE** and Transcendent Goals
2. Sound **PRINCIPLES** and Efficient **PROCESSES**
3. Responsible **PROFIT** with Multiple Usages
4. Sensitivity to **PEOPLE** and Societal Needs
5. Respect for the Natural Ecology of **PLANET** and Systems

A final word. Many business leaders also are influential in national politics, or in local concerns such as education, poverty relief, social justice, and similar causes. By understanding how deep values systems (rather than surface-level manifestations) shape such issues, and by getting to the bottom of such issues to the core "memetic DNA" codes that are in actual fact shaping the social systems, those business leaders can increase their influence profoundly.

Many organizations, enterprises and foundations have moved beyond charity and want to make the kind of investments that have a long-term, sustainable effect rather than short-term, cosmetic outcomes. Don Beck describes this process within his "MeshWorks" and "Transpartisanship" initiatives.

Moving Forward

We celebrate the potential of human beings to learn, grow, and evolve our consciousness. We started FLOW to channel our passionate commitment to our personal commitment to learn, grown, and evolve our own consciousness, and to inspire and support others to do the same.

We encourage you to open your heart wider and extend love and compassion further. We invite you to join the expanding FLOW community or other communities of like-minded and open-hearted individuals and organizations, where you can collaborate and contribute to the upward evolution of human expression and endeavor, creating integral businesses and organizations that address the critical challenges we face in the world today.

We are especially excited about the millennial generation, those of you born between 1982 and 2000 (see the book *Millennials Rising* by Howe, Strauss, and Matson). While the dates are not hard and fast, many of our younger readers are collectively very aware. Many of you are already moving into Second Tier (in terms of the Spiral Dynamic map outlined above) and you have barely entered your third decade! This generation has the potential of moving into Second Tier in significant numbers, and of participating in a dramatic surge in the upward flow of human development.

We at FLOW propose to assist you to liberate your entrepreneurial spirit for good, and we intend to work with you to create sustainable peace, prosperity, and happiness for all, in our lifetimes.

Here are a few resources if you'd like to learn more:

- *Spiral Dynamics: Mastering Values, Leadership, and Change*, by Don Beck and Christopher Cowan
- *Spiral Dynamics Integral: Learn to Master the Memetic Codes of Human Behavior*—a *Sounds True Audio Learning Course*, by Don Beck, Ph.D.
- *The Crucible: Forging South Africa's Future*, by Don Beck and Graham Linscott
- *A Theory of Everything*, by Ken Wilber
- *Essential Spirituality*, by Roger Walsh
- *Motivation and Personality*, by Abraham Maslow
- *The Farther Reaches of Human Nature*, by Abraham Maslow
- www.flowproject.org/
- www.spiraldynamics.net
- www.humanemergence.org
- http://integralinstitute.org/
- www.itp-life.com/
- www.zaadz.com.

Chapter 14

Areté and the Entrepreneur

Brian Johnson
Philosopher and Entrepreneur, Founder of Eteamz, Zaadz, and Philosophersnotes

Some believe there is nothing one man or one woman can do against the enormous array of the world's ills—against misery, against ignorance, or injustice and violence. Yet many of the world's great movements, of thought and action, have flowed from the work of a single man. A young monk began the Protestant reformation, a young general extended an empire from Macedonia to the borders of the earth, and a young woman reclaimed the territory of France. It was a young Italian explorer who discovered the New World, and 32-year-old Thomas Jefferson who proclaimed that all men are created equal. "Give me a place to stand," said Archimedes, "and I will move the world." These men moved the world, and so can we all.

—ROBERT F. KENNEDY, TWENTIETH-CENTURY
U.S. POLITICAL LEADER

If we—as enlightened entrepreneurs—are going to change the world, we must start with ourselves. We must strive to live at our highest potential while using our greatest strengths in the greatest service to the world.

The classic Greek philosophers had a word for the process of self-actualizing and striving to reach your highest potential. They called it *Areté* (pronounced ar-uh-tay).

In fact, *Areté* was one of the most important values in classic Greek culture. Guys like Socrates, Plato, and Aristotle taught that the meaning of life was happiness and that the way to achieve happiness was to live with *Areté* (also known as excellence, striving to reach your highest potential).

I believe that by looking at the universal truths taught by philosophers, religions, and current psychological research, we can find the keys to self-actualizing, happiness, and creating businesses that can move the world.

With that, I offer you a quick overview of the universal truths that I have discovered in the course of my studies and that I strive to apply in my life. I hope you enjoy.

What one can be, one must be.

Abraham Maslow,
Twentieth-century psychologist

Your mind will be like its habitual thoughts; for the soul becomes dyed with the color of its thoughts. Soak it then in such trains of thoughts as, for example: Where life is possible at all, a right life is possible.

Marcus Aurelius,
Second-century Roman emperor,
Stoic philosopher

The Attitude Principle

It all begins with accountability. Unless you're willing to take absolute responsibility for your life, there is no hope. Seriously.

If you're going to blame a bad economy or a bad childhood or a bad whatever for your problems, then you won't come close to reaching your potential. Sorry to break the news.

Having said that, if you're willing to quit being a victim and to start taking control of how you think about and interact with the world, then you're on your way to doing anything you set your mind to.

Open up the Dhammapada, the core text of Buddha's teachings. Flip to the first lines. The very first words are "Our life is shaped by our mind. We become what we think."

That sums it up pretty well, eh?

And, scientists have done all kinds of research on this. They talk about "locus of control"—also known as, where you place control. Do you put control outside of yourself and have what they term an "external locus of control"? Or, do you take responsibility and have an "internal locus of control"?

Not surprisingly, you can test rats and humans and you'll find that, to the extent you place control outside of yourself, you will be significantly less happy, less successful, less all the things you want to be, than if you internalize control.

Philosophers have commented on the subject exhaustively as well—from ancient Greek philosophers like Epictetus to Buddha to more recent guys like James Allen and contemporary gurus like Steven Covey. Of course, we can't always control what happens in our lives, but we can always control how we perceive and respond to what happens. And, oh, what a difference that makes.

> *Man's ideal state is realized when he has fulfilled the purpose for which he is born.*
>
> *And what is it that reason demands of him? Something very easy—that he live in accordance with his own nature.*
>
> Seneca, First-century Stoic philosopher

The Vision Principle

Okay. You've assumed control. No more whining from you.

Now that you've taken that step, what are you going to create for yourself? What's your ideal life? What's the ideal you? What are you doing on a daily basis? Who are you around? How much money is in your bank account? What kind of physical shape are you in? What do you look like and feel like?

Sounds simple, eh? Of course it sounds simple, but in my experience, people have a pretty hard time with this because they lack clarity in terms of who they are and what really fires them up.

We're so used to doing what we think other people want us to do that we haven't taken the time to truly understand who we are and what we want. In short, we lack self-awareness. We'll get you thinking more about what you want and create a vision of your ideal.

Only by much searching and mining are gold and diamonds obtained, and man can find every truth connected with his being if he will dig deep into the mine of his soul.

James Allen,
Nineteenth-century philosopher

The Self-Awareness Principle

Self-awareness. Our third step. Remember Socrates? The Oracle of Delphi in ancient Greece? What did they teach us?

"Know thyself," of course. Well, how well do you know thyself?

What are your greatest strengths? What are you most passionate about? When are you most naturally yourself? What are you most proud of? What gives you goose bumps? If you were absolutely guaranteed to succeed, what one thing would you dare to dream?

I can't begin to stress how important self-awareness is. Again, all kinds of scientific research has been done on this subject. Psychologists have often wondered why IQ isn't that well correlated with success and happiness in life and several authors have explained the keys to what Robert Sternberg calls "Successful Intelligence." In its simplest form, he says that the most successful people in the world know their strengths and know their weakness; they create a life around their strengths and spend enough time on their weaknesses so that they're not liabilities.

Basically, they know themselves.

Martin Seligman, the past president of the American Psychological Association, professor at the University of Pennsylvania, one of the most preeminent psychologists alive and the founder of the current positive psychology movement, recently wrote a book called *Authentic Happiness*. In it, he boils down Aristotle's good life to a simple formula (ridiculously simple but backed up by some impressive philosophical and scientific data).

His axiom: Know what he calls your "signature strengths" and use these strengths as often as possible throughout your daily life. Sound simple? It is in theory. Tragically, most people don't take the time to figure out what they are and even fewer actually consciously build their lives around them.

So, what are your greatest strengths? Are you creating a life around them? We'll check out some more theory and walk through some assessments and exercises to get you knowing thyself more than ever before.

> *The unexamined life is not worth living.*
>
> Socrates,
> Fifth-century BCE Greek philosopher

> *Life is growth. If we stop growing, technically and spiritually, we are as good as dead.*
>
> Morihei Ueshiba,
> Twentieth-century philosopher, martial artist

The Goals Principle

Alright, so you've assumed control of your life, you're creating a vision of your ideal self and you're focusing on gaining greater self-awareness. Now what?

Now, it's time to bring the theory down to reality. It's time to set goals. Odds are you don't have absolute clarity on exactly who you are and what you want in your life. Welcome to the club. Something like less than 5 percent of the U.S. population actually sets written goals.

That doesn't mean you're off the hook. It means you need to get to work. Start by setting goals. Your goal can be as simple as getting out of bed tomorrow morning when your alarm goes off—and before you hit snooze three times! (Why is that so hard sometimes?) Or it can be more complex, like getting in shape, losing 10 pounds and running a 5k in four months.

The bottom line is clear: You need goals. I'll tell you more about why goals are so grand and also teach you a thing or two about how to actually set goals and all that good stuff. For now, let's assume you have goals . . . now it's time for action.

Good thoughts are no better than good dreams, unless they be executed!

Ralph Waldo Emerson,
Nineteenth-century American philosopher

The Action Principle

What's the use of having absolute clarity of who you are and what you want if you lack the power to take action? It's time to follow the advice of another prominent Greek entity, Nike, and "Just do it."

Unfortunately, it's not good enough to just do it. You have to get in the habit of just doing it impeccably. Impecc-a-what? Impeccably. The word literally means "without sin."

And, that's what you need to do. You need to do your best. Every single moment—from putting your socks in the hamper to putting a dish straight into the dishwasher.

Trust me. When you get in the habit of doing every little thing to the best of your ability, you will do some amazing things.

That's action. It's powerful. In fact, there's nothing more powerful than having the ability to do what you need to do when you need to do it. That's probably why one of my heroes, Leonardo da Vinci, said that "One can have no smaller or greater mastery than mastery of oneself."

Imagine having absolute self-mastery aligned with absolute clarity of vision of what you want to manifest. If you're willing to dream big enough, it's the stuff legend is made of.

Be not afraid of going slowly but only afraid of standing still.

Chinese Proverb

Energy: The capacity for work or vigorous activity; vigor; power.

American Heritage Dictionary

The Energy Principle

It's hard to take consistent, impeccable action if you don't have that much energy. I like to say that you're going to have a hard time reaching your potential if you have a hard time getting out of bed in the morning.

Now, optimizing our health isn't rocket science. We all know what we should be doing (at least 90 percent of it!) but tragically few of us actually do it. Use your impeccability from above to master the fundamentals of nutrition and exercise. Build habits that will last you a lifetime and then put this part of your life on autopilot.

The best way to make a fire with two sticks is to make sure one of them is a match.

Will Rogers,
Twentieth-century cowboy and actor

God turns you from one feeling to another and teaches by means of opposites, so that you will have two wings to fly, not one.

Rumi,
Fourteenth-century Sufi mystic

The Wisdom Principle

Alright, now you've got some momentum: You've taken control, got some more self-awareness and a game plan that you're executing.

Whatever you do, don't freak out the first time (or the hundredth time) you drop the ball. Of course you're going to screw up. If you don't, then something's wrong! Don't view every challenge as a life or death event. View every situation as another opportunity to learn, another opportunity to grow. Success and failure are much less important than what you're learning.

Life is our classroom. That guy cutting you off and honking on the way to work? He's just another teacher—teaching you how to remain cool when others are stressed out. Thank him for the lesson. Move on. Don't get caught up in his issues.

And, you've gotta spend some time learning. Turn off the TV for an hour every night and open a book or open a journal. Learn. Write. Think.

Everything in the universe is a pitcher brimming with wisdom and beauty.
Rumi, Fourteenth-century Sufi mystic

Each and every master, regardless of the era or place, heard the call and attained harmony with heaven and earth. There are many paths to Mount Fuji, but there is only one summit—love.

Morihei Ueshiba,
Twentieth-century philosopher, martial artist

The Love Principle

Alright, so we're well on our way to thinking and living *Areté*. Good work.

We've got to remember one very important thing: None of this is anything without love. It starts with loving ourselves. To the extent that we can realize that we're not perfect and we never will be, we can forgive ourselves for our faults and have a little (perhaps even a lot?) more compassion for everyone else around us who is struggling with the same challenges.

We also need to remember to look outside of ourselves and think about how we can create a life that allows us to share our gifts with the world.

Remember Seligman? The guy who wrote *Authentic Happiness*? Well, he told us that if we want a happy life we need to know our strengths and use them as often as possible in our daily lives. We'll be more happy if we can do that. But, if we want to have a truly meaning-ful life, we need to use our strengths as often as possible and do so for something greater than ourselves.

We need to give back to the world. We've gotta show the love.

It's not enough to have lived. We should be determined to live for something. May I suggest that it be creating joy for others, sharing what we have for the betterment of personkind, bringing hope to the lost and love to the lonely.

Leo Buscaglia,
Twentieth-century Doctor of Love

Anything may be betrayed, anyone may be forgiven. But not those who lack the courage of their own greatness. . . . It does not matter that only a few in each generation will grasp and achieve the full reality of man's proper stature—and the rest will betray it. It is those few that move the world and give life its meaning—and it is those few that I have always sought to address. The rest are no concern of mine; it is not me or "The Fountainhead" that they will betray: it is their own souls.

Ayn Rand,
Twentieth-century Objectivist philosopher

The Courage Principle

Living with *Areté* starts and ends and is driven every moment by courage—by our willingness to grow, to evolve and to challenge ourselves to be who we are capable of being, moment by moment by moment.

Nothing is more important and nothing is more challenging.

Society does anything but support our growth, our individuality, and our greatness. We're told from the day we're born that we need to behave a certain way, wear the right clothes, drive the right cars, live in big houses in the right neighborhood, get the right education and the impressive job and the beautiful spouse and 2.2 kids and all that other nonsense. It's enough to drive anyone insane.

You have to be willing to jump from the normal and risk looking like an idiot as you grow. As Maslow says, "You will either step forward into growth or you will step back into safety."

Which way are you headed?

You're packing a suitcase for a place none of us has been.
A place that has to be believed to be seen.

U2,
Twentieth-century rock band

Now that we've covered some of the high-level stuff, how about some tips on how to apply these principles to our day-to-day lives?

The Attitude Principle

Smile. Isn't that nice? It's amazing what a smile can do. I once read about a study where depressed people were split into two groups—one group looked into a mirror and smiled for 30 minutes a day for 30 days. That's it. Just looked at themselves and smiled. The other group didn't. At the end of the study, the smilers were significantly more happy than the other group. Cool, eh?

Lesson: smile. Now. Tickle tickle. Gimme a little smile, will ya? There ya go! That wasn't so hard now was it?

Say Yes! Quick exercise: Take a moment and say, "No!" out loud right now. Say it. Seriously. "No!" Say it again. "No!" Again. "No. No. No. No. No."

Thank you. Alright. So, how do you feel?

Now, say, "Yes!" "Yes!" "Yes! Yes! Yes! Yes! Yes!"

Do you notice a slight difference? When you say "No" do you feel yourself shutting down, collapsing in? How about when you say "Yes!" Do you feel your whole body and spirit being lifted?

Amazing, isn't it? Lesson: Say "Yes!" more today. Go for it. Live a little.

Act "As If." Who do you want to be? What's your ideal? Are you enlightened? Are you wealthy? Are you in perfect physical shape?

Whatever it is, get that image. Then, on a moment-to-moment basis, act as if you already were that person. What would the enlightened being that you are do in this moment of tension? Perhaps breathe in, breathe out, gain perspective and maintain equanimity. Good. Then act like that enlightened person *now*.

How about that perfectly healthy person that you imagine? Good. What would he do right now? What would he eat? How often would he exercise? Perfect. That's what you do now.

Act as if. Moment to moment to moment. And, sooner than you think you won't be acting anymore. How amazingly cool is that?

The Vision Principle

Dream. In the words of one of my favorite teachers, James Allen:

"The greatest achievement was at first and for a time a dream. The oak sleeps in the acorn, the bird waits in the egg, and in the highest vision of the soul a waking angel stirs. Dreams are the seedlings of realities."

So, what are you dreaming of today?

Know What You Want. What's your intention? What do you want in your life? What do you want in this moment?

Quick tip: You're a *lot* more likely to get it if you know what "it" is. So what is it?

Regain Your Balance. Here's an exercise I often use to capture the importance of having a clear intention to regain our balance:

Stand up. Put your arms straight out. Make sure you're in an area that's big enough that you can spin around. Alright. Now, spin. Give yourself a good 5 to 10 to 15 spins—whatever it takes to get you a little off balance. Alright. Now once you get there, I want you to stop spinning. Then, I want you to do two different things.

First, I want you to put your hands together like you're praying and stare at your fingertips—it brings you back to balance *amazingly* quickly. Then, I want you to quit staring at your fingertips and instead I want you to look all around you—up, down, far away, to the right, to the left . . . just look everywhere. Notice how that makes you feel. If you're like me, it probably makes you nauseous.

For me, this is a perfect metaphor for having a clear intention in our lives. When things get stressful (that is, when we're spun around), we have a couple of options: We can look all around us to get a sense of perspective (which usually leads to more confusion/nausea); or, we can focus on what we know to be true, what our intention in life is, what the purpose of that experience is, and so forth—that clarity brings us back to balance as quickly as staring at our fingertips.

So, the next time you're spinning—have a clear intention: Know that your highest intention is to grow as a more enlightened, loving, balanced, growth-oriented human being (or whatever it is for you) and come back to that to regain your balance.

Try it out! Methinks you'll dig it.

The Self-Awareness Principle

Quit Worrying About What Others Think. That's a big one. Really big. Really, really, really big.

First of all, let's be clear about one thing: You're worried about what someone else thinks of you, right? Okay. Now, while you're doing that, what do you think they are worried about?

Hah. Exactly. They're worried about what you think of them. But you're so busy worrying about what they think of you that you're not even spending much time thinking about them. You follow that?

To be honest, whether or not that's true all the time is irrelevant (although I do think it's true most of the time). In any case, if you're going to live your life dependent on the good opinion of others for your happiness then, uh, I'll put it to you bluntly: You're screwed.

There's *no* way you can please everyone all the time. Even someone who wins an election by a landslide still had 30 or 40 percent of the people who disagreed with her.

Further, and I'd say much, much, much more important, by worrying about what other people think of you and working hard to try to please them, you're losing the essence of who you are—you're expressing such a small fraction of who you truly are. That's not cool. So, quit worrying about what other people think of you. Pretty please.

Be Authentic. Authenticity. Did you know that the word "authentic" literally means to be your own author. Be you. Don't pretend to be anything else. Pretty please.

(One of my friends and favorite teachers, Dan Millman, taught me that—along with a lot of other stuff woven through here. If you aren't familiar with Dan's work, you can check him out at www.danmillman. com and I recommend you start with *Way of the Peaceful Warrior* (which was released as a movie starring Nick Nolte in June 2006) and then go from there! Thanks, Dan!).

Quit Comparing Yourself to Others. It's really a pointless exercise. It automatically creates a strained relationship with whomever you're comparing yourself—you've either gotta be superior or inferior to them, right? Neither is a good basis for a loving relationship.

If you need to do any comparison at all—do it with your potential self! In the words of William Faulkner, "Don't bother just to be better than your contemporaries or predecessors. Try to be better than yourself."

Follow Your Bliss. Those three words capture the message of Joseph Campbell—the amazing mythology guru and mentor to George

Lucas who based much of *Star Wars* on the classic archetypal journeys Campbell discovered.

It's rather simple. Three words: 1. Follow. 2. Your. 3. Bliss.

Key words: "bliss" and "your." Not someone else's idea of your bliss. Not what you think should be your bliss. Not what you think would impress the crowd or appease the family. *Your* bliss. What truly gets you giddy.

Oh yah, "follow" is kinda important as well. Get out there and follow your bliss! (Pretty please. Thank you.)

The Goals Principle

Step Forward. Abraham Maslow broke it down for us in simple terms. He told us that in any given moment you have two options: You can step forward into growth or you can step back into safety. Pretty simple, really. Become aware of your behavior.

Become aware of the decisions you are making every moment of your life—the decision to speak authentically (step forward into growth) or to say what you think you should say (back into safety). Pay attention to your decision to either go out for the run you promised yourself or to make up an excuse as to why you just can't do it today.

Become aware. Become conscious of who you are, the decisions you're making, how you're expressing yourself and what you're actually doing. Your destiny is shaped by your moment to moment decisions. Choose wisely. Step forward.

Push Yourself. In the words of William James, the nineteenth-century U.S. philosopher and psychologist, "You have enormous untapped power you'll probably never tap, because most people never run far enough on their first wind to ever find they have a second."

How about we tap that power? The way to do it? Push yourself a little harder. Let's take a quick look at the "Training Effect"—a concept used to build your body—and see how it applies to our lives.

The same principle that applies to building muscles in the gym applies to building excellence in our lives: In order to grow, we must consistently push ourselves just a little bit past our current comfort zone. In exercise physiology parlance, this is called the Training Effect. The principles involved?

Overload: You must "overload" your body with more stress than it can currently handle. (Not too much as this may lead to injury, but enough so you're out of your current comfort zone.)

Overcompensation: Your body is smart. It doesn't like to get its butt kicked. So, what does it do? It overcompensates and repairs itself so that next time it's stronger—and capable of withstanding the level of stress you put on it previously.

The training effect explains how muscles grow, how your heart is trained to beat more efficiently, and how your lungs are trained to distribute oxygen more efficiently. It's also the same principle that dictates growth in other aspects of our lives: from our ability to give presentations at work to our ability to have challenging conversations with our significant other at home.

Go out and train. Push yourself a little further today.

Fill Your Water Pot and Hit the Rock. Every great teacher will advise you to build habits and to consistently train yourself to do your best.

The Buddha says it so beautifully when he reminds us that: "Little by little a person becomes evil, as a water pot is filled by drops of water. . . . Little by little a person becomes good, as a water pot is filled by drops of water."

I think the stonecutter is another perfect metaphor for the process of growing into our full potential. You may have heard the story:

A stonecutter hits a rock with his hammer. The stone splits. The casual observer sees this and thinks, "Wow. That guy is really strong. I can't believe he broke that huge rock with a single blow!"

The reality (obviously) is that the stonecutter didn't break it in a single blow—he'd been hammering away at that rock for a long time. Many, many blows went into the rock before it finally split.

Most people see someone who has achieved some level of success—whether it's enlightenment or celebrity status or financial wealth—and think, "Wow, they sure must be lucky."

Obviously, the stonecutter isn't strong enough to break a rock in one blow and no one is lucky enough to reach any level of excellence without an equally diligent and consistent effort.

So, hit the rock. Again. And again. And again. You will break the rock. (Oh, and by the way, quick FYI: Once you're done with that rock get ready to start swinging at the next one.)

The Action Principle

Floss. Not kidding. It's all about the little things, I'm telling ya! A number of years ago I asked a mentor of mine what one thing he would recommend. His advice: Do the little things to the best of your ability—from putting a sock straight in the hamper to washing your dishes immediately to flossing your teeth. His point: there are no little things and when you get in the habit of living at your highest potential with the mundane things, it becomes second nature for the bigger stuff.

So, floss your teeth. It'll build strong habits and even make your trip to the dentist a lot more pleasant! (Seriously: It's fun to have a dentist tell you how good your gums look!)

Pay Your Bills with a Smile. Never let a dollar come in or go out of your hands without gratitude. Thank whoever gave you the money and whoever gave you the services or products you're paying for. Honor the exchange. Think about how many people you're supporting as you circulate energy in the form of money. Make it a spiritual practice.

Create a New Habit. Right now. What one thing do you know you should be doing that would most dramatically change your life? Think about that: What one thing do you know you should be doing that would most dramatically change your life? Okay. Commit to creating that habit. Now.

Stop! So you just created a new habit that would most beneficially change your life. Now, the question is: What one thing do you know you should stop doing? You might have more than one. But what *one* thing do you know you just simply need to stop doing? It's not serving you anymore (not that it ever did). If you want to live with consistent happiness what *must* you stop doing?

You got it? Good. Write it down. Say it out loud. Whatever you gotta do.

Now *stop* doing it. Now. Forever. The next time you feel the urge and you feel your habituated self pulling you so strongly toward that behavior. *Stop. Stop. Stop. Stop.* It might be helpful to replace that old behavior with a new, more positive one.

Say you tend to yell at people you love when you get stressed. Catch yourself doing it (there's that awareness again). Pause, then pick something new to do. Maybe smile, take a deep breath or two. Whatever it takes. But the bottom line is simple: Pick that one thing you need to stop doing and stop doing it.

Phew. Good work. (This one's gonna be tough . . . but do it!)

Move! Take Action! I often imagine a powerful river with a stream of water that is moving. How beautiful is that? How pure and powerful? Contrast that with a little stagnant pool of water just sitting there—not moving. It's gross. Scum gathering on top, bugs cruising all around. Yuck.

The difference between the two? One's moving and the other's not. Lesson: Move! Flow! Don't get stagnant and invite the scum. Especially when you're stressed and don't feel like doing anything but lying in bed and moping. That's *exactly* when you need to make sure the pond scum doesn't start to grow! Move, move, move.

Go Straight at Your Problems. There's a great story in John Bunyan's book, *Pilgrim's Progress*. It goes something like this: The main character experiences all kinds of challenges and tough situations on his metaphorical spiritual quest in life. The cool part is that he's blessed with a shield. This shield miraculously protects him against everything in front of him. Nothing can harm him as long as he approaches it head on. That magic shield works wonders—provided he goes straight at the challenge. If he runs away, he loses its magical powers.

I think that's amazing. And, so true. Have you ever noticed that those huge problems you've had seemed to vanish the moment you tackled 'em head on? (I mean really head on not vacillating kinda sorta head on!) The things that really kick our butts are the ones we avoid. Lesson: Don't show 'em our ol' butts! Take 'em head on. Trust in the powers of your shield.

What problem have you been running away from? Tackle it head on.

The Energy Principle

Breathe. Often. You know—that whole oxygen and carbon dioxide moving through your body thing. It's good for you. Seriously. Stressed? Slow down. Take a deep breath in. Exhale. Ahhhh. Shoulders up! Shoulders down. Breathe in. Breathe out. Now isn't that nice? I think so, too. So does every cell in your body that you just nourished.

Tip: Ever watch a baby breathe? Notice how the baby's belly just goes up and down? Up and down . . . now that's a nice, deep breath—that's how you want to breathe. It's called breathing into your diaphragm. Babies get it. Somewhere along the line, stress moved our breath up and up until we were taking shallow breaths and barely getting any air. Eek.

Try this: Put your hand on your belly. Try to keep your chest still while you make your hand on your belly move in and out. Why should you care? Because right there at the bottom of your lungs is where all the real friendly little lung guys hang out waiting to collect the most oxygen for you! (That's the scientific description.) Seriously, breathe deeply. Increase oxygen. Reduce stress.

Sweat. You get sweaty today? I hope so. Our bodies were made to move. We, uh, weren't really designed to be sitting in front of a computer or in a car all day long. Get out and move! When you pump blood through your vessels and air through your lungs, it's like taking your insides to a car wash. (Even comes with an air freshener . . . oh, wait . . . that comes after the shower.)

Drink Plenty of Water. You drinking water today? Bare minimum is 64 ounces per day—that's 8 cups. Your body needs water for everything from releasing toxins to maintaining skin health. If you're not drinking enough water, your energy level will drop and you'll be more likely to get headaches.

Your brain and your heart are especially sensitive to even the slightest levels of dehydration. If you don't drink enough water, your blood volume will be affected, requiring your heart to pump harder to circulate blood throughout your body. The chemical and electrical signals in your brain need water. You'll feel tired and lethargic if you're thirsty.

Tip: Drink at least eight cups of water every day for a week. You'll be surprised with the boost in your energy levels. Trust me.

The Wisdom Principle

Meditate. Slow down. Breathe. Quiet your mind and your body for a moment or two or three. Whether it's for 20 minutes in the morning or night (or both) or 20 seconds at a stoplight, take a deep breath in, exhale, clear your mind.

Turn Off Your TV. (Better yet, never turn it on.) Love this quote by Bill Hicks, an American comedian: "Watching television is like taking black spray paint to your third eye."

Guess the average emotion of your average TV viewer. Mild depression. Yikes. Makes sense though, eh? Your soul knows that you're just avoiding life when you plop down to watch some fictional drama unfold or distract yourself in the myriad of numbing selections. Turn off your TV please and . . .

Open a Book. And read it. Read anything good lately? Hope so. Take some time. It's fun. Your brain will thank you. Looking for some good picks? Check out http://brian.zaadz.com for some of my favorites.

Be Consistent. One of my favorite lessons from training my body is the idea that you want to focus on consistency over intensity. It's not about getting all fired up one day and going off at the gym for an hour and a half . . . and then waking up the next day unable to move!

It's much much, much, much, much better to just show up. Put in your 20 minutes, your 30 minutes, your 40 minutes. Whatever. Just do it consistently.

Aristotle made it pretty clear: "We are what we repeatedly do. Excellence [also known as *Areté*] then, is not an act, but a habit."

This applies to all aspects of our life. Quite simply, we are what we consistently do.

Sure, it's a lot more fun to jump into the latest fad diet or hit the gym for an intense workout once a week or go to a motivational seminar or yoga retreat, but the question is not how intensely we get into any given workout or week of dieting or weekend of yoga . . . it's all about whether we have the self-mastery to do the things we know we should be doing consistently—moment to moment and week in and week out.

Be Inconsistent. So, now that we're clear on how important consistency is, be inconsistent.

Well, at least be willing and able to be inconsistent. It's so easy for us to get locked into a way of thinking or to maintain an opinion simply because we strongly felt a certain way at one point. But, my God! If you can't break free and give yourself the power to change your mind, your job, your strategy, your relationships, whatever . . . you, uh, are kinda screwed.

I love Emerson's comments on the subject:

A foolish consistency is the hobgoblin of little minds, adored by little statesmen and philosophers and divines. With consistency a great soul has simply nothing to do. He may as well concern himself with his shadow on the wall. Speak what you think now in hard words, and to-morrow speak what to-morrow thinks in hard words again, though it contradicts every thing you said today. Ah, so you shall be sure to be misunderstood. Is it so bad, then, to be misunderstood? Pythagoras was misunderstood, and Socrates, and Jesus, and Luther, and Copernicus, and Galileo, and Newton, and every pure and wise spirit that ever took flesh. To be great is to be misunderstood.

So, please do us all a favor and don't be a hobgoblin, okay?

Embrace Opposites. You know, yin and yang, light and dark, night and day, high tide, low tide, consistency, inconsistency. Stuff like that. Life is full of opposites. Learn to live in a state where you appreciate it and see that you simply can't have light without dark; you can't have a day without a night; can't have a summer without a winter (well, I guess in California you can but you know what I mean!). The more you appreciate this the less you're gonna be taken away by your sadness, despair, hopelessness. Transcend it and you're even more golden.

The Love Principle

Be Nice. Have you ever heard about the effects of kindness on your brain? Wayne Dyer shares the amazing science of kindness in his book *Power of Intention.* It goes something like this:

> Serotonin is the drug that makes you feel good. It's what all the pharmaceutical companies pump into those wonderful little anti-depressants. It's also a little drug God decided to pump through our brains when we do things he/she/it likes. It's kinda like a little reward for good behavior, you know?

Anyway, get this: When you do something kind for someone else, the person you're helping has serotonin released in her brain—she feels happier. So do you. Good news! Two more serotonin-induced happier people in the world! Woo hoo! But the most amazing thing is this: Not only do you and the person you helped feel better, so does some random person who happened to watch your act of kindness.

Serve. It's so easy to spend all of our time asking what we can get out of a situation instead of what we can give. I don't know about you, but I feel stress when I'm just focused on myself. The moment I get out of my own little set of fears/issues and start thinking about how I can serve and give to those around me, my stress seems to evaporate. Amazing.

Try it out. The next time you're stressed, step back. See how you're focused on yourself and how you may not get what you wanted. Flip the situation around and see how you can give all of yourself to the situation. Irony here, of course, is that when you truly give yourself to the world, you'll get more than you ever dreamt of in return.

Reminds me of one of my absolute favorite passages from Viktor Frankl's *Man's Search for Meaning*:

> Again and again I therefore admonish my students in Europe and America: Don't aim at success—the more you aim at it and make it a target, the more you are going to miss it. For success, like happiness, cannot be pursued; it must ensue, and it only does so as the unintended side effect of one's personal dedication to a cause greater than oneself or as the by-product of one's surrender to a person other than oneself. Happiness must happen, and the same holds for success: You have to let it happen by not caring about it. I want you to listen to what your conscience commands you to do and go on to carry it out to the best of your knowledge. Then you will live to see that in the long run—in the long run, I say!— success will follow you precisely because you had forgotten to think about it.

Be the Change. What do you want to see in the world? More peace? More love? More kindness? According to Gandhi, the answer is simple: We must be the change we want to see.

You want world peace? Bless the person who cut you off and honked at you on your way to work. Wish them a safe journey instead of getting caught up in their anger and impatience.

You want more kindness? Smile at the person who might be frustrating you. Open the door for someone, pick up a piece of trash. Be kind. Simple but not easy. Be the change.

Say **"Thank you, thank you, thank you, thank you, thank you, thank you."** Go to bed with these words on your mind, wake up with them and pop 'em in often throughout the day. As you say these words, you'll find your mind discovering all the wonderful things for which you're grateful. It's amazing.

Reminds me of Meister Eckhart's wisdom: "If the only prayer you ever say in your whole life is 'thank you,' that would suffice."

The Courage Principle

Ask Yourself: What would I do if I wasn't afraid? Then do it.

Ask Yourself that Question Again. Then do it again. And again. You do that 10 times and I guarantee you you'll be a different person. Do it every moment and you'll be telling your story to the world. In the words of Ralph Waldo Emerson, "Always, always, always, always, always, always, always do the thing you fear and the death of fear is certain." God, I love that.

Shine. Are you shining today? Good. Marianne Williamson would be proud, 'cause:

Our deepest fear is not that we are inadequate. Our deepest fear is that we are powerful beyond measure.

It is our light, not our darkness, that most frightens us.

We ask ourselves, who am I to be brilliant, gorgeous, talented, and fabulous? Actually, who are you not to be?

You are a child of God. Your playing small doesn't serve the world.

There's nothing enlightened about shrinking so that other people won't feel insecure around you.

We are all meant to shine, as children do.

We are born to make manifest the glory of God that is within us.

It's not just in some of us, it's in everyone. And as we let our own light shine, we unconsciously give other people permission to do the same.

As we are liberated from our own fear, our presence automatically liberates others.

Now get out there and shine!

Chapter 15

The Creation of Conscious Cultures in Support of Human Flourishing

Michael Strong
CEO and Chief Visionary Officer, FLOW

Much of the animus against the free enterprise system is that it encourages shallow, materialistic values. But every human being who aspires to be an empowered creator must realize that there is no anonymous "it." Everything we see around us is created by choices made by you and me, our friends and families, and billions of other mostly decent human beings around the world.

One often encounters criticisms of contemporary society that accuse our culture of caring too much about money, materialistic goods, appearance, power, or various other shallow appetites. Sometimes these critics then express anger with capitalist society. But there is no need to be angry with anyone. We can begin today to create a world in which people are primarily focused on love, compassion, community, wisdom, beauty, and any other ideals. By our moment-to-moment decisions and interactions we can begin to create the world we want right now.

At present, many people seem to believe that money, power, and formal status (for example, a title such as "Professor so-and-so," or "Chief Undersecretary so-and-so") are required to get their esteem needs met. But this is an entirely arbitrary approach. Human beings are tribal animals that have been genetically programmed to seek hierarchy and status within their tribes. But the wonderful thing about the world today is that we can create new tribes with new standards for the distribution of status.

One of the insights of the second tier of Spiral Dynamics is that there are, and will always be, social hierarchies. But at the same time, we must realize that we can continually work toward focusing our hierarchies of value ever more clearly in alignment with the True, the Good, and the Beautiful as we understand them.

No one forces us to watch television. No one forces us to be envious of the clothes, cars, or homes of other people. No one forces us to pay attention to the activities of the wealthy and powerful. No one forces us to buy anything. Beyond a very modest supply of food, every individual is completely free to make daily choices that reflect that which they believe to be the True, the Good, and the Beautiful around them.

It is true that, because we are tribal animals, it is easier to make positive choices when we are members of tribes who support our choices. It is difficult for most of us not to drink if all of our friends drink, to avoid popular entertainments if all of our friends talk only about popular entertainments, and so forth. But each and every one of us can be a cultural entrepreneur who supports the creation of new cultural hierarchies in which only those things that are authentically valuable receive attention, financial support, and cultural sanction within our tribe.

Lynne Twist, in *The Soul of Money*, reminds people to let their money flow where it needs to go to give them fulfillment:

> Grounded in sufficiency, money's movement in and out of our life feels natural. We can see that flow as healthy and true, and allow that movement instead of being anxious about it or hoarding. In sufficiency we recognize and celebrate money's power for good—our power to do good with it—and we can

experience fulfillment in directing the flow toward our highest ideals and commitments. When we perceive the world as
one in which there is enough and we are enough to make the
world work for everyone everywhere, with no one left out, our
money carries that energy and generates relationships and partnerships in which everyone feels able and valued, regardless of
their economic circumstances.

Lynne Twist, *The Soul of Money: Reclaiming the Wealth of Our
Inner Resources,* W.W. Norton & Company, 103

Twist is working to liberate people from a cultural hierarchy in
which they feel locked into believing that they need ever more money
and goods. Her talk of "sufficiency" shows her to be a cultural entrepreneur who is working to focus us on using money to do good
instead of staying frozen in traditional cultural norms that encourage us
to hoard money.

Her advice, and example of cultural entrepreneurship, concerning
the flow of money may likewise be applied to our flow of love, attention, and respect.

Teachers in training sometimes learn a disciplinary technique
known as "extinction." This is fancy jargon meaning that if a kid is
misbehaving, sometimes the best way to deal with it is to ignore it.
And while there are certainly some kinds of misbehavior that must be
addressed by means of disciplinary action, rarely do we tap into the
power of focusing our attention on people's best behaviors and ignoring their worst behaviors.

Many people who aspire to do good spend a great deal of time
thinking about these things and perhaps a great deal of time in personal
development. And yet in many cases, their attention continues to remain
focused on the same behaviors and issues as before, and their daily habits of personal and professional interaction remain largely unchanged.

But culture and status hierarchies are made up of thousands of
unconscious choices that we make every day. Who do you look at
when you walk into a room? What headlines draw your attention?
What behaviors do you notice in a meeting? What comments make
you angry? To whom do you give compliments and why? Is it possible that sometimes you ignore people for whom your attention might

be an important gift? Are you directing your attention to the right words, emotions, thoughts, glances, and energies in every interpersonal interaction?

Our presence around children is especially important; they learn far more from our behavior than from our words. How, and toward what, we express approval and disapproval are especially important. What do you notice about them? What do you compliment? What aspects of their lives do you ask about? When they observe you, as they always do, in what kinds of activities and emotional states do they find you? What future social realities are you creating with every twitch of your eyebrow or grimace that crosses your face?

Stop, for a moment, and write down your ideal of a perfectly healthy and well human world:

_____

_____

_____

_____

_____

Now consider first what kinds of purchasing, investment, hiring, and employment decisions would need to be made in such a world; what criteria should be used in making such decisions.

Because of various commitments or constraints, you may not be able to change all of your financial decisions to be immediately in alignment with your ideals, but it is important to focus on the extent to which your decisions are so aligned. Then, over time, you can gradually bring your reality into alignment with your ideals.

Now for the most difficult one: Review your human interactions in the past 24 hours. Consider exactly where you directed your attention, or where you allowed your attention to be taken. Now consider where your attention would have gone if it were perfectly in alignment with your ideals; write down your ideal patterns of focus in human interactions.

Would you have focused on anything different than you did or ignore anything that you allowed to occupy your attention?

It is good that we live in a world in which people are increasingly conscious of the financial choices that they make. The next frontier is to live in a world in which people become increasingly conscious of the attention choices that they make. The upward flow of human development will proceed far more quickly and far more deeply, if we support ourselves and others by means of moment-to-moment acts of recognition of kindness, insight, patience, love, and beauty than if we talk about personal development and socially responsible choices while allowing our attention to be drawn primarily by acts of anger, hatred, manipulation, or shallow sensation.[*]

We are responsible every moment of every day for creating the culture we see around us. Each of us has a responsibility to be a powerful force for positive change by means of our moment-to-moment interactions with every human being we encounter.

I say this as someone who aspires to this ideal and who constantly fails. I need the best in you to draw out the best in me. And, in turn, I will strive to give you my best, in hopes that I am supporting you, however partially, to manifest your best.

Anger is rarely, and resentment is never, a reflection of our best selves. More powerfully positive cultures are not created by means of chronic anger and resentment. While particular individuals in particular situations may rightly deserve your anger, with respect to any frustrations you have with society or culture or the system, it is a far more valuable contribution to sublimate your anger into motivation to make the world a better place. Become an entrepreneur of new cultural hierarchies more in alignment with your ideals.

Some people are perfectly content with existing status hierarchies. For some people, it is utterly okay with them that Donald Trump is respected for being rich and gaudy, or President Bush is respected for being powerful, or Noam Chomsky is respected for being a famous intellectual. Let them enjoy their status hierarchies. Let them be.

Other people are frustrated and unhappy with existing status hierarchies. They believe that there is something morally bankrupt about a society that respects wealth, power, or position. Wonderful! Let them criticize by creating. Let them create new educational institutions, new communities, new ideals, and new status hierarchies.

---

[*]This is why the issue of education is so crucial, and why education is primarily about creating a more positive culture and not about the transmission of data.

There are open source communities in which Linus Torvalds is the ultimate hero. There are athletic communities in which Lance Armstrong is the ultimate hero. Riane Eisler wants to create a "partnership society" instead of a patriarchy or a matriarchy. Go Riane!

Is it easy to create new communities with new status hierarchies? Not at all. No one ever claimed that worthwhile achievement was easy, ever. Is it worth attempting? Of course.

The only Greek expression that I remember after two years of Greek is *Ta Kala Xalepa* (that which is beautiful or noble is difficult and worth striving for).

We need to create an honorable, pluralistic ethos according to which we acknowledge that many people are dissatisfied with many things in our society—fine, we welcome dissatisfaction as the source of craving for the good. But we never accept whining or criticizing of others or critiques of society. If you don't like it, go fix it, go create a world, a community, a subculture in which your ideals can be instantiated, realized, in which you can show us what your vision of beauty and nobility looks like. Create a new social reality, so that I can see your dreams come true. I want to see a world in which billions of dreams are coming true constantly.

Criticize by creating.

As far as we can discern, the sole purpose of human existence is to kindle a light in the darkness of mere being.

Carl Jung

Chapter 16

Liberating the Entrepreneurial Spirit for Good™

Jeff Klein
Executive Director and
Chief Activation Officer, FLOW

M ind is the forerunner of all things," observed the Buddha. At FLOW, we give great credence to mind—to ideas and the words we use to represent them. We believe they have great power, as they guide our actions, which shape the world. When we say that FLOW is dedicated to "liberating the entrepreneurial spirit for good," we know these words represent a powerful intention with profound consequences.

We believe that the liberated entrepreneurial spirit, embodied by millions if not billions of people, can effectively address the challenges and opportunities facing humanity, leading to sustainable peace, prosperity, happiness, and well-being for all, in our lifetime.

We understand that, to effectively liberate the entrepreneurial spirit for good, we have to address the idea individually and globally. In this chapter I'll address the following questions, relating to FLOW's purpose—liberating the entrepreneurial spirit for good:

- What does liberating the entrepreneurial spirit for good mean?
- What are the conditions that foster liberation of the entrepreneurial spirit for good?
- What are the factors that constrain the entrepreneurial spirit for good?
- What can we do to overcome these constraints?

What Do We Mean by "Liberating the Entrepreneurial Spirit for Good"?

Let's look at the words, and the ideas they represent, beginning with the subject of the phrase, "spirit," and its modifier, "entrepreneurial," continuing with the verb, "liberate" (liberating), then the modifying "for good," and finishing by putting them all together.

Spirit: Vital principle or animating force for human beings. Origin: Latin *spiritus*, breath; *spirare*, to breathe.

Entrepreneurial: Undertaking an endeavor, assuming risk, innovating, creating wealth by combining things in new ways. Origin: French *entreprendre*, to undertake.

Entrepreneurial Spirit: An energy or animating force that activates the human potential to create, innovate, explore, endeavor, passionately pursue vision in spite of challenges, obstacles, and risks.

Liberate: To set free, release, unleash. Origin: Latin *liberare*, liberate, free.

For Good: Two meanings. 1. Positive, desirable, beneficial, constructive. 2. Permanently, forever, once and for all.

Liberating the Entrepreneurial Spirit for Good: Once and for all, unleashing the human potential to create positive outcomes through courageous innovation, exploration, and endeavor.

Human beings have the extraordinary ability to envision something that doesn't exist, and through passion, audacity, ingenuity, and persistence, to create what we envision. We have the added ability to imbue our vision and pursuit with intention to serve, enhance, and benefit—ourselves and others. We believe this ability to envision and manifest vision is among the most powerful abilities of homo sapiens. It is one of the core factors contributing to our individual growth and development and to the elevation of our communities, societies, and species.

What Are the Conditions that Foster Liberation of the Entrepreneurial Spirit for Good?

Part of our work at FLOW is to celebrate accomplishment of the entrepreneurial spirit in business, social service, the arts, and all channels of human endeavor and expression, through individual entrepreneurs and entrepreneurial cultures and eras. As Michael illuminated in his piece, the Industrial Revolution and the Information Age were substantially catalyzed by young, entrepreneurial "tinkerers."

We also seek to understand and promote the forces and factors that foster the entrepreneurial spirit to catalyze such profound shifts. Among the factors we have identified and that we are focusing on through our programs are:

- Access to capital and other key resources, including high quality information.
- Economic freedom (including the rule of law and secure property rights) as well as freedom, more broadly speaking, and protection of essential human rights.
- Entrepreneurial culture, that provides education, training, mentorship, networking, and cultivates inner resources of imagination, creativity, initiative, and so on.

With respect to the "good" part of the equation, as John Mackey outlines in Conscious Capitalism, and as his work through Whole Foods Market exemplifies, establishing the higher purpose of enterprise (in general and specifically for an individual enterprise and entrepreneur) and recognizing and addressing the interrelated system of stakeholders in an enterprise, leads to a dynamic, evolving system that explicitly addresses the good in its decisions and through its actions.

What Are the Factors that Constrain the Entrepreneurial Spirit for Good?

By amending our mistakes, we get wisdom.
By defending our faults, we betray an unsound mind.

The Sutra of Hui Neng

In our pursuit of liberating the entrepreneurial spirit for good, we must overcome many levels of limitations undermining our ability to fully express our entrepreneurial spirit for good. These include:

- Personal constraints: Inherent or learned, self-imposed and sustained—such as fear, doubt, and laziness.
- Collective/systemic constraints: Imposed by systems, structures, culture, and institutions; including cultural norms and related context of attitudes and behaviors, and legal, financial, and political systems.

More specifically, some of the personal constraints include:

- Fear
- Doubt
- Delusion
- Complacency
- Ignorance
- Overindulgence
- Addiction to distraction
- Arrogance
- Disinterest
- Unwillingness to learn
- Weak moral and ethical core
- Weak skills
- Lack of confidence
- Diffidence
- Lack of discipline
- Lack of imagination
- Anger toward yourself and others
- Avoidance
- Shame
- Blame toward yourself and others

These personal or internal restraints feed voices inside that say "I can't," "I won't," "Why bother," and so on, which paralyze us, limit our perspective, and our sense of what is possible in the long run and even in our next steps.

Here are some systemic constraints:

- External control (including regulations, monopolies, unfair competition, cheating, collusion)
- Cultural norms
- Social pressures
- Bad information (including lies)
- Limited access to resources
- Degraded resources

What Can We Do to Overcome These Challenges and Constraints?

That which we persist in doing becomes easier for us to do. Not that the nature of the thing itself has changed but our power to do it has increased.

Ralph Waldo Emerson

To address personal, internal constraints requires awareness, courage, discipline, dedication, personal growth and development, as well as collaboration and support from others.

To address the external, systemic constraints requires rigorous analysis, extensive dialogue and process, collaborative effort, and even societal transformation. As Michael Strong reflected in his opening chapters, human beings have historically risen to the occasion, and continue to address and overcome seemingly insurmountable challenges.

The way to overcome obstacles to liberating the entrepreneurial spirit for good—for yourself and in support of others—begins with personal responsibility and practice. It is and has always been, "a small group of highly motivated individuals who have changed the world" to paraphrase Margaret Mead. And these thoughtful, committed citizens build on their personal, internal resources to do their transformational work in the world.

Following are some core skills and attributes we can cultivate to support us as we seek to liberate the entrepreneurial spirit and to have a positive impact in and on the world:

- Passion, patience, and persistence
- Vision, wisdom, and discernment
- Compassion, courage, and collaboration
- Faith, creativity, and discipline
- Introspection, reflection, and inner work
- Authentic power, self-restraint

And among the tools and practices that support us as we embody and employ these skills and attributes are:

- Conflict mitigation, mediation, and resolution
- Thoughtful use of speech
- Planning (without attachment to plans)
- Establishing measurable goals (and rigorously tracking our progress in an iterative process)
- Assessing and tracking the condition of the environment and our relationship to it
- Employing feedback mechanisms throughout our work and organizations
- Organizing our activities
- Keeping track of our commitments and ensuring that we live up to them

Developing consistent personal practice is essential to cultivating the entrepreneurial spirit for good within yourself. As we brush our teeth, wash our hands, keep our kitchen sink clean, eat well, drink plenty of water, and so on, certain personal practices can provide a strong core of support for our pursuit of entrepreneurial liberation for good.

Personal practice supports our efforts to develop many of the skills and attributes listed above. Finding practices that best support you is a matter of personal choice, guided by intuition, teachers, trial and error. To a considerable extent, what specific practices or paths you choose doesn't really matter. As Carlos Castaneda recounts the counsel of his teacher, Don Juan, what matters is that "it has heart."

My personal practice over the years has evolved to reflect changes in my perceptions, needs, and circumstances, but has consistently included physical, mental, emotional, and spiritual activity, including Yoga, meditation, martial arts, gardening, hiking, running, reading, dancing, parenting, and on.

Practices such as these can help to develop a strong nervous system that can withstand and weather the endless stream of stress we face in entrepreneurial adventure. They help to build a resilient immune system that can ward off illness and enable us to persevere with health and vitality. They provide deeply rooted moral and ethical fiber, which sustain steady and consistent behavior. And they help us to keep our word to ourselves and to others, which is among the most essential skills for well-being and success.

When challenges and crises arise, we have the strength, stability, and flexibility to adapt, maintain focus and intention, sustain energy and persist. And when joy arises, we can embrace it in a sustained and grounded way rather than burning out with excitement.

With respect to building community, developing organizations, and, perhaps, catalyzing positive social change, it is imperative that we cultivate skills for communication, cooperation, and collaboration. I have found awareness, listening, dialogue, writing, and facilitating skills to be especially helpful to foster effective communications, cooperation, and collaboration.

> Though I do not believe
> that a plant will spring up
> where no seed has been,
> I have great faith in a seed.
> Convince me that you have a seed there,
> and I am prepared to expect wonders.
>
> Henry David Thoreau

We have great faith in the entrepreneurial spirit that resides in each of us. We encourage you to look to us and others for ongoing inspiration and support and, most important, to continually look inside yourself to find the inspiration that resides in your heart, and to follow it with passion and purpose.

You can't connect the dots looking forward; you can only connect them looking backwards.

So you have to trust that the dots will somehow connect in your future. You have to trust in something—your gut, destiny, life, karma, whatever. This approach has never let me down,

and it has made all the difference in my life.

Steve Jobs

Chapter 17

The FLOW Vision for the Twenty-First Century

Michael Strong
CEO and Chief Visionary Officer, FLOW

I present a vision in three acts:

Act I: A Tale of Two Activists, a concrete vision that is taking place in the here and now.

Act II: The Global Consequences of FLOW, activism from today through 2040.

Act III: A concrete vision of a school in 2060 as a result of the FLOW activism through 2040.

The vision is a very specific road map for those who believe that the future described herein is worth creating.

Act I: A Tale of Two Activists
(A Vision for the Here and Now)

Consider Julian, Activist A. Angered by social injustice and environmentally unsustainable commerce, and inspired by earlier generations of activists, Julian graduated from college determined to make a difference in the world. He got a job as a canvasser for a social justice organization at below minimum wage (indeed, the organization pleaded with the government for an exemption to pay its employees below minimum wage). After 18 months at this job he obtained a better job, working for a nonprofit, as a community organizer in a poor, Hispanic community.

This was a far more satisfying job than going door-to-door; the women of the community often brought him burritos for lunch and he felt valued by the community as he fought city hall to ensure that they got their fair share of parks and recreations dollars and quality water and sewage services. He was still paid just slightly more than minimum wage, but the satisfactions of the job made it all worthwhile. After five challenging years in this position, constantly battling the government, Julian fell in love with a woman he met at a protest march, and they married and decided to raise a family.

He went back to school for a couple more years to get a teaching credential while still working as a community organizer, then went into public school teaching, finally earning a modest but comfortable salary. He started out idealistically as a young teacher, and was supported by his principal as he tried out innovative methods that developed critical and creative thinking and emotional intelligence in his students. That principal was then transferred, and his new principal, concerned with the low test score gains at the school, required all faculty to be trained in a form of direct instruction, in which the teacher's entire day was scripted. Instead of teaching creatively, Julian was now forced to read out loud from an instruction book, which told him what to say and specified how the students were to respond.

His autonomy as an educator was nonexistent. He quickly came to hate his job but conscientiously tried not to expose his frustrations to his students. He looked into taking a job at a nearby private Montessori school where he could teach in a way that had integrity and rewarded his creative intelligence, but it would have required a 40 percent pay cut and the loss of his retirement. By this time he and his wife had a child and a mortgage, and he couldn't afford to leave the public schools.

Julian vacillated between rage and depression day after day, year after year. In his quietest, most honest moments, he wondered if he had wasted his life. Although he and his wife contributed $50 they couldn't afford to Greenpeace each month, and they only bought ecologically conscious products, he knew he wasn't making much of a difference in the world. But he also knew that he couldn't stomach selling out to corporate America even if it meant that he could give more money to activist causes. Was there no alternative between dying a slow death of the spirit and selling out?

Consider Patrice, Activist B. Patrice, who was a freshman the year Julian graduated, was likewise angered by social injustice and environmentally unsustainable commerce. For a time, she attended the same activist meetings as Julian and went to the same protest marches. Then one day she attended a FLOW speech on campus that mostly just confused her. The speakers seemed to have an honest commitment to making the world a better place and introduced her to many new concepts she had never heard before, but they also were unabashedly enthusiastic about free markets. It was weird stuff, but she couldn't quite reject it out of hand.

For the next several months she read FLOW materials and argued with members of the campus FLOW group about free markets and sustainability and innovation and entrepreneurship and advertising and consumer sovereignty and personal responsibility and personal growth and just about everything else it seemed like. Gradually, as the FLOW worldview came into focus and she came to understand the potential for global change provided by FLOW, she became excited. She saw how she could have an enormous positive impact on the world, be a much happier person, and, indeed, have a blast and live a prosperous life, while making the world a better place. Although Julian and her other activist friends mostly cut her off in anger when she quit attending their meetings (she had gotten to the point where she found the anger and righteousness at those meetings tedious), she didn't care anymore. She was busy making things happen.

Patrice became a leader in the FLOW movement. She organized a FLOW Happiness and Well-being chapter that supervised internships at various local new private and charter schools that were creating happier, better places for kids to learn. Although occasionally a placement or a school didn't work out, for the most part she constantly heard stories of how happy the schools were to have extra help, how meaningful the interns found the experiences, and most of all how young people's lives were being changed. The students who worked at these schools became school choice activists, working vigorously on behalf of educational vouchers, tax credits, and more liberated charter schools. She later found that many of the interns she set up went on to create their own chains of schools based on the new educational approaches learned in these cool laboratory schools.

She also organized FLOW Open World groups that coordinated campus entrepreneur clubs with do-gooders eager to address social, economic, and environmental issues in developing communities throughout the world. There were already several dozen bright, ambitious young men who were busy creating web-based businesses in their dorm rooms. In her former life she would have despised these geeky guys for not joining her at antiglobalization protests. But now she was organizing many of her former protester friends to create online education and training for people around the world. Through Open World they were working with teenagers in Sri Lanka, microentrepreneurs in Bolivia, and a tech park in Kyrgyzstan, to develop a wide range of skills and establish positive relationships beyond their local communities. Her goal was to develop the teenagers' skills to the point where the campus geeks would hire them to work on their web businesses.

She encountered significant challenges in addressing cross-cultural communication issues, and sometimes it seemed as if her team had to learn how to explain the entire modern world to people in other countries so that they could be effective employees and collaborators. But when the first poor people in Sri Lanka, Bolivia, and Kyrgyzstan received their first $5 PayPal payments invariably they would send her Open World team the most effusively grateful thank-yous.

More impressive, a remarkable number of them, once they started earning $50 per month or so, began donating money back to the project. They felt both grateful and rich and wanted to give back.

Both the geek entrepreneurs and the former antiglobalization protestors were so overwhelmed by this display of generosity by those so much poorer than themselves, that they began holding a weekly "Upwing" party to which each person was required to bring someone of the opposite political persuasion as a date. Each "Right-Left" couple paid $20 to get into the party, $10 of which went directly to scholarships for students at private schools in the developing world (where tuition was $20–40 per year). These parties and this movement began spreading to campuses across the United States, and within a few years they were producing millions of dollars for scholarships around the world.

Initially, the campus environmentalists were hostile to the Open World project because they thought that it just meant more economic growth that would be destructive to the environment. A low point was when one of the Upwing parties was disrupted by a protest with signs proclaiming: "Don't Sleep with the Enemy," "Beware: Capitalism is a communicable disease," and far more vulgar slogans. This became awkward after Oxfam officially supported the Open World project, but there were still very negative attitudes toward Open World among some of the environmental groups.

Patrice realized that she needed to do some outreach, so she held FLOW sustainability workshops and one-by-one twisted the arms of key players in the campus environmental movement to attend. The workshops first clarified the distinction between those resources that were in serious danger of depletion due to tragedy of the commons problems and those that were not due to the fact that they were owned. They then presented ways to address tragedy of the commons problems and how to persuade businesspeople that property rights solutions to such problems were good business.

They held panel discussions featuring FLOW leaders, environmentalists, economists, and businesspeople that revealed openness to practical environmental solutions on the part of all parties. Patrice then created a campus sustainability chapter that supported property rights solutions, a green tax shift, and environmental entrepreneurship without the rage and exaggeration that too often undermined the credibility of some of the traditional campus environmental groups. Patrick Moore, the founder of Greenpeace who had quite publicly given up the

destructive approach many years ago, became a campus hero among the
FLOW Sustainability group. Greenspirit, Moore's newer, more positive
organization grew rapidly, and students joined Moore in supporting a
growing forest products industry to reduce atmospheric carbon.

One of the implications of the FLOW sustainability approach
was price rationing to ensure that resources were not depleted.
Although price rationing did eliminate sustainability fears, it created a
new concern: The poor would not be able to afford basic resources.
Patrice adroitly led those new recruits who were most concerned about
this issue to create the Affordability Group. This group worked on creating a campaign to reduce unnecessary building and zoning regulation
that caused housing to be so unaffordable. Once the members of this
group understood that they had an effective strategy for reducing housing costs for the poor by 50 percent or more and that housing took up
60 percent or more of the housing budgets for poor people, they were
more willing to support price rationing policies that could result in
higher gasoline prices, higher energy prices, and higher water prices.

Their big victory was to rewrite the housing regulations for
New Orleans and then to get Wal-Mart to partner with a manufactured housing firm and several innovative architects. The day Wal-Mart
signed the contract to purchase 500,000 elegant modular homes to
retail for $4,999 each the entire Affordability movement around the
country celebrated. The next day the world was dumbfounded when
Wal-Mart announced that it would give away the first 50,000 units to
New Orleans families who wanted to return if the Affordability Group
could legalize affordable housing in 10 other urban areas. Remarkably,
with efforts going on in 50 cities, within 6 weeks 10 new cities had
legalized affordable housing, through reducing unnecessary regulations, and by the end of the year 35 of the 50 cities had legalized such
housing—and Wal-Mart stock went up 10 percent.

Patrice had previously thought of graduate school after graduation, but by the time she graduated she found herself on the board of
directors of 11 organizations, 6 nonprofits and 5 for-profits. She had
received significant shares of stock from each of the for-profits. She
also found herself to be in high demand as a speaker and consultant and
found that she could earn a good living showing other groups how to
apply FLOW principles. A couple of years later one of the Open World

for-profit companies went public and she became a multimillionaire before she was 30. But she was far too busy to even notice.

When she married a fellow FLOW entrepreneur they raised their children in both the United States and Tanzania, where she was setting up an Open World project to save the chimpanzees. One of her best FLOW friends, whom she had placed at a school as an intern, had become one of the greatest educators on earth, leading a chain of 50 for-profit schools that were havens of creativity and well-being. When Patrice was not traveling she would simply go and spend time at her daughter's school because it was such a beautiful environment. And, logically enough, she helped her friend to open up a franchise of the school at the Open World zone in Tanzania. She was gently envious at her daughters' opportunity to learn a local Tanzanian dialect while learning to speak to the chimpanzees as well.

Life was such a spectacular experience she usually forgot her role in transforming the world for the better—until she happened to have lunch with her old friend Julian.

Of course, Julian quit his public school job the next day. But that is another story.

Act II: The Global Consequences of FLOW Activism from Today through 2040

This section consists of three parts:

  I. The Growth of Peace and Prosperity around the World.
 II. The Growth of the Well-Being Industry in the United States.
III. Progress toward Global Sustainability

We start with the first section because we need global peace and prosperity for all, but the vision is ultimately not satisfying if it is based merely on mindless materialism. Thus we also need to envision a growing well-being industry; the United States is used as an example, though other nations might move first on this. And, finally, global peace and prosperity would not be sustainable if we destroyed the environmental conditions needed for life in the process; thus, a parallel process describing progress toward global sustainability is also included.

I. The Growth of Peace and Prosperity around the World

Campus activists target specific regions in which to develop their peace and prosperity initiatives: There are activist groups devoted to Asia, Europe, Oceana, Africa, and the Americas.

Asia

2010: The Asia group begins an aggressive campaign to reduce trade barriers and to increase trade across national boundaries throughout Asia in the name of peace and prosperity. Student groups protest trade barriers and government control of the economy in Japan and Thailand. Idealistic young entrepreneurs from the West pour into China and, in the midst of the old regime, help to create thriving enterprise zones throughout China. While creating wealth for hundreds of millions of Chinese, they also deliberately transmit an understanding of the FLOW vision of peace and prosperity. The entrepreneur movement in India is becoming politically credible and powerful as people recognize how much wealth is being brought into India. FLOW chapters develop on campuses throughout India. India's Special Economic Zones (SEZs) become increasingly focused on idealistic visions of a better life for all.

2020: As the Chinese realize that, with the right legal environment, they will quickly become the wealthiest nation on earth, the entire Chinese mainland becomes the most dynamic free market region on earth: There are thriving markets in education, health, insurance, community design, construction, policing, and management. Meanwhile, despite tremendous wealth creation in India, attitudes are still slow to change. Gradually the socialist structure of India is being dismantled, but many entrepreneurs are frustrated. Gradually more and more talented young people in India focus on the ideal cities being born in their increasingly independent SEZs.

2030: As the Chinese juggernaut takes off, with Hong Kong, Singapore, Japan, South Korea, Vietnam, and Thailand all deeply integrated, the issue of Taiwan gradually disappears as Taiwan becomes another important gear in the powerful Chinese wealth machine. Indian leaders, seeing China leap from behind to become wealthier than India so quickly, are finally beginning to act more assertively to support markets beyond the SEZs. As the FLOW ideology spreads, there are some forward-thinkers who are even discussing trade as a means of building more peaceful relations with Pakistan. A shocking paper is published on the possibility of "economic government" in the disputed Kashmir region, which would allow people to choose by means of private enterprises which government controlled them. The border between India and Pakistan soon develops into one of the most innovative regions of the world due to dozens of private SEZs with essentially complete legal autonomy; the very concept of nation-state evaporates in the region.

2040: A leader in North Korea appears who realizes how easy it would be to move from a place of poverty, weakness, and embarrassment to one of wealth and dynamism. Without losing face, he follows the Chinese model of deep market activity. As a latecomer to the game, he chooses to out-do even the Chinese, and North Korea starts to make startling gains in wealth as the most perfectly-designed deliberate market economy ever begins to take off. India becomes a "nation" of competing, independent ideal cities, a Nozickian utopia of utopias. Because trade with India has become so profitable, Pakistani businessmen protest ongoing government restrictions and hostilities toward India. The FLOW student movement reaches Pakistan as well, and student groups are demonstrating for peace and free trade with India. The Pakistani government pretends to remain hostile, while giving on all essential issues, thus setting the foundation for a lasting peace with India.

Europe

2010: The Europe groups starts by trying to transmit the FLOW vision to European student groups. There are a few bright stars: Bjørn Lomborg and Johan Norberg are among the leaders of a brilliant new student movement in Europe. But the backlash is tremendous and powerful. Most student groups remain virulently leftist. Estonia and Ireland are becoming the wealthiest, most vibrant, and exciting centers of culture and innovation in Europe.

2020: The core FLOW group in Europe is steadily developing. Despite the substantial welfare states in Scandinavia, the most powerful FLOW leaders are based there. Several state-sponsored universities have dynamic FLOW research centers. The FLOW energy in Scandinavia has spread to Britain, where Irish thinkers both in Ireland and Britain are the intellectual leaders of the British FLOW movement. The Czech Republic and Hungary are centers of first-class FLOW intellectual work as well. Throughout Eastern Europe, idealistic young entrepreneurs are working together with government leaders to create super-economies. The greatest resistance continues to come from France and Germany. Russia is wealthy through oil and gas, but still largely unfree. People refer to France and Russia as third-world countries.

2030: The standard of living in Japan, Taiwan, Singapore, and Hong Kong has long surpassed that of Europe. As the newer Asian miracles make it clear that the standard of living in China, Thailand, and Vietnam are rapidly surpassing Europe, more Europeans begin to take note. Moreover, as the United States, Canada, and Australia are now recognized as the leaders of the FLOW social justice movement due to their incredible receptivity to immigrants, European countries are becoming increasingly ashamed of their chauvinistic socialism and realize that opening their borders and their labor markets would produce more social justice than did the "gated community socialism" of the twentieth century. Most of Europe is now developing a quite obvious market momentum. Although the Left still controls France, it is becoming embarrassing. There are FLOW student protests against the aging leftist leaders and intellectuals in Paris.

2040: Europe is changing as it opens its markets. Young people are now openly ridiculing the leftist history of Europe in the twentieth century. Europe is becoming radically multicultural as large numbers of Arab and African peoples enter the European market. European intellectual life begins a dramatic ascent as the brightest young people have become brilliant FLOW theorists; people wonder if the FLOW intellectual leadership has definitely passed to Europe. Russia is starting to come to life because of trade with its highly successful neighbors. In Germany, the Netherlands, and Scandinavia, radical community experiments are taking place. Americans living east of California are shocked by the exotic combinations of lifestyles that are developing. German intellectuals write long treatises defending the most innovative (and bizarre) "lifestyle corporations" that create new ways of living that shock the old. Music and art suddenly become explosively new and exciting in Europe. Ireland is producing poetry and literature and film and virtual reality experiences that delight the world. France is obviously trying to play catch-up while trying to save face.

Oceana

2010: Australia and New Zealand are leaders from the start. Both nations continue to receive large influxes of immigrants and to experience large increases in their standards of living. Because the FLOW consciousness is so well developed there, immigrants from Indonesia are constantly returning home with new understandings of how government can work and how businesses can be created so that peace and prosperity will be available to all. Thousands of young people from Australia and New Zealand are setting up their own businesses with partners in Indonesia.

2020: As Australia and New Zealand develop distinctive cultures that combine Anglo, Aboriginal, Asian, and south Pacific traditions, people from all over the globe visit the region to experience the food, the ambiance, the culture, the communities. One hasn't really lived until one has visited the "Oceana potpourri." Australia is becoming a global economic heavyweight due to the massive increase in population and wealth.

2030: The Indonesian government is steadily becoming less corrupt because of the ongoing influence of FLOW entrepreneurs. Islamic radicalism is increasingly marginalized. The world's largest Islamic population is becoming a global model for Islamic integration into modernity. Indonesians become proud of the regional brilliance for culturally-evolved tourism and contributes an Islamic experience that is bringing in increasing numbers of tourists and intellectuals.

2040: Oceana has become a peaceful, happy, dynamic place in which to live, to visit, and to do business. Australia has a reputation as one of the most effective economies on the planet. Indonesia is the first large nation in the Islamic world to become committed to entrepreneurs and markets, and Islamic leaders regularly visit the country to see how it is being done.

Africa

2010: The African experience remains largely grim. Botswana has become ever more free market, and people are beginning to call it "the Estonia of Africa." There are bright spots in South Africa, where an open repudiation of socialistic measures has begun, and in Libya, where Quaddafi's son has decided to create the first successful Islamic market society.

2020: South Africa has begun to become a serious market force and South African students, leaders, and intellectuals are trying to persuade other African nations to implement the market reforms that have given them so much success. Libya and Egypt are gradually integrating into the global economy. Throughout North Africa young Islamic entrepreneurs who have returned from Europe are starting to promote FLOW ideas. Open World experiments in Tanzania are starting to produce remarkable growth there within the small Open World zones. Senegal develops a striking market momentum and begins to pull ahead of the rest of west Africa.

2030: A surprise break for Africa: A Senegalese FLOW billionaire, made wealthy through the striking growth in pro-market Senegal, has made an arrangement with the leader of Kenya to purchase several million acres for a FLOW model state in exchange for a large cash price plus consulting and educational services for the Kenyan government. Idealistic young people from all over the world arrive to help launch "the Kenyan experiment." As businessmen begin to take the Kenyan government seriously, businesses start to locate in Kenya, both within the FLOW experiment and throughout the country. South Africa has become a strong, modern economy and its neighbors are starting to imitate it as well as to benefit from the strong trade ties.

2040: The Kenyan experiment has excited the world. Although North Korea is a close second, the Kenyan experiment is showing more dramatic levels of economic growth than have ever been seen anywhere. Kenya as a whole is starting to show a healthy economy. With North Africa becoming economically successful, Kenya being a global model, and South Africa having become a major global economy, most of the rest of the continent is experiencing strong pressure internally and externally from businessmen, political leaders, and student groups to begin developing just societies.

The Middle East

2010: Other kingdoms within the United Arab Emirates (UAE) have followed the lead of Dubai in creating free zones and attracting billions in oil money in the process. Oman is developing market-based ecotourism and flourishing as well. There is little progress elsewhere.

2020: Kuwait and Qatar have followed the model set by UAE and Oman; they are both receiving billions in investment dollars. Egypt is moving in this direction as well. There are rumors that the young professionals in Iran, Iraq, and Saudi Arabia are looking enviously at their wealthy and dynamic counterparts in UAE and Oman.

2030: The Dubai model has conquered much of the Middle East. Syria, Lebanon, and Jordan remain committed to hostility toward Israel rather than modernization, but even here the growing influence of commercial peace throughout the region is becoming increasingly compelling. Business ambition, rather than religious fanaticism, has conquered the region, despite occasional ongoing violence.

2040: Although anti–Israel rhetoric still exists, and an occasional act of violence, the general push is toward progress and commerce. The rest of the world outside Africa, Russia, and France, has become so wealthy and successful that Islamic pride has now shifted to outdoing the Chinese in terms of a commitment to market progress. They have a long ways to go, but now that their extraordinary oil revenues (due now to very high oil prices) are devoted to real investment, they do have some advantage in the race.

The Americas

2010: Mexico, Chile, Costa Rica, and many of the Caribbean economies have all become substantially integrated into the U.S. economy due to free trade agreements. All are visibly developing. FLOW student activists have fought to stop the drug wars that have destroyed Colombia and Peru; it appears as if a drug decriminalization movement is about to pull the plug on drug cartel profits. U.S. campus activism still includes many leftist groups due to the ongoing presence of the "tenured radicals," but there are strong FLOW groups at most campuses. It is increasingly recognized that tariffs, subsidies, and border controls are shameful evidence of social injustice. There are student protests whenever illegal aliens are arrested or when employers are sanctioned for employing them. It is widely recognized that border controls on human beings contribute more to slavery and human degradation than does any other practice.

2020: The United States has become a largely bilingual nation. After significant resentment, the FLOW idealists have helped turn the attitude around to one of celebration of the Hispanic influence. The obvious increase in wealth in Mexico helps: Anyone who refuses to celebrate the increased standard of living comes across as a cruel bigot. Mexico, Chile, Costa Rica, and the Caribbean are all approaching a

U.S. standard of living. Other nations throughout Latin America are eliminating corruption and instituting solid market reforms. FLOW intellectuals, activists, and entrepreneurs are pouring across borders throughout Latin America. FLOW idealism has finally penetrated the campuses and opinion leaders; there is pressure on the government to liberate education and health care. The teachers' unions and American Medical Association are waging aggressive campaigns, but everyone knows that they are fighting a losing battle.

2030: The entire Americas are becoming wealthy and integrated. Although spots of profound poverty remain, optimism pervades the hemisphere as people see the progress that is being made. The United States itself is becoming a miracle of education and well-being as free markets in health and education are starting to come to life. Bright young people are swarming into the fields and large, idealistic, entre-preneurial corporations are offering "lifestyle contracts" that integrate education, health, insurance, and residential options in interesting and appealing packages.

2040: The Americas enjoy a decent standard of living throughout. Large U.S. lifestyle corporations have enormous research and devel-opment budgets devoted to designing better ways to make human beings happy and well. U.S. corporations are contracted throughout the world to improve well-being. Their only serious competitor is The Kenya Corporation, whose lifestyle product is even more original than is that produced in the United States.; the average income of a Kenya Corporation employee is 50 percent greater than is the aver-age income of members of its nearest competitor, and life expectancy is 10 years longer. An Australian/Indonesian conglomerate is develop-ing a "South Pacific Delight" package that looks formidable even to the producers of "Hawaiian Blend" and "Marin Medley" among the hedonists. *Mormon Glory* is a best-seller throughout Latin America and has made inroads into Africa. It has been banned in the Arab nations. Most of Latin America is still loyal to the Catholic Church, which has become far more effective at creating well-being than it ever was in its first 2,000 years of existence due to the pressure of a competitive mar-ket. *Confucian Discipline* is a best-seller in U.S. inner-cities and maintains dominance in Chinese markets around the world. *Bubba's Good Times* dominates the market throughout the southeast United States but does not sell well internationally except for a few odd cult followers in Italy and the Ukraine. Tibetan Buddhism has colonies throughout the Americas. *Life is God*, based on Sufi mysticism, has attracted a devoted following among educated Americans, Europeans, and Iranian Muslims.

The leading lifestyle corporations periodically attempt to ban additional experimentation, but the FLOW ethic has become so firmly rooted that people are outraged when the existing corporations attempt to limit access to newcomers. The Innovators is a large organization, known for the intellectual brilliance of its members and for producing diverse and experimental lifestyle options that push the boundaries in every direction. Although the more traditional companies hate to admit it, many of their best new ideas regarding art, education, the wellness industry, and community structure come from The Innovators.

II. Focus on the Growth of the Well-Being Industry in the United States

2010: Campus activists focus on fighting for changes in law and attitude that will allow the entrepreneurs to market well-being. Priorities include school choice and the complete elimination of government-mandated licensure in all fields. Government restrictions on the health and insurance industries are coming under attack. Campus groups work with inner-city communities to create innovative solutions to housing and safety while activists fight those zoning and building code obstacles to better housing and legal rules that reduce public safety.

The role of universities is questioned; some students protest harmful and idiotic courses, others simply desert harmful courses. A league of FLOW professors, very small at first, promotes coursework that will make the world a better place. Student groups rate the value of courses that undermine well-being. As some courses consistently receive negative ratings, those professors are gradually left with small cadres of angry leftist loyalists that no one takes seriously anymore.

After the final political battles over No Child Left Behind have dis-illusioned everyone about government control of education, a serious educational freedom movement has begun. Young people, students, and young parents alike, are aggressively pushing for a radically open school voucher program. It looks as if it may pass.

2020: Finally, in 2015, substantial educational freedom was granted to U.S. citizens. Thousands of the brightest young people in the United States begin to flood into education; billions of dollars worth of capital begins to support their projects, and interesting, effective, exciting ways of schooling children begin to be developed. University education departments are so obviously obsolete that most of them are either closing down or being taken over by the education corporations. Because of the revolution in education, more and more pressure is being focused on the medical field. The AMA is frightened. Meanwhile, there are interesting small experiments in which innovative entities take over the management of cities and residential areas. Legislators in Nevada are proposing that state government be managed by these legislative innovators.

2030: U.S. education is becoming a global force to be reckoned with. Although Chinese diligence and innovative education in China may leave us behind for some time to come, most observers consider the United States to be driving the future in terms of K–12 education. As educational institutions cultivate healthier habits, graduates from many institutions receive discounted health insurance. The health industry has been partially deregulated, and as a consequence specialists in healthy living have joined forces with K–12 educational organizations and insurance companies to create lifestyle plans that often include discounted food options, massage, bodywork, meditation, exercise, vacations, entertainment, and so forth that, in combination, result in significantly reduced rates of heart disease, cancer, obesity, and other lifestyle diseases of the twentieth century. Residential corporations work closely with lifestyle suppliers. Nevada state government has been contracted out to a legislative innovator; this corporation has various contracts with several different lifestyle providers and residential corporations to create custom legal environments appropriate to different customer groups throughout Nevada.

2040: The average U.S. citizen currently earns $100,000 per year in 2004 dollars and average life expectancy at birth is up to 120 years. More important, most people thoroughly enjoy life. Private corporations manage most towns and cities. Women and children can walk alone through the streets of any city in the United States day or night and be perfectly safe. People look and feel healthy and trim. Learning and culture are alive and vibrant. Most people work when they want to, for as long as they want, where they want. Physical and emotional stress is rare except when deliberately chosen. People devote an increasing percentage of their time and incomes to developing their mind, body, and spirit. Suicide and depression, violent crime, and spousal and child abuse are all almost nonexistent. Because these trends are even more dramatic in Nevada, New Hampshire and Arizona have also contracted out government management to innovative corporations: The feeling is widespread that we have only begun to learn how to live well.

III. Progress toward Global Sustainability

2010: The scientific community is beginning to learn the economic principles that form the basis for FLOW. Several universities around the world have developed joint programs between science, engineering, economics, and law in order to begin to develop intelligent solutions to environmental problems. Environmental trusts, based on Peter Barnes' *Capitalism 3.0*, are beginning to be created around the world to protect diverse commons. Widespread support develops for a green tax shift using geonomic principles and for innovative property rights solutions and solutions to commons problems as proposed by Elinor Ostrom.

2020: Groundwork is being developed for flexible, intelligent, legal frameworks that protect the environment while providing incentives for technological innovation. Global frameworks addressing issues relating to air, water, and biological diversity are being developed by international teams of scholars.

2030: Combinations of governments, NGOs, universities, private corporations, and individuals are creating contracts that allocate resources in ways designed to improve the environment. Participation is voluntary, and levels of participation in the agreements vary widely based on the quality and intelligence of the contract design. As this trend becomes more obvious, consortia of scientists, engineers, lawyers, and economists band together to produce better contracts and monitoring provisions. Chinese private communities are leading the way in purchasing their services.

2040: "Sustainability Contracting" has become a global business. Several different companies offer environmental design and enforcement contracts. Most nations, cities, and other political units, as well as most major corporations, are signatories to one or several of these contracts. International underwriters provide substantial discounts to entities that sign credible environmental contracts. Those few nations and corporations that have not signed typically face large insurance costs and are vulnerable to larger liability suits when they violate another nation's or corporation's environmental well-being. While this field is highly complex, combining many different types of technical expertise, an innovation dynamic has developed that is producing concretely better results. Most people experience a natural environment that is healthy, aesthetically satisfying, and filled with vibrant, diverse ecosystems.

Act III: A Concrete Vision of a School in 2060 as a Result of the FLOW Activism through 2040

I have a feeling we're not in Kansas anymore.

Dorothy Gale in L. Frank Baum's,
The Wizard of Oz

By 2060, schools have become almost unrecognizable to people from the early twenty-first century. Indeed, most young people learn academic content quickly by means of software or by means of brain implants and develop their other human characteristics, including superb intellectual skills, healthy culture, and habituation, in deliberate, chosen communities.

On my 100th birthday I apply to visit The Wellness Community. This community is known for growing the best organic computers, for its eco-habitats, and for its healing resources. The community sells custom evolved computers to major clients around the world to manage complex organizational systems. Its own inhabitants are managed by their evolved organic computers to ensure constant improvements: The system automatically monitors brain waves, gene activation, hormonal levels, immune system functioning, and hundreds of specific biochemical markers in order to optimize well-being. The inhabitants' immune systems are such that they almost never become ill; the community spends almost nothing on health care. The inhabitants have developed habits that prevent the onset of chronic diseases; combined with new techniques to slow aging processes, the life expectancy of people from this community is 160 years and growing. Because of its profound expertise in human well-being, sick people from the mainstream culture pay for limited recuperation periods in the community. There is a long waiting list to have one's children accepted by the community, despite the fact that it is beginning to replicate itself as fast as it can while maintaining the integrity of the community structure.

There are 10 levels of this type of community. After a comprehensive physical and emotional examination, it is determined that I am capable of visiting the sixth level. Prior to entry, I must undergo a six-day preparation period during which I live in a special chamber in which my diet, activity, and sensory input are carefully managed. The preparation includes exercises, meditation, bodywork, a soundtrack that combines music and mythical experience, special baths, and mineral and vitamin treatments. Apparently, before they began preparing outsiders to visit these communities, some people would have heart attacks, or experience mental breakdowns, or become incontinent, or otherwise lose control over basic functions. It is explained to me that visitors from regular life are not prepared for the intensity of experience available in the community.

I awaken. As I transition from dream-state to consciousness, I am first aware of warm lights and fragrant tropical smells, then waves of distant sounds, waterfalls, surf, voices, and singing in the distance. I then feel female fingertips almost, but not quite, touching my temples and my ankles. Gradually a warm energy begins to flow back and forth from my head to feet and back again, initially small and gentle, and gradually with greater and greater warmth and intensity. Finally, I open my eyes and am helped to sit up. I am given a flask of cool, silky liquid, which I drink slowly. And I look around. I am in a semi-enclosed space with a waterfall crashing over a bright green, moss-covered cliff. At the base of the waterfall is a small, deep pond, and then a short river flows through a sandy beach and into the ocean. There are transparent sheets of a clear substance that partially enclose the space; I've been told that climate control is achieved by means of a combination of changes in the air flow through the crystal sheets combined with the activation and deactivation of heat-producing or absorbing microorganisms that live in the moss on the waterfall. The level six community in which I have been permitted entry is devoted to young people between the ages of 13 and 25; I am told about 300 live in this community, visiting their families whenever they please. They are scattered around the space, some alone, some in small groups. Some are reading, some are using a technical device, some are engaged in some type of martial art, some are preparing a meal, and some are diving through the waterfall into the pond. There are caves off to the side that apparently contain study quarters for those who want isolation or technical equipment.

What is most striking is the constant singing and music. It varies and undulates constantly. Sometimes there are high-pitched solos, then group a cappella, then a flute. Sometimes drums start and then chanting. Sometimes the music emanates from one corner of the enclosure; at other points voices and instruments appear from all different places. The patterns are strange and unfamiliar; every moment flows seamlessly into the next, there are no sharp changes, and yet the whole set of sounds is constantly changing. Somehow the group as a whole seems to know what should come next.

The sound is accompanied by waves of emotion that are felt throughout my whole being. Sometimes, for no apparent reason, I feel deliriously joyful, and then apprehensive, and then I start to laugh, realizing that laughter is bouncing all around the enclosure. At one point I feel a burst of bright orange anger; my guide points to a group of young people swinging across the cliff. She said that the anger is caused by one of the students taking an irresponsible risk, and her mentor corrects her sharply. I asked why I feel the emotions of the community so directly and intensely, and she explains that they have been working on an experiment in radical emotional openness; my preparatory period was designed to allow me to open up so that I could sense, at least partially, the community's current project. The various biochemical sensors and organic computers were then determining the ways in which this particular phase of emotional openness improved or diminished both individual and communal functioning and well-being. I feel a wave of happiness that literally knocks me down onto the ground; I have to be helped back up. My guide explains that people from the outside world, whose limbic systems have been so thoroughly contaminated by our upbringing in the still chaotic world, are not fully capable of experiencing life in the community. She laughs and says that perhaps a level six community is a stretch for me. She then says that she has visited a level seven community and almost been knocked over herself.

I looks enviously at these young people bursting with health and well-being and become dizzy from the music and the smells. I know that many of them will eventually leave this community in order to create more level one communities that will allow more and more people to begin a path of deeper happiness and well-being. And I know that this is but one of thousands of experiments going on around the world, and that I will never know a fraction of the well-being projects that are being developed everywhere.

About the Contributors

John Mackey is Chairman and CEO of Whole Foods Market, an $8 billion Fortune 500 company, and a "Fortune 100 Best Companies to Work For" every year since 1998. Whole Foods is one of the top 12 supermarket companies in America and the world's largest natural foods retail chain. John Mackey was named the Ernst and Young Entrepreneur of the Year for the United States in 2003. John is the co-founder, with Michael Strong, of FLOW.

Michael Strong is a pioneer in education and independent learning. He is the author of *The Habit of Thought: From Socratic Seminars to Socratic Practice*, and the founder of innovative Socratic, Montessori, and Paideia schools and programs in Alaska, Florida, California, Texas, and New Mexico. His public school programs increased female minority critical thinking scores, on a test that is highly correlated with the College Board SAT, by as much in one semester as the average high school student gains in four years of high school. Another of his schools had 6th, 7th, and 8th grade students successfully passing AP courses. Moreno Valley High School, the charter school for which Michael was the founding principal, was ranked the 36th best public high school in the United States on the Washington Post's 2006 Challenge Index. Prior to his career in education, Michael was writing a dissertation on "Ideas and Culture as Human Capital" under economics Nobel laureate Gary Becker. Michael is co-founder and serves as Chief Executive Officer and Chief Visionary Officer of FLOW.

Candace Smith (formerly Candace Allen), a high school teacher for 26 years in Pueblo, Colorado, has won national, state and local recognition— her numerous awards include the Enterprising Teacher of the Year in Colorado in 1989 and the 1993 National Milken Award for innovative approaches to education and quality improvement processes in the classroom. As an educational consultant, her expertise was in economics education, quality improvement processes, including the employment of Socratic seminar methodology. Today, Candace continues the same path of inquiry that led her in the exploration which culminated in the paper, "The Entrepreneur as Hero." Her passion is interaction in conversations regarding the great questions of civil society, and she especially enjoys Liberty Fund conferences. Candace travels extensively on her own ventures, and with her husband, and plays a significant role in the preparation and execution of their appearances. She volunteers as Vice President for the International Foundation for Experimental Economics, a foundation that her husband, Vernon Smith, started in 1997.

Muhammad Yunus was born in 1940 in Chittagong, a seaport in Bangladesh. The third of fourteen children, five of whom died in infancy, he was educated at Dhaka University and was awarded a Fulbright scholarship to study economics at Vanderbilt University, where he earned a Ph.D. in economics. In 1972 he became the head of the economics department at Chittagong University.

Professor Muhammad Yunus initiated the Grameen Bank Project in Bangladesh in 1976. From Dr. Yunus' personal loan of $27 to 42 poor people in Bangladesh in the mid-70s, the Grameen Bank has advanced to the forefront of a growing world movement toward eradicating poverty through microlending. Replicas of the Grameen Bank model now exist in almost all the countries in the world. It is estimated that more than 110 million borrowers receive microloans each year around the world today, the majority of them women.

Professor Yunus is the recipient of numerous international prizes for his work, including the 2006 Nobel Peace Prize, shared with Grameen Bank.

Kartar Singh Khalsa began his career at Golden Temple 1973 baking granola, after starting the company with others in a spiritual community committed catalyzed by the teachings of Yogi Bhajan, renowned master of Kundalini Yoga. Kartar subsequently worked in every department, including a stint as the deliveryman, driving a semi up and down the West Coast. He assumed the role of CEO in 1996, and under his helm Golden Temple has doubled its business over the past four years, and continues to grow at an impressive rate.

A former engineering student at Oregon State University, Kartar is as well-informed about profit margins, technical manufacturing specs, and brand positioning, as he is about the service role of business, the power of spiritually based values in the conduct of business, and the responsibility of business to elevate human well-being—a reflection of his decision to leave college to pursue a spiritual path and the practice of Yoga.

The primary products of Golden Temple, include Yogi Tea, the number one tea brand in the Natural Products industry, Golden Temple Granola, the number one bulk granola in the United States, and Peace Cereal, a fast-growing brand of packaged breakfast cereal, created to promote peace through business, and sponsor of Working for Good.

Donna Callejon As COO of Global Giving, a web portal that allows donors to give to specific social entrepreneurs around the world, Donna oversees activities designed to attract, retain and serve GlobalGiving's community. This includes business and partner management, development of technology and infrastructure for globalgiving.com and over a dozen custom websites, and internal operations. Donna also serves on the Board of the Washington Area Women's Foundation and previously served six years on the board of Business for Social Responsibility. In a prior life, Donna was a senior executive and member of the Operating Committee of Fannie Mae. From 1996 to 2000, she oversaw the company's strategic planning, business development and international consulting efforts, and prior to 1996 led the core purchase and securitization business, including marketing, product development, customer technology and negotiated transactions. She holds a B.S. in Managerial Economics from UC Davis.

Hernando de Soto is the founder of the Instituto Libertad y Democracia (Institute for Liberty and Democracy), a Peruvian think tank that has been described by Bill Clinton as "The most promising anti-poverty initiative in the world." De Soto has written two books: *The Other Path: The Economic Answer to Terrorism*, and *The Mystery of Capital: Why Capitalism Triumphs in the West and Fails Everywhere Else.*

In 1999 *Time* magazine chose de Soto as one of the five leading Latin American innovators of the century. *Forbes* magazine highlighted him as one of 15 innovators "who will re-invent your future." The *New York Times Magazine* wrote, "To the leaders of poor countries, de Soto's economic gospel is one of the most hopeful things they have heard in years." The *Economist* magazine identified the ILD as one of the top two think tanks in the world. He is the co-chair, with Madeleine Albright, of the U.N. Commission on the Legal Empowerment of the Poor.

For his efforts, the Peruvian Marxist terrorist group Shining Path targeted him for assassination, bombing his offices and machine-gunning his car. Today the Shining Path is moribund, but de Soto remains very much alive and a passionate advocate.

Brian Johnson has always been passionate about understanding what makes great people great and applying the truths they embodied to make his little dent in the universe. After selling his last business (Zaadz) and traveling for a bit, he decided to give himself a Ph.D. in Optimal Living with a Specialization in Greatness and Bliss. You can follow his work at PhilosophersNotes.com.

Dr. Don Beck has been designing transformational practices for more than thirty years in corporate, institutional and governmental settings worldwide. He is perhaps best known for his work as originator of Spiral Dynamics®, a unique values-based model that charts the emergence of human nature—an integral, bio-psycho-social approach which offers Natural Design and MeshWorks Solutions that are ecological, systemic and life-affirming. He founded the concept and practice of Large-Scale Psychology, and is actively engaged in global geopolitical macro-transformations, at present most notably in the Middle East, Mexico, and Latin America. He played a major role behind the scenes in the design of moving South Africa nonviolently beyond Apartheid.

Beck is co-author of *The Crucible: Forging South Africa's Future* and the seminal book *Spiral Dynamics: Mastering Values, Leadership and Change*. He is a sought-after keynote speaker and has addressed corporate and political leaders worldwide. His interests range from working with National Football League teams to exploring new levels of consciousness.

Jeff Klein serves as Executive Director and Chief Activation Officer for FLOW—a position he has held since November 2005. Jeff and Michael Strong serve as the core producers for FLOW, collaborating to conceive and produce the FLOW programs—Peace Through Commerce®, Conscious Capitalism®, and Accelerating Women Entrepreneurs™. All three programs are examples of the work he continues to do through his own company, Cause Alliance Marketing.

Jeff has worked in marketing and business development in the music, natural products, and fitness industries, building companies and talent including Private Music, Yanni, Seeds of Change, Spinning, and ChiRunning. He has designed cause alliance marketing programs for The Esalen Institute, The National Geographic Society, GlobalGiving, the Institute of Noetic Sciences, and Peace Cereal.

Jeff graduated Brown University, with an AB in International Relations. His first book, *Working for Good: Making a Difference, While Making a Living*, will be published by Sound True in the Fall of 2009.

Index

Note: Bold page numbers indicate material in figures or tables. Page numbers followed by an *n* indicate material contained in footnotes.